Edward Hedican is a Professor Emeritus of anthropology at the University of Guelph, Ontario, Canada

Edward Hedican is a Professor Emeritus from the University of Guelph, Canada, whose primary field of study is cultural anthropology. For most of his career he has conducted research among the Indigenous peoples (Anishinaabe or Ojibway) of northern Ontario in the subarctic region around Lake Nipigon. He has also studied the history of Irish immigrants to Canada in the post-famine period which involved an in-depth analysis of various genealogical, census and demographic documents in both Ireland and Canada.

The following book is primarily a summary of the various aspects of his anthropological career extending over a fifty-year period and the significant lessons that he learned during the course of his professional field of study.

Dedicated to "Jud" Epling, Richard Salisbury and Ken Dawson who inspired me to travel along the path less travelled in life.

Edward Hedican

BEYOND THE BEATEN PATH

50 Years of Anthropology in Canada

AUSTIN MACAULEY PUBLISHERS™

LONDON • CAMBRIDGE • NEW YORK • SHARJAH

Ordering Information
Quantity sales: Special discounts are available on quantity purchases by corporations, associations, and others. For details, contact the publisher at the address below.

Publisher's Cataloging-in-Publication data
Hedican, Edward
Beyond the Beaten Path

ISBN 9781685628895 (Paperback)
ISBN 9781685628901 (Hardback)
ISBN 9781685628918 (ePub e-book)

Library of Congress Control Number: 2023913875

www.austinmacauley.com/us

First Published 2023
Austin Macauley Publishers LLC
40 Wall Street, 33rd Floor, Suite 3302
New York, NY 10005
USA

mail-usa@austinmacauley.com
+1 (646) 5125767

For my son, Shaun Hedican, who resides on the Rocky Bay Anishinaabe Reserve in northern Ontario, I am grateful for his insights and perspectives on life in the Lake Nipigon area. Thanks to Karen Hurson who helped me with proof reading and generally lent her support for my various writing projects. My long-time friend and colleague of more than forty years, Stan Barrett, Professor Emeritus at the University of Guelph, has always been very supportive of my research, often lending encouragement and advice, and to him I am very indebted. Also at the University of Guelph, Tad McIlwraith has been very helpful sharing his ideas with me on current Indigenous issues.

Table of Contents

Preface

Have you ever wondered what it would be like to be an anthropologist? There is a certain mystery about the profession, since anthropologists often travel to out-of-the-way parts of the world that might be considered exotic, dangerous, or otherwise mysterious to most people. Of course, there are many misconceptions, such as the view of the anthropologist in khaki-colored shorts, wearing a pith hat and accompanied by a string of baggage carriers trailing behind him as depicted in a *Far Side* cartoon. This book describes my own life in anthropology carried on over five decades. My career was not necessarily typical in terms of specific details, but it does involve extensive field research as well as various other activities, such as appearing as an expert witness in a Supreme Court land claims case, that were unique in certain ways.

The photo on the cover of this book depicts several log cabins and a trail between them. The photo was taken in the mid-1970s when I was conducting a period of anthropological research in a small Anishinaabe community in northern Ontario situated north-west of Lake Nipigon. At that time, everyone lived in log cabins, and there were no cars, trucks, or electricity in the village. For the most part, the people lived then by hunting and fishing with occasional periods of wage work on the nearby railway. In the intervening years, amounting to about five decades, I have kept in touch with many people. Just a few days ago, in fact, I was discussing the present state of the village with the current chief on Messenger, who was just a baby girl when I first lived there. The old adage about the years flying by seems appropriate in describing my experience.

The image in the photo of the trail winding its way between the cabins in the village suggests to me the well-worn path of life. Another interpretation is that the path suggests a metaphor about research in anthropology, which is to say, that in order to create new ideas one is required to seek out new trails to follow 'beyond the beaten path'. In anthropology, as in life itself, it is easiest to stick to the tried and true; to stick with what we already know and are familiar with. Yet, if one tries something new, to move beyond the beaten path, then our life holds the possibility of being even better. Of course, there are risks involved in traversing the new trail, but even then there are opportunities for new learning experiences. In any event, if we only stick to same-old, same-old, holding to what is already known, then that is all we will ever get out of life.

New discoveries require an adventurous spirit, one willing to move beyond the known ground, and from there you take your chances. As we learn new lessons, we are also presented with new opportunities for growth. This book, then, is about my attempts to move away from the beaten path of intellectual ideas and research, to embark on a road less travelled to use a familiar phrase. While this book is at least partly autobiographical, by the very nature of the subject matter and the time span involved, there are other goals that I consider more significant than a simple rendition of my life experiences. There are a number of important themes that provide a structure to this book.

Perhaps the most salient of these is a discussion of the manner in which field research in anthropology, called ethnography, is linked to larger theoretical issues. The particular details of everyday life during the course of our research may be interesting in themselves, but as a basis of scientific study they are relatively meaningless unless they can be tied in some way to the more encompassing general patterns that illuminate arrangements in social and cultural life.

A second theme is about the various people who have influences one's research career in anthropology, both during the actual fieldwork, as well as our academic mentors who provided much need guidance through our research. It is important to acknowledge that we alone are not responsible for any success that we have in our intellectual careers, because what we are able to do is built upon the efforts and accomplishments of those who came before us, in a long stream of thought and action extending into the past.

Thirdly, this book covers five decades of anthropology in Canada, especially as this time period focuses on Indigenous issues that have evolved over this time period. The discussion begins with such important land marks as the Hawthorn Report of the mid-1960s, and then traces various episodes, such as Prime Minister Trudeau's White Paper of 1969, the James Bay Cree and their involvement in the Quebec Hydro-electric Project of 1975, continuing to discussions of the Ipperwash Protest and the resulting Linden Inquiry of 2007, the so-called Oka Crisis and the establishment of Nunavut in the 1990s, followed by Prime Minister Harper's apology of 2008, and then Prime Minister Justin Trudeau's contemporary Indigenous policies.

Throughout this period, there were also various land claims taking place in the courts and several chapters discuss my own involvement as a so-called 'expert witness' in the Supreme Court in 2015, as well as my role as a land claims 'facilitator' for the Whitesand Band in northern Ontario in the 1980s. My attempt here is to portray the life of an anthropologist in Canada through various phases of one's career. In addition, each of the chapters includes a section on 'lessons learned' as well as a summary in the Epilogue of ten of the most important of these.

Chapter One
Introduction

The title of this book, *Beyond the Beaten Path*, is meant to suggest that new knowledge is generated by pursing courses of action that have not been followed before. If you wish to find new ideas, then it is necessary to discover your own path, one that other people have not travelled on previously. It is for this reason that I chose for my research site an Indigenous community that existed outside the governmental structure of the Indian Affairs department because this type of community had not been studied beforehand. This chapter introduces the community where I took up residence, some of the research interests that I investigated, and the various persons who provided information that facilitated my research goals at the time.

As such, in my study of an Indigenous Anishinaabe community in northern Ontario, which is situated about 300 kilometers north of Thunder Bay, I usually began my day as many people do by making a cup of coffee. Then, weather permitting, I sat on a small bench in front of my cabin so that I could watch the comings and goings of the village population. In my direct line of vision, there is a small field with an old store, on my left near the railway tracks which bisects the community is a water pump and where several women were lining up, chatting, with small children running about. To the right is a trail down to a large lake. I see an elderly man dragging a wash tub, probably full of fish, from his canoe, and along the path small log cabins with people walking between them. Most of the people I'm sure do not give much notice to all this activity since it goes on in more or less the same manner on most days.

On one of these days, though, I began to wonder why I was waiting for the women to finish filling their water buckets before I went and filled mine. Then it dawned on me; perhaps I did not want to be seen mingling with the women; could there be some aspects of local mores and attitudes that I was missing? I wondered. For one thing, as a single man in the village, I was quite conscious of not raising suspicions or jealousies among the married men that I was at all interested in their women. Then I was also aware, when I finally came around to thinking about it, that the reason that only women went to the water pump was because there was a certain division of labor in the community that I had previously not given much thought to.

As a general rule, it was women who handled the household duties relating to cooking, child care and so on.[1] On the other hand, one might not expect to see a woman setting out on a hunting expedition, although this was entirely possible and probably happened more than I thought. The thought crossed my mind that there were relatively mundane everyday activities going on right under my nose that I had not previously given much attention to, but which probably were a key to understanding social processes in the village at a more widespread level. As it turned out these thoughts were just passing ones. I had more important matters to occupy my attention, or so I thought.

So this is one of the problems, I now realize, with field research in anthropology[2]—we do not give much attention to everyday affairs even though they can have deeper significance in our research. We tend to concentrate on the more noticeable, more salient events, those activities that people give special attention to and are considered significant in some way. Even in the wider sphere of theoretical orientations[3], our attention might be to discuss our research in terms of the manner in which our results pertain to societal evolution, conflict theory, structural functionalism or postmodernism. Our gaze is seldom removed from the big picture, and so we miss out on the possible significance of the ephemeral, quotidian or common place aspects of everyday life.

The Ethnographic Narrative

The description portrayed above concerning my observations made from my cabin's bench about people going about their everyday tasks could be seen as presenting an account of my ethnographic fieldwork in terms of a narrative format. My intention here is to explore aspects of ethnography that are not normally presented in a more formal, 'scientific'[4] version of anthropological descriptions of everyday life. Although such reflections are not rare in the anthropological literature, there is none that I am aware of for the boreal forest region of Canada's north. In an historical sense, then, the anthropology of northeastern North America has not generally benefited from the short of 'behind-the-scenes' reports that other readers have available to them for other parts of the world.

As far as the ethnographic narrative is concerned, it has become an increasingly important part of social anthropology as fieldworkers explore new ways of presenting their experiences in diverse cultural settings. For whatever reason, such experiential accounts in the northeastern part of North America are either quite rare or virtually nonexistent. Simply on a pragmatic basis there is much that we can learn from such accounts, since they provide information that is not normally included in a more formal ethnographic version of a community study. We can learn, for example, about how ethnographers' everyday experiences influence their intellectual perspectives, about how anthropologists interact with their informants in social settings, about the living problems that they encounter, and, in general, about the unique flavor of that particular ethnographic 'present'.[5] All in all, these accounts provide a useful backdrop to understanding how the more formal account was conceived and carried out, aside from the fact that such inter-cultural experiences tend to be interesting in their own right.

It is also important for me to point out that my life experiences described in these pages are based on factual events that occurred while conducting research among the Anishinaabe people living in an isolated region where they live in tents and log cabins (at the time of my fieldwork in the 1970s), do not possess cars or trucks, as there are no streets or roads here. At the time of my fieldwork, there was a limited access to seasonal wage work but for the most part they subsisted by hunting and fishing, as they have always done in the past, and rely little on store-bought foods. It is also important to add that these Indigenous peoples do not live a life untouched by modern society. They have some use for modern technology, such as snow machines and up to date hunting equipment, but they are still living a life in the bush when I conducted my research as their ancestor did.

Another important point is that this book is not only about the research results that I was able to uncover during the course of my fieldwork, but also about my reflections of my activities over the last several years. Such reflections have suggested to me that it has become increasingly evident that anthropologists should attempt to describe how the personal experiences of their fieldwork have effected them, not only as professionals but also as people who are immersed in the ebb and flow of everyday life. As much as anthropologists attempted to portray their situation in the past, they are not unattached from the settings of their work, they also influence the people around them and, in turn, are similarly affected by the people with whom they interact and by their research experiences. Therefore, the intent of this ethnographic narrative is to present what is probably an all too rare study of Indigenous fieldwork in terms of actual events, and then to examine these events and episodes in the context of the ethnographer's experiences in fieldwork. It is a matter somewhat of how much we would like to shape events, and how much we are willing to let them shape us in turn. As in life itself, we do not know what will happen next, but we always hope that something happens (to paraphrase Margaret Mead) and must be prepared for it.

It is a basic fact of research that fieldworkers need particular events and situations, in order that these become studies and analyses which are then placed in a larger context. As Hortense Powdermaker (1966: 296) explained, anthropologists "write out of their immersion and participation in a particular situation from which they have been able to detach themselves. But they write of the particular…the particular illuminates the human condition." One might also add that these 'particulars' sometimes come to us unannounced, on our door step, but mostly we have to go out and seek them, to reach out for the stuff and details of everyday life. In this sense, we can also appreciate what Clifford Geertz (1973: 24) meant when he talked about ethnography becoming 'imprisoned in the immediacy of its own detail'.[6]

It is in the documentation of this detail, in the 'writing of culture', that some controversy has been generated in the discipline, especially as it comes to portraying the 'other' in an ethnographic narrative. For example, there are those who would see ethnography and fieldwork in the context of power relations. The issue here is what has been called a 'crisis of representation', which is to say, "the explicit discourse that reflects on the doing and writing of ethnography" (Marcus and Fischer 1986: 16). The challenge here is to "all those views of reality in social thought which prematurely overlook or reduce cultural diversity for the sake of the capacity to generalize or to affirm universal values" (ibid: 33). Furthermore, scholars such as Lila Abu-Lughod (1991) have been particularly critical of certain phases of anthropology for exaggerating uniqueness and 'particularism' (á la Franz Boas), of, in their opinion, overly emphasizing cultural differences, which translate into 'inferiority'. It is essentially their viewpoint which is at the heart of certain ongoing criticisms in anthropology and elsewhere against the concept of 'culture'.

Furthermore, if culture is "an ensemble of texts, themselves ensembles, which the anthropologist strains to read over the shoulder of those whom they properly belong" (Geertz 1973: 452), then we can pretty well dispense with the idea that culture is a universal concept, belonging to all people, in all societies. In Geertz's terms, the job of the anthropologist was to read and interpret this text that is written in 'shaped behavior'. If cultures are like texts, then it follows that embedded in each culture is its own unique interpretation. Thus, our task in creating ethnographic narratives is to elucidate this 'unique interpretation', and in so doing transcend the commonplace, the everyday nature of human behavior.

It is therefore evident that the so-called post-modernist approach in anthropology is much more than an issue concerning literary style; it is about cultural portrayal and representation.[7] It does question anthropological authority and calls for a 'dialogic' approach. And besides, it is clear that even post-modernist ethnography is controlled by some authority—the fieldworker. In the context of the present discussion, I would support the post-modernist argument that the construction of ethnography is largely a matter of organizing our "reflexive understandings" of the fieldwork experience. Thus, this process of constructive understanding becomes central to the problem of verification in fieldwork, given that quite different accounts of the same "reality" can be expected.

This issue of cultural portrayal has much to do with what we choose to write about, or not write about, and the ensuing ethnographic narrative that eventually unfolds from the stance or position that we decide to take. Writing involves a certain perspective, like an artist composing a painting— considerable thought is apt to go into the process. Barrett (1996: 232) suggests, for example, that "a great deal of reflecting, planning and organization must precede writing. My own approach is not to write a word of the actual manuscript until I have worked out the entire thing in my head." Without sounding cynical about his approach, one could only hope to attain this level of competence and memory. In this sense, the writing process of a fieldworker is something akin to that of a novelist.

Yet, we are reminded that, "The business of writing up fieldwork has always been a controversial part of anthropological research…And today, perhaps more than ever before, anthropologists pay close attention to how language shapes and influences their work" (Chiseri-Strater and Sunstein 1997: 277–278). I bring these matters to the reader's attention in the hope that one can begin to appreciate the inherent difficulties about describing just about anything pertaining to another culture, especially when one is using a language, terms, and concepts from a culture different from that which is being described in the first place. In other words, the intrinsic difficulties of cultural translation are manifold and inherently complex.

Anishinaabe Country

The area of northern Ontario that is the focus of this book is a rugged region consisting of some 800,000 square kilometers of glacially scoured Precambrian shield covered with coniferous forest and numerous lakes and streams. North of the Canadian National Railway (CNR) mainline through Ontario live about 50,000 people, almost exclusively Anishinaabe and Cree. Most of these northern Algonquians[8] live in relatively isolated settlements of under two thousand people, which are usually situated on the larger lakes and rivers. Generally, the northern Anishinaabe live between the southern area of the Canadian Shield, just north of Lake Superior, up to the Albany River, where there is a gradual cultural merging with the Cree (Rogers and Taylor 1981: 231–243). Since most roads from the south end at the CNR line, the usual mode of transportation in the area is by boat, snowmobile, and bush plane. Today, access to the internet and other forms of electronic communications have tended to lessen the isolation which was prevalent for the last generation of residents. While there are many local schools, often high school age children attend school in the larger centers such as Thunder Bay.

For the most part, the Anishinaabe of northern Ontario have subsisted on fishing, trapping, and wild rice harvesting, but all of these activities do not have the income potential to adequately support the growing population. In addition, store-bought foods found in the local stores are much higher in cost than is the case in comparable areas farther south. As a general rule, at present there is an acute lack of jobs suited to the remote location, skills and life-styles of the Indigenous people of the area, causing many young people to seek their fortunes farther south. While there is some variation from place to place, welfare and social assistance, along with other forms of transfer payments, forms a substantial proportion of a community's disposable income. The tourist industry, government sponsored community work projects, and commercial fishing provide the main sources of employment. Trapping, once the main stay of most Anishinaabe villages, and the major form of income, now has been mostly reduced to part time activities for more elderly residents as the fur industry has gone into decline because of competition with synthetic materials and various animal rights protest movements. While not readily evident in most government reports, almost every community nonetheless has a sizeable 'hidden' economy involving subsistence hunting and fishing, firewood collection and the manufacture of local products such as snowshoes, sleds, leather products, and various types of handicrafts.

The history of the northern Anishinaabe and the Cree over the last several centuries has been dominated largely by the fur trade, and their interaction with the Hudson's Bay Company. This territory, previously known as Rupert's Land, extends roughly from Lake Nipigon north to Hudson Bay. For almost 200 years, fur merchants were the only Europeans with which the northern Anishinaabe had to contend. However, after about 1850, an increasingly wider array of outsiders could be found traversing Anishinaabe territory. Government agents came to sign treaties and settle land claims, missionaries arrived to introduce new religious beliefs, and surveyors plotted the future course of railways, roads, and mineral development (Bell 1870). The Indigenous people who were living north of the Robinson-Superior treaty limits, signed in 1850, negotiated one of the largest land settlements in Canadian history when they signed the James Bay Treaty in 1905. During that same summer a survey crew for the Canadian Transcontinental Railway (now called the Canadian National) was mapping a 200-kilometer strip of land westward from Lake Nipigon, just north of Lake Superior (Collins 1906). And by 1910, an anthropologist, Alanson Skinner (1911), had arrived to document some preliminary aspects of social and economic change in the area.

Completion of the CNR in 1912 afforded an opportunity for independent fur traders to reenact a process that had occurred during the height of the Hudson's Bay-Northwest Company rivalry. A hundred years after the amalgamation of the two companies in 1821, backwoods entrepreneurs once more attempted to circumvent trade, which in northern Ontario had previously gone to HBC posts on the Albany-Attawapiskat River systems (such as Fort Hope, Lansdowne, and Osnaburgh House), or to posts in the Lake Nipigon drainage area. Independent fur traders chose their positions with some foresight, locating on the shortest canoe routes from the Albany River to the CN rail line.[9]

The Genesis of Collins

Collins was the terminus for one of these routes, and as such was an ideal location for the establishment of a rail line trading post. For the Anishinaabe trappers in the area, competition among the operators of rail line posts, coupled with less expensive freight overhead because of the proximity to the railway, meant a lower cost of living. In addition, rail line trading posts could offer a more varied supply of trade goods, and higher fur prices, than their more northerly Hudson's Bay Company competitors. It was factors such as these that contributed to the early success of rail line fur trading posts, and provided the economic incentives which drew large numbers of Anishinaabe trappers to various rail line locations.

Collins Store in 1967
Photo Courtesy of Anita Patience

Although the first trading post in Collins did not open for business until 1921, almost a decade after completion of the CN line, residents relate that permanent log structures were not constructed on Collins Lake until the end of the 1930s. The years before World War II were a period of resurgence in Anishinaabe geographical mobility in northern Ontario, a demographic pattern reflecting population increases and consequent pressure on the land and its resources. For most of the time during the five-year period from 1941 to 1945, a sizeable proportion of the Fort Hope (now called Eabametoong First Nation) population was absent from the home community for treaty payments (Baldwin 1957; Driben and Trudeau 1983). Of those absent from their home reserve, about 50 percent of these were stationed in the vicinity of Lansdowne House, an HBC outpost of Fort Hope some 60 kilometers to the north.

The remaining 25 percent were scattered throughout the territory, primarily at points along the Albany River or the rail line. By 1945, 31 Fort Hope families had settled at various rail line locations. Since that time 18 of these Fort Hope families remained to form the nucleus of the present (1970s) Collins community. For the most part, these families stayed at Collins only during the summer months living in tents, returning to their trap lines for the winter. It was only with the establishment of a school at Collins in 1960 that there was any widespread construction of more permanent log houses, and the year-round occupation of the village.

As such, Collins is an Anishinaabe community formed by the migration of northern Indigenous people, mostly from Fort Hope (Eabametoong), during the war years to the Canadian National Railway line. In general, the genesis of settlements such as Collins can be attributed to increases in the population densities of northern reserve communities, and the resulting competition for trapping territories and other diminishing resources, such as fish, game, and firewood. Migrants to the rail line sought to extricate themselves from the restrictions and uncertainties of a limited resource base by moving to areas where there was a greater opportunity to supplement subsistence production with income earned through wage labor. As such, the construction of the tourist lodge project at Whitewater Lake (described in Chapter 4) to the north of Collins could be seen as a culmination of this long term switch from subsistence hunting to increasing wage labor opportunities, although the local economy was nonetheless comprised of aspects of both sources of income when I conducted my fieldwork in the 1970s.

Economic Change

It is therefore important to note that the eventual movement away from a subsistence-trapping economy to an ever-increasing emphasis on wage labor was a relatively long term process. The first opportunities for wage employment in the area, aside from occasional trading post work, began with the CNR construction just after the turn of the twentieth century. There are no surviving records to indicate the extent to which Indigenous people were employed during the railway construction stage, but the number was probably small given the short duration of possible employment, and the fact that most people in the Lake Nipigon area at this time were still actively engaged in the annual subsistence cycle of summer fishing and winter trapping. One observer at the time noted that there were a number of Indigenous men working in the railway camps, but only for short periods of time: "The bunkhouse itself in the Canadian hinterland signifies an intrusion upon his former domain. Camp activities of whatever kind mean ultimately a narrowing of privileges and customs that for so long have marked his mode of life" (Bradwin 1928: 116).

After the construction stage of the railway, full-time maintenance jobs generally went to outsiders. Over the last generation or so, many outside workers have transferred to sections closer to the larger urban centers eschewing the isolation of the lonely northern railway camps, with Indigenous people tending to fill these vacancies. Aside from railway work, the trading post in Collins employed casual workers to cut firewood, to maintain and store fish in the icehouse, and to transfer furs and supplies back and forth from the rail line. The spasmodic nature of production and wage work cycles is illustrated by the following description of economic trends in Collins during the 1950s:

The trading-store owner bought a thousand dollars' worth of fish from four families in 1954, no fish in 1955. Blueberries bring from $1.50 to $2.00 a basket, and the amount taken varies greatly from year to year. Ten guides were employed in 1954, six in 1955, at ten dollars a day, for about ten days each. The lumber mill at Fee Spur employed twenty in 1954, but only two in 1955 (Baldwin 1957: 92).

Decades later, railway maintenance and activities related to the construction of a tourist lodge at Whitewater Lake accounted for virtually all of the full-time employment for village residents. Railway work also accounts for most of the geographical mobility of the local labor force since men are employed at various locations on the 'sections' on the CN rail line from Nakina to Sioux Lookout.

By paying attention to the various types of occupations available for Anishinaabe workers through the years, general trends have become discernible in the development process. Casual or seasonal employment has become less prevalent as demand has increased for more regular, full-time employment. In conjunction with this new preference, such activities as hunting and fishing, while still important as an income producer in the local economy, benefited from labor-saving technology such as snowmobiles and more efficient water craft. This is especially true for the more affluent workers in the community who have the resources to most effectively exploit aquatic and faunal cycles, and thereby reduce their costs through country food production.

Other forms of casual employment which were quite prevalent a generation ago, such as berry picking, firefighting, and tree planting, now have little preference among Indigenous workers. In fact, Collins leaders have told government officials that they will not tolerate the conscription of young men in the community for summer firefighting because their removal from the local labor force is disruptive of ongoing construction projects and that these workers are crucial to the community's long-term development goals. As such, these goals would tend to be compromised by the indiscriminate commandeering of local workers. Presumably the Ministry of Natural Resources now recruits fire fighters from the more isolated, less economical developed regions of the north where there still exists a demand for wage employment of this kind.

All in all, my research in Collins indicates that this is a northern community that is, in a certain sense, half-way into the Euro-Canadian economy, and the other half maintains contact with the people's traditional social and economic roots. It is an accepted fact that wage work has become an ever-increasing facet of the local economy because of the necessity of purchasing modern goods of various sorts. In the small, relatively isolated Indigenous communities that are spread throughout northern Quebec and Ontario, and other regions of the boreal forest belt, there is not the same lack of proximity to a traditional economic life that was probably already forgotten by the grandparents of southern Indigenous people generations ago.[10]

24

This fact, I believe, has important implications for the formulation of governmental policy for northern areas. While economist and other government advisors who lack first-hand familiarity with Indigenous conditions in the north are apt to concentrate on the flow of money and the purchase of goods in the market place, anthropologists who have lived in northern Indigenous communities are more apt to be aware of all the various sorts of activities that engage people in the pursuit of the goods and services that support their way of life, regardless of the presence or absence of cash transactions, which is especially the case with the important role that the subsistence economy plays in maintaining a healthy life style for northern residents.

For those conducting research into the economic life of northern Indigenous settlements, the economist's narrower perspective on economic change has an unfortunate aspect to it. Any attempts to simply duplicate an industrial wage economy in northern areas is apt to draw attention away from other important areas of concern, such as the benefits to be derived from an efficient use of local resources, and the contributions of traditional economic activity to the viability of northern Indigenous community life. From the economist's perception, in a developing economy there is a trend toward full-time wage work and occupational specialization. It is no doubt true that over the long run, that is since the end of the twentieth century, this trend has been occurring in northern areas to a larger and larger extent. Yet it is also the case that in many northern settlements the pattern of economic diversity not only remains a strong one, but also remains a preferred situation because it tends to lessen dependence on the outside for food, fuel, and other renewable resources.[11]

Northern Studies in Anthropology

From an anthropological perspective, the history of ethnographic research in northern Ontario has been rather sparse, at least compared to other areas of Canada (Rogers 1981: 19–29). This research has consisted mostly of various ethnological sketches and surveys in the early part of the twentieth century, and then shifting later on to more involved, problem-oriented research. Ruth Landes (1937), a student of Franz Boas, conducted fieldwork in the Kenora-Rainy River area in the 1930s, thus initiating a period of more intensive ethnographic work. This was followed in the 1940s by Irving Hallowell's (1992) focus on the Anishinaabe of the Berens River area near the Manitoba border. Later ethnographic accounts of the northern Anishinaabe were produced on the basis of fieldwork carried out in the 1950s which focused on various community studies, such as a focus on social and economic change for the Pekangekum band (Dunning 1958, 1959) and Round Weagamow Lake (Rogers 1962, 1966, Rogers and Black 1976). At an earlier date, as mentioned previously, Alanson Skinner conducted a survey along Lac Seul and the Albany River.

Farther south, Baldwin (1957) conducted a study of social problems in the Collins community, northwest of Lake Nipigon. In more recent times, an ethnohistorical account was written concerning the Osnaburgh Band (Bishop 1974). For the most part, Rogers's (1962: 2) comment that "so little field work has been done in this area northern Ontario that comparison and generalization are impossible" is still largely true today. It is no doubt unfortunate, but there has been little published on the contemporary Indigenous peoples of this area for nearly a generation after the work of Dunning and Rogers. A focus on emergent leadership among the Anishinaabe along the Canadian National Rail line continued a trend of more focused or problem-oriented work (Hedican 1986). There have fortunately also been several studies of more recent note, such as Driben and Trudeau's account of the impact of government programs at Fort Hope (now called Eabametoong), Driben's (1986) ethnography of Aroland, a community similar to Collins situated on the CN rail line, as well as my own continuing work in the area (Hedican 1990, 2001, 2008, 2017) which extended for three decades from the 1970s to the early 2000s.[12]

Current Economic Challenges

Northern Ontario in recent years has also been the subject of various resource development projects and future proposals, the most prominent of which is known collectively as the *Ring of Fire*.[13] This region is near the Attawapiskat River in the Kenora District which extends about 70 kilometers east of the First Nation community of Webequie and due north of the Albany River, west of James Bay. There are three First Nations communities in this area that would be directly impacted by mineral exploration and development, namely Marten Falls, Webequie, and Neskantaga (Garrick 2010). All of these

First Nations suffer from depressed economic conditions in one way or another, such as high unemployment, low per-capita incomes, and lack of employment possibilities. As Tony Clement, former Treasury Board president and FedNor minister, acknowledge in 2013, the Ring of Fire area is home to some of the 'most socioeconomically disadvantaged communities in all of Canada'.

Mr. Clement also stated that "chronic housing shortages, low education outcomes and lack of access to clean drinking water jeopardizes the ability of local First Nations to benefit from significant economic, employment and business development opportunities associated with the Ring of Fire developments." Nevertheless, the Ring of Fire, according to Clement, represents a "once-in-a-life time opportunity to create jobs and generate growth and long-term prosperity for northern Ontario and the nation" (Ontario Ministry of Natural Resources 2013). Thus, the Ring of Fire development is seen as a possible significant economic benefit to the area, but there are infrastructural challenges that could blunt the possible benefits that the mining activities could bring to the region. Bob Rae, former Ontario premier, was appointed to represent the First Nations impacted by the mining developments as their chief negotiator which suggests that the Government of Ontario has taken these developments in northern Ontario in a serious manner (*Globe and Mail* 2013).

Thus, it is fair to indicate that resource issues are becoming ever more prominent as mining companies are discovering the untapped mineral wealth of Ontario, especially in northern areas. The Ring of Fire is such a situation involving mining companies anxious to move forward beyond the exploration stage, while First Nations people in the area argue for a slower process in which the Aboriginal rights promised by past treaties are honored. There is also the potential conflict in Anishinaabe country between development companies involved in the mining and forest industries and those Indigenous interests, such as the development of the tourist industries in places such as Collins, and the possible harm that could occur to the environment. In northern Ontario, one might conclude that an uneasy balance is taking shape between those Indigenous people who seek employment opportunities and those that seek a balance between economic development and preservation of the relatively pristine environment of the northern subarctic. Choosing from among these diverse opportunities will no doubt make for difficult choices for the Anishinaabe population of future generations.

Research in Anthropology

Anthropologists who are conducting fieldwork in a community setting usually arrive with a research agenda and a certain number of objectives. They also commonly arrive with a hypothesis, or set of hypotheses, about what they expect to find through their research. These hypotheses are not what one could call 'preconceived notions', rather, they are well-founded ideas built upon existing academic literature. However, the researcher also seeks new ideas, which is the reason or reasons for conducting the research in the first place.

In the midst of an immersion in the academic literature, the researcher arrives with some idea about what to expect; however, an absorption into the everyday life of a community can be a disconcerting experience. First, one requires a place to live, and a search for what are termed 'key informants' who can serve in the information gathering process[14]. One soon realizes that there are various social activities happening that were not initially expected. The anthropologist begins to become immersed in the activity of everyday life with the result that the initial research expectations could begin to recede in the background of living priorities. Some researchers even find new and interesting aspects of community life to study that they had not initially expected, and a shift in research priorities could take place. For most people, though, one slowly settles into the flow of community life and start to sort out ways in which to gather the information to support or reject their initialresearch priorities.

Anthropologists, once they begin to adjust to their new lives as community members, partly in and partly out of this new social system, begin to realize that one of their biggest concerns is learning how to translate what they are witnessing in everyday life into certain patterns, into larger themes, that can be utilized as the basis for larger descriptions of everyday life. The minutiae of everyday life may have some interest, but it is usually far too disconnected to form overall patterns in a person's mind unless one is more rigorous is defining what is needed to discuss the hypotheses that one brought to the fieldwork experience in the first place. In the midst of all these adjustments to the community, one also needs to be an opportunist. Events will occur, or one will meet new people who can aid in setting the research in a somewhat altered direction. Flexibility in the face of a community's everyday activities is a necessary component of successful fieldwork.

For whatever reason, there has been far too little discussion in the academic literature of anthropology about the manner in which the details of everyday life are transcended or transformed into larger patterns that can be appropriately used as a basis for theoretical discussions. There are times when a certain 'burst of insight'[15] is involved, a sudden perception of an event that was not realized before. At other times, the research process is more systematic. Information is gathered in a methodical manner much akin to putting together the pieces of a large jigsaw puzzle. In any event, it is pretty much up to each anthropologist themselves to work out the details about how this transformation from the bits and pieces of everyday life are transformed into useful patterns, configurations or other designs that have real explanatory power when it comes to defending the researcher's ideas in the arena of academic scrutiny as a peer-review process.

The overall purpose of this book, then, is to suggest the analytic techniques that I used in my own fieldwork in northern Canada as methods of transforming the details of everyday life in an Indigenous community into larger theoretical patterns. The rationale for such a book is based on a discussion of the manner in which everyday life is transformed, as a step-by-step process into larger spheres of discussion, into the eventual ethnography that finally emerges from the veritable quagmire of detail in which the researcher is apparently immersed. Thus, the first rationale for this study is to discuss the manner in which field data concerning everyday life in anthropology is transformed into ethnographic and theoretical discussions. On this basis, this book would serve to fill a gap in the literature focusing on the methods that anthropologists use to gather information in their field studies. Second, there is also a paucity of descriptions by anthropologists who have worked in northern Canada concerning such matters as their living conditions, relationships with Indigenous community members, and ethnographic goals. In this regard, such a book would contribute to the history of ethnographic studies in Canada of which there is little existing literature.

Anthropologists often live in small communities engaging in what is called in the discipline *participant observation*.[16] On a daily basis, notes are usually kept on the everyday goings on of community members, most of which are probably fairly routine in nature. People visit each other, trade for things, herd animals, fish and hunt, in other words all the sorts of activities that make up everyday life. While notes may be kept on these various activities, there is usually also a more specific purpose to this sort of research that the anthropologists wish to investigate. Thus, on the one hand there are the quotidian events of day to day living, and on the other, data collection with a more refined or specific purpose in mind.

After a fairly extended period of time spent engaging in community life, the anthropologist then writes up a report of his or her findings, called an *ethnography*.[17] This research report is usually comprised of the specific details which interested the anthropologist in the first place, such as some aspect of social life, politics, economics or some other matter. In this way, most of the details noted on the daily life of the community members are not particularly relevant to the overall objectives of the investigation and are soon forgotten as the major themes take precedence over the mundane details of communal life in the village or town. As a process of research it is important to discuss the changes that are made from the events of everyday life to the more prominent theoretical details in anthropological research.

Another purpose of this book is to help explain, on the basis of my own field research among the Indigenous inhabitants of a small community in northern Ontario, how transitions are made from the details of daily life to the broader explanations that take place in social anthropology. It details, for example, a central activity in this community pertaining to the construction of a tourist lodge (in Chapter 4), and the local leadership which facilitated this endeavor, based on everyday living in the community. The goal is to provide a much needed investigation into the transitions that take place between the observations that anthropologists makes on people's daily lives during the course of field research and the more abstract or theoretical themes that they eventually deduce from these everyday events.

Studying Everyday Life

In the academic literature, various authors have shown an interest in everyday life as a methodology in itself (see Berger and Luckman 1966; Kahn 2011). A focus on everyday life, according to Brinkmann (2012: 4), requires that we operate on the "fundamental assumption...that there is no clear difference between 'doing a research project' and 'living a life'." In a similar vein, anthropologist Tim Ingold (2011: 240) advocated that we try to minimize the traditional divisions between theory and method. Rather than have our research dominated by a theoretical agenda, Ingold suggests that "there is no division, in practice, between work and life. An intellectual craft is a practice that involves the whole person, continually drawing on past experience as it is projected into the future."

The term 'everyday life' has entered the literature in the social sciences from several different sources. One of the more significant of these is the classic work by Irving Goffman (1959) on *The Presentation of Self in Everyday Life*. There is also Lefebvre's (1968) *Everyday Life in the Modern World* and de Certeau's (1984) *The Practice of Everyday Life*. In these works, there is a focus on the mundane details of human interaction as the key to understanding social processes (Brinkmann 2012). A focus on everyday lives becomes even more central in the modern era, when society "has been broken apart and reconstituted as everyday life" (Ferguson 2009: 160). In the late nineteenth century, there was also a particular social science focus on everyday life that began with the University of Chicago when there was a need to understand people's experiences in urban environments (Jacobson 2009).

In terms of a general definition of everyday life, we could follow Ferguson's (2009: 164) suggestion that everyday life refers to "a host of routine activities, private and public, carried out on a regular, if not actually daily, basis; such as eating sleeping, working, commuting, shopping and so on." Furthermore, he adds, everyday life is "the inclusive arena in which occasional, incidental, and unusual events *also* take place" (ibid). One might also point out, though, that everyday events do not have to be entirely reoccurring events because, as an example, we might only be divorced once in our life yet this does not make such an event that extraordinary in people's everyday lives. Still, it is not easy to define everyday life. In Elias's (1998) characterization, as an example, it is suggested that everyday life can be contrasted with such areas as public life, exceptional events, holidays or the life of the privileged class.

On the other hand, Scott (2009) sees everyday life as taking place in a particular 'space', such as work and living spaces. One of the difficulties in defining everyday life is that it is our principle or paramount reality; in a sense it encases our entire being, it is ubiquitous. It is seemingly everywhere like a fish immersed in its aquatic world; since we cannot imagine another form of existence; it could even go largely unnoticed. Similarly, in Dreier's (2008) terms, everyday life is a 'zone' where we lead or conduct our lives.

In an attempt to define the diverse experiences of everyday life, Maffesoli (1989) suggests following three characteristics. First, the researcher is a participant in everyday life and not just a spectator, so that the researcher writes from the vantage point of their participation in the social world; second, the research into everyday life is based on human experiences; and third, studying everyday life requires the researcher to adopt an attitude of 'conceptual audacity' such that an analysis of the mundane world becomes intellectually challenging and thought-provoking. In this sense, a conceptual audacity can "break the closure of the political-economic logic which still underlies many analyses" (1989: v).

One of the main problems with studying everyday life is that there is so much that we are prone to take for granted. In this sense, it is very difficult to understand what is obvious to us. As Hall, Lashua and Coffey articulate:

How are we to know that which we begin by taking for granted? This is precisely no problem at all when it comes to 'doing' daily life, in everyday ways—fluency here follows from our unconscious familiarity with the mundane—though much harder when it comes to knowing the everyday and making it the explicit object of attention and understanding. Here the everyday resists, or rather eludes, scrutiny. Attending to the everyday can require an estranging sensitivity, one that is more often found in the arts than science (2008: 1021–1022).

One of the strategies that one can take to overcome these difficulties, as suggested by Noblit and Hare (1988), is to continually stress the obvious, by 'making the obvious obvious'. Another suggestion, that made by Parker (1996: 190), is what he calls taking a 'step back'. Parker argues that taking a step back is a crucial part of any study of everyday life, which consists of producing a critical distance between the researcher and the event (or object) in order that we may come to an understanding of the relationships among the phenomena under study. Or, in Richard Rorty's (1991: 175) terms, the "way to re-enchant the world…is to stick to the concrete."

A number of contemporary scholars, such as Gardiner (2000, 2009), Highmore (2002), Sherington (2006), and Pink (2012) have made attempts to critically discuss and synthesize the work of twentieth-century theorists and their perspectives on everyday life. Such everyday life studies have also taken an interdisciplinary approach with attempts to describe the manner in which everyday life research has emerged from different scholarly traditions. Thus, there are a number of different perspectives that have drawn from studies in philosophy, anthropology, sociology, among other disciples (Howes 2003, Edwards et al. 2006, Hubbard et al. 2004, and Schatzki et al. 2001). In particular, there have been several anthropological studies (i.e., Stoller 1989, Howes 1991, Seremetakis 1994) which have considered details of everyday life in their approaches, but these have not been very numerous, compared to other disciples, such as psychology, and sociology especially. We might, however, make special note of anthropologist Tim Ingold's (2000) attempts to bring the philosophy of Maurice Merleau-Ponty to the study of sensory perceptions in our everyday lives. It is also worth noting that according to Ingold's position, the manner in which we understand the world is not based on a single perception but a multiplicity of these as our experiences are modified, or vary, by different physical and social contexts. In this regard, our sensory perceptions developed in everyday life are to a large extent 'culturally constructed'.

One might also note that many interdisciplinary approach to everyday life are largely historical in nature, rather than focused on the development of theoretical themes. There has also developed to a certain extent a disjuncture between cultural studies of everyday life and other approaches taken in the social sciences, suggesting that a multidisciplinary synthesis of approaches may be a long way off. As an example, Highmore suggests that scholars have started "thinking about an area of life that manages, for the most part, to avoid scrutiny," (2002: vii) by shielding their work behind sometimes inscrutable disciplinary boundaries. He also takes note of the ever increasing number of cultural studies of everyday life, which, as could be the case with social anthropology, have researched the details of people's everyday lives in developing countries but have not developed similar approaches to the lives of people in modern, Western, urban contexts.

There is an opportunity, as Moran (2005) suggests, for anthropologists to focus research in European ethnology on everyday life in a profitable manner. Overall, the problem according to Pink's (2012) assessment is not the interdisciplinary nature of everyday life studies, "Rather it is that there has been little joining up of these bodies of work theoretically or empirically. The study of the theory of everyday life is often undertaken in isolation from the ethnographic and qualitative literature on everyday life thus, we need to seek to make connections between these approaches."

I would contend that this is an important suggestion for anthropologists, so that they might broaden their studies to include ethnographies of everyday life in a variety of cross-cultural perspectives. On another point, it has been noted that when anthropologists focus on everyday life, it often has been focused on the material aspects of life, which is to say, on approaches to consumption, rather than more explicitly on the social aspects of everyday life (Shove, Watson, Hand and Ingram 2007: 2–11; see also Casey and Martens 2007 and Highmore 2001 on the topic of material culture and everyday life).

In sum, the study of everyday life can be described as focusing on the mundane, the routine or the habitual. There has been a tendency in the social sciences, as I suggest is the case with anthropology, to ignore the unexceptional, to concentrate on the 'big' events, to the neglect of what people commonly do on an everyday basis. I hope to demonstrate in this book, on the basis of my own fieldwork among Indigenous peoples in northern Ontario, that looking under the surface of the quotidian events in life can be rewarding in an empirical sense. Such a focus can aid us in understanding larger social issues that apparently lie hidden because they are regarded as so ordinary as to be unworthy of serious inquiry. It is apparent that such has been the case with social anthropology because of the minimal attention that has been paid to the everyday lives of people as evidence by this gap in the academic literature of the discipline.

Beginning Fieldwork

It amazes me at times that certain twists of fate place us in a position in life that seem totally inconsequential at the time but eventually have a dramatic impact on the course of our lives. There was a time when my younger brother William had a short term teaching position in an Indigenous community called Collins which is situated on the Canadian National Railway line about thirty kilometers west of the north shore of Lake Nipigon in northwestern Ontario. He phoned me one day in April, 1972, saying that he would soon be leaving the community and that I should come for a visit during the following weekend.

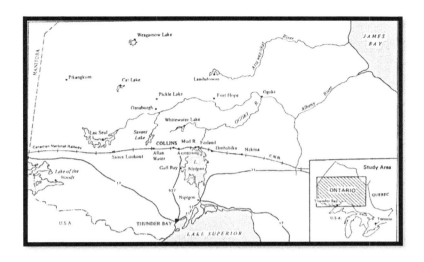

Map 1 Northern Ontario

When I arrived, it became evident that most of the residents in the community continued hunting and fishing for their daily subsistence needs, lived in small log cabins with no electricity or running water, and that there were no roads, cars or trucks in this place. He portrayed the situation as one that probably would not exist very much longer in northern Ontario among the Indigenous (Anishinaabe) people. From Thunder Bay, there was a three hour drive up to the CNR line at Armstrong and from there I boarded the passenger train for the twenty-minute ride to Collins. My brother greeted me at the train and introduced me to an elder in the community named Peter Patience. Peter operated a small store in the community and was the postmaster. After a while, he suggested that I stay in the community after my brother left since he could provide some short term employment for me utilizing my university skills at letter writing and engaging in discussions concerning various plans that he and his brothers had for the economic development in the future.

Peter Patience (left) and Haimish Patience (right) with sister Sarah
c. 1975 photo courtesy of Anita Patience

Peter explained that he and his other two brothers, Donald and Haimish, had originally been born in Fort Hope (now called Eabomatoong) up on the Albany River as did many other people in the community. When he was a child, his father, who had been an employee of the Hudson's Bay Company in Fort Hope, decided to move to Collins as an independent fur trader. When I arrived in Collins, there were about 150 people living there compressed between the rail line and the north shore of a lake called Name-Sakehegun (Trout Lake). Peter explained that his father had passed away recently and so he and his two other brothers were attempting to provide a transition in the village economy from trapping and occasional guiding to a wage economy. The brothers, he explained, had been in contact with various provincial and federal government departments in an attempt to secure grants to facilitate this economic transition. Their primary goal was to construct a tourist lodge at Whitewater Lake situated about seventy kilometers north of Collins.

I kept in touch with Peter and others in the community for several years and eventually an opportunity arose in 1974 which gave me the time to conduct an extended period of doctoral research in northern Ontario, and so I thought that the goal of the Collins' people to construct their tourist would be an interesting project to investigate. I discussed this plan with Peter and he said that the community would welcome someone who could document their efforts at community development. The various notes that I kept in my field diary were never meant for publication; however, reading them after a period of reflection, I began to realize that a discussion of these writings could be the basis for an interesting dialogue concerning the methods anthropologists use to transcend the gap between observations of community members' everyday lives on the one hand, and the eventual formulation of more abstract themes on the other.

Ethnographic Setting

When the Canadian National Railway line was built through northern Ontario in 1911, along the north shore of Lake Nipigon and on to Manitoba, several 'free traders', that is traders not employed by the Hudson's Bay Company, began to construct trading posts along the new railway line beginning about 1920. The rail line trading posts offered distinct advantages over their more northern competitors. The Hudson's Bay Company usually imported their trade goods from England at a much greater expense than their rail line competitors, so that economic advantages were a distinct aspect which began to draw trappers from the more northerly areas, such as those living along the Albany River.

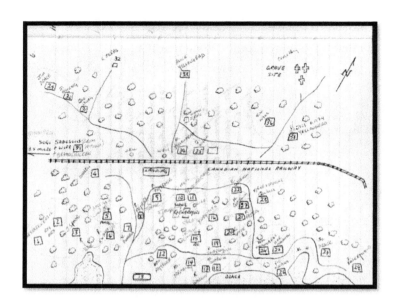

Map 2 Plan of the Village of Collins

Collins was the name given to one of these incipient communities, named after a CNR surveyor. The name originally only referred to the railway section houses which were spaced along the rail line about every thirty kilometers or so. The new fur trading establishment was a convenient spot on the railroad for transferring goods and passengers, and offered lower prices for trappers' goods, and paid higher fur prices because of the reduced transportation costs than the more established HBC posts farther north. As such, Collins drew trappers and their families southward, farther and farther away from their original home communities in the north. In the initial periods, the trappers traded at the rail line posts then began the long trek by canoe back to their home communities on the Albany River. Before long many of these trappers decided to spend the summer months on a large lake near the Collins post, then travelled back to their trap lines in the fall, thus forsaking the Hudson's Bay Company. After a while, a community of perhaps a hundred or so people began to form the beginnings of the Collins population, many who had originated from the Albany River area, but later joined by others from nearby Lake Nipigon.

Getting Started

My fieldwork began when I received a message from Peter Patience, who was one of the directors of a local development group called the Ogoki River Guides. He mentioned that his brother, Donald Patience, had been staying in Thunder Bay for the last several weeks meeting with various government officials in an attempt to raise funds for the construction of a tourist lodge north of their community. I subsequently met with Donald at the Royal Edward Hotel the following evening. He filled me in on various details concerning his dealings with a potential fund raiser of theirs who were employed with ARDA (Ontario's Agricultural Rural Development Agency).

The following morning, we packed up our belongings and headed for the Thunder Bay Airport. From there, we travelled by TransAir to Dryden, in the western area of northern Ontario. We then hired a taxi to take us to Sioux Lookout on the CNR line and from there took a six-hour train ride to Collins. Peter met us at the train depot, which was not much more than a small landing. Peter is a store keeper in Collins, a business which he inherited from his father, as I mentioned who was a former Hudson's Bay Company fur trader from Fort Hope. His residence is attached to the store along with several small rooms to accommodate guests. After a supper of lake trout and potatoes prepared by his wife Dorothy, we talked well into the evening, after which I settled into one of the spare rooms.

Edward Hedican (L) and Donald Patience (R) c. 1975

After breakfast the following morning, Peter took me outside and pointed to a small log cabin across a field adjoining the rear of his house. He explained that the house was owned by a fishing guide named Sogo Sabosons who spent his summers several kilometers away maintaining a group of cabins owned by American tourists. Peter thought that I should make an arrangement with Sogo such that I would live in his cabin if I helped repair it and let him occasionally stay there. Later, I walked down the railway tracks to Sogo's place, introduced myself and the reason for my visit. Before long we had arrived at an arrangement similar to Peter's suggestion. Now I felt settled into the community. I was busy for a week or so repairing the roof, installing a new window, constructing some shelves, and before long had a comfortable place to live and hopefully to meet members of the local community.

Lessons Learned

Life is a learning experience, or at least it is supposed to be. 'Live and learn' is the old expression. This is true in life but especially so when one is conducting research in the social sciences. While it should go without saying, research in which there are no lessons is not very valuable. Research is conducted so that certain issues can be explored, and in this way others will not necessarily duplicate what came before, and thereby have something to build upon. This is the way science proceeds, through trial and error. Even when the results of research do not validate one's hypothesis or previous presumptions at least that is a result worth discussing. One way or another one should be reflective and attempt to assess one's lessons—were these lessons useful? Did they lead to new discoveries? Was there something in these lessons that can be built upon for the future? It is for this reason that each of the following chapters will conclude with a section called 'Lessons Learned' as a way of summing up the goals and objects of the research that is reported.

There is an old saying attributed to Confucius to the effect that "choose a profession you love and you will never have to work another day in your life." Of course any profession has its problems, yet for those who have found their 'life's calling', then the struggles can seem worthwhile when we are trying to achieve our goals in life. As far as I was concerned, as a beginning undergraduate student I felt lost, not knowing where I wanted to go in life. I found an introductory anthropology class intriguing, at least more than other subjects that I was taking at the time. In my second year, I decided to switch my major from history (I'm still interested in this too) to anthropology and 'go for broke', as the saying goes. Most of my fellow students said that I was crazy —"How many jobs are there in Canada for anthropologist," they asked. Their point was obvious, but I also realized that if I didn't find a subject that I was interested in, then I was not likely to put in a full effort.

That weekend when I went home to visit my parents, my father was reading his newspaper as usual and my mother was engaged on the other side of the couch with her daily crossword puzzle. "Well Eddie," my father asked, "what's up now?"

"I switched my major," I replied, "I'm now an anthropology major!"

My father lowered his paper, and looked over at my mother, "Marge, do you think Eddie could at least take a subject that we can pronounce?"

My mother responded, "Oh, it's okay, Ed same name as me, Eddie's going to study the Egyptians."

My father, unimpressed, raised his newspaper again, "Well, as long as Eddie gets a job out of it."

Both of my parents passed away years ago, and if I saw them again, I'd say, "Yes, I did get a job out of it, and much more. Here I am retired and writing another book just for the fun of it." The lesson here is that everyday life is far from boring when you find something interesting to do. The day I decided to switch my major to anthropology was one of those life decisions that is made by students every day, but it was one of those decisions that certainly changed my life for the better.

Conclusion

For the most part, it has been fairly common for anthropologists to conduct their research in remote areas of the world with relatively small populations. For many decades, anthropologists attempted to cover numerous aspects of community life, once referred to as anthropology 'in the round', however in more recent times their research has become much more problem oriented. In other words, as a preparatory stage before field work, anthropologists spend as much time as they can analyzing previous research reports with the goal of finding an entry into a particular field of study, either because there is a gap in the existing literature, or a new interpretation may be called for. In any event, anthropologists today commonly prepare to investigate some specific issue that they hope can be developed into a wider perspective.

However, as most researchers begin to realize, once they begin their investigation in the field, new ethnographic issues are apt to emerge, or new, more interesting, problems begin to materialize. In these cases, the research begins to follow a new tract, sometime radically different from their original proposed plan of action. It is these unexpected or fortuitous events that make field studies so rewarding. Eventually findings are gathered together, arguments broached, and a report is prepared. It is important to indicate, though, that such a process involving data collection and articulating the research findings is not simply a matter of 'writing up' the results. Nor is this a matter simply of creating fictions, literary texts or interpretations as the post-modernists of the Clifford and Marcus (1986) era were prone to suggest.[18]

Anthropological investigations, it could therefore be suggested, are not simply a matter pertaining to the 'creation' of research results. There are important conceptual transitions that need to be made which transforms the specific details of everyday life into the broader abstractions and patterns that can be utilized in an attempt to generalize beyond the characteristics of the community itself. For whatever reason, anthropologists in my opinion have been averse to discussing how they accomplish such transitions, as if they possibly fear that discussing them will reveal some fault in their analysis. Therefore, an important lacuna in the anthropological literature involves a discussion of the transition between the details of everyday life and the final, usually more abstract, conclusions that eventually emerge in the author's publications. This present book, then, aims to provide an analysis of these transitions using my own field work experiences while living and learning among the Anishinaabe of northern Ontario. This was the manner in which I tried to discover new knowledge, by moving 'beyond the beaten path', and seeking a direction that was different from that which others had travelled. However, it is necessary to point out that our search for new knowledge is built upon the discoveries of those who proceeded us, individuals who we could call 'our academic mentors'.

Chapter Two
Our Academic Mentors

Almost every day of my life, I spend a few moments during the day giving thanks for the opportunities that have presented themselves which helped me get ahead a little so that I could build a career as an anthropologist and support my family. Of course, there is this saying that "You make your own breaks in life." This platitude is no doubt true to some extent because if you do not take advantage of the opportunities that are presented to you in life then you will not get very far. However, this saying is only half of the issue; we may well get ahead in life by making breaks for ourselves, but these breaks are often presented to us because other people in our lives have prepared the conditions which made these so-called 'breaks' possible.[19]

It is also important that we spend some time at introspection during our day to reflect on the course of our lives and to give thanks for the various turning points that helped us along the way. These turning points, or 'defining moments', as I call them are pivotal slices of time when, if we follow the intuition involved, lead us along a different path in life. What is interesting about these defining moments is at the time that they are presented to us they might not have seemed that important, but upon reflection, perhaps even many years later, we realized that they were very significant in the course that our life took. Here are some of those turning points, or defining moments, that were the most significant in my own life and I would encourage you as well to think about how your own life was transformed in some manner because of the decisions that you made along the way, or will still make in the future.[20]

Life's Defining Moments

I had never failed a grade in all my school years until the final one in high school. It seemed as if I was becoming more and more disillusioned with the importance of education in my life as time when on until I finally slipped under the bar which caused me to have to repeat my final year of high school. I found it humiliating to now have to attend classes with all those younger students who had been following me along throughout my school years and I resolved to quit the academic life forever.

In my family, you were not allowed to hang around your parents' house if you were no longer in school, or working, so off I went to Winnipeg in an attempt to find a job in the mines of northern Manitoba in 1967, Canada's Confederation year. At that time, the INCO (International Nickel Corporation) in Thompson, almost a thousand kilometers north of Winnipeg, was hiring and so I thought this would be my start at being an adult in life. By mid-July, I was living in a trailer camp with several thousand other men and starting out in the labor pool. After three or four months, I found a job on the surface in the Sampling Department. There was considerable overtime available then because of a shortage of men and so the money was good. Before long I took a part-time second job driving a large truck on the mine site.

The money was rolling in but I could hardly see a future here. As I looked around I saw men in perhaps their mid-thirties who looked much older. The chemicals in the refinery where I now worked, I reasoned, would no doubt reduce my life expectancy. On one particular evening when I had a lunch break during an afternoon shift, I pulled a book out of my rear pocket that a fellow worker had given me. I remember perched high up on some steps away from all the turmoil below me.

The book was called *Black Like Me* (1962) by John Howard Griffin (1920–1980). It detailed the story of a journalist who wanted to experience what it was like to live the life of a black person in the segregated south of the United States at a time when racial discrimination was particularly virulent. On the back cover is a statement, "This book will certainly change some lives," and as it turned out I happened to be one of those whose life was changed by reading this book. In 1959, John Griffin went to see a dermatologist who gave him a prescription for pills which darkened his skin color, which for all intents and purposes changed him into a black-looking man.

During the course of his research, Griffin was able to learn from other black men what their daily lives were really like in the deep southern states. If he had conducted his research as a white reporter, no one would have ever given him any information on their actual views. In turn, he was constantly shocked by his contact with white men in the region and their deep-rooted contempt for their black neighbors. Griffin refers constantly to the 'hate stare' to which he was subjected, and he also underwent a number of frightening and deeply shocking incidents.

At the time of the book's publication in the early 1960s, his account evoked deep reactions. Threats against his life caused him to have to move his family and elderly parents from his hometown in Texas to Mexico. He was also severely beaten by members of the Ku Klux Klan and at one time an effigy of him was hung up in the main street of the town where he lived. These were the days of open discrimination, some enforced by existing laws and others by custom backed up by the implicit threat of violence by whites. Blacks at times had to walk miles to find one of the few 'colored rest rooms' and had difficulty trying to find places to eat or drink or even simply to sit down and rest. As a white man when Griffin entered a store he was greeted with smiles and polite conversation, yet, as a black man, he was greeted with silence and hostile stares if he was even served at all. An effigy of him was even strung from the traffic light on Main Street. A cross was burned on the lawn of the black school near his house. Griffin also received death threats and was denounced as a traitor to the white race.

As I read on I was stunned by his description of such discrimination, yet I was also curious about the transformation this journalist underwent to gather the information that formed the basis of his book. There was no doubt that it would take considerable courage to do the things he needed to do to engage in this sort of dangerous investigation. By the time I had finished reading Griffin's book, I had decided that I needed to get out of this mining job and try to build a better future for myself.

My first step was to apply to Lakehead University in Thunder Bay. I was told by the registrar's office that my high school grades were too low for normal admission, but if I waited until the following year they would consider my application as a so-called 'adult student'. So it was on that basis that I managed to enter university with a very weak academic record, hardly a student that anyone would have had much hope for in being successful in his studies. Yet, I always knew that the nickel mine awaited me if I failed to make a go of it as a university student, so I persevered, and for the first time in many years actually put some effort into my studies.

P. J. Epling

As I mentioned earlier, eventually I changed my major from history to anthropology, which I'm sure my father regarded with some humor. By now, my grades were in the respectable 'B' category, but by my third year, with much more essay writing, I managed to achieve several 'A' grades. Then in my third year I experienced another one of those life changing turning points. An anthropologist by the name of Philip 'Jud' Epling had just been hired for a one-year appointment as he was on his way later to the Epidemiology Department at Chapel Hill, University of North Carolina. 'Jud' as he was called, had spent the previous several years at the University of California, Irvine, and had traded a year with a colleague at Lakehead. I remember asking if he could give me a reading course and he regarded me with skepticism, but finally after some cajoling on my part he agreed to take me on.

We met on a weekly basis in his office and discussed various readings that he had assigned. One day he grabbed a pile of papers off his desk and said "read this. These are the proofs for an article that several colleagues and I have written which is scheduled to be published in a month or so in *American Anthropologist*." I was a bit shocked by the request. I had never before met a professor who had the credentials to publish papers in what is still regarded by many as the most prominent journal in all of anthropology. I was also intrigued to see what it took to publish in such a prestigious journal.

That evening I cautiously read through this rather complex material. The article was entitled 'Genetic Relations of Polynesian Sibling Terminologies' by P.J. Epling, Jerome Kirk, and John Paul Boyd (*American Anthropologist*, 1973: 1596–1625). As the abstract indicated:

Relations between anthropology and linguistics are explored through the examination of the taxonomy and phylogeny of a small lexical set (sibling terms) within the Polynesian genetic/culture unit using traditional and mathematical techniques of historical semantics and ethnology...Beginning with the lattice of all possible partitions of sibling terms, assumptions are developed which reduce the number of terminologies (4140) to a small number (146), based on conjunctive concepts (1973: 1596).

"Yikes," I thought, "this is a mouthful. How can this even be anthropology?" But I persevered. I was particularly interested in several charts in the paper and tried to duplicate these using my rudimentary mathematical skills. Jud had suggested that I take a course in differential calculus which was a great help in augmenting my computational skills. At first, the charts seemed incomprehensible to me, so I went to the library and found a book which introduced the basic principles of information theory entitled *The Mathematical Theory of Communication* (Shannon and Weaver, 1949), which was the classic work on the subject, as well as some more recent studies on the topic.

My approach was to use the information measures indicated in their paper, then use this material to compute figures in their table, in order to see if I could achieve the same results as the authors did. It was slow going, but eventually I was able to duplicate their technique. However, there were several instances in which the numbers that I calculated did not match those in their table. I tried repeatedly without achieving any success. I was certainly despondent with my efforts.

The next day when I went to meet Jud in his office to discuss the paper, I thought at first that I should cancel our meeting. I knocked on his door and took a seat. "Well?" he asked, "how'd it go, does the paper make any sense to you?"

I looked down.

"What's the problem?" he asked.

"I can't seem to figure some of the numbers out," I responded.

"Oh, yeh, give me that," and he grabbed the paper from me with mock anger. "I'm sure it's simple to explain." Jud then began to stare at the paper, raising his glasses, then lowering them, becoming more agitated by the moment, grabbing his calculator, then punching in some figures, and getting more perturbed by the second. I thought I should leave, because he's going to blow his top.

Finally, he settled down. "Congratulations, Ed," he remarked, "as much as I don't want to admit this, you've discovered some mistakes in our paper. I'll have to contact the other authors immediately because we have to make some changes right away before this paper gets published. Do you realize what you've done? Jerome Kirk has a degree in mathematics and he never found this problem, it would be a great embarrassment to us if the paper was published with these mistakes. Thanks."

For all the other times that we met from then on, he regarded me in an entirely different light. I tried to explain to him that all I was doing was checking the results in the paper to see if I could duplicate them, nothing special. "No," he said, "it takes a singular mind to discover mistakes like these, you have a certain skill that is valuable, ever think of going to grad school?"

"No," I thought, "never." So, from that point on, he began to write letters of recommendation for me, touting what he thought were special skills, but I remained unconvinced of my abilities. After all, this was just one instance, and all I was doing was trying to duplicate their results, not formulating anything new on my own.

Much to my surprise, his endorsement, as an upper-level scholar in his field, was enough to secure a letter of acceptance from several universities. I chose McMaster University in Hamilton because they offered me a small scholarship, and before I knew it I had left Lakehead and moved to southern Ontario, while Jud left Thunder Bay for Chapel Hill. We corresponded frequently, and I made plans to develop a MA thesis using the methods of information theory that Jud was an expert in.

Jud and I became friends and he even purchased a car from my dad's garage in Nipigon. Before my move to Hamilton, I travelled down to Chapel Hill to visit him and his family. I was very saddened to hear from his wife that Jud had a tragic accident in his backyard when he was filling up his lawn mower while smoking a lit cigarette. Maybe what I learned most from Jud was that you should try to have confidence in yourself and not be afraid to reach for lofty goals in your academic career and in your everyday life (see his obituary, *Anthropology News*, 1973. 14 (7): 4).

On my graduation from Lakehead University in 1972, I sat in the Fort William Gardens hockey rink waiting for the proceedings to begin. A longtime friend of mine from Nipigon sat next to me reading the graduation agenda. He shoved my shoulder, "Hey Ed," he said, "you're everywhere in here. Look!" I was startled to find that I had won the Arts Medal and the Governor General's Gold Metal for the student with the highest grades in the graduating class for that year. I had not expected this to happen in a thousand years. The medals were present by Bora Laskin, Chief Justice of Canada's Supreme Court. I looked up and felt Jud's smiling gaze from above. My skin shivered.

Margaret Mead

I was hardly settled into my Hamilton apartment when I heard that the American Anthropological Society meetings were being held that fall in Toronto, at the Royal York Hotel. All of the grad students at McMaster were very excited to attend because they expected to see any number of famous anthropologists there walking around and giving papers at the various sessions. This was the first time that I really felt part of the anthropological community and attended as many of the sessions as I could. Jud had told me that if I ever got the chance I should say hello to a friend of his from California, named Kim Romney.

On one of the evening sessions, I heard there was a large party going on in one of the top floor rooms. I decided to take my chances and so I knocked on the door. A man opened it and loud noises and billowing smoke flooded through the door's opening. "Yes, what can I do for you?" the man asked. "I'm looking for Kim Romney," I shouted into the mass of people. "Who wants to know?" came a reply from somewhere in all the clouds of smoke. I decided that this was my chance so I burst into the crowd.

"Over here, kid," came a voice from the floor, "watcha want?"

"Jud told me to say hi," I answered.

"Well, sit down here with us," came the reply from a row of men sitting on the floor. A hand motioned me over. "I'm Kim" the voice said. "Who are you?"

"Jud told me to look you up, if I had the chance," I said in reply.

"Well grab a seat and sit on the floor, heh, heh," he joked. "Plunk yourself down here, and how's Jud these days?"

Kim reached up and pulled me down to the floor. "Here, have a swig," and he shoved a bottle in my hand.

"Hey, meet Marvin Harris," who was now sitting next to me. I couldn't believe what was happening. Just last year I was trying to figure out what to do with my life, and here I was sitting beside one of the most famous anthropologists in the world. Marvin Harris indeed. I couldn't believe my good fortune. We all talked most of the night as I was introduced to others in the crowd by Kim. Needless to say I never made it home that evening as most of us just lay on the hotel floor for the night.

By the next evening, after attending sessions all day long and not having any sleep the night before, I decided to drive back to Hamilton and skip the evening sessions. I was walking down a hall on one of the top floors. The setting sun light shone brightly through a large window at the end of the hall. I saw a blurry figure approaching me silhouetted against the sun. The figure was unmistakable with her tall staff with the 'Y' on top, and her large flowing cape—it was Margaret Mead for sure.

Margaret Mead with her iconic staff and cape

I wanted to run away. There was no one more famous in anthropology than Margaret Mead. I told myself that this was the chance of a life time and I could not miss it for I would forever regret it. Quickly, I made up a plan. I confronted her face to face and said, "Dr. Mead, Ruth told me to say hello." I was referring to Ruth Landes, one of the older professors at McMaster who had been a friend of Margaret's when they were both students of Franz Boas back at Columbia University in New York. It was a bold-faced lie but I didn't care—I was not going to miss this opportunity.

"Oh," she said, somewhat startled by my approach, "and how is Ruth these days?" At that point she grabbed my arm and pulled me along. "Young man, do you mind accompanying me down the hall to a room where I have to give a speech?" she asked. To tell the truth, I do not remember much more. We walked along slowly, and then suddenly two large doors flung open leading into a large auditorium that contained hundreds of people. Upon seeing Margaret Mead, they all jumped to their feet, clapping loudly; there was a thunderous roar. She seemed to just float up onto the stage as if being raised by an updraft of air.

I slunk away after this, in more or less a state of shock. I was in a daze driving home. "Did this really happen," I thought, "was that really Margaret Mead I met and walked with?" And I sat beside Marvin Harris, I couldn't believe this took place and I'm sure back among the grad students that no one would take my improbable stories seriously.

There can be little doubt that Margaret Mead was the most influential cultural anthropologist of her time. Her impact extended far beyond the discipline of anthropology, in the same manner that Albert Einstein, say, was to physics, or Babe Ruth to baseball. She was a controversial figure as well. With her views toward sex in Samoa, Mead was a dominant figure in the 1960s sexual revolution. As well, in 1976 Mead was a key participant at UN Habitat, which was the first UN forum on human settlements. But it was her book *Coming of Age in Samoa* (1928) that drew both praise and condemnation.

A New Zealand anthropologist named Derek Freeman wrote a disparaging attack on her South Pacific research five years after Mead's death in *The Making and Unmaking of an Anthropological Myth* (1983). Mead's supporters at a special session of the annual meeting of the American Anthropological Association called Freeman's book 'poorly written, unscientific, irresponsible and misleading' (Shaw 2001). However, in a *New York Times* article, John Shaw (2001) concluded that while Freeman's views of Mead's Samoan research were no doubt upsetting to many in the anthropological community, they nonetheless had 'generally gained widespread acceptance'. On the other hand, anthropologist Martin Orans (1996), while critical of Freeman's critique of Mead, still thought that her study was insufficiently scientific to support her conclusions about sexual attitudes in Samoa. Even by 2009, though, the controversy was still worthy of commentary, as in Paul Shankman's conclusion that:

There is now a large body of criticism of Freeman's work from a number of perspectives in which Mead, Samoa, and anthropology appear in a very different light than they do in Freeman's work. Indeed, the immense significance that Freeman gave his critique looks like 'much ado about nothing' to many of his critics (2009: 41).

Shankman's view was that Freeman picked only the data that appeared to support his conclusions and that he largely misrepresented Mead's research about Samoan culture. One also has to wonder about the reasons that Freeman waited so long to publish a critique of an out-of-date book, after the author had died, and which was largely written for the lay reader in any event. Perhaps his target was not Margaret Mead after all, but the faults of the modern world and the West, was an idea sometimes expressed.

One suspects that Mead's future reputation will have more supporters than detractors as time goes on. Thirty-two years after her death, in a *Scientific American* article, John Horgan (2010) wrote that "Margaret Mead's Bashers Owe her an Apology," noting that "Her writings helped inspire feminism, the sexual revolution, the human potential movement and other countercultural trends during the 1960s…Mead deserved a Nobel Prize for her achievements." In terms of Margaret Mead's legacy, she was inducted into the National Women's Hall of Fame in 1976, and later, in 1979, President Jimmy Carter posthumously awarded her the Presidential Medal of Freedom. By the 1960s, Mead became the voice of liberalism, writing a monthly column in *Redbook*, and appeared from time to time on the Johnny Carson TV show.

As far as my own view of Mead is concerned, I think one of her most important books, one not mentioned very often, is her study of the generation gap in *Culture and Commitment* (1970). If you grew up in the 1960s, you know what I'm talking about. Our parents had survived the Great Depression and the Second World War. Men often wore crew cuts and their generation loved Frank Sinatra. My generation wore raggedy bell-bottoms, scraggly long hair, listened to the Beatle ("Love yah, yah, yah",) marched against the War in Vietnam, and spouted 'make love not war' slogans.

One of Mead's central points is that some degree of commitment on the part of the researcher is essential to the viability of fieldwork in anthropology. What she had to say about the 1960s is still relevant today, which is that in her time it was becoming increasingly difficult for people to find themselves within the conflicting versions of our culture (think Trump, GOP, January 6th

2021, and white nationalism), a situation that also makes it difficult for people to make choices about which ideals, if any, they should commit themselves to.

For the anthropologist, the issue of commitment is an especially important one if the discipline is to inform people about different, competing ideological forces. "It is my conviction," Mead explained that "in addition to the world conditions that have given rise to this search for new commitment and to this possibility of no commitment at all, we also have new resources for facing our situation, new grounds for commitment" (1970: xii). Her sense of optimism, tempered by a sober realization of human frailties, was the foundation of her life's work, and the basis for her outspokenness on such wide-ranging issues as nuclear disarmament and generational conflict.[21]

So, when I met Margaret Mead quite by accident in 1972 I felt that I was in the presence of a superstar. Here was an anthropologist with an international reputation who was willing to put her career on the line by criticizing the war in Vietnam, supporting the campus protests of university students, and promoting the rights of women. While she is known for her fieldwork in Samoa, her book *Culture and Commitment*, in my opinion, is a classic text which outlines the basic principles of today's public anthropology.

Thus, when I became a university professor myself, I wanted to devote my time to promoting the initiatives that anthropologists like Mead began so many years before. She devoted her work to combating racism, promoting cultural tolerance, and instilling the idea of cultural relativism into the discipline of anthropology. Eventually, I felt the need to write a book, *Public Anthropology: Engaging Social Issues in the Modern World* (2016), in an attempt to explain to students how contemporary anthropological research becomes public research. So while this book offers an overview of disciplinary discussions about becoming more relevant to the world beyond the academy, it is also about many other areas of research in today's world that students are interested in.

What this summary of research demonstrates is how anthropology has become well immersed in the public issues of our time, in the same manner that Margaret Mead showed her commitment to making the world a better place to live in. For me, this interest in public issues was instilled in my mind from that first meeting in that long hallway at a hotel in Toronto when I saw Mead's unmistakable image shrouded in her cloak and walking stick. On that evening, she took a young student by the arm, which in turn, also took his mind into the realm of new possibilities for his life.

A Modest Discovery

After completing my BA at Lakehead, and being accepted for the MA program at McMaster in Hamilton in 1972, I spent the summer working on Jud's paper in *American Anthropologist*. I was still trying to figure the basic principles of information theory as it was applied to kinship systems. Although this was a novel application, nonetheless it was simply another version of a classification system, so the same basic principle applied to kinship as classification systems in biology. During that summer I attempted to apply the information measure to a set of Athapaskan (or Dene) sibling terminologies with the intention that this study would form the basis of my MA thesis.

Basically, what I was attempting to do was measure the manner in which information gain in kinship terminologies is influenced by the complexity of the kinship system itself. For example, if a sibling terminology were to increase its size from, say, two terms to four terms, would the information gain remain constant, I wondered? So, as I was measuring the information in all these Athapaskan sibling terminologies I stumbled more or less by pure accident on a fundamental problem or trend; as the sibling terminology increased in size, there was a corresponding decrease in information gained. I could not find any information in the literature concerning this apparent anomaly so I decided to make this discovery the basis of my thesis.

When I eventually presented my thesis to the anthropology department for examination, it was rejected. The basis for the refusal was that the anthropology department could only find two members who were even willing to read my thesis, claiming that the mathematics in the thesis was beyond the scope of their expertise. This caused me to scramble around the university and eventually I found a member of the engineering department who taught a course in information theory, who agreed to be on my committee. For him, the problem was that he did not understand the kinship principles involved, however as far as the use of information theory was concerned he regarded this usage as fairly rudimentary.

This is what happens in academia if you combine several disciplines together, or go beyond the accepted disciplinary boundaries, you will run into problems of acceptance of your ideas. Happily, for me, my thesis defense went well with the help of the engineering professor and I passed my MA. I never returned to examine the anomaly that I had discovered again until at least ten years later. I had the idea that I should write a paper on my modest discovery. When the paper was completed, I sent it to the journal *Ethnology*, which I considered almost as difficult to publish in as *American Anthropologist.* My approach was to send the paper to this journal, have it reviewed, and, thinking that it would probably be rejected, send it somewhere else. So here is another one of those unexpected moments in one's life which could be regarded as a turning point of sorts and which happens only rarely in one's career.

On my birthday, if you could believe, I received a phone call from the editor of the journal. He explained that they were all very excited at the *Ethnology* office to receive my paper, that I had made an important discovery in kinship studies, and that they wished to publish this paper in the very next issue. Of course, I was astounded, surely they had the wrong number, or the wrong person. No, was the reply, but he had a few questions. He did not think that I realized the scope of my discovery, which is to say, that as a kinship system becomes more complex, information gain tends to diminish with the addition of more terms. In other words, if one were to make a graph of this phenomenon, the information gain does not proceed directly upward at a forty-five-degree angle, as one would expect. What happens is that the upward trend begins to 'bend' the more the line on the graph extends upward, much like the concept of a 'limit on an upper bound' in calculus.

The editor told me that he did not think that I realized the implication of this discovery, that not only did this 'bending' with decreasing information gain occur with sibling terminologies, but that the same principle applied to *all* taxonomic systems. "No way," I responded, "if that were the case then surely it would have been discovered decades ago!" His reply was that it was one of those quirky things in mathematics that goes undiscovered because it remains, in a way, 'hidden' in the calculations. In any event, he said that I should be given credit for this discovery, however he wanted to rewrite the conclusion of my paper reflecting this wider application involved. And yes, the paper did come out shortly after and can be found in the following reference (Hedican 1986b).

To this day, I am still a bit shocked at what happened. I was even told that a decade or so later this paper was referenced in *Scientific American* as an example of the limitations on human cognitive processes. As it turned out, I never pursued these ideas again because I was more interested in conducting more conventional fieldwork in northern Ontario; however, this incident does show the serendipitous nature of some scientific discoveries, which occur, as in my case, by perseverance and a bit of luck.[22]

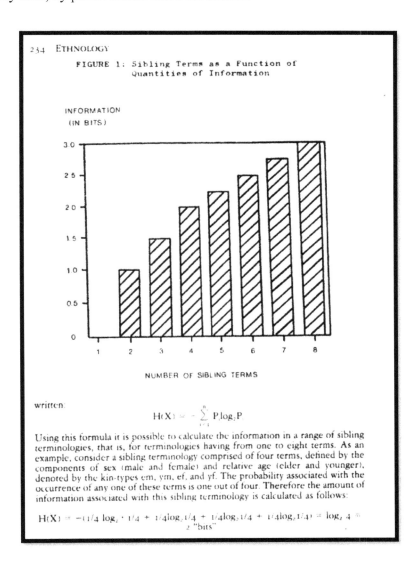

FIGURE 1: Sibling Terms as a Function of Quantities of Information

INFORMATION (IN BITS)

NUMBER OF SIBLING TERMS

written:

$$H(X) = -\sum_{i=1}^{n} P_i \log_2 P_i$$

Using this formula it is possible to calculate the information in a range of sibling terminologies, that is, for terminologies having from one to eight terms. As an example, consider a sibling terminology comprised of four terms, defined by the components of sex (male and female) and relative age (elder and younger), denoted by the kin-types em, ym, ef, and yf. The probability associated with the occurrence of any one of these terms is one out of four. Therefore the amount of information associated with this sibling terminology is calculated as follows:

$$H(X) = -(1/4 \log_2 1/4 + 1/4 \log_2 1/4 + 1/4 \log_2 1/4 + 1/4 \log_2 1/4) = \log_2 4 = 2 \text{ "bits"}$$

A Simple Chart Leads to a Big Idea

I enjoyed being a student at McMaster University and was determined to continue my graduate studies there by pursuing a doctorate program in the anthropology department. So confident was I that I had made a solid impression on the department's anthropology faculty that my application would be readily accepted that I never even applied to another university. However, I was startled to be notified that my application for further graduate studies had been rejected. The letter gave no reason for the refusal other than to say that there were many other good applications to choose from, but nothing to indicate any deficiencies of my own on my part. Needless to say, I was very disheartened.

Possibly, I thought, the rejection had something to do with my Master's thesis and its mathematical orientation. I immediately had to pull myself together. I subsequently sent off an application to McGill University. In short order, I received a phone call from Professor Peter Gutkind, one of the anthropologists, saying that my application had been accepted and that he wanted to personally welcome me to McGill. Of course, I was startled at this turn of events. As it turned out McGill was a much better fit for me and my academic interest than McMaster ever would have been. As a learning experience, the thought also crossed my mind that rejection in one instance could lead to better fortunes in another.

Richard Salisbury

Driving into Montreal for the first time was a daunting experience for a boy from small town northern Ontario. It looked like everyone was participating in a Lemans car race, cutting in and out with break neck speeds. You get used to it though. It did not take long before Montreal was my kind of city. I loved the ethnic mix, the Jewish bakeries along Park Ave., the small pubs along Sherbrook St. On Centre St., the crowds were packed on the weekends, and window shopping along Côte St. Catherine was fun as well.

More than anything McGill was my kind of university. Big library collections, all the small buildings hidden here and there. One of them was on McTavish St. and was called the Programme in the Anthropology of Development which was directed by Richard Salisbury. Here was an anthropologist with an international reputation, he seemed to have been everywhere and knew everyone. His fieldwork in the New Guinea Highlands was legendary, and his first ethnography, *From Stone to Steel* (1962), on the study of Saine economic and political development, remains a classic work and was referenced in just about every introductory text book that you would come across in those years.

Richard Salisbury was born in Chelsea, England, in 1926 and served in the Royal Marines between 1945 and 1948, after which he attended Harvard University and the Australian National University completing his graduate studies in anthropology. He came to McGill University in 1962 and in 1974 was elected to the Royal Society of Canada. Salisbury was also involved in McGill's administrative programs, serving as the Chair of the university's Anthropology Department (1968–1970, Director of the Programme in the Anthropology of Development (PAD), and Dean of Arts (1986–1989). Among a long list of his involvement in academic associations, he was President of the Canadian Sociology and Anthropology association (1968–1970), the American Ethnological society (1980), and the Society for Applied Anthropology in Canada (1986).

Richard F. Salisbury
(1926–1989)

I knew it would be a hard sell but I thought that I did not come this far not to have the best as my thesis director. He kept saying that he was busy, had many other doctoral students, and would not have much time for me. I was undeterred. I kept showing up at his office, asking questions, before long he caved in, "Ok," he said. I felt that I did not travel all this way from Thompson, Manitoba, to Montreal not to have the best that a university could offer. After a year of courses, and then a fieldwork exam, I was off again to northern Ontario, to the place that I knew. We called him 'Doc', I wrote a lot of letters to him and he answered every one of them, offering valuable direction. Another book of his, *Vunamami: Economic Transformation in a Traditional Society* (1970) was one of the few books I took to Collins with me. He kept telling me, "Give us the details, we want to see the details. After you've written a description about something, add some more details. Fieldwork is all about the details, worry about your theories later," he urged. I'm not sure what I would have done without his guidance, thoughtful suggestions and practical wisdom (see Hedican 1990a; Silverman 2004).

Salisbury, throughout his academic career, searched for complementarity or a middle ground on which disputing parties could find a basis of common or mutual understanding, was one his more important contributions to anthropology, I thought. In a debate going on at the time concerning the substantivist-formalist debate in economic anthropology, he cautioned that "What may be ignored is the degree of complementarity between the two analyses" (1973: 92). In one of his articles entitled, "The Anthropologist as Societal Ombudsman," in David Pitt's book, *Development from Below*, Salisbury analyzed the manner in which disputes are settled involving the Cree of northern Quebec and the Tolai of New Guinea. Both of these activities, he suggested, "imply a somewhat new role of the anthropologist as an intermediary in trouble situations between central agencies and local groups" (1976: 255). As another of his students who came after me, Colin Scott, indicted that Salisbury's position was clear: "confrontation doesn't get you anywhere—words heard more than once as we discussed current events" (1990: 18). Salisbury's approach was always transactional in nature, he expected disputing parties to formulate their positions and then work out the structure of future relationships (1977a).[23]

Another one of his themes was that anthropologists would be best served if they avoided choosing sides in conflict situations: "I am convinced that when an anthropologist commits himself to one side only, he nullifies many of the benefits that his professional training could give to that side" (1976: 257).[24] There were times later in my career involving land claims disputes in northern Ontario that I wish I would have heeded this advice and avoided the difficult choices involved. Salisbury's warning was that we must avoid becoming active participants in disputes because it will only further exacerbate the problem, and ultimately undermine any contribution that the anthropologist might make in solving human problems.

Richard Salisbury moved to McGill University in the early 1960s where he continued his emphasis on basic research coupled with attempts to place research in a more general context of discussion. This interaction between theory and research ultimately led to new directions in the application of anthropological studies of public policy. In his keynote address to the National Social Science Conference in 1975, he warned that:

If the verdict on social science knowledge is that there is a large store of it, that much of it is related to outdated issues, and that what is relevant to current policy issues is not recognized as applicable, the question of how far it is used in policy making is very simple to answer. Hardly at all (1975: 3).

Nonetheless he ended his paper on a familiar note, "The problem is how co-existence can work equitably...Everyone needs knowledge of how to resolve conflicts" (1975:12); advice that can never get old or be made irrelevant.

Salisbury set high standards that were difficult to emulate, but it was also part of his legacy that he left us with a role model which is imbued with the admirable qualities of intelligence, empathy for others, and a sense of integrity that he brought to his life's work. The enduring strength of his work largely emanated from the fact that he never became aloof, pretentious, or autocratic, despite his success. Overall he relied on the lasting strength of anthropology itself: fieldwork, participation, and knowledge gained through first-hand experience. A quality that I appreciated perhaps above all else was that Salisbury never forgot what it was like to conduct fieldwork, and this is the source of perhaps his greatest contribution to anthropology that he instilled in a generation of anthropology students. He gave students financial and intellectual support, insisting always that basic research be placed in the larger context of practical and theoretical issues.

There was much that went on behind the scenes that no one knew about—but his students remember. Always you knew he was there, thinking about his students. When I was conducting my fieldwork in northern Ontario in a community of small log cabins, without electricity, or really no means of communicating with the outside world except by letters, it would have been easy to forget why one was there in the first place, given the constant search for firewood and food. Then, unexpectedly, one of Salisbury's letters would arrive, to snap me back to reality so to speak. His letters kept me in touch with a sense of purpose, encouraging me on with his 'gentle reminders'. By the end of the winter of my fieldwork, with spring starting to melt the snowdrifts, one of his letters arrived with the following news:

May 22

Dear Ed,

We decided to make you an award of a nine-month research assistantship (currently the rate for Ph.D. students is $325 per month) after you return from the field. Although this will presumably be in September, we are beginning the period of payment in June to make use of some expiring funds. We hope that you will not object to having a nest egg on your return from the field.

Good wishes with the fieldwork.

Dick

The cliché of the impoverished student was no joke when you were living week to week, sometimes even day to day, stretching out your meals. A letter such as this was a god-send. I was now ready to continue my fieldwork with renewed vigor. Then, another letter arrived almost two months later, that provided pivotal information on what I should be doing in my fieldwork, the sort of encouragement that is apt to give one a renewed sense of direction and purpose:

July 4

Dear Ed,

I would add a gentle reminder about the possible usefulness of reports. You obviously have some ideas about (a) different perceptions of development, (b) the role of leaders, their perceptions and followers' perceptions, and (c) the organization of productive tasks. Are you sure you are writing these ideas down? Are you discussing them with people in the field? One month from now will you remember how your thinking developed now, so that you could trace out the development? Are you confident you have the right data to be able to support your ideas in the arena of seminar papers or discussion with colleagues? All of these questions, if you answer 'no' to any of them, suggest to me that writing down in very preliminary form what you are thinking and formalizing would assist you in many ways.

At a minimum, I am suggesting that sitting down and 'talking' to paper (at a time like when it is raining, or when you feel depressed) and trying to think abstractly about the practical reality which you are very tightly involved in, is useful in focusing your work as you go along. It is easy to get right out of academic, theoretical thinking completely.

Good luck, and I hope to hear from you,

Dick

This is the sort of letter that has acted as a sort of touchstone for all the other work that I've done since. Every once and a while I pull it out, not in a sentimental way, but as a manual or set of guide-lines for doing the job right. The following month there was a follow up to this letter containing much of the same useful advice:

August 25

Dear Ed

I enjoyed your August 18th letter. If you have short pieces on all the topics you list, you need only some editing for a full report on your research. I can't really comment, of course, without seeing them, but they seem to indicate some creative and empirical thinking about the interplay of local and national actions over development issues. Have you looked back at some of the early ones, comparing them with later ones to see how your thinking has developed? Or to see how mutually consistent the early and later ones are?

Good luck,

Dick

When we got back from our fieldwork, our discussions continued with one another in small groups gathered together in the evenings at various student's apartments. Richard Salisbury was a frequent visitor at these gatherings, usually sitting on the floor with the rest of us, encouraging us to talk about our ideas in these informal gatherings. With our mentor's help, we felt that we were not alone in the world with our ideas, that we were being supported, and that everything was going along the way it should.

Philip C. Salzman

Philip Salzman was another member of the Anthropology Department at McGill University who was supportive of my research endeavors and an important member of my dissertation committee. We had several common interests, especially in the area of informal leadership structures in communities without readily identifiable political roles. I found it interesting that his ethnographic research among Baluchi pastoral nomads who live in Iran, Pakistan, and Afghanistan was in certain ways similar to my own research in Northern Ontario. These nomads live in the harsh desert conditions of Baluchistan, meaning 'land of the Baluch', in sparsely populated groups which usually inhabit agricultural oases or herding camps in the desert plains and mountains.

One would not think that the small Baluchi herding populations living in desert conditions would not have much in common with the Anishinaabe of northern Ontario who inhabit the moist forests of the eastern Subarctic. However, anthropologists often find cultural and social similarities that one would not expect because of similar causal conditions in ecological and economic characteristics. As an example, both the Baluch and the Anishinaabe have constraints placed on their social and economic conditions due to environmental conditions. This is not a matter of environmental determinism, but of 'possibilism', a concept that was introduced into anthropology by Franz Boas. As he explained, "environmental conditions may stimulate existing cultural activities, but they have no creative force…the same environment will influence culture in diverse ways" (1940: 266; see also Milton 1996: 45–46).

In our discussions, we looked at our various experiences in researching the topic of environmental influences. The Baluch lived in an arid environment, so their constraints were mainly determined by the availability of water which was essential for sustaining the life of their domesticated animals. For the Anishinaabe in the subarctic forests, there were seasonal variations in the availability of food resources which effected their social organization. In the winter months when food was scarce and travel difficult, they broke up into smaller family groups to spread more evenly across the land. In the summer months, they gathered together in larger groups, especially around lakes with abundant fish to live on. It was interesting to explore these quite diverse cultural situations and then discover that the ecological constraints acted in similar ways in these two quite different cultures.

Discussions of leadership also led to some interesting findings. We talked about the topic of 'encapsulation', for example which was originally introduced into the anthropological literature by Fred Bailey, especially in his book *Stratagems and Spoils* (1969). From Bailey's perspective, leaders plot strategies to outwit opposing leaders and thereby gain 'spoils', in the sense of resources and followers. The assumption here is that leaders who are able to offer their followers more rewards than other leaders are able to gather a larger following and thereby be more successful (see also Hedican 1986d). When we compared notes, Salzman and I were able to come to some similar conclusions about leadership in the two different societies in which we had conducted research. In my own case, I found that leaders in Collins were dispensing jobs, a very valuable resource, to attract followers and thereby build up political capital (Hedican 1991). In a comparable manner, Salzman (1974) described how tribal chiefs were attempting similar tactics.

The concept of 'encapsulation' was also an important political force in both of our research settings (Bailey 1969: 144–182). What Bailey calls 'encapsulated political structures' involved political groups in a minority, usually ethnically different population which are encapsulated or enclosed by a larger political entity. In these cases, the local leaders were mostly able to maintain their traditional political structure, but were encapsulated by a larger and more powerful political system which exercised a significant degree of effective control over them (Salzman 1999: 31–35). In the age of British colonialism, it was common for the British authorities to try to control the minority groups under their dominion by either co-opting the leaders of the minority group, or if that did not work, then installing their own leaders who were sympathetic to them.

A classic example of this strategy occurred when the Hudson's Bay Company (HBC) installed leaders called 'trading captains', to influence the fur trade between the Cree, who lived near the coastal forts, and the Indigenous people who lived farther away (Morantz 1982). The HBC, recognizing the influential role of the Cree vis-a-vis other Indigenous groups, nominated some of the more dominant Cree as 'trading Captains', and outfitted them with special coats and gave them special privileges about the trading post. Others were designated as 'homeguards' who led hunting parties and provided food for the posts (Francis and Morantz 1983: 41–45, 81–83). So influential were the Cree that their language became a *lingua franca*, or a language adopted as a common language of the fur trade era. Since their economic position between interior Indigenous groups and the Hudson's Bay Company allowed the Cree to wield much influence, and thereby gain materially from this role, they were unlikely to give up their location without a fight. As far as the European traders were concerned, when Indigenous people such as the Cree acted as middlemen on their behalf it also assisted the European's needs as well:

It served the European traders to cultivate a middleman status among Indians living near the main posts whose own country had become depleted as in the case of the Cree. By utilizing Indian middlemen, the expenses of transporting goods into and out of interior areas and the necessity of maintaining garrisons and other establishments were avoided (Hickerson 1973: 25).

There is evidence (such as in Rogers 1965: 272) that the emergence of such leaders seems to be based on acculturative factors which were dependent upon the degree of contact. Such leaders were able to secure power from several sources. If they were of mixed ancestry, since near the fur trading posts fur traders often married Indigenous women (see Brown 1976. ,1980), this was also probably a fact explaining their influential positions.

In the case of the Baluch, Salzman explained, in 1928 the king of Iran "sent an army into Baluchistan to 'pacify' the unruly tribes and bring them securely under control of the crown" (1999: 31). This 'pacification' of the Baluch resulted in alterations in the local political structure. As an example:

The chief, who in the past depended entirely upon his tribesmen and tribeswomen for support, now had new external resources. As the *middleman* (emphasis in the orig.) between the tribe and the state, the chief took on new roles as an *intermediary*, acting as a channel for communicating messages between the state and the tribe, as a *mediator*, bringing the tribe and state to mutually acceptable compromises on courses of action, and as a *broker*, advocating to the state on behalf of the tribe and its needs (1999: 32).

So these were the sort of conversations we had on a fairly frequent basis. Usually they were quite informal. I would be just walking down the hall way and he would call me in. Sometimes we just talked for several minutes, or at times, several hours. We would usually just begin a conversation of something in everyday life, then give examples, and then one of us would draw a comparison to another similar situation. We started, then, talking about some ordinary situation, and from there draw in other ethnographic examples, and before you knew it we had some sort of theory that explained a number of cases.

Philip Salzman was big on talking about real life events and even wrote a book on the topic called *The Anthropology of Real Life Events in Human Experience* (1999). As he explains, "My good fortune was to be at the right place at the right time, benefiting from events that I did not author and could not control…Of great interest for us is the impact an event has on people's lives, the way it directs lives, shapes them, terminates them, liberates them…In real life, things happen, and these things sometimes impose circumstances that transform people's life" (1999: 3).

Actually, before reading this quote, what he describes is the very reason that I found myself writing about him in the first place. It was not so much about all our conversations, although they were indeed stimulating and served as a learning experience in their own way, it was that Philip Salzman was responsible for one of those great events, or defining moments, that fundamentally changed my life.

Let me explain. There was this one Friday that I had an almost overpowering urge, or compulsion, to travel down to McGill's anthropology office. I lived quite a way up on Côte de Neige so I did not really want to make the trip, figuring there would be no one there anyway. But the urge got the better of me and so off I went to the bus stop.

As I expected on this Friday the halls were barren. I quickly walked down the hallway with thoughts of picking up my mail. All at once there was someone shouting at me. I turned around and it was Philip Salzman shaking a newspaper in the air. Apparently he was pointing to a job add. "Have you ever heard of Guelph?" he asked.

Well I've been here for over forty years now and raised four children. I often wonder what would have happened if I had not followed this over powering urge? Something would have happened but it would not have been a job at Guelph. And it might be crazy to think this way, but "was somebody or something directing me?" As Salzman said in his quote above, you need to be at 'the right place at the right time', and my life was indeed transformed—that's the key to good fortune.[25]

Lessons Learned

There are several lessons here. First, never turn your back on an opportunity. I heard once that 'things happen for a reason'. That reason may not be immediately obvious. Opportunities open the door to other events, and so on. You will never get anywhere in life by hiding out in your room feeling sorry for yourself.

Second, never give in to fear. Fear is the great destroyer of opportunities. Often our first urge when confronting a difficult situation is to run away—'fight or flight'. It seems naturally built into our psyche. I do not mean that we should always be in fight mode, but we should be prepared to accomplish things by overcoming the trials and tribulations in life. Fear may be there in life to warn us of danger, but we never know what may lie behind this apparent danger. To accomplish anything in life we must be willing to acknowledge our fears and understand their source and power over us. It's like the medieval stories of dragons guarding a pile of diamonds. Sometimes we may have to make the attempt to slay these dragons, real or imagined, with our little swords.

Third, give thanks for life's 'defining moments'. These are gifts and should be acknowledged. These gifts are largely the result of favors bequeathed to us from our academic mentors. The role that they have played in our lives should not be taken for granted or forgotten.

Conclusion

Would it be accurate to regard my life's story as a sort of Horatio Alger narrative? Am I an anthropological revisiting of 'Ragged Dick'? In the typical Horatio Alger book a teenage boy improves his circumstance in life by virtuous behavior and hard work. However, when you look under the surface, the real reason for the boy's success is due to some accidental or serendipitous circumstance which works to the boy's advantage. The boy, for example, finds a sum of money which he returns to what turns out to be a wealthy person who presents him with a handsome reward. Or, the boy saves someone from a run-away carriage, resulting in turn to a rich compensation. So, there is a Horatio Alger myth involved in these "rags-to-riches" stories of ill-fated youth such as Ragged Dick who, through circumstances not of their own making, are able to dramatically improve their fortunes in life.

From my own perspective, the latter interpretation of the Horatio Alger success stories are the correct ones, which is to say, that certain 'defining moments' are largely responsible for one's success in life. You may work your fingers to the bone, as the old saying goes, but to be efficacious in life one nonetheless requires opportunities without which no amount of hard work will suffice in the achievement of one's chosen endeavors.

So, as a way of summarizing these defining moments for me, I offer the following instances without which I would not have been able to achieve whatever success I have thus far made of my academic life:

1. Reading John Griffin's inspiring account in *Black Like Me* and then deciding to quit my employment in the mines and seek my future course in life at university. The parable of Griffin's investigation of a life so foreign to him, and the courage it took to pursue his social and racial investigation, inspired me to think in similar terms.

2. My fortuitous chance meeting with Jud Epling when he was only going to stay at Lakehead University for that one year which coincided with my fourth and final year as an undergraduate student. Reading his article on Polynesian kinship, and its imminent publication in *American Anthropologist*, during which I was fortunate enough to discover some pivotal errors in several of the tables. This discovery,

in turn, lead to effusive letters of recommendation by Epling which opened the door to various graduate programs.

3. Meeting Margaret Mead in the hallway of the Royal York Hotel at the exact moment that she was on her way to deliver a speech. One moment one way or another would have meant that I would have missed her altogether. Meeting her inspired me to aim for more socially conscious academic goals than I would have otherwise attempted, especially in areas of 'culture and commitment'.

4. Rejection of my graduate application at McMaster University eventually led to a much better fit for me at McGill University where I met Richard Salisbury. His research on 'development and culture change' became the bedrock of my future academic pursuits in northern Ontario.

5. Philip Salzman locating a job offer from the University of Guelph which I had not previously seen, and therefore would probably not have had the opportunity to apply for, leading in turn to a forty-year career.

Therefore, I set out these 'defining moments' as evidence for my opinion that opportunities in life are just as important, or possibly even more so, as any amount of hard work that one is willing to engage in. In fact, I have watched the careers of many professors who I have become familiar with over the years who were very hard workers but who nonetheless never seemed to have achieved very much academic success because they either lacked opportunities to display their talents, or were for whatever reason not able to take advantage of certain fortuitous circumstances that were offered to them.

Chapter Three
Fieldwork as a Rite De Passage

Near the turn of the last century, a folklorist named Arnold van Gennep proposed that people in various societies go through phases in their lives that he called *rite de passage*. The most obvious application of this proposal was in reference to transitions in religious ceremonies, such as a confirmation ritual in the Catholic Church, but in later years the approach has been broadened out to include other transitory phases in society as well. In van Gennep's scheme that status changes that individuals go through in their life cycle involve the stages of separation, marginality, and reincorporation.

By the 1960s, anthropologist Victor Turner, on the basis of his research among the Ndembu of Northwestern Zambia and the nature of symbolism in human societies, suggested that interstitial periods between the transitory stages be called a case of 'liminality'; meaning, in Turner's words, when individuals are "betwixt and between all recognized fixed points in space-time" (Turner 1967: 97). He also describes a phase in which a person has left one status but has not yet entered another, or a limbo-type period in which normal social relations and even time itself is placed on hold, as in "a moment in and out of time" (Turner1969: 96).

In the history of social or cultural anthropology, large scale changes were taking place in the discipline at about the time of Gennep's proposals. The phase referred to as the Unilineal Evolutionary stage had come under heavy criticism because it apparently lacked concrete evidence for its underlying propositions, i.e., that all societies would go through the same stages of evolution. This period was also called the 'Armchair' period, used in a pejorative manner, to refer to research based on the unfounded speculations of travelers, missionaries and other types of unsubstantiated, discursive reporting. In order to support anthropology's conclusions about human societies and culture, research became based on first-hand ethnographic fieldwork, most notably conducted by Franz Boas in his classic work *The Central Eskimo* (1888) and Bronislaw Malinowski's research among the Trobriand Islanders in his *Argonauts of the Western Pacific* (1922).

In due course, ethnographic fieldwork became the *rite de passage* for professional anthropologists. To properly enter the discipline, it was expected that an ethnographic study be conducted among the members of a society different from their own, that they would attempt to learn the local language, and participate to the extent that was allowed in the various customs of that culture. As Watson comments:

…the personal significance of fieldwork for the anthropologist is that there is a powerful lobby within the profession…that one cannot be an anthropologist without having undergone the *rite de passage* which is constituted by fieldwork…yet we know surprisingly little about it: how understanding of the other occurs is insufficiently documents and still not fully understood (1999: 2).

"It is not surprising," Epstein (1967: vii) adds, "that preparation for fieldwork has come to be seen as an essential part of the training of students in the subject, and fieldwork itself as a unique and necessary experience, amounting to a kind of rite de passage by which the novice is transformed into the rounded anthropologist and initiated into the ranks of the profession" (1967: vii). In other words, ethnographic fieldwork became the 'liminal' phase in the transition from neophyte to full-fledged anthropologist.[26]

In this chapter, we explore Turner's concept of liminality in anthropological fieldwork, and in people's everyday lives. The metaphor of a door, by which one enters into a liminal phase, is explored for its explanatory value. Then, in the latter portion of the chapter, ethnographic fieldwork's relationship to theory building in anthropology is discussed, especially in terms of such contrasting methodologies as inductive (propositions made on the basis of specific observation in fieldwork) versus deductive (reasoning which starts with general propositions and is subsequently applied to particular instances) research strategies.

Knock, Knock, Strangers at The Door

There are probably few events in our daily lives more common than hearing a knock on the door (or the door bell ringing). Few of us would probably not give much thought to who might be on the other side of the door, or if there are dangers lurking there. Most of the time when we open the door a small tyke thrusts a handful of chocolate bars up to us, wanting a donation to her soccer league, or two religious proselytizers shoving a copy of the Watch Tower under our nose, asking if we want to be saved. It could also be a disgruntled neighbor complaining once again about our barking dog in the back yard, which we would be happy to take back in doors if only we were not so bothered with all these intrusions in our life.

However, there is the odd chance that answering the front door could involve much more than we could ever expect. Take this example from my own family history. My great grandfather's brother, Barney Hedican, was a foreman on a cattle ranch in Gilt Edge, Montana. One day a cowboy rode into Gilt Edge, got a haircut at the local barber shop, and then inquired where he could find Barney Hedican. The barber then pointed the way to the Hedican residence on the edge of town where Mrs. Hedican kept a boarding house. The cowboy subsequently rode out there and knocked on the door. When Mrs. Hedican came to the door and opened it, the cowboy shot her twice and killed her on the spot. A boarder upstairs heard the shooting and started down the stairs. When he got to the kitchen, the cowboy shot him too, then turned the gun on himself. No one ever knew who this cowboy was or why he went on this killing spree.

This shocking incident in which Emma Hedican was shot and killed by a complete stranger was a thorough mystery. The boarder who was also shot eventually recovered from his wounds. A newspaper account of the incident, in the *Fergus County Argus* (March 25, 1903), reported that the coroner's jury returned a verdict that Mrs. Barney Hedican and W. D. Patterson, the shooter, were victims of a double tragedy. Apparently Patterson left a letter stating that Mrs. Hedican in reality was his wife, and that he intended to slay her because she was not faithful to him. Patterson claimed that he married Mrs. Barney Hedican in Denver on September 2, 1902. In another twist, United States Senator Patterson of Colorado is said to be an uncle of the dead man. The claims of the shooter were never verified. And, to add to this tragedy, Barney

Hedican was later convicted of stealing horses and was sentenced to eight years in prison. Then, on the very day of his release, in which his sentence was pardoned by the state governor, Barney was killed by a dynamite explosion on a road works project.

Now, I am not suggesting that answering a knock on their door led the Hedican family to all this unfortunate misery in life. Obviously one could answer the same door thousands of times and never suffer such a fate. What I am suggesting though is that even in a mundane, everyday life existence unimaginable tragedies can occur. Everyday life contains both the commonplace and the exceptional occurrences. One never knows from moment to moment the fate that everyday life holds for us. For the most part, we probably would never give much thought to the endless possibilities, trusting that the odds of suffering some tragedy simply by answering our front door are rather small and not worth worrying about.

The Blue Light Saloon

On the evening of March 30th, 1893, two men who were grappling with each other fell through the doors of the Blue Light Saloon in Ashland, Wisconsin, onto the street outside. One of these men was a gambler known as the New Orleans Kid. According to the newspaper accounts at the time (*The Ashland Daily News*, March 30, 1893; and *The Ashland Daily Press*, same date), the New Orleans Kid showed up at the Blue Light gambling rooms and tried to hold up the hotel keeper. About one o'clock in the morning a search by police officers began which located the culprit at another establishment, the Fashion Saloon. There he was brandishing a large .44 caliber revolver which was subsequently taken away from him by Officer Kennedy who had just arrived at the scene. Then a scuffle ensued in which the gambler lunged at Officer Kennedy in an attempt to regain possession of the revolver.

At about the same time, another policeman, Officer Ed Hedican, arrived at the scene of the fracas in which the gambler was resisting arrest. Officer Hedican then attempted to aid Officer Kennedy who was trying to handcuff their man. As the newspaper indicates, with a headline detailing the stunning report, "Ed Hedican Shot [27]and Almost Instantly Killed this Morning": "During the scuffle which followed the gun accidently exploded, the bullet entering Hedican's stomach below the heart. The gallant officer staggered for a moment and then fell to the sidewalk, almost a corpse, for within an hour he died" (*The Ashland Daily News*, March 30, 1893). The newspaper described this tragic series of events further: "Poor Ed is dead—shot while on duty and with a bullet from a revolver in the hands of a brother officer."

Several days later another Ashland newspaper (*The Ashland Daily Press*, April 3, 1893) provided details of Ed Hedican's funeral:

"The funeral of Ed Hedican yesterday was undoubtedly the largest ever held in Ashland and was a token of the universal respect and esteem in which he was held. The funeral cortege was over a half hour in passing a given point…there were two bands in line. Nearly 100 carriages followed in the rear…the body was buried in the Catholic cemetery. Four brothers and a sister of the deceased officer attended the funeral. As an officer he was ready at all times to do his duty and fear was an unknown quality to him."

There is an important point here regarding this unfortunate incident concerning our everyday lives. The episode described above is certainly not one that an average citizen would be expected to deal with in the usual course of everyday events in their lives. However, people do die every day, in very large numbers (nearly 150,000 people die per day worldwide, usually from cardiovascular disease). Police officers especially are well aware of the mortal dangers intrinsic in their chosen profession. In the year 2020, there were over 300 police officers killed in the USA in the line of duty, in 1930 there were even more (312), with over 22 thousand total deaths of police officers since statistics were kept.

In other words, in the USA at least, the death of a police officer killed in the line of duty is an almost everyday occurrence. This is a profession in which deadly circumstances are virtually an everyday event. So it is important then, when discussing everyday life, to examine the situation for the individual or individuals concerned because not all people's lives have the same inherent danger. Yet, there are circumstance beyond our control. Simply opening a door is an everyday occurrence for all of us, and we are not likely cognizant of the dangers inherent in this mundane, everyday act. Even so, each of us only dies once in our lives, which is perhaps an odd way of phrasing it.

Liminal States

According to Arnold van Gennep's concept of *rite de passage*, rites have three stages: separation, liminality, and incorporation. The second phase, the *liminal* period, is one of transition (characterized as a 'threshold') between the other two phases or segments during which a person leaves one state but has not yet entered into the next. According to Victor Turner, "The attributes of liminality or of liminal *personae* ('threshold people') are necessarily ambiguous" (1969: 95). In addition, as van Gennep theorized, a society is composed of multiple groups.

To illustrate his schemata, he utilizes a metaphor, "as a kind of house divided into rooms and corridors" ('chaque société générale peut être considerêrée commode maison divisée en chambres et couloirs') such that when a person leaves one group to enter another, van Gennep visualizes this as an individual changing rooms (1960: 21). He also visualized a territorial passage, or a crossing of borders, which would occur if one were to travel into a culturally different region. Furthermore, it is obvious that a person cannot enter a room without first opening a door. For the purpose of my own analysis here, I conceptualize a door as the entry point into a transitional or liminal state, a place of ambiguity, or even a site of cultural interaction and exchange.

So my purpose here is to suggest that the theme of opening doors also leads to endless possibilities of what might actually happen in every life. Doors are sites of transition from one state to another, from the inside world to the outside, or, in the case of Emma Hedican, from life on the inside to death on the outside. One can never know with any degree of certainty what will transpire when crossing a boundary. There was a case some time ago of a woman who slammed her front door shut only to have a loose air conditioner which had been improperly installed in an upstairs bedroom fall on her with disastrous results. At least, that was what a murderous husband wanted the crime scene to look like, until a wary detective uncovered the plot.

Thus, doors are sites of liminality. In anthropology, *liminality* (from the Latin word *līmen*, meaning 'a threshold') is the quality of ambiguity or disorientation that occurs in the middle stage of a rite of passage, when participants no longer hold their pre-ritual status but have not yet begun the transition to the status they will hold when the rite is completed. Turner is considered to have "re-discovered the importance of liminality." In 1967, he published his book *The Forest of Symbols*, which included an essay entitled *Betwixt and Between: The Liminal Period in Rites of Passage*. For Turner liminal states are 'neither here nor there'; they are 'betwixt and between'. Within Turner writings, liminality began to wander away from its narrow application to ritual passages in small-scale societies.

In the various works he completed while conducting his fieldwork amongst the Ndembu in Zambia, he made numerous connections between tribal and non-tribal societies, sensing that what he argued for the Ndembu had relevance far beyond the specific ethnographic context, as outlined in his book *The Ritual Process* (1969). It is not my place here to engage in a prolonged exegesis of Turner's work on liminality. The point is that one may begin with such a simple everyday occurrence as opening a door and find a wider, theoretical significance that could be explored further. It is no doubt true that the simple act of opening a door does not normally lead to such catastrophes as indicated here, but such events have happened, and could again even though the chances are relatively small. However, if one of these events did happen to you personality, it could be the most significant event in your entire life.

Doors, then, can be understood as sites of ambiguity, as an interface between the known and the unknown, between light and dark, or even between life and death. According to Turner (1967: 97) to be 'betwixt and between' is to be situated in a symbolically ambiguous state in which one is no longer able to hold on to their old social status, yet does not assume their new status (Turner 1964; see also Thomassen 2009). In his *Revelation and Divination in Ndembu Ritual* (1975), Turner clearly acknowledges the role of Arnold von Gennep's *Rites of Passage* (1960 [1909]) in formulating his concept of liminality when he says:

Let us go to Arnold van Gennep for his liminality…Inner space, like outer space, has boundaries, and these often prove to be the boundaries of symbolic systems…Today's liminality is tomorrow's centrality. Consideration of the negative instance provokes science to a grasp of general laws (1975: 33).

Furthermore, liminality is imbued with contrasts, such as light and dark, or white and black. Turner points out that Jesus himself was associated with whiteness at his transfiguration. Quoting Matthew (17:2) "and his face did shine as the sun and his garments became white as snow…the finding of the empty tomb takes place at 'liminal' times, between day and night…and between night and day" (1975: 189; see also Thomassen 2009).

In *Rites of Passage*, van Gennep 'grounded the similarities in ceremonies in the very fact of *transition*' (Thomassen 2012: 244). Transitions from group to group or from one social situation to the next are, according to von Gennep, a 'fact of existence'. As he explains further, "The universe itself is governed by a periodicity which has repercussions on human life, with stages and transitions, movements forward, and periods of relative inactivity" (1960: 194). However, at the time when von Gennep was an active academic he engaged in polemical sparring with Émile Durkheim and Marcel Mauss which tended to diminish the influence of his ideas in the intellectual circles of his time. As Thomassen explains, "Arnold von Gennep's larger anthropological project was not widely known, and that is certainly also due to the fact that it was shipwrecked. Von Gennep never became a founder of anthropology because of these feuds with more influential figures in French academic circles such as Émile Durkheim" (2012: 242–243).

Over the last several decades there has been an ever increasing interest in von Gennep's concept of liminality, especially as it has been interpreted by Victor Turner (Thomassen 2009, 2012). As Wels, van de Waal, Speigel and Kamsteeg indicate: "Amongst his multifold contributions to the development of anthropology as a discipline, Victor Turner became particularly famous for introducing concepts that have more or less become part of the standard lexicon of any anthropologist…but above all 'liminality', in any conversation among peers has almost become an initiation protocol in itself. 'Liminality' particularly seems to remain one of Turner's enduring legacies in the anthropological conceptual repertoire." (2011: 1).

From anthropological usage, the concept of liminality has apparently spread out in a multiplicity of directions and inspired much academic debate about its usefulness in the process. The problem with liminality and its conceptual use by Victor Turner is that there have been problems with defining what precisely the term means. As Wels et al. suggest, "a 'liminal phase' could thus refer to almost anything in which there was a normally short lived period of upending of a prior hierarchy and during which power reversals occurred, or at least appeared to have occurred" (20011: 1).

This reference to 'almost anything' appears justified since the liminality concept has been associated with identity reconstruction (Beech 2011; Yang 2000), gender studies (Mackay 2006; Madge and O'Connor 2005), nursing sciences (McGuire and Georges 2003), international conflicts (Rumelili (2003), religion (St. John 2008) and organizational studies (Tempest and Starkey 2004), among various other studies expounding on rites of passage (i.e., Willett and Deegan 2001). In fact, the proliferation of liminality as a research focus has spread into so many areas previously unanticipated in Turner's original notion of the concept that such authors as Balduk (2008) have shown a distain for the concept because of its 'anything goes' characteristic. Yet, for many, "it is what makes it an endearing concept—precisely because of its possibilities for flexible adaptations and application" (Wels et al. 2011: 1).

My Cabin's Door

With such a wide range of usage, I therefore feel confident in expanding my dialogue of everyday life using the concept of doorways as points of transition in my ethnographic fieldwork, at least as an experimental option. On a less dramatic instance of door 'happenings' during the course of my fieldwork, I would like to relate details of the following occurrences. One of these involved my attempts to solicit information from youngsters in the village. Children were always coming up to me wanting to know what I was doing in their village, where I lived and so on. When they came around to my cabin, I occasionally distributed cookies to them which tended to open up discussion about what was happening in the village.

Children, I noticed, appear to be able to pass from household to household rather unobtrusively in ways that adults would never be allowed to do. Children are often also seen by adults as inconsequential and so are apt to discuss all mater of affairs that would not occur with other adults. This, I notice, gives children a certain amount of power in the village's information flow—they are privy to much of the goings on in everyday life that others would not notice and even see as significant because of their often inconspicuousness nature. As such, one over hears scraps of conversation that are sometimes spread around by children. It is not that one needs to pry children for inside information, they usually just blurt it out, possibly as a way to become noticed or be regarded as important.

There was a little cat and mouse game that we used to play. When I was doling out cookies in front of my cabin, a rather large group of youngster would gather. When I was finished, I made a show of replacing the cooking bag near my front door, on a lower shelf. Then later I would leave my door open a crack. I would hear furtive noises outside and I knew my little subterfuge was working. Inevitably a small brown arm would search around cautiously through the door and into this lower shelf. "Ah ha," I thought my little trap did not fool them. Then I would rush over and grasp the wrist which occasioned much squealing. Other children would grasp the child's waist and try to pull him or her out of harm's way. A tug of war ensued, in which I would overly dramatize the event, with much huffing and ruffing. Eventually I let the child's arm go, spin open the door and there they were, this small crowd of apparent villains. This was followed by a further distribution of cookies. After awhile this scenario became a sort of drama enacted with renewed vigor.

In an attempt to interpret my interaction with these Anishinaabe children, and the ongoing 'cookie stealing episodes' as a process, as development in the course of social relations, I found it useful to revisit Victor Turner's well known (in anthropology at least) concept of 'social dramas'. In Turner's words, social dramas "represent sequences of social events, which, seen retrospectively by an observer, can be shown to have structure" (1974: 35). In his (first) chapter on 'social dramas and ritual metaphors', he postulates that "although we take theories into the field with us, these become relevant only if and when they illuminate social reality…sometimes ideas have a virtue of their own and many generate new hypotheses" (1974: 23). I found this comment most instructive. We do not always need *a prior* theory to make sense of our new found social reality in the field; there are times when intangible ideas emerge on their own, as we observe social events, and as such become the basis for abstract thought.

To summarize, Turner suggests that social dramas "are units of harmonious or disharmonious process, arising in conflict situations." Typically, they have four main phases:

1. *Breach* of regular, norm-governed social relations;
2. A phase of mounting *crisis*;
3. *Redressive action;*
4. *Reintegration* of the disturbed social groups (1974: 37–41).

To reiterate, my relationships with Anishinaabe children during my field work in northern Ontario became characterized by the setting of a central 'stage', focused on my cabin door, with 'actors', comprising myself and the children, enacting social dramas. My main observation is that serendipitous acts in which cookies were distributed to children, became codified or ritualized into a social drama. Turner's characterization here is instructive in interpreting the course of events. First, the children engaged in a *breach of social norms* by trespassing on my place of residence, and attempted to steal my property. Second, continual attempts by the children to steal my property lead to a phase of *mounting crisis* in our relationship. Third, the children were apprehended in their acts of pilfering which resulted in *redressive action* in which my relationship with the children was 'set straight', when the cookies were freely offered, therefore obviating the need for the thefts. Fourth, our relationship was "reintegrated" when we once again resumed amicable relations.

Thus, as far as Turner's abstract thesis regarding social dramas is concerned, I found it a useful tool in interpreting the everyday relationships between children in my research site and my own position as an observer of social interaction. Perhaps not everyone would agree with my usage in this instance, however I would nonetheless argue that an analysis of social dramas, and even that of the concept of liminality, broadened the scope of my research in thought-provoking ways that I had not initially anticipated. Thus, once again, the study of an everyday life experience during fieldwork provided an opportunity for a more abstract interpretation of events.

There were several other events, that tend to fall into the same category, that I wish to mention briefly to illustrate the connection between everyday occurrences and broader theoretical issues or interpretations. In the the first of these instances I was abruptly awaken in the middle of the night, say about 2 am, but by a man who burst through my door, took several steps forward and abruptly fell face first onto the floor. Of course I was shocked very quickly into consciousness by this sudden intrusion. I put on some clothes, lit my lamp and proceeded to shut my front door. I then took the lamp and placed it down by the man's face, at which it was clear to me that the man was an Anishinaabe individual who was also a foreman on the Canadian National Railway, and therefore one of relatively high status and income in the community. We did not have a particularly close relationship, however I have questioned him in the past about hunting and fishing returns as well as his employment on the railway.

I sat down on the edge of my bed for a few minutes trying to figure out what was the meaning of this rather peculiar visit. I bent down once more and could tell immediately that he was inebriated. His wife, I also knew, regularly attended the local Anglican church and was likely not willing to tolerate drunkenness in her home. One the other hand, most other people in the village would not tolerate this intrusive behavior either. On a few occasions, when there was instances for some general partying in the village I would hear guns discharged which I took to mean a warning to the rabble rousers to stay clear of particular houses. But why my house?

My interpretation was that since there were few other places in the village where he would be welcomed in this particular state of inebriation, for some reason he felt that I might at least tolerate him. Here I might apply a few insights derived from Victor Turners concept of liminality. In the first place, unlike just about every other person in the village I was a person 'betwixt and between'. What I mean is that while I was clearly not an Anishinaabe I nonetheless lived like one. Few Euro-Canadians, such as the police, social workers, or government officials, ever spent more than a few hours in the village—they were there strictly for business and left as hastily as possible. So one way to look at my position as an anthropological researcher was that I was in this liminal state—neither totally in or totally out of the local society.[28]

Of course there were anthropologists who occasionally crossed the line, perhaps taking a native wife, assimilating as best they could, and never returning to their previous status in life. However, I was not one of these. I was therefore not 'in transition' between two societies, just 'partly in, and partly out'. My position in the village was therefore an ambiguous one and this foreman obviously, given few other alternatives, felt that I would tolerate his presence. As it turned out, when I awoke in the morning, this intruder had left during the night, and the incident was never mentioned to me again. In other words, my front door was an entry point into a luminous state, where he felt safe because he was no longer on Anishinaabe territory, yet not really on white man's soil as well, just some point 'in-between'.

In another incident, there was a knock on my door. When I opened it, a young man was standing there with his hands outstretched. He said his father wanted me to have these objects that he held in his hands. He tried to motion that I should cup my hands together, and when I did he poured into them a number of small silver objects, and then abruptly left without any further explanation. I took these over to my table so I could see them under better light. There were perhaps about a dozen small rings. When I examined them closer, they were all marked with a stamp, 'Washington, DC' followed by a series of numbers. Then it dawned on me, these were the leg bands from geese that his father had probably recently shot.

So, I begin to ponder the situation. A young man hands me some strange objects through the passage way of my front door. Then, surprisingly, I begin to notice a conceptual passageway as well. Then a sequence of thoughts. The bands were from wild geese that people were eating. These geese were part of a wider diet of country food, including probably fish, waterfowl such as the geese, and various animals. This diet is an important part of the local economy because without it people would have to rely on Euro-Canadian foods, at much great expense. In other words, country food was in itself a source of income, especially if you begin to tally up the worth of such food. Remember also, that this country food is composed of high quality protein, without modern additives, and chemical, and therefore has a very high replacement value.

As my thinking progressed one thought led to another. It starts with a small apparently insignificant element—the geese bands—and can be extrapolated further into an analysis of the local economy. As such, I wondered what country food was worth in Canadian dollars, as a replacement cost. This caused me to seek in earnest any information on hunting and fishing. At every chance, I asked questions from local hunters and fishermen about their month to month subsistence activities. I wanted specific details which I kept in a separate notebook. In another notebook, I kept details on wage income in the community and was hoping at one point to compare the two.

My main point which I noticed tended to be absent from the exiting literature is that hunting and fishing could be considered as a form of wage work, and not just an idle pastime, or as a recreational activity, as with Euro-Canadians. At the end of a year, I was able to put together a summary of all this economic data. The conclusions were: (1) the total country food production when considered as replacement costs at a store amounted to 20 percent of the total cash income in the community including transfer payments. In other words, country food production increased the wage income of the community by 20 percent. In turn, this additional income could be used to purchase equipment (rifles, chain saws, fishing nets) which could then be used to increase proficiency of country food production; (2) the highest productivity in country food production was among men with the highest earned incomes in the village. This surprised me. I thought that it would be the less employed men who have the time to spend on subsistence productions.

Then I conducted some interviews. The men with the higher cash incomes could afford to increase their country food production by using better equipment and, probably most importantly, could afford to travel usually by plane to the less utilized areas in their territory where hunting and fishing returns were the highest. Men with less income were forced to hunt near the village, in areas that were highly utilized and less productive of hunting and fishing effort.

To summarize, a young man comes to my door and hands me, through the passage way, some strange silver bands. These bands set in motion a series of research questions about subsistence production and its relationship with cash income in the community. The results of the subsequent inquiries and the resulting analysis of the data obtained from these queries led to significant results that were hitherto not previously reported in the ethnographic literature. In other words, what would appear to be a rather trivial everyday event concerning geese bands, when investigated further and at greater depth, resulted in research opportunities that were not otherwise anticipated. In this case, it was not a theory which informed the data, but the other way around; the research data led to significant abstract ideas that could then be tested on a wider ethnographic scale.

Here is another example of one such occurrence which serves to make my point about the significant of routine, everyday events which nonetheless turned out to have a significant impact on my research endeavors. I mentioned previously that I had seen an elderly fellow hauling fish from his canoe. My interest here was almost exclusively related to my interest in documenting what is usually referred to as subsistence production or country food collection. The larger picture here would be to gather research details on a larger theme, which is to say, on the relationship to local food production as an aspect of acculturation studies. In other words, the idea would be to relate the quantity of local food collected to a hypothesis about possible assimilation into the large Euro-Canadian society. So with this goal in mind I began to proceed down to the lake shore hoping to be able to count the fish that the elderly fellow had caught that morning.

On my way down to the lake, I was intercepted by Donald Patience, one of the local leaders, who wanted to know where I was going. After explaining my purpose, he suggested that I go into his cabin for a moment because he wanted to explain something to me. "You need to spend more time getting to know the people here," he said. "All you do is talk with us the local leaders but you seem to avoid most of the ordinary people," he said, which I took as an admonishment. "Take that old guy down by the water, his name is Samson Basketwang," Donald explained, "I'm sure he is curious about you, and why you are here asking all these questions."

"Oh, I don't know about that," I responded, "he probably doesn't speak any English."

"All the more reason why you should visit him, anyway, what are you here for, if it isn't to get to know the community?" Donald asked.[29]

Yes, Donald had a point, I thought, there is no point in being far too cautious. "Look," Donald went on, pulling a small box from under his bed. "There are four or five beer here, take this over to Samson's place, it will help to break the ice. When you come back, let me know how it went," he suggested.

So off I went feeling quite nervous about the whole affair. "Oh, well, what have I got to lose," I thought, trying to buck up my courage. This was one of those fieldwork opportunities that I did not want to be ruined by my apprehensions.

Samson's cabin was at the far end of the village so I had some time while walking to reflect on my timid approach to research. I needed to be a bit bolder, I conceded if I was going to get anywhere. Donald was probably right. However, as I approached their home I became increasingly concerned over what might happen. It was quite conceivable that they would misinterpret my intentions, ask what I wanted, and shut the door. Then, I thought, I would become increasingly apprehensive of having this incident repeat itself with other residents. Word might get around that this strange white guy was going around the village disturbing people for reasons that were not comprehensible, I should have stayed with the people I know, I reasoned, with the situations that were familiar to me. I almost turned around but for whatever reason continued on my quest.

As it turned out I was really glad that I did. With my knock on the door, Samson did open it in a cautious manner, with a quizzical look on his face. His wife Annie was sitting on their bed, apparently stitching some beads onto a leather glove. When I raised the small box of beer, his face brightened. He took me by the elbow and guided me to a seat by the window. There is no doubt that we struggled with communication. I had been taking almost daily lessons in Anishinaabe from a young man in the village, but my communication skills were obviously quite poor. Nonetheless, it was also apparent they this elderly couple appreciated my somewhat feeble attempts at learning their language. As it turned out, Annie knew more English than I originally had expected. We prattled away in a friendly manner, mixing hand gestures along with facial expressions and phrases with an odd mixture of English-Anishinaabe terms.

Annie, I noticed, often laughed away but always guarded her mouth with her hand when doing so. At one point, she brought out from under the bed a package of cigarettes, tailor-mades, which in this village were almost as valuable as money, as most people only smoked what were called 'roll-your-owns'. Even though I was not much of a smoker, I took one anyway as a sort of peace offering, recognizing also the role of tobacco in Indigenous societies. The time seemed to pass quickly, and I mentioned that I needed to use their out house. Me too, Samson indicated. Outside I noticed several deep holes around the yard, with dogs of various sizes chained up around a central stake. Samson tripped, falling over in the mass of chains. In an attempt to rescue him, I also fell, we rolled around together laughing. Finally, I pulled him up and we both dragged ourselves away from the dogs who were intent on licking our faces to the bone.

I will never forget this day, even though I never considered this fortuitous meeting worthy enough to make a description of it into my research notes. It just seemed one of those fun times in life that happens all too infrequently. We make new friends, when we overcome somehow our inhibitions and are rewarded.

Several days later, when I finally saw Donald again, I described my meeting with the Basketwangs. He said, "So, told you so, for the most part we're friendly people here." Then I asked quite accidently about Annie's persistent gesture in which she shielded her mouth when laughing. "Oh," he said, "odd that you should notice this, but there was something important here that you might not recognize. People are really sensitive here about any slights, about anyone making fun about them, or becoming the butt of jokes. People here carry resentments for a long time. So, people cover their mouths when laughing so as not to suggest that they are laughing at you. Not so long ago there used to be witchcraft and spells about such things. The Anishinaabe are a proud people and don't take kindly to being made fun of."

And then another thought occurred to me, "What about all those dogs that Samson keeps," I asked, "what's the story there?" Donald paused for a moment, "Well, Samson used to have all those dogs carry him through the snow on a sled, but the sled wore out. Anyway he can't afford a snowmobile, what with the high cost of gas, oil, maintenance fees and a place to store it. He loves his dogs and wouldn't think of shooting them. So he feeds them fish from the lake. When you think about it, the dogs don't really cost him anything, just his labor to feed them."[30]

This explanation was thoughtful and made a lot of sense. I remembered a book called *The Snowmobile Revolution* (Pelto 1973) about the mechanization of reindeer herding among the Lapps of Scandinavia. This study is about "the processes of change which occurs in situations wherein societies abandon locally available sources of energy for those which must be acquired from the outside…the consequences have been disastrous…the main point to be made is that, with the snowmobile revolution, the Lapps have joined the growing numbers of people for whom a return to energy autonomy is nearly impossible" (1973: 168). In this light, Donald's observations were quite perceptive. He was able to link a single case of technological change in his community with wider economic trends.

Assessing Turner's Liminality Concept

For those who might be skeptical about Turner's liminality concept and its usefulness in anthropological situations during field research, this of course is quite understandable. To use his concept of liminality requires a certain 'leap of faith'. All in all, we are led to the question, "How have anthropologists assessed his concept?"

As a starting point, it should be noted that a great many anthropologists have used this concept solely on the basis of its popularity alone, from which we would be led to assume that the concept has a fairly wide acceptance in the discipline. As Wels et al. conclude in their review article, the widespread use of Turner's liminality model "testifies to the extent to which it is stimulating and refreshing to revisit what has become a 'household' concept in anthropology, such as Turner's liminality" (2011: 3).

Other anthropologists would apparently agree with this assertion concerning the popularity of Turner's liminality concept. As an example, in Dan Jorgensen's review of Ashley's edited collection, *Victor Turner and the Construction of Cultural Criticism*, he asserts that "anthropologists have assimilated Victor Turners ideas so thoroughly that they are hardly mentioned these days…it is hard to imagine treatments of symbolism that fails to make at least tacit notions of liminality" (1992: 196). Furthermore, Weber apparently tends to agree suggesting that "liminal (or 'liminality') has become *the* as in orig. key word in current American Studies and in cultural studies scholarship in general…I, too, found Turner's theories of ritual process to possess formidable explanatory power" (1995: 533). However, Jorgensen (1992: ibid.) concluded that Turner's influence is, generally, 'not apparent in most of the essays' that he read in Ashley's collection.

In my experience, having taught anthropology for over four decades, the idea that Turner's liminality concept has become one of those 'household' ideas in anthropology would have to be thought of as an exaggeration. If by this statement it is meant that the liminality concept stands beside such fundamental terms as ethnocentrism, participant observation, or Boas's historical particularism, then this is simply not the case. Perhaps a third-year theory course in anthropology would be a more appropriate university level for any extended discussion of such a topic, but probably not at the introductory level. I have an array of recent introductory texts on my bookshelf and leafing through the index of each of these I notice that most have a brief mention of liminality, sometimes in association with Turner's discussion of symbolism, but most with regards van Gennep's focus on rites of passage.

Most introductory texts do not specifically link liminality to Ndembu rituals which was Turner's focus, but to the more familiar (to university students) educational rites of passage between childhood and adulthood. It is understandable that Turner's concept of liminality be discussed in terms which can be comprehended my by introductory anthropology students, but such usage does mask the complex mix of usages, and the clash between symbol, structure and contradictions that would appear to be an integral part of Turner's initial African ethnographic applications.

Thus, there appears to be a certain degree of ambivalence with the treatment of Turner's liminality. In Barrett's assessment, he attempts to explain the reasons why symbolic anthropology "occupies a minor place in this study…Without the clash between symbol and structure, or the working out of basic contradictions among the shifting, often irreconcilable norms that guide and rationalize behavior by actors who strive to better their positions in a constantly changing world, dialectical anthropology cannot thrive" (1984: 209). As such there is a certain contradiction in the role of an actor in a ritual, which is to say that an emphasis on the 'native viewpoint' may lead to distortions or even errors of interpretation. In other words, there may be a certain validity to the idea that even natives to a particular culture may not fully or *really know what's going on*, at least at a wider, more comprehensive, level. As an example, it is fair to ask about the extent that any individual actor is functionally aware of what produces the institutional arrangements in their society.

To further explain what is meant here about the relationship between knowledge and societal structure we can rely on Turner's own words: "The participant is likely to be governed in his actions by a number of interests, purposes, and sentiments, dependent upon his specific position, which impair his understanding of the total situation. An even more serious obstacle against his achieving objectivity is the fact that he tends to regard as axiomatic and primary the ideals, values and norms which are overtly expressed or symbolized in the ritual" (Turner 1964: 28). The question, then, becomes "who among us *really knows* what is happening in our society, at least at a certain abstract level?"

If we are willing to concede that most participants in a society are unlikely to be aware of the causes of their behavior beyond a quite limited sphere of events, then this opens up a Pandora's box of related issues, especially when we are dealing with such complex societal issues, as structure, organization, and symbolic actions. If we are willing to concede, as I suggest most of us would, that society is composed of a variety of interpretations (in Geertz's 1973 terms) of most phenomenon, then one wonders if anyone has control of these interpretations of events, and, if they do, how does power relate to the control of a society's narratives? This is exactly the issue that Weber raises with regards Victor Turner's interpretation of liminality. It is important, Weber argues, not to lose sight of "the battle over narrative power, the fight over who gets to tell the story, and from which position" (1995: 532). Furthermore, borders and international positioning is an important factor, as Spierenburg suggests in an article on 'The Politics of the Liminal...' that "transfrontier parks constitute liminal spaces where international borders no long matter" (2011: 81). In turn, Weber's (1995) retort is that this suggestion ignores culture as a political manifestation.[31]

Essentialism and Culture

This discussion concludes with a brief discussion of perhaps the most important issue with Turner's work over all, that of *essentialism*. Sidky defines this term as "the propensity to reify ideas and concepts as if they represent the essence or inherent qualities of the things to which they refer" (2004: 424). Here lies the problem. As anthropologists attempt to provide abstract interpretations of the myriad cultural idiosyncrasies of an individual society, they have a tendency to 'strip away' the very characteristics that make that society unique. Salzman explains further: "We anthropologists rely on abstraction to move beyond the confusing welter of daily life and its infinite variety of particulars," but there are "serious interrelated problems with this abstract way of thinking about people and their lives. One is that we often end up reifying 'culture' and 'position' by treating these cognitive abstractions of ours as if they were forces that made people do one thing or another" (1999: 92–93). In other words, in order to comprehend the myriad detail of everyday life, there is a tendency to focus on one main cultural feature as the 'essence' of a people's lives.

In the process, the cultural characteristics that make the people in a particular society relatively unique are minimized or disregarded altogether in an attempt to present an abstract model. We are often left, then, with a view of a society as if it were homogeneous and logically consistent, whereas the truth of the matter is that human societies are frequently 'messy', contradictory, and fragmentary. This point of view leads to another problem. By only looking at essential details, and ignoring the fragmentary nature of real social life, we are apt to be fooled into thinking that societies are relatively unchanging in their nature and consisting of permanent patterns. To the contrary, we should be well aware that people's everyday lives are changing all the time; that nothing is fixed, that life is an ever changing river of possibilities and contradictions. To think otherwise is to engage in self-deception.[32]

Now, returning to Turner's concept of liminality, Deflem comments that "*liminal* as in orig. phenomena are predominantly restricted to 'primitive' tribal societies" (1991:15–16). Then Spiegel adds, "liminality being seen and applied to all 'betwixt and between' social situations…created a tendency toward it being used to perpetuate a crude and by now passé primitive-versus-civilized/modern view of societal types" (2011: 11). In other words, the abstract nature of the liminal concept, and attempts to apply it to all kinds of behavior, by necessity involves an essentialist attempt to reduce the peculiarities of cultural phenomena to an almost preposterous level.[33]

All that we are really left with in Turner's liminality concept is the idea of individuals stuck in a limbo or status-less position (the betwixt and between), in which a person has left one status but has not entered another one. Obviously, then, this extension of the liminality concept allows it to be used in such a variety of situations that depart radically for Turner's original intention when he studied Ndembu ritual that one is left to wonder if it means anything at all. To make the point more emphatically, Sidky suggests that "The Liminal *persona* as in orig. is defined by a complex and sometimes 'bizarre' set of animal or natural symbols, such as bird feathers, grass skirts, animal masks, and the like" (2004: 313). In addition, liminality has been linked to death and invisibility, a state 'out of time', and 'in and out' of a society's social structure.

Sidky has a long list of weaknesses of Turner's approach. The principle one is "the problem of validation or replication...How is Turner (1974: 36) sure that he has accessed the 'models' or 'metaphors' carried in the actors' heads that figure in the 'social dramas' he used as units of analysis?" (2004: 319). Further problems concern Turner's "inferences drawn from human behavior," and finally, "there is the difficulty posed by the multivocality of symbols...symbols are open to different interpretations"...such that there is then a tendency to write ethnographies that 'lend themselves to the production of wonderfully imaginative and clever stories, especially if the ethnographer is inclined toward the idea of ethnography as fiction, as is the case of present-day postmodern interpretivists'. "How do we know," Sidky asks, "whether the interpretation offered is just clever talk" (ibid).

In the end, though, Sidky has a positive view of Turner's place in anthropological history, despite his long list of complaints. He is particularly impressed with the fact that Turner's interpretations are actually based on fieldwork, on an examination of real life, on everyday events among the people of an African society, as opposed to the 'fictions' created by many postmodernists. Social anthropology, when it comes right down to it, will survive or fade away in the course of time, based on an accurate observation of human behavior in many cross-cultural settings, and not just on the imaginative power of creative writers. In other words, if you have not the time for all the myriad predicaments, informant temperaments, language-translation impediments, and conceptual complications that fieldwork entails, then perhaps you might be better suited for another profession.

Fieldwork and Epistemology

There is no doubt then that Turner's liminality concept has several problems associated with its usage. No one ever said that living in another culture and trying to interpret what is going on is an easy task. In fact, there are a number of publications that critically examine the practice of fieldwork specifically, or the state of theory and the discipline of anthropology (such as Sanjek 1990). One might also note Cerwonka and Malkki's (2007) attempt to draw theory out of ethnographic experience as it unfolds, especially in terms of people's everyday lives. Even so, despite the difficulties of attempting application of the liminality concept to real life situations, Sidky nonetheless feels that "Turner's approach is to be commended because it requires immersion in and an empirical understanding of another culture that takes into account observational sociological factors. Turner never attempted to bypass the required hard work in the field" (2004: 319–320).

This discussion of Turner's liminality concept has important implications for social (or cultural) anthropology as a whole. Which research design to cultural issues are we to take? On the one hand there is the top down or deductive method in which one begins with a problem to investigate, develops a hypothesis and then tests it in the field. The other tactic, the inductive one, is to select an area or people to study then through the experience of fieldwork allow issues to emerge through the course of the study. As Barrett indicates, "Probably most anthropologist have been (and continue to be) opposed to a deductive approach on the grounds that problems and themes should emerge from the fieldwork setting, rather than being imposed by the investigator" (2009: 78). The approach favored in this book, and in my own career, is the 'bottom up' or inductive approach in which fieldwork is a central concern in data or information gathering.

We might therefore say that anthropological fieldwork has significant epistemological implications—how we know what we know issues—and that our main conceptual concerns in the discipline are intrinsically tied to fieldwork. In fact, I would go so far as to assert that our fieldwork activity is the basis for all debate, and is the final arbiter about methodological issues in social anthropology. Since many anthropologists gather information on their subjects of interest mainly on the basis of first-hand experience through field research, then the interrelationship between fieldwork and the creation of knowledge in the discipline is a matter of some epistemological interest. For as Ulin (1984: xi) rightly indicates, "Fieldwork or participant observation has led many anthropologists to struggle with epistemological problems related to understanding other cultures as part of a dialectical process of self-understanding."

It might also be correctly argued, that for the last several decades at least, anthropologists in their writings are now showing a much greater interest in the methodological issues raised by field research, especially in ethnography's depiction of the point of view of the 'Other' which is at the center of discussion in contemporary anthropology. In Abu-Lughod's words, as she explains:

Culture is the essential tool for making other. As a professional discourse that elaborates on the meaning of culture in order to account for, explain, and understand cultural difference, anthropology also helps construct, produce and maintain it. Anthropological discourse gives cultural difference (and the separation between groups of people it implies) the air of the self-evident (1991: 143).

In an ironic twist of fate, since anthropologists such as Franz Boas for the last century have argued against equating race and culture, there is a suggestion promulgated among scholars such as Abu-Lughard that culture has become a virtual equivalent of race (Brumann 1999: 2). Note, for example, Visweswaren's (1998: 76, 79) use of the term 'cultural racism', and his suggestion that "we not mourn the passing of the modern concept of culture." Thus, it is debates such as these that might propitiously be investigated during fieldwork in everyday settings in an attempt to investigate important epistemological issues in the disciple.

Since many anthropologists view the concept of culture as the central core of the sub-discipline of cultural or social anthropology, then an investigation of the importance of the culture concept during fieldwork would be of immense value as a point of debate which might well influence the future of the discipline. In addition, we can regard the debate about culture as a multifaceted one, and which might well portent a rupture in anthropology which could be at the center of the call for a distinct break with the past, and a disappearance of existing paradigms and old-order authorities such as the culture concept. One should not ignore the fact that there is presently in social anthropology a crisis over how 'other' people are portrayed, what has come to be known as a 'crisis of representation' (Marcus and Fischer 1986:16) which is to say 'the explicit discourse that reflects on the doing…of ethnography'. What is at issue over the last several decades in social anthropology is a challenge to "all those views of reality in social thought which prematurely overlook or reduce cultural diversity for the sake of the capacity to generalize or to affirm universal values" (Ibid 1986: 33).

As one might expect, there has been a certain amount of vitriolic back-lash in anthropological circles from those who see a diminished role for fieldwork if the post-modernist view prevails. For example, it has been suggested that the 'challenges to ethnographic authority' represented by the postmodernist trend in anthropology represented by Marcus, Clifford and Fischer has unfortunately led many contemporary anthropologists to abandon fieldwork in favor of what has been referred to as 'strategies of theoretical puppeteering, textual analysis, and surrogate ethnography'. Alternatively, it is argued that the power and knowledge attained through the fieldwork experience be enhanced, not diminished —"fieldwork yields important insights outside the reach of textual analysis," Borneman and Hammoudi assert (2009:1). They also point to the importance for ethnography of describing the "daily concerns and concrete actions of people: that is, in their subsistence activities, family structure, marriages, relations with parents, siblings and neighbors…the intensive, intimate, reflexive engagement with the quotidian" concerns of everyday life (2009: 9–10). "Fieldwork experience," they conclude, "provides for a special kind of reflexive experience and perception" that the post-modernist perspective does not offer (2009: 19).

On this basis, one might also reasonably conclude, using Marcus and Fischer's phrase "for the sake of the capacity to generalize" is furthermore central to the manner in which fieldwork is conducted, and that the relationship between the portrayal of everyday events and the possible generalizations that are likely to emerge from the analysis of these events. Thus, fieldwork is fundamental to resolving current debates concerning the manner in which people in difference cultures are portrayed in anthropology. It is likewise imperative that the centrality of fieldwork as portrayed in the characterization of everyday events is not replaced by attempts to reduce ethnography simply to a set of literary skills and 'constructed truths', but that sound analysis founded on accurate observation and meaningful participation provide the basis for reasonable conclusions of human social and cultural life. With regard to Watson's comment that "the implication seems to be that we would do well to spend more time on the intellectual analysis of what we have and be less obsessed by the collection of data" (1999: 19), this juxtaposition which posits data collection with intellectual analysis is misplaced—we obviously need both types of endeavor to be successful. Facts are useless by themselves, without context and interpretation, and by the same token, intellectual musings without sound evidence to support them amounts to mere speculation.

A Fundamental Problem

The fundamental problem in anthropology is the simultaneous notion of cultural uniqueness and the underlying similarity of *Homo sapiens*. "The great natural variation of cultural forms is" Geertz asserts, "the ground of its deepest theoretical dilemma: how is such variation to be squared with the biological unity of the human species" (1973: 22). As social anthropologists seek to further articulate the 'particularistic' nature of cultural variation, or as Geertz (1973: 24) suggests, anthropology becoming 'imprisoned in the immediacy of its own detail', there is therefore a corresponding trend which minimizes our commonalities as a species. A balance between the two perspectives—biological and cultural—is a predicament for anthropology since one starts to emphasize one aspect over another, it also then tends to minimize the importance of the other.

By focusing anthropological fieldwork on the everyday necessities of human life—food getting, conciliatory patterns of behavior, functional interrelationships—we begin to find common ground between the two seemingly polar attractions in human societies. Using such an approach, which is to say, concentrating research efforts on what every human needs to do every day to maintain life is one method of drawing these two seemingly disparate aspects of human life closer together, and thereby serve to move toward reducing anthropology's 'deepest dilemma'. As Geertz explains, "To an ethnographer the shapes of knowledge are always ineluctably local, indivisible from their instruments and encasements" (1983: 40). If we agree with this assessment, then it is to the local situations of everyday life that anthropologists' focus should return, and not to the grand conjectural schemes of today's version of the 'armchair' theoreticians.

An anthropologist's approach to fieldwork probably is a matter, as much as anything else, on how one broaches the question of human existence, the sorts of training and experiences one has, and whether or not one is predisposed to viewing humanity in a micro or macro perspective. As Scholte (1972: 438) has suggested, "The ethnographic situation is defined not only by the native society in question but also by the ethnological tradition 'in the head' of the ethnographer." The suggestion, then, is that anthropologists see in their fieldwork situations what they are trained to see, but not necessarily what is 'factual' or 'in the heads' of the people who are living their everyday lives in plain view of the ethnographer. In this sense, ethnographic research is all a matter of what one chooses to observe, and then how this view is 'crafted' to present a view of society which conforms to a predetermined 'theoretical' point of view. It is for this reason that many anthropologists prefer an inductive—from the ground up—approach to their research.

In addition, there are those who suggest that the problem is not with fieldwork approaches *per se*, but in the methodology in use. As an example, in an apparent criticism of Geertz's 'interpretive' approach, Renner explains that "the absence of an empirically convincing theory and methodology has as its consequence the fact that there can be no program for the direction in which research should proceed" (1984: 540). This is a view reinforced by others, such as Lett's comment that "the most significant deficiency in Geertz's interpretive approach is its lack of explicit theoretical and methodological guidelines" (1987: 117).

Such comments bring to the forefront the division between anthropologists who bring to their fieldwork set 'theoretical and methodological guidelines', and those who prefer to see in their fieldwork an opportunity to observe and participate in a community's daily life events and on this basis form more abstract generalizations, if warranted on the basis of evident 'social facts'. In this regard, one is reminded of Durkheim's assertion that "Sociology does not need to choose between the great hypotheses which divide metaphysicians. It needs to embrace free will no more than determinism" (1938 1895: 141). He also noted that "the great sociologists…seldom advanced beyond vague generalities on the nature of societies, on the relation between social and the biological realms" (ibid: lix).

We also should note Marvin Harris's opinion that "One must agree completely with Durkheim that from an operational point of view, the idiosyncratic or historical instance is merely the observational raw data out of which the categories of sociological discourse are constructed by the community of observers" (1968: 471). In other words, particular 'instances' are the "raw data" upon which more universal or abstract themes are developed, rather than the inverse. The conclusion is that one builds abstract ideas through observing the peculiarities of everyday life in community settings, rather than through what Scholte (1984: 542) referred to as 'the reductionism and ethnocentrism of traditional science'.

Fieldwork and Reflexive Understandings

Any anthropologist who has ever conducted fieldwork soon realizes that their knowledge of community life does not come to them in neatly packaged themes or categories. Instead, knowledge gained is largely discontinuous, it comes in bits and pieces, mostly when we are thinking about something else. It is for this reason that Robin Ridington's (1990) study of the Dunne-za entitled *Little Bit Know Something* is apt to resonate with other ethnographers because it "blends Indian voices with my own into a continuous narrative which in turn blends my voice with that of academic anthropology" (1990: xiv). For the Dunne-za say that people speak from the 'authority of their experience'. In other words, their knowledge comes to them through direct experience which, in turn, empowers a person to live in this world with intelligence and understanding. Knowledge does not come before 'direct experience', but precedes it, and then the two aspects—experience and knowledge—interact in a dialectical fashion, one contributing to the other, and advancing the whole forward in time (see also Ridington 1988: 98–110).

Here is an example of the sort of situation that I encountered during my own fieldwork. In an Anishinaabe village of small of cabins in the far reaches of northern Ontario, I lived in my own cabin a mere four or five meters square but nonetheless comfortable enough. I had a small desk in one corner accompanied by an overturned garbage can with a pillow on top, which served as a seat for my visitors. There was also a small bench situated near the front door so that at first people to feel a bit nervous or shy about visiting could keep their distance. However, most people eventually moved over beside my desk because the candles and coal oil lamp made it hard to see even at four meters.

Another reason for moving closer was so that they did not have to speak so loud, especially when someone wanted to tell me a bit of information not commonly known, in which instance they would motion with a wiggly fore finger that I should come closer so that they could mention a special 'secret' in my ear. I always found it somewhat odd that someone would tell me, an outsider, one of their closely guarded snips of information. Possibly it was to let me know that they were sincere, or to gain my confidence, I was never sure.

This cabin was the place where much of the information about village life was gathered, as just about everyone showed up beside this desk at one time or another, often spending long hours recounting their memories, perceptions, frustrations and insights. One must remember that nobody was really rushed, especially in the evening, and a visit to me could be seen as a form of entertainment. Talking with other people, especially strangers who had additional bits of information from the outside world, was sort of like listening to the news on television, which of course they did not have here at this time. Taken as a whole, it all seemed to me like a jumble of fieldwork, entertainment, and relaxation to help fill in the long winter evenings. Late at night the flickering lamp made the shadows and shapes in the room flow back and forth as if they were made of liquid matter.

On one occasion, a middle-aged man grew serious as he pointed to the corner of my cabin where the wood stove was situated and he asked if I had seen it. The bottom of the stove had begun to rot out, and the glowing embers inside cast eerie twinkles of light across the ceiling. "What?" I asked. "You know, the *cheebuy* ('ghost' in Anishinaabe)," he said. This *cheebuy* was apparently that of Ed Pidgeon, the one-armed former occupant of the cabin, whose death to this day had remained a mystery in the community. Now this fellow was starting to make me nervous, because while I had to admit that Ed Pigeon's apparition had not revealed itself to me, I also realized that through the long winter months I had to spend many hours alone in this cabin, and one never knows what tricks the mind is apt to play as we work our way through the manifestations, real or imagine, of the so-called culture shock experience.

This cabin and the people who came and went were part of my life decades ago, yet the scene remains with me, sometimes in vivid detail. The cabin itself has long been torn down, the result, it is said, of the drowning of Sogo

Sabosons, a later owner. The cabin had to go because they did not want his ghost wandering about the village. Without the cabin, the reasoning went, Sogo's apparition would not have a place to settle down and would move elsewhere.

It would not be true to say that events such as these have had any sort of permanent impact on my psyche as an anthropologist, but it is the cumulative nature of such happenings that have a subtle molding effect. They are a touchstone to an alternate reality that is after all these years still only poorly conceived and apprehended on my part. It is as if in the beginning of our fieldwork we are not allowed a true glimpse of the magnitude and scope of the reality enveloping us. In any event we are usually too naïve, young and immature to fully appreciate what is going on, so our mind's eye secretly files various occurrences away for safekeeping as it were, for retrieval later for reflection, with the possibility that at some later stage in our development we might be in a position to make a more profound sense of these happenings. So these little snippets of time are hauled out on occasion and presented to us for some sort of closer scrutiny and analysis.

The trouble with all this is that we are now years down the road in life, and the accuracy of our recollection, even with the aid of written field notes, logic tells us, should be regarded with some degree of skepticism. We have a seemingly clear grasp of the detail of some events, but other aspects have been forgotten altogether. What this means is that we are faced with the task of trying to reconstruct the reality of the original fieldwork, and all the other "realities" that have emerged over the years as we reflect on our experiences and what they mean in some wider, objective sense. How merry, we are led to think, must be the life of the logical positivist for whom the content of observation tends to be free of conceptual contamination. It is no wonder that Nietzsche called this 'the dogma of *immaculate perception* [emphasis mine]'.

We are therefore left with a question about the manner in which anthropologists come to the sorts of understanding and explanations that they do. One facet of this problem is what Barrett has referred to as 'the illusion of simplicity', which is to say:

The Interplay between the contradictory nature of social life and the mechanisms that conceal it indicates the vast complexity in the midst of which our lives unfold...But anthropologists spend their lives trying to prove that order exists. This mistake is not restricted to anthropologists or to their analysis of primitive society. It is probably intrinsically related to the attempt to establish a positivistic science of society (1984: 195).

It is no doubt true that many anthropologists perceive of themselves as 'doing science'. However, science can be thought of in terms of a broad range of scholarly activity. For instance, as Pelto (1970: 30) indicates, "No sharp lines can be drawn to differentiate the so-called hard sciences from other disciplines...somewhere in the middle of this conceptual domain is the matter of methodological verification—the sets of rules whereby useful knowledge can be accumulated and pyramided into a more powerful understanding of the universe." There is no doubt that this issue of 'methodological verification' has become the focus of controversy concerning the believability of anthropological research and the basis on which anthropologists accept generalizations of human behavior.

Lessons Learned

One of the main lessons that I learned from conducting my ethnographic research in northern Ontario is that the construction of ethnography is largely a matter of organizing our "reflexive understandings" of the fieldwork experience. It is a process fraught with difficulties of interpretation as we attempt to grapple with the accumulation of "realities"—our and that of the 'Other'—that have built up over time. The fact that we are able to provide plausible accounts of our experiences is perhaps a minor miracle in itself. Our success depends pretty much on how we are able to organize our understandings. We group them together in various ways, by discussing issues and problems that are encountered, and thereby build up larger spheres or facets of the account we seek to portray. Thus, this process of constructive understanding becomes central to the problem of verification in fieldwork.

The various incidents that are discussed in this book highlights the possibility, even probability, that quite different accounts of "reality" can be expected in anthropology. However, it would be a mistake to conclude that ethnographies are by their very nature unreliable documents because of the matter of methodological verification. As an example, if we take the various incidents that I encountered in the Anishinaabe village that was the site of my research, and those that I was a participant in, it becomes quite obvious that one could never duplicate these situations because they were unique in their own right. In addition, each of the participants, myself included, brings a different perception of what occurred because of cultural background, age, gender, economic status, and so on.

As an example, in attempting to provide an explanation for the interaction of Donald, Samson and myself, it is evident that while Donald himself owned a snowmobile, he could afford to do so, unlike Samson's case. Thus, the Collins community was becoming bifurcated into those who were able to keep up with technological change and those who were not. It was a matter of what economists call *opportunity costs*, which is to say that every economic change involves costs that one may or may not be able to afford.

On a related theme, one is also reminded of Marvin Harris' (1966) arguments relating to India's sacred cows. Using cows to pull plows may seem inefficient to the Western mind when tractors are available. And, like the snowmobile, tractors involve similar costs while cows require almost no maintenance. They feed themselves by eating the grass along the roadways, provide traction for plows, and their dung is a valuable source of fertilizer. Tractors may plow their fields quicker than cattle do, but then again the farmers' plots are small, therefore the tractor might sit idle in a shed for long periods of time and as such are not very economical to own. I see snowmobiles in a similar light.

So there I was, another lesson learned that I did not expect, just by observing everyday life, about noticing the small, mundane aspects of human interaction, which ultimately led to wider societal characteristics and economic issues that most people would probably never notice. A few simple observations and questions about everyday life can lead to a much wider field of inquiry that one would not likely notice in the first place if we tended to regard the commonplace and ordinary goings-on in life as inconsequential and not worthy of special notice. As a result of these little instances I've begun to look out for unusual occurrences even apparently trivial ones and attempt to arrive at a larger picture of the flow of everyday life that most people would not normally give much attention to.

There is another important lesson that I learned concerning the use of concepts in anthropology. In the normal course of my research, I must admit that I have been more than a little hesitant about using concepts, or theoretical paradigms, that did not seem to neatly fit into my ethnographic perspective. This intellectual inhibition I now see has limited my ability to expand the scope of my ideas. So the lesson is, try to think 'out of the box', as the expression goes. It is interesting to explore concepts that one might not be familiar with; who knows, it may help to explain certain issues or problems that you are working on. As an example, Victor Turners concept of liminality at first appeared too implausible for me to use as a productive tool in studying everyday life. However, upon reflection, and using the concept as a tool of analysis, it now makes a certain amount of sense. Of course I will leave it up to others to assess the efficacy of its use in this instance. In sum, an important lesson here is that even when there exists some degree of consensus among anthropologists concerning problems of definition, the subjective interpretations by anthropologists about what patterns he or she actually sees in the field is a matter of some variation.

Certainly one of the main lessons that ethnographic research has for anthropology is that the search for general statements of the structure of knowledge may be precluded by the very facts of cultural variation. There would appear to be few cross-cultural generalizations that could be made concerning such things as proper conduct, morality and, ultimately, truth. There is then an epistemological dilemma or contradiction in the task of anthropology. If our concern is with epistemology as the theory of knowledge, with the pursuit of basic questions concerning the search for truth, then we might have to be prepared for the development of 'culturally embedded' methodology that would be capable of dealing with the sorts of variations in points of view, in accepted traditions and 'truths' that anthropologists have to deal with. What all this suggests is that there is some validity to Peter Winch's argument made many years ago that it is not empirical verification that confirms what is in agreement with reality, but rather it is intersubjective communicative competence that constitutes reality in each social matrix. As he suggests, "Indeed…social relations are expressions of ideas about reality" (1958: 23). In other words, we might profitably examine social relations for clues to the manner in which reality, and truth, are perceived from culture to culture.

Ultimately, if we are willing to entertain a phenomenological (reality exists only as it is defined by human observers) point of view, and thus forsake positivism or nomothetic inquiry (approaches geared toward producing generalizations or scientific laws) in the search for 'truth' in anthropology, then we are prone to see theoretical issues as a matter of polar opposites. Then, in turn, there is a dilemma in anthropology since we may be unwittingly, and perhaps wrongly, persuaded by the view that either many logical possibilities exist for a "real" interpretation of any phenomena, or that, on the other side, that only one interpretation must prevail. Furthermore, we could be led to ask why must an 'objective' account—the 'real' or 'true' one—be provided by only one spectator: can there not exist a number of valid subjective accounts?' In addition, is there not the possibility of a cross-cultural 'scientific' perspectives such that a scientific observation could have been made by any number of observers.

Therefore, as so often happens in anthropology, we return to fieldwork as an ultimate arbiter of our disputes. The reason for this is that much of the turning point for debate centers on the methodological issue of how knowledge is created by the researcher in the field. However, when we discuss such methods as participant observation we tend to become apologetic, hoping that no one will seriously challenge what might appear to others to be an unsophisticated, crude and maybe even an inappropriate method of gathering information. As another example, when we talk about unstructured interviewing, we realize in our hearts that it requires considerable skill to conduct, and that it is probably our greatest aid in the field, yet we may have difficulty in describing what we are doing in a manner that does not always seem to be rambling, undisciplined and lacking purpose.

Of course, at times our methods do have some of these characteristics, which may not always be such a disadvantage, since it could leave open the possibility of serendipitous discovery than more "rigid" approaches would not be capable of making. And so one of our main lessons concerning fieldwork is that the task of anthropology is not aided so much by the cultivation of methodology as it is in some other discipline because such a task is neither sufficient nor necessary for a successful research endeavor. We come to learn, with experience, that there is much more that goes into the making of a successful field trip than an armful of specific tools for eliciting information; intuition, that undefinable quality, is perhaps most important of all.

Revisiting van Gennep's *Rite de Passage*

This chapter organized a number of my field work experiences; mostly mundane situations of everyday life, into a broader, more abstract frame of understanding. The theoretical inspiration for the organization of these events derives from several sources, mostly connected to one another. Initially, the stimulus for this endeavor derives from the work of Arnold van Gennep, an early twentieth century French theorist, and his concept of *rite de passage*. In van Gennep's conceptualization of life's passages, these are akin to a person going from room to room in a building. As such, in this chapter I have extended his metaphor further by focusing on the entry point between rooms, or different states, in which a door symbolizes the *threshold*, the literal meaning of the Latin term *limen*, or a passage way between states of being.

Victor Turner was at least partly famous for his emphasis of van Gennep's middle state, that of liminality, or as he describes, "neither betwixt or between." I would suggest that the life of anthropologists could be seen as existing in such a liminal state. While they are conducting their ethnographic research, they are 'partly in their own culture and partly in another'. This is a state of ambiguity, as a transitional state, in which normal expectations are suspended. I also see much of my own field work among the Anishinaabe of northern Ontario in a similar light. The door of my cabin could be interpreted as an ambiguous, transitional state, neither in one culture or another. Information passes through this transitional zone, by various members of the Indigenous community. All of this reasoning is an attempt to interpret the everyday life of an anthropologist who is a collector of information, but also one who must interpret and place in context this material.

This is also what Paul Stoller (2009) refers to as 'the power of the between'. It is the anthropologist's fate, Stoller suggests, to always be between things: countries, languages, cultures, even realities. But rather than lament this situation, he celebrates the creative power of the between, showing how it can transform us, changing our conceptions of who we are, what we know, and how we live in the world. Stoller begins with his early days in the Peace Corp in Africa and his more recent struggles with cancer. In all, his book *The Power of the Between* is an evocative account of the circuitous path his life has taken. As Stoller summarizes:

Indeed, anthropologists are always 'between' things—between 'being-there', as the late Clifford Geertz put it and 'being-here', between two or more languages, between two or more cultural traditions, between two or more apprehensions of reality. Anthropologists are the sojourners of 'the between'. We go there and absorb a different language, culture, and way of being and return here, where we can never fully resume the lives we had previously led (2009: 4).

And yet, dwelling in the between, or what Arnold Van Gennep and then Victor Turner called the liminal, can also be illuminating. As Vincent Crapanzano wrote:

The liminal has often been likened to the dream…It suggests imaginative possibilities that are not necessarily available to us in everyday life. Through paradox, ambiguity, contradiction, bizarre, exaggerated, and at times grotesque symbols—masks, costumes, and figurines—and the evocation of transcendent realities, mystery and supernatural powers, the liminal offers us a view of the world to which we are normally blinded by the usual structures of social and cultural life (2003: 58).

All-in-all, fieldwork by its very nature is an ambiguous experience for the anthropologist. Part of the ambiguity stems from the ethnographer's attempt to bridge the gap between objectivity and subjectivity in fieldwork, which could be described as a liminal area in itself, an epistemological state of 'in-betweenness' in a methodological sense. The general lack of discussion of this problem in the discipline has meant that anthropologists have become the subject of criticism on this account, such that 'ethnographic accounts are by nature one-sided, although based on dyadic interaction', according to Manyoni (1983: 227). As he explains further, "Defined in stranger/host terms, the informant-ethnographer relationship is the pivot upon which the whole anthropological enterprise in any given community revolves. Success in fieldwork may hinge precisely in the nature of this relationship" (1983: 230). Similarly, Watson adds that "it is clear that anthropologists feel secure and comfortable in their role of professional stranger which, even if it requires constant explanation, does not demand self-justification: in other words, the anthropologist's role is taken for granted by the anthropologist" (1999: 13).[34]

The fact of the matter, for a variety of reasons, is that not everyone is suited to the role of anthropological fieldworker. In the first place, one needs to be a good listener and be empathetic to the informant's situation. People who are braggarts, or who want to dominate a discussion will probably not be a success as ethnographers. In other words, there are personality traits that one either has or does not have, that probably cannot be instilled in a university methods course. Watson, who examined the close relationships that anthropologists establish with informants in the field suggests that "the quick rapport and seeming inwardness which a good ethnographer established in the field is, however, counterbalanced by the arduous and painstaking work of the marginal anthropologist" (1999:7).

Aside from personality traits there also life experiences to consider that might allow one to feel comfortable in cross-cultural situations. As an example, Hortense Powermaker in her book *Stranger and Friend* suggests that her own life experiences were an important factor in her career choice as an anthropologist: "Long before I ever heard of anthropology, I was being conditioned for the role of stepping in and out of society. It was part of my growing-up process to question the traditional values and norms of the family and the experiment with behavior patterns and ideologies" (1966: 19).

In a similar vein, Clyde Kluckhohn suggests that "The lure of the strange and far has a peculiar appeal for those who are dissatisfied with themselves or who do not feel at home in their own society" (1957: 1). Anthropologists are described by Stan Barrett (1979) as 'marginal academics', choosing to exist outside of the mainstream of conventional intellectual life of the university. He also suggests that some anthropologists intentionally contribute to an aura or sense of mystique and adventure, regaling the guests at departmental parties with their stories of the strange foods, social customs, dress and sexual practices of those living in 'primitive' tribes. In addition, Gottlieb (2012) provides a description of those he refers to as the "restless anthropologist" who moves from one ethnographic situation to another, never really satisfied with their living conditions or relationships with informants. Then there is Behar's (1998) account of the 'vulnerable observer', seemingly caught between cultural worlds, in a limbo state, in which the functioning rules are nebulous or even invisible.

Anthropologists who collaborate with informants as partners rather than as subjects are another kind of continuing engagement that blurs the distinction between the ethnographer and those who previously might have been the objects of an ethnographer's gaze (as described in Amit 2000; Boellstorff 2008; Gershon 2009; Hastrup 1993; Lassiter 2005). In my own fieldwork, I would find it difficult to classify all the people in one community in the same manner. With the leaders of the Ogoki River Guides organization, for example, there was not much of a collaborative relationship than existed with, say, hunters, or religious specialists. With the ORG leaders, I was primarily interested in their development projects; this was the area that I was trained for at McGill's center for 'The Anthropology of Development' headed by Richard Salisbury.

I performed certain services for the ORG leaders, such as writing letters to government officials for them in a more professional style than they were capable of. We also discussed strategic approaches to various problems, such as certain recalcitrant workers, accessing various government projects. In turn, they provided me with statistics on incomes, the place of origin of certain workers, or kinship ties between families living on the construction site at Whitewater Lake. In other words, we found ourselves engaged in a mutually beneficial relationship; I believe we thought of ourselves as belonging to the same team with the same goals of developing the local economy.[35]

So, while anthropologists in academic circles could be regarded as scholars 'betwixt and between', as people partly in and partly out of both their own and another culture, they nonetheless ultimately depend upon their success as fieldworkers as a determining factor by which their accomplishments may be gauged. It is fieldwork that is primarily responsible for the anthropological emphasis on the uniqueness of human cultures, and for the relativistic view that in its own way each human society has a view of the world in its own terms, that 'makes sense' from their people's point of view. It follows, then, that fieldwork poses certain epistemological problems for anthropology about how knowledge in a general sense is to be studied. It also follows that a central problem for anthropology is that fieldwork tends to induce us into the belief that all knowledge is relative, or even further, that reliable knowledge is not possible.

Conclusion

It is fieldwork which poses broad, comparative questions, even when new orthodoxies tell us they are obsolete. It is fieldwork which brings surprises, such as the possibility of ghosts in a northern Ontario cabin. My fieldwork encounter with the Anishinaabe man in my cabin, and our discussion about whether or not I was aware of Ed Pigeon's apparition near the stove, was a problem because I had not initially come to the community to study ghosts, religion or any other such phenomenon. My central concern at the time was with politics, leadership and economic development, so I did not pay particular attention to what my visitor was talking about. It was only later, when I began to reflect on my fieldwork experiences, that this ghost episode would creep into my consciousness. When it did so, I was belatedly forced to ponder some very fundamental issues concerning my fieldwork experience, such as: to what extent did our concepts of 'ghost' coincide, if at all? What 'message' was he actually trying to communicate to me concerning the ghost phenomenon?

It was these sort of everyday experiences that later posed problems for me later in my fieldwork when I began to realize that the man was not just posing a rhetorical question about ghosts, as to whether or not I was able to see one, but that he was actually 'seeing' it and wanted me to be party in some way to this, for him, 'normal' everyday experience. As the months went by, I also began to realize, in ways that were not immediately obvious to me in the initial stages of my fieldwork, that the Anishinaabe people took the existence of 'ghosts' as pretty much a routine matter, like seeing dogs, trees, and so on. For them, it was sort of belaboring the obvious to have to point out to the anthropologist the existence of ghosts in my cabin.

Over the years this experience academically haunted me—a piece of fieldwork flotsam that was not part of my original research plan. The issues raised were issues of comparative epistemology—the translation of *cheebuy* 'ghost', Anishinaabe belief in and experience of this *cheebuy* concept, the rationality or irrationality of their 'knowledge' of such phenomena. Since the question of evidence is also central to the pursuit of epistemology, we are thus confronted with the challenges that our sources of knowledge brings us from the fieldwork experience. In all, as Watson summarizes, "reflection at a temporal and spatial distance from our experience within a different cognitive and experiential context inevitably brings about further reformulations and recasting of our thoughts and ideas and the best way of expressing them" (1999:1).

If nothing else, anthropology teaches us that life is full of chances and opportunities. We never know from one moment to the next what will happen; there are no guarantees. For the most part, we are taught to take advantage of the chances that appear in our lives, professional or otherwise. However; we do not know the outcome of our choices, all we only know in a general sense are the vague odds of this or that occurrence happening. So, the next time you hear a knock on the door, it will probably be just another benign encounter; nonetheless, be wary of the capricious nature of human existence.

Chapter Four
The Tourist Lodge at Whitewater Lake

The ethnographic experience portrayed in this chapter describes fieldwork conducted in a remote part of northern Ontario between Lake Nipigon and the Albany River called Whitewater Lake. Whitewater Lake is situated about 350kms north of Thunder Bay. It was part of a historically important chain of lakes and rivers in the fur trading era, as it was a major transportation route linking the interior of northern Ontario with the Hudson's Bay Company fur trading posts on James Bay via the Ogoki and Albany Rivers. Today, while still in a remote and relatively inaccessible region, it is known more as an attraction for adventurous canoeists and fisherman than for its productivity in beaver pelts. It was because of the relatively pristine environment and abundance of pickerel that the Indigenous residents of Collins decided to build a tourist lodge at Whitewater Lake, hoping to establish a tourist industry that would form the basis of a reliable local economy.

I had the good fortune of arriving in Collins when the tourist lodge project was still in the planning stage, so there was an opportunity for me to study various aspects of the construction process from its initial inception to eventual completion. The various facets of this lodge construction that interested me concerned the Collins leadership group's organization, called the Ogoki River Guides Ltd., and its negotiations with government officials over the funding of the lodge (it eventually cost over a million dollars to build). Also of interest were the economic aspects of the construction phase, such as the structure of work crews and their duties, as well as the larger sphere of the social organization of family life in and around the lodge site.

It should be pointed out from the outset that the term 'Whitewater social organization', as used here, refers to the Anishinaabe population on the construction site. There were also a number of non-Indigenous workers on the construction site as well, such as plumbers, electricians, construction bosses and an engineer, however, for our present purposes they are not included in this discussion of 'social organization'. If one is wondering at this point about the social network used to gain entry into the camp at Whitewater Lake, and the reason why the camp population chose to interact with me in the context of my anthropological field research, it should be indicated that for several years previous I had developed a working relationship with the leaders of the Ogoki River Guides in their attempt to formulate an economic plan to revitalize the local economy.

In this regard, my primary interest, as a general research problem, was on the topic of 'emergent leadership and economic development'. However, it is probable that the Indigenous people of Collins saw my research in a somewhat more circumscribed manner, that is, as documenting the structure, activities, and projects involving the Ogoki River Guides organization. From my own perspective, I saw these two facets as largely coterminous with each other. The people of Collins saw my research, I believe, in a positive light, which is to say, as documenting an Indigenous 'success' story, as opposed to the usual gloom and doom perspectives commonly written about in the Canadian news media.

On this basis, there was a ready co-operation among the Collins people to contribute to my research at Whitewater Lake, and the construction of the tourist lodge, which was a source of great pride among the Anishinaabe people. The engineering firm that was to oversee the construction of the tourist lodge facilities which was selected by ARDA, the government agency which was funding the project. Without much consultation with the Ogoki River Guides leadership on this matter, the role of the engineers was at times a source of conflict between ARDA and the ORG personnel. Collins leaders saw this 'top down approach' of government as fulfilling a commonly held stereotype that Indigenous people were not capable of managing their own affairs, and on this basis were not consulted on many aspects of the construction process, especially in the hiring phase of outside workers. This seemingly paternalistic attitude on the part of the Ontario government personnel was therefore one of the negative aspects of the 'negotiation' process, and was a source of strife between the various Indigenous and non-Indigenous parties involved. As an anthropologist, I was well aware of this contentious issue and strove where possible to separate myself and my activities from that of the Ontario government, and to align myself where possible with the ORG leadership.[36]

Flying Up to Whitewater Lake

When I first arrived in Collins it was not long before Peter, Donald's brother, suggested that I take a flight up to Whitewater Lake, some 60 kilometers north of the community, which was the site of ORG's tourist lodge construction. A float plane had arrived in Collins from nearby Armstrong loaded with supplies for the lodge. The pilot, Alonzo Nuttall, was well known in the area. In fact, one does not often realize the benefits of being an anthropologist with roots in the area of their study. As an example, Alonzo's son and I were from the same home town of Nipigon. We often went fishing together as teenagers and played on the same hockey team. This is a pattern that one finds in many small-populated northern areas that many people from the south might not realize. It is common to find people you know from other circumstances and in various walks of life while engaging in seemingly unrelated activities.

As we travelled through a bright sunny sky, overlooking the vast forest cover below, the pilot told me about the construction site. Alonzo explained that an area in the southern part of Whitewater Lake had been cleared and that workers were just beginning to arrive for the summer season. As we approached the site, one could see a large log building which was the storage shed, the beginnings of a foundation for the main lodge, and several large tents that he explained was the location that the single men stayed. He also pointed to several other cleared areas on the main shoreline and on a nearby island. These areas, he suggested, were sites for the tents that would be erected for workers and their families. The site supervisors thought that if workers lived with their families nearby the construction site that this would provide stability to the work environment and alleviate the possible boredom that was bound to happen in such an isolated environment.

When I returned to Collins that evening, a research plan began to emerge in my mind. While a study of the construction site would form a major focus of my Whitewater Lake research, I also thought an interesting research tactic would be to study the emergence of the tent set-ups for the workers' families. As such, I would then be in a position to study the social patterns of the work environment virtually from the beginning, as these patterns emerged, and so did not want to waste this opportunity. This is an important part of anthropological research. One needs to find opportunities that could be interesting while they are happening so that the process of their evolution could be studied as they were actually taking place.

One needs to always be thinking about opportunities for sociological analysis on the spot because such prospects for in-depth research may not occur frequently. This is what I mean by studying everyday life—being able to perceive patterns as they emerge and to take opportunities to study these patterns through time. As in life itself, we do not often know what will happen next, but we always hope that something happens and we must be prepared for it.

Obviously, it is difficult to please everybody, however there is little doubt that anthropology needs to describe the details of life, because ultimately these particulars are the most interesting aspects of social life, rather than continually engaging in esoteric theoretical debates which are not grounded in the 'facts' of life. To be successful, one is required to weld together both 'facts' and larger theoretical patterns to be successful. At least, this is what I learned from my experience, and the research goal that was aimed for in my Whitewater Lake study.

Defining Research Objectives

As such, the plan of action was to document as accurately as possible the various people who arrived at the construction site and then seek out patterns of their interaction as a way by which I could define the research objectives of this fieldwork. From there, on the basis of these concrete details, I would then attempt to formulate a description of larger social patterns. This issue of social and cultural portrayal has much to do with what we choose to write about, or not write about as the case may be, and the ensuing ethnographic narrative that eventually unfolds from the stance or position that we decide to take.

Writing involves a certain perspective, like an artist composing a painting, since considerable thought is apt to go into the process. In this regard, Barrett (2009: 260) has suggested that "a great deal of reflecting, planning and organization must proceed writing". In this sense, the writing process of a fieldworker is something like that of a novelist. Yet, we are reminded that "The business of writing up fieldwork has always been a controversial part of anthropological research…And today, perhaps more than ever before, anthropologists pay close attention to how language shapes and influences their work" (Chiseri-Strater and Sunstein 1997: 277–278).

However, fortuitous circumstances also play an important role in ethnographic research.[37] As previously reiterated, I had the good fortune of arriving in Collins when the tourist lodge project was still in the planning stages, so there was an opportunity for me to study various aspects of the construction process from its initial inception to eventual completion. There were various aspects of the lodge construction process that interested me, so I began to itemize these so that there was a concrete focus to my research, otherwise it is difficult to know what to concentrate on. One of these main aspects concerned the Collins leadership groups' organization, called the Ogoki River Guides Ltd., and its negotiations with various government officials over funding for the lodge construction. Also, of primary interest were the economic aspects of the construction phase, such as the structure of work crews and their duties, as well as the larger sphere of the social organization of family life in and around the lodge site.

In this way, that is in terms of prioritizing which areas of the lodge construction which I wished to investigate, I was able to rank my research goals. This involved, then, a three-part process: first, establish concrete areas of interest; second, itemize these areas of interest into spheres that could be investigated; and three, collect information that would support these research goals so that my ideas were based on concrete facts and not mental suppositions. This three-part process would then allow one to defend your hypotheses and larger theoretical themes in the realm of the peer review process, as Richard Salisbury mentioned in one of his letters to me.

The tourist lodge construction site at Whitewater Lake was characterized by a social organization that largely defined the work activities that were necessitated by the construction process itself. In other words, the construction process involved a hierarchy of individual workmen, such as foremen, skilled craftsmen and laborers. However, there were other facets of the camp organization that were not directly tied to the construction activities, composed of the wives and children of the workers who had set up about a dozen campsites of varying size in the vicinity of the construction site. These families lived in tents, and engaged in a certain amount of hunting and fishing to meet their subsistence needs. In this regard, the Whitewater social organization had a much more 'traditional' appearance than the Collins community situated near the railway line to the south. But such appearances can be deceiving, since there is no reason to assume that because of similarities in the physical set up of an Anishinaabe bush camp that there is by necessity any similarity to the more traditional social make up of such camps as well; this would be a matter for further investigation and analysis.

One of the research problems that I began to work on at Whitewater Lake was the social composition of the bush camps, and how they compared with other Indigenous residential groups in the past, as described in the previous ethnographic literature in subarctic anthropology (as for example, in Bishop 1974; Dunning 1959; Hallowell 1992; and Rogers 1962). Thus, my research strategy was to document the characteristics of the Whitewater Lake social organization in terms of kinship ties and the step-by-step evolution of the camps. This research approach, as a consequence, further involved a related research objective, which is to say, the extent to which the wage economy at Whitewater was a determining factor in group composition, and the degree to which economic factors in previous decades, such as that which existed in the previous fur trade period of the 1950s and before, were noteworthy factors in group composition.

A significant factor in my pursuit of these research goals pertains to Roger's (1966: 2) previously mentioned comment that "so little field work has been done in this area of northern Ontario that comparison and generalization are impossible." It is no doubt unfortunate as far as the ethnographic record of northern Ontario is concerned, that there has been little substantive published work on the Indigenous peoples of this area for several generations of scholars. As such, my research objectives tend to be reinforced by a lacuna in the northern cultural and social record of Ontario.

In summary, my research objectives initially focused on the social, economic and economic characteristics of the Anishinaabe village of Collins, but by necessity, when I first arrived to conduct this study it became obvious to me that I needed to broaden my focus of investigation by also including the quite different community setting that was emerging at the construction camp at Whitewater Lake. Anthropologists may have certain objectives that initially motivate their initial research interests, but to be successful they also need to become flexible enough to take advantage of new opportunities as they may emerge. In this manner, new research perspectives were therefore necessitated by these different settings, which in turn forced me to be innovative and intellectually creative in ways distinct from those utilized in my approach to the Collins community itself.

Levels of Abstraction

The research problems that presented themselves to me were different in each of these two separate settings, yet both had to be tied together at a higher level of abstraction. So, in this sense, I decided to focus the fieldwork problems in the different settings to issues relating to social organization, economic pursuits, and leadership characteristics. In a curious sort of way, I was also intrigued by the Collins-Whitewater dyad. For Collins people, it was evident that the activities at Whitewater Lake were a return to a nostalgic past of fondly remembered bush life. Of course, whatever the people at Whitewater Lake were feeling about resurrecting an idyllic past of survival in the bush, as their grandparents had endured, for them I contend this was largely an illusion. The lives of the grandparents were a matter of survival based on their bush skills, whereas the workers and their families who were living at Whitewater Lake were more akin to a summer camping trip.

Whitewater Lake Construction Site, 1975

As such, I sensed that much of the appeal for Collins people of life at Whitewater Lake was an ideal amalgamation of the traditional and modern worlds. At Whitewater Lake, people could engage in the wage economy and make a decent living, while at the same time, enjoy the outdoor life of fishing, camp fires and fresh air. There was also the appeal of an optimistic future in which people could continue their life in the bush while simultaneously engaging in economic activities that they enjoyed and over which they had some measure of control. As a fieldworker, I participated in this dream to some extent. I shared in the Anishinaabe vision of a better future, one that made sense in the shared image of the 'good life', as they perceived it.

The more I reflected on my experience as a fieldworker at Whitewater Lake, the more I began to realize that my analysis would require the articulation of what could be termed different 'levels of abstraction'.[38] What I mean by this term is that there were day to day living experiences that were occurring at the Whitewater constructions site, that is the relatively mundane activities of preparing meals, washing clothes, minding children and so on, but there were also conceptual matters as well. These conceptual matters pertained to the people's perceptions of what was occurring at the Whitewater camp in terms of revisiting or renewing a past life that was fondly remembered by their grandparents, an idolized life that no longer existed, a life seen as better than they were living today.

All of these perceptions, of course, were filtered through the mists of time, somewhat oblivious to the fact that generations ago Indigenous people at times starved to death in the bush for lack of food, or suffered an early death because of injuries or child birth, problems that modern Indigenous people were not likely to have to contend with. Even though Collins itself was as far away in the bush as most southern people could imagine, the people still had a safety net of medical aid, government services, and transportation that their ancestors did not have the advantages of in their lives years ago. In this sense, what one may regard as a life of deprivation is a matter of perception, historical distance and mental constructs about one's place in the modern world.

Studying the Whitewater Campsite

For anyone who has taken a flight in a bush plane over the northern forest, one is apt to experience an odd mixture of excitement, semi-panic and sleepiness. The seemingly endless drone of the float plane's engine is hypnotic, creating a sense of torpor, as one speeds along the tree tops of an apparently endless blanket of forest below. There are images of streams, rock outcroppings, sightings of an occasional moose or bear, but mostly it may seem monotonous. On the other hand, one may realize that this is a dangerous adventure, there is only one engine which could malfunction at any time, the distance from the plane to the forest below is relatively short, and a sudden drop in altitude could have catastrophic consequences. If you are old enough, you might remember the Martin Hartwell story—broken limbs, slow starvation and, in his case, cannibalism. At any moment, at least to the neophyte traveler, one could expect the sudden 'thwop, thwop' sound as the propeller disengages, and then the inevitable dive bomb to the crash landing below. For the most part, though, there is a tendency to become sedated by the lack of typological relief to the country below and its coniferous forest, since it was not long before, in geological terms at least, that the glaciers scoured the land flat and then left melted pools of lakes and rivers.

The flight from Collins to Whitewater Lake took about an hour's time. It appeared that we had hardly gotten airborne when the plane's motor slowed down and my mind snapped back to the reality of our plane circling around the bay at the southern end of Whitewater Lake. Over the roar of the motor, the pilot pointed out the various features to me—a cleared patch of ground on which the main lodge would eventually be built, clumps of white canvas tents huddled here and there, and small boats with outboard motors streaming across the water. The pilot motioned to the other side of the bay, as he twirled a device to lower the rear flaps. "That's where all the people are camped," he said, "do you see the smoke coming up through the trees? Somebody will see our plane and come and get you by boat—you can't walk over there, it's too swampy at the end of the bay." The pilot quickly landed, unloaded his supply at the construction site, and before I knew it he was taxing his Beaver plane into the wind. Up he went in as much time as it would take to park one's car at the mall. I stood still for a moment, watching the bush plane ascend into the sky, its motor becoming ever quieter until it disappeared into a pin point into the setting sun.

"Where was I?" It was getting dark and there was no one in site. Suddenly I realized that I was becoming immersed in a cloud of mosquitoes and black flies. There was no one around, there was just a few digging tools left scattered about and it was becoming darker by the moment. I tried yelling, but to no avail. The bugs were already crawling around my neck and up the sleeves of my jacket. Desperation was starting to set in. Quickly I gathered up some leaves and twigs and without much hesitation, lit this little pile into fire. Smoke billowed up. Where was the rescue party, as the pilot promised?

It did not take long before I could hear the noise of an outboard motor. A man jumped out of his small boat—"What are you doing here," he wanted to know. "We didn't expect any visitors." I tried to explain that I had been talking to Peter who suggested this trip. "Why?" he wanted to know, are you a worker, or government guy? Now I was faced with the task of trying to explain what an anthropologist does and decided to make up a story. "Peter wanted me to talk to a few of the workers, to try to find out when they were coming back to Collins." This seemed to make sense since there were no phones up here and as this was before the cell phone era. "Oh, okay," he said, apparently accepting the explanation. "There's still some food left over from supper, if you're hungry?" When we arrived at the other shore my guide suggested I talk with the site engineer about staying in his tent, as he was alone. I learned that his name was Tim and that he was from New Zealand—his older brother worked for an engineering firm from Toronto called Group-33. "Get some grub, from the kitchen tent" Tim suggested and we'll talk about what is happening here.

I looked round. This was apparently the single men's camp ground. There were eight or ten white canvas tents, scattered about, pitched on plywood platforms, with plywood side walls, so that one could walk around inside. Some tents were erected over a frame of spruce poles with the walls a meter and a half above the ground. A small kitchen area was crowded into the central area of the camp, with several picnic tables arranged near the tent. Tim explained to me that there were quite a few other families camped along the shore and on an island across from the bay. These tents were off-limits to the single men so he didn't know how many people lived in these accommodations. We talked for a while before climbing into our sleeping bags. He said that there were mosquitoes in the tent but they had no effect on him. Apparently Tim had been taking some pills that reduced the effects of the bug bites. Despite growing up in northern Ontario, I had never heard of such medication and wondered why.

Gathering Field Data

We were awoken fairly early the next morning by boat motors and another plane landing with supplies. I noticed that several single men were lined up with plates and cutlery in their hands waiting for breakfast. Without hesitation I filed in behind them and was shown where the utensils were laid out. There was some porridge, left over fish from last night's supper, and some fried potatoes to eat. I couldn't believe how hungry I was. Back at our tent, Tim wanted to know about my visit. "Who do you work for?" he wanted to know.

At this point, I explained that I was from McGill University and was conducting a study of northern Indigenous social and economic change. I must admit that I was not particularly candid but tried to piece together a plausible explanation. Research grants from the university supported my trip (this was true), but then I said that the Ogoki River Guides had given me the task of assessing their construction project (only vaguely true). "Oh," he asked, "you work for the Patience brothers?"

"No, not exactly," was my reply. "I saw myself as an independent observer, but I wasn't here to criticize anybody," and this was the answer that I thought might alleviate any suspicions he had. My colleague, Stan Barrett at the University of Guelph, when he was conducting a study of the white supremacists in Ontario, called this approach 'deceptive candor'. It seemed to fit my explanations to Tim, not exactly lying, but missing elements of truth as well.

Now I had to figure out a way to travel over to the island where various families were setting up their tents, realizing that those from the single men's camp were prohibited from going there. I asked a worker down by the dock if he could ferry me over to the island, which he did without question. When I landed, I noted several men and women from Collins that I knew briefly from my time there setting up my log cabin. I walked over to them and said, "Peter wants to know where everyone is living, so I'm here to make a diagram." Without any trepidation, one of the women said, "Sure, there's Sinclair's place, and over there is Harriett's tent" and so on. So, the deceptive candor approach seemed to work, and I would leave it to the research ethics boards to pass judgement on the technique. The question here is, "How does one resolve a possible ethical issue during fieldwork when one is so far removed, thousands of kilometers away, from any possible means of communication?"

Over the next several days there were numerous bush planes arriving which carried workers, equipment and other supplies. I set to work recording the comings and goings of the various people involved. I was particularly interested in the manner in which a camp was forming on an island site across the bay from the single men's base camp and felt fortunate that I was able to arrive at the construction site just as the workers and their families were arriving. There are times when an anthropologist needs to seize a fortuitous opportunity, even though such research may not have been part of the original plan.

My field notes are filled with comments about the various kinship relationships, and what their possible significance could be. The people themselves seemed to feel that they had just moved where 'they felt like it', however, I felt that there were underlying patterns involved that they were probably not particularly aware of. In the beginning, I was disappointed that these patterns did not emerge readily from my note books. It appeared to me that other ethnographers of previous generations (i.e., Dunning 1959, Rogers 1962, for example) appeared to have such consistent patterns involved in their explanations of community life, something like the working of a pocket watch, and yet here I was struggling with so many contradictions and unresolved sociological problems.

As it turned out, there was an important lesson for me here, and this is to try to accept the 'field data' as it is, as you properly recorded it. It is the differences that one finds from the work of previous ethnographers, rather than the similarities, that are most important and are apt to lead to new insights. Nobody in anthropology wants to hear that you travelled to a new research site and found exactly what had been previously discovered by researchers that came before you. In other words, revel in the differences and hope that many of them emerge in your own research. These 'new insights' in the case of my own particular field study had to do with the way people employed the pre-existing flexible social relationships back in their home community of Collins to adopt to the conditions of the wage-work setting at the Whitewater Lake construction site.

The island site was initially occupied by two sisters, their husbands and children. The extended family of one of these husbands arrived (his mother, single brother, and two sisters). Later on one of the sister's husbands landed with his own parents. I began to make kinship diagrams of the various relationships, and found an intricate pattern of family ties involved as the camp social organization developed. Here is an example of one of these kinship diagrams taken from my original hand-written field notes. The emerging formation of this camp seemed to me to be an opportunity to develop a hypothesis about the formation of residential groups under conditions of a wage-work economy, but still in a bush-oriented environment. I then wrote this preliminary hypothesis after the kinship diagram in my field notes.

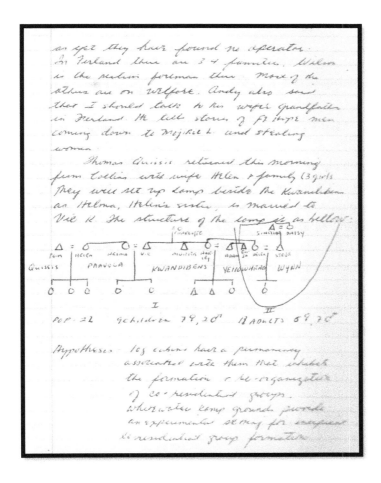

Kinship Diagram from Whitewater Lake Field Notes

When I was finished documenting the arrival of the various workers and their families, I noted their position on a sketch map of the lower end of Whitewater Lake, as indicated below:

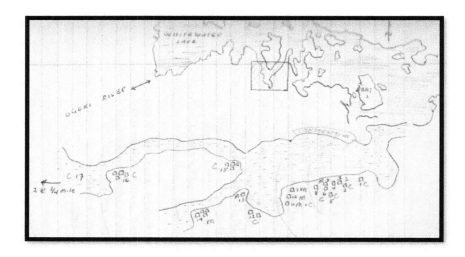

Map 3 Location of Whitewater Lake Summer Camps

The numbers on the map correspond to the various families inhabiting the construction environment, the small squares are the number of tents that each family grouping set up, and the letters are meant to indicate family groupings. Then an itemized list was made of the various families at this end of Whitewater Lake which correspond to the number of the sites indicated on the above map, as indicated from my field notes below. From here, I began to work out what I saw as various social patterns, as a way of establishing in a preliminary manner, some general principles. My approach involved three different steps, as indicated below:

CAMP

1. FRANK PETERS + JANE GOLDWIN
2. HAMISH PATIENCE + HARIETTE GOLDWIN
       3 CHILDREN
3. JIM BAYLEY
4. CECE HOUSE
5. ED GOLDWIN + MARCEL LOUISIS
6. STEVE GOLDWIN, STEVE + TOM LOUISIS
7. OLIVER BELMORE (ARMSTRONG)
8. UNOCCUPIED
9. EUGENE SHADWAY KEESIC (MUD RIVER)
10. RAY NUDIN (MUD RIVER)
11. DOUG SIMOGWAY + BERT COOK
12. SAUL CHEESE + WIFE SOPHIE
       4 CHILDREN
13. ANDY WILLOWBY + WIFE MARY
       4 CHILDREN   BOW

14.   (MUD RIVER - ARMSTRONG)
    a) FRANCIS DANIEL + WIFE (CHARLIE'S BW)
    b) CHARLES SHADWAY KEESIC + WIFE
           6 CHILDREN
    c) JOHN NUDIN + WIFE
       HOWARD NUDIN
    d) MERRIN WANAHAMIC
        DON NUDIN
        WAYNE SHADWAY KEESIC
        DENNIS SHADWAY KEESIC

CAMP.

15. a) STAN SLIPPERJACK + JEAN BASKEINANG.
    b) CHILDREN
    c) RUBINA SLIPPERJACK ; CLARA SLIPPERJACK
    d) COOK TENT

16. a) VICTOR KWANDIBENS + WIFE BELMA (FRAWLA)
       2 CHILDREN GIRL
    b) MORRIS KWANDIBENS + GRL SPARK
    c) ADAM YELLOWHEAD + WIFE HARIETTE (KWANDIBENS)
    d) 3 CHILDREN - 2 boys - 1 girl

17. a) SINCLAIR WYNN + WIFE DAISY
    b) STEVE WYNN + WIFE HELEN (KWANDIBENS)
       1 CHILD - GIRL
       ELIJA YELLOWHEAD

    POPULATION AT SITE - 66
    BEAR LAKE -
    KWANDIBENS KEESIC -
    WIFE 5 CHILDREN
    JIM KWANDIBENS - WIFE
    + CHILD   8
    POPULATION ON LAKE   74
    AT SHADWAY KEESIC L
    end of 1952 - DAISY

    POPULATION IN AREA   81   (83 if those from Collins)

Occupants of Whitewater Lake Summer Camps

Step 1: Describe the Relationships

Thomas Quissis returned this morning to Whitewater Lake from Collins with his wife Helen and family (3 girls). They will set up camp beside the Kwandibens family as Helma, Helen's sister, is married to Victor K. The evolution of the Kwandibens' camp began with Victor, his wife Helma, and widowed mother Charlotte. Victor's brother Morris, a single man, joined them shortly after from the base camp. Next, Victor's sister, Harriette, and her husband Adam Yellowhead set up their camp. This camp is further augmented by Harriette's sister, Helen Wynn, and her husband Steve. Steve's parents, Sinclair and Daisy Wynn, then moved close by. This camp is completed when Adam's brother, Elijah, a single man from the base camp, moved in with the group. Sinclair's wife Daisy is a sister to Adam and Elijah Yellowhead.

The following day I attempted a preliminary analysis of the relationships in this camp, trying to account for their formation in light of various historical, cultural and economic conditions.

Step 2: Account for the Patterns

August 28

An analysis of the structure of this co-residential group demonstrates the significance of the solidarity of brothers in the alignment of residence patterns. There is also operative a solidarity of sisters as well, provided that their husbands have no close male kinsmen in the area. This is indicated by Thomas Q's and Adam Y's decision to join the Kwandibens group even though Thomas has a brother and father in the area—both of whom are widowed and live in the base camp—and even though Adam's sister lives close by. However, Adam's single brother Elijah moved into the Wynn section of the camp. The solidarity of male kinsmen is further indicated by Steve W.'s decision to take up residence in his father's part of the camp, rather than close to his wife's family, i.e., the Kwandibens.

An attempt was then made to push this preliminary analysis into a wider sphere of discussion, by way of trying to outline a hypothesis to account for the formation of this particular camp on the basis of more general historical factors.

Log cabins have a permanency associated with them that inhibits the formation and reorganization of co-residential groups. The Whitewater camp grounds provided an experimental setting for incipient co-residential groups formation. There is a paucity of material in the literature on the evolution of these groups. Also, the significance of certain relationships, such as a number of dominant brothers as the core of the co-residential group, tends to be assumed beforehand.

One may argue that changes in the structure of co-residential groups have resulted from acculturation and an entry into the Euro-Canadian wage economy. In the fur trade economy, a group of brothers who were good hunters and trappers contributed the most to their group. It is assumed that the evolution of these large families began with a group of brothers about whom concentric rings of relatives through marriage became attached to these patrilateral kinsmen. The wage economy allows for less dependence upon hunting and fishing for survival as more food can be store-bought than is possible on a trapper's income.

Hypothesis: The evolution of residential groups in the context of a wage-work economic system tends to develop on an *ad hoc* basis, depending upon pre-existing relationships with individuals already settled into the work camp.

This, then, was the general pattern of analysis by which I proceeded. First, there was a documentation of particular cases taken as accurately as possible. Two modes of analysis then took place; first, examining the various inter-relationships and general patterns of the specific details involved in the internal patterns of the cases; then, second, resorting to more wide-ranging thinking about what these specific instances could possibly mean in the larger context of the literature on Anishinaabe sociology and cultural practices.

Tommy's Guiding Camp

On the construction site, a make-shift store had been constructed to provide for the needs of the various families in and around the construction site. While purchasing some items here, I encountered a man who I had known previously from Collins, but had not noticed on the construction site before this time. His name was Tommy Wastaken (now deceased) and he explained to me that he had been working for the summer as a fishing guide for an Armstrong tourist outfit and was not affiliated with the Whitewater project. He also explained that he had driven his boat over to pick up some supplies and wanted to know if I wanted to see some of the lake by boating with him over to his guiding camp, spend the night there, and return with his wife the next day who was returning to visit some relatives.

This was a good opportunity I thought to gain a wider perspective on the happenings at Whitewater Lake so off we went. Shortly after leaving Tommy took out his Winchester rifle and steadied it at the stern of the boat. He explained that if he saw a moose swimming across the lake he would attempt to shoot it—one must be prepared, Tommy said, for any eventuality when it comes to hunting for food. I did not realize that it was getting so late as we sped off into the semi-darkness. I wondered how safe it was to travel in these conditions with the possibility of logs and rocks emerging unseen through the water.

In no time at all, we were in complete darkness, as there was not much of a moon out. The star light glistened off the waves, the motor hummed along at a steady roar, and I marveled at how Tommy could find his way through this channel, around this island and so on, mile after mile in the nondescript terrain that was hardly visible by now. It took about two hours for our trip, the motor slowed its pace, and my hearing started to return. I noticed a long section of land jutting into the lake with what appeared to be several white canvas tents pitched near the end of the peninsula. Another thing I noticed was the rather eerie sight of long strands of moss blowing in the wind, like so many beards of decapitated men, hanging from the branches of several nearby trees. It puzzled me what this was all about. Tommy paid no attention to this strange sight, as he hurried to haul the boat up on shore, "Well, here we are, make yourself at home," he said with a snicker.

There was also the oddest sight, to my mind at least, of an electric wringer washing machine sitting out here in the middle of nowhere. It was evidently hooked up to a small generator, and was probably brought in by plane, but it was no doubt of immense practical help to the women of the camp, especially if they had small children. The tents housed several families and were set up on plywood platforms. The wind blew incessantly, the sides of the tents flapped loudly most of the time, and I wondered if I would get used to the noise. Then I remembered the mosquitoes which were so prevalent at the construction site, and thought no more about the reason why we were camped on this long, windy finger of land protruding out into the lake.

Tommy pulled back the opening flap of his tent, and we crawled into a dimly lit area. His wife, named Otsie, a nick name for Elizabeth, hardly looked up. She was busy attending to a baby who was stretched out on its back, and then I realized what the dried moss was used for—it was used as a lining for the child's diaper, whose bottom was wrapped in a sort of 'bag' as they called it. The baby was then stuffed inside the opening of a cradle board, or *tikenahgen*, which had several laces sewn up in front and highly decorated bead work all over the outside leather. There seemed to be some nervousness about me watching this operation, but it wasn't long before we were all asleep, sprawled out across the floor. Then I noticed the baby in a sort of swing, tethered to the roof of the tent, which was swung back and forth by a leather strap pulled back and forth by Otsie. Up in this contraption the baby never made the slightest noise all night.

My first introduction to the morning was to hear the crackling fire outside, and the smell of bacon frying in a pan. In short order, there was an elaborate breakfast set out before me. I appreciated the effort although I didn't feel that hungry. It struck me that this was the sort of shore lunch that the tourists would eat before their fishing trips, and, as a *Shaganash* (or white man), maybe Otsie thought this was what we expected to eat every morning. Before long we were back in the boat skipping across the water, away from what I began to call in my head this 'moss bag retreat'.

Otsie was just as adept as her husband at skirting around islands, and maneuvering through the channels. Even though it was now daylight, I felt just as confused about the terrain as the night before. Heaven forbid, I thought, if you ever became lost out here. Soon enough, travelling what appeared to me at break-neck speed, we arrived at the large dock at the construction site. Otsie skillfully guided the boat up to the dock. I then grabbed my old, green pack and skipped out, uttering a short "Thanks," as I left. That was the only word we had ever said to one another. She smiled, put her head down, and sped off to visit her relatives.

A Frightful Journey Home

At the construction site, as we entered the first week of September, the weather suddenly became colder and wetter, so that we seldom saw many planes arrive any more. Most of the people huddled around large outdoor fires, rubbing their cold hands, and discussing their predicament. The main problem was that the camp's food supplies were dwindling rapidly, and men were beginning to take time off work to hunt and fish to provide food for their families. Eventually the weather cleared, and I remember the first plane was carrying a load of sliced bread, which was distributed one loaf to each family. We quickly stoked up the fires and began to make toast, eating one slice after another until all the bread was gone.

Families with school age children were anxious to return to Collins, and there was a steady stream of flights leaving Whitewater Lake over the next few days. The cold, wet weather was closing in again, so a priority departure schedule, of an implicit nature, was developed. This meant that the sick and elderly were allowed to leave first, followed by women and children, older people and so on. I was on just about the last plane to leave the construction site, and was the only passenger. "Hey Ed," the pilot shouted, "Haven't seen you in years. What are you doing up here anyway?" Then I remembered that the pilot and I were students in high school together at Red Rock—small world, they say.

Cargo, tools and other supplies destined for Armstrong filled the plane. It took us quite a while to become airborne, as there was not much of a headwind and we were carrying so much extra weight. The wings teetered back and forth, the flaps extended fully down, and with a loud roar of the motor we barely cleared the low spruce trees near the shoreline. This turned out to be one of the scariest flights of my life. A light rain rapidly turned to heavy snow. We were suddenly faced with a complete white out and the pilot, who had no instruments of any kind to guide him, not even an altimeter, was at a complete loss to explain to me where we were or where we were going.

It was like trying to fly inside one of those little Christmas toys of a winter scene that you shake back and forth to make a snow storm inside. I thought the end would surely come here, in this bleak land of swamps and endless coniferous forest. I had sudden glimpses in my mind of crashing and setting up a makeshift camp. Images of a Martin Hartwell type of existence flashed before me.

I looked over at the pilot. He was lost in concentration, peering this way and that, as if there was some peep hole that he had overlooked that would magically restore his vision. All at once, "We're going down," he yelled, over the steady roar of the engine. I wondered to myself, "Down? Where to?" The nose of the plan began a gentle, swaying descent. The pilot then sharply pulled up on his throttle stick as we began to skirt dangerously over the tops of the trees below. "There's an old cutting road around here somewhere," he explained, as he motioned with his finger down to the snow covered terrain below. I could see little but a stream of green directly below the plane, and a sheet of white above with the realization that we were skimming along near the tops of the pine and spruce trees.

It was all a harrowing experience, but before long we flew over the familiar line of railway tracks and began our descent into Caribou Lake near the town of Armstrong where the air base was situated. The pilot seemed to have forgotten the adventure while we were still landing on the lake below, skimming over the waves. He gave no sigh of relief, as one might expect, but began instead to quietly banter about the upcoming weekend and what his life was like since we were students.

For this pilot, I sensed, experiences such as this one were pretty routine, these experiences happen in the course of his everyday life, or 'business as usual', one might say. But for me it was an entirely different matter, and certainly not something that I could classify as an everyday event. After the pilot left, I sat in the plane for a few moments, drew in a deep breath, and reflected on this shocking experience. There are times evidently when fieldwork can involve such heart-pounding adventures, and such grave risks to one's life. Of course, I started to question why I was doing this research in the first place, or what I might be doing wrong when my life was placed in such danger. I gave my head a shake, and snapped out of my day dreaming. It probably just wasn't my time yet, I thought, and stepped hesitantly out of the plane onto the dock.

Macro-Local Historical Perspectives

An important aspect of field work concerns the relationships between what is happening at the local level and the larger sphere of macro-level processes. During the period during which I conducted most of my field work around Collins and the Whitewater Lake tourist lodge project (1974–1975), the most important Indigenous concerns at the national level in Canada involved the Hawthorn Report (1966–1967), the Trudeau government's White Paper (1969) and, a decade later, the Bill-C 31 proposal to amend the Indian Act (1985), and the Sechelt (*Shishalh*) Band in British Columbia municipal approach (1986).

To review the social and political situation in Collins, it started as a transitory summer gathering place around a fur trading post on the CNR line. In 1960, DIAND built a school close to the trading post which required more permanent houses to be built for the Anishinaabe residents. As time went on, the grandparents stayed behind to look after the school children so their sons and daughters could return to their trap lines. Also, as the years passed, the people of Collins began to lose contact with their home reserves—mainly Fort Hope (Eabamatoong) on the Albany River and the Whitesand Reserve on Lake Nipigon. There were also Anishinaabe women who had lost their Indian status because they married a non-status person. Her children, as a result, also were denied Indian status, and this trend began to proliferate so that by the 1970s in Collins only about 60 percent of the population retained their status. The community of Collins did not have any legitimate right to be situated around the fur trading post since the land was mostly owned by the CNR or the federal government as Crown lands.

When the Hawthorn Report was published in the mid-1960s, it contained the shocking, for this time, recommendation that "Indians should be regarded as 'citizens plus', meaning Indigenous people were not only citizens of Canada but possessed 'certain additional rights' because of treaties and other land cessation agreements. One must remember that Indigenous peoples with status under the Indian Act were not even allowed to vote in federal elections until 1960 because they were not really even considered to be Canadian citizens. In other words, their position in Canada was ambiguous. In any event, Indigenous organizations began to form in the 1960s using the term 'citizens plus' as their banner or rallying point against what was widely perceived to be the assimilationist policies of the Trudeau government and the White Paper of 1969.

The statement issued by the Indian Chiefs of Alberta in 1970, also called *Citizens Plus*, soundly rejected any suggestion that a termination policy would ever be considered by the Indigenous people of Canada. As Weaver states, "Predictably, the policy caused shock and alarm among Indians. Even though they were an unorganized minority, they responded with a clear-cut rejection of the White Paper" (1981: 4). From that point on, it was as if a tidal change had occurred. Now there was talk, not about disposing of the Indian Act, but on ways by which it might be changed or even strengthened so that its provisions would be more amenable to the aspiration of the country's Indigenous people.

During the period of July, 1968 to May,1969, Indian Act consultation meetings were held. Weaver pointed out that:

Although there was little consensus on the Act's revisions…Indians wanted their special rights honored and their historical grievances, particularly over lands and treaties, recognized and dealt with in an equitable fashion. Equally important, they wanted direct and meaningful participation in the making of policies that affected their future…Indians responded to the White Paper policy with a resounding nationalism unparalleled in Canadian history (1981: 5).

The White Paper approach with its termination agenda was officially abandoned by the Trudeau government in the spring of 1971.

Over the next decade of the 1980s there was clearly emerging a different approach to the position of Indigenous people in Canada which was more conciliatory in its emphasis and less based on ideas of colonial suppression. In 1982, the Constitution Act, in Section 35, recognized the "aboriginal peoples of Canada and the existing aboriginal and treaty rights of the aboriginal peoples of Canada are hereby recognized and affirmed." In 1985, Bill C-31 was passed with the stated attempt to amend the Indian Act so that it was less sexist in its orientation. The central idea was that the bill would end discrimination against Indian women, and bring the Indian Act into line with the Canadian Charter of Rights and Freedoms. With the passage of Bill C-31, the Indian Act was amended so that neither Indian women nor men would lose their status upon marriage to non-status individuals. Then in 1986, the Sechelt Band near Vancouver, British Columbia, adopted a plan to remove their reserve lands from the jurisdiction of the Indian Act, which in effect, allowed the band members to adopt a municipal model of government.

All of these national-level initiatives had an effect on the Collins community either directly or indirectly. Perhaps the most important effect was that for the first time Indigenous communities such as Collins, even though they were not directed under the provisions of the Indian Act, then became recognized as a sort of municipality under provincial jurisdiction. Before this time, Collins appeared to have no legal rights whatsoever as its members were simply regarded as squatters living upon land to which they had no legitimate rights.

The Hawthorn Report suggested that Indigenous people such as those inhabiting Collins probably had some rights, although these were not clearly defined, since their ancestors had signed treaties with the British government and Collins was situated on lands that they have inhabited 'since time immemorial'. For the first time, representatives of federal and provincial governments were willing to listen to their concerns, in the spirit of 'citizens plus', which initiated a process that is still going on today.

At the time in the 1970s that I was beginning my field work, I began to realize that Collins was a unique community that was not described before in the ethnographic literature. What I mean is that anthropological research was only conducted on reserves because these were officially recognized, and so descriptions of places such as Collins were hidden in a sort of political obscurity because its members lacked official status. My fieldwork, I thought, was an excellent opportunity to describe a type of Indigenous community in Canada for the first time. There were so many questions that needed answers. As an example, since Collins was not regulated by the Indian Act, then what sort of leadership, if any, took place I wondered?

When I first went to Collins in 1972, to visit my brother who was there on a one-year teaching contract, I found out that three Métis brothers were in the process of forming a leadership organization called the Ogoki River Guides, Corp (ORG). The purpose was to have a recognizable body that would act as an administrative focal point through which outside interests could make contact with the community and through which negotiations could be conducted. The brothers were the sons of a Scottish fur trader father who had formerly worked for the Hudson's Bay Company in Fort Hope, and their Anishinaabe mother who was the daughter of a former chief of the band. Thus, the brothers drew skills, and prestige, from several sources, such as a certain business acumen derived from their father's business experience, and through their mother, a knowledge of Indigenous language and culture. For these reasons, the brothers were ideally suited to represent the Collins community, although they were not officially elected to their positions as would have necessarily been the case if they lived on a reserve which required an elected chief and council.

On my first visit to Collins, in 1972, I was asked if I wanted a summer job. The idea was that I would help the brothers compose grant proposals designed to generate employment, write letters to various government officials, and otherwise engage in strategy discussions. They wanted whatever literary skills I could offer, since their education was limited, they said. Not having another alternative source of employment for the summer, I said, "Sure, I would be happy to work here for a few months." This is the way that I learned about ORG's goals, government contacts, and strategies for achieving their economic objectives.

Later, during 1974–1975, when I was to eventually spend eighteen months in the community on an extended doctoral research project, these sessions were a valuable source of material for me. I had access to their records concerning the various grants they received and the employment funding coming into the community, material which would otherwise not have been available to me. Overall, earned income amounted to about 75 percent of the total, and transfer payments the other 25 percent. There were several aspects of government funding that I found interesting. In Collins, during 1974, almost 25 percent of the cash income came from CNR employment, another 25 percent from the tourist lodge construction, 25 percent from various transfer payment, and another 25 percent from other miscellaneous projects. Income from trapping amounted to less than 1 percent of the total. The store business which had been inherited from their Scottish father, less than 6 percent. Welfare/temporary relief accounted for less than 1 percent (Hedican 1986a: 62–78).

One can now see how valuable accurate statistics are when arriving at conclusions. As an example, the notion of a welfare ridden northern community was totally false. Trapping had virtually disappeared as a source of income, despite the relatively isolated location of the community. However, according to my records, the economic or cash value of country food production, which was calculated separately, amounted to about 20 percent of

Collins' total income. The implication, therefore, was that if community members were no longer able to hunt and fish, but needed to replace country food with that bought at the store, then their level of income would decrease significantly in terms of their cash outlay.

The ORG strategy was primarily based on the tourist trade—a renewable resource. The community would have trouble surviving without the full-time employment of the railway. Finally, most of the government-sponsored projects, which are the ones in which ORG competes with other communities for employment grants, came from provincial sources. Despite the high percentage of Indigenous people in the community with status according to the Indian Act, the federal government in the form of DIAND contributed virtually nothing to the economic welfare of the community.

This fact led me to examine the possible municipal connections, not only in this community, but elsewhere in northwestern Ontario. A fortuitous find was a provincial government document, dated 1974, and entitled *Bill102, an Act to Provide for the Incorporation of Communities without Municipal Organization*, produced by Ontario's Department of Treasury, and otherwise known as *The Northern Ontario Communities Act*. I found that this document included a treasure trove of information on Indigenous communities in northern Ontario that were not reserves under the Indian Act and as such were largely hidden from public scrutiny.

Here is some interesting statistical information on northwestern Ontario available during my time of fieldwork in the mid-1970s. Overall there were some fifty-three Indigenous reserves and settlements, meaning these have direct connections with the federal Department of Indian Affairs and are under the Indian Act. Twenty-five percent (19) of these have a resident population of about two hundred people. There are also about a dozen small towns and villages with a high Indigenous population, such as Sioux Lookout, Armstrong, Savant Lake, and Nakina (Hedican 1990b).

There are also various Indigenous settlements which I have termed 'Indigenous non-reserve settlements', or which the Ontario government terms 'unorganized communities'.[39] These communities are often situated on Crown lands and are usually administered by Ontario's Ministry of Natural Resources (the name at the time of my study). These settlements usually have a high percent of Indigenous people and lack formal procedures for forming councils or electing local officials. From what I was able to determine, about ten percent of the population lived in these so-called unorganized communities, of which Collins is an example. It also means that such communities have connections to a multiplicity of government agencies, both federal and provincial, that have some form of influence or jurisdiction over them.

The overall problem for these villages is that they lack some sort of municipal or township status which would allow for the settlement to be surveyed and individual lots sold to the inhabitants. There is also consequently no way in which individuals can build up equity in private properties that could be used as a basis for financing. If its residents had title to the land, a village such as Collins would then be in a position to participate in the services and improvements available from the provincial government. In addition, if local government groups existed, these could form the basis for local decision-making bodies and administrative structures capable of coordinating changes in the village as a whole.

During the time of my fieldwork, the document called *The Northern Communities Act* (Ontario 1974) indicated that:

It is a generally accepted principle of government operation that the provincial government will contract to provide for essential service or basic social and physical services only to those communities which have some form of legally recognized self-government in unincorporated communities, and that there were well over a hundred such communities in the rural areas of northwestern Ontario (Ontario 1974).

The point that I wish to make here is that this document was written at least a decade before the Sechelt Band in British Columbia left the confines of the Indian Act and became a municipal entity. In northwestern Ontario during the 1970s, there were over a hundred Indigenous communities that appeared to be virtually abandoned by the federal Indian Affairs Department and would have benefited for incorporation as municipal government entities. The overall conclusion that one could reasonably draw from the forgoing discussion is that there were ample opportunities for researchers to link local level developments in northern Ontario with the wider national events occurring in Canadian Indigenous issues.

Lessons Learned

My fieldwork experiences at Whitewater Lake provided me with a unique opportunity to learn how to conduct ethnographic research in a quite isolated environment in northern Ontario. As time went on I began to see Whitewater Lake as a small social, economic and political laboratory where one could try out and experiment with new ideas. The evolving social organization of the construction camp was a good example of the way my ideas changed and developed over time. Part of this development was reflected in my attempts to see my own fieldwork in a historical context, which is to say, how my ideas were different from, or a continuation of the work of previous researchers. As an example, R.W. Dunning had previously conducted fieldwork (in the 1950s) among the Anishinaabe who were living in the community of Pikangekum which was situated near the Manitoba border. Dunning had studied the composition of hunting groups, which he called 'co-residential groups', noting that "The new population grouping is less bound by environmental strictures and consequently changing social norms are free to develop more uniformly along lines of a sociological form rather than an environmental control" (1959: 108).

My strategy here was to utilize Dunning's observations on Anishinaabe social structure as a hypothesis that I could use to initiate my own study of the social groupings at Whitewater Lake. I expected that there would be important differences in the nature of the Anishinaabe social organization from Dunning's earlier period to my own, and I intended to use these differences to launch my own analysis. In Dunning's time of the mid-1950s, for example, the families were mainly fur trapping units, and the ebb and flow of family life followed the dictates of this economic pursuit. At Whitewater Lake, however, there was more mobility in family life because the workers were participants in a wage economy, even though the people still lived in the bush, as the people did at Pikangekum. For my part, I was able to document the forms and shapes of family organization from the ground up, as the family units evolved, with each successive wave of flights from the Indigenous communities to the south.

Some families quickly located their camp beside one or more other families, usually linked by some form of kinship ties, while others chose a more isolated location, away from the other members of the camp. Using Dunning's phrase about population groupings developing along 'lines of a sociological form', I was curious about what sorts of decisions members of the various families were making when they chose the location for their camp site. As one might guess, the reasons for each family's particular decision on where to locate their camp were quite varied. Some expressed a desire to be with other family members, such as brothers or sisters, while others wanted to be near friends from their home communities (this camp was composed primarily by residents of Collins, but also comprised those from Armstrong, Ferland, as well as a scattering of other places). It was also evident from my interviews on the subject of decision-making regarding camp locations that some people chose their sites simply because they did not want to be near particular people, or some just wanted to be left alone.

After several months of field work, I was able to put together a fairly complete picture of the emerging social organization of the Whitewater camp, and to make some reasonable attempts to explain the nature of this emergence, based on several earlier studies of Anishinaabe life in northern Ontario. This, then, was my fieldwork strategy. Collect as much accurate information as possible, on a firsthand basis, using whatever techniques seemed most appropriate, or were apt to yield the productive results at that time.

If it meant being perched up in a tower all day so that I could observe the flow of work activities on the construction site, then that's what I did. I also participated to the extent that I was able, or allowed to participate, in many of the camp's activities—eating meals with the workers, fishing sojourns after work, or chatting it up around a camp fire in the evening. Conducting interviews (usually of the more informal kind, called 'unstructured') was an important part of my research strategy as well, in order to obtain firsthand information from workers, crew bosses, the construction foreman, and the women and other family members of the workers in the various campsites in the vicinity of the tourist lodge. In other words, I employed primarily the more conventional fieldwork methodology of participant observation supplemented with additional data gathering techniques involving questions and answers.

There was a plan or research design that I also worked on, which evolved over time, so that there was a purpose for the information that I was gathering. This design had three primary facets to it: 1) study the economic and political strategies of the Ogoki River Guides leaders along with their goals and objectives; 2) research the economic and organizational facets concerning the construction of the tourist lodge; and 3) examine the structure of social life, including workers and their families at Whitewater Lake. This overall view of the research with its three-pronged approach allowed me to keep in focus the rationale for data collection and, at a later date, integrate the three research areas into a larger theoretical argument.

As a concluding statement, from my fieldwork experiences at the construction site situated at Whitewater Lake I learned that it is the documentation of specific details of everyday life that was the most important aspect of my study. These particulars of everyday life provided the concrete foundation that one can return to over and over again for subsequent re-analysis and interpretation. The other modes of analysis are also important in their own way, but for different reasons. The analysis taken in the field of specific cases of everyday life serves more to provide an orientation for what one is doing, than to lay out in any specific way the wording of the analysis that will eventually take place at the write-up stage.

What this preliminary analysis does is force you to think about general patterns and arguments while actually living in the field (as Richard Salisbury suggested to me in one of his letters). In turn, this has an effect on what field materials you are apt to collect, because you are then in the practice of constantly thinking in terms of general patterns and issues. The preliminary analysis will probably be changed later, sometimes in a major way, but it does have the side effect of allowing you to see the way your thinking has changed over the course of the fieldwork, the way ideas get started, and how they relate to the types of issues that one begins to think are important during a very preliminary stage of the data collection phase.

Conclusion

My field notes written during this period of my anthropological career are filled with comments about the various kinship relations, and what their possible significance could be. The Anishinaabe people themselves seemed to feel that they just moved where 'they felt like it' and I was disappointed with their lack of a more 'structuralist' orientation to their explanations, however implausible that would be. Other books on the Anishinaabe of northern Ontario (Dunning 1959; Rogers 1962, for example) appeared to have such consistent patterns involved in the explanations of community life, and yet here I struggled with many contradictions and unresolved sociological problems.[40]

As it turned out there was an important lesson for me here, and that is to try and accept the 'field data' as it is, as one properly recorded the details of everyday life. It is the differences that one finds from the work of previous ethnographers, rather than the similarities, that are the most important and are most apt to lead to new insights. These 'new insights' in the case of my own particular field study had to do with the way people employed the pre-existing flexible social relationships at Whitewater Lake as they lived their lives on an everyday basis, apparently oblivious to the larger overarching sociological patterns of life that are sought by anthropologists.

If I could regard my fieldwork as successful, it was because there was a plan or research design that I also worked on, which evolved over time, so that there was a purpose for the information that I was gathering. I was not just sitting around waiting for things to happen, as I tried to be more proactive in my approach. This design had three primary facets to it—studying the economic and political strategies of the Ogoki River Guides leaders along with their goals and objectives, the social and organizational aspects concerning the construction of the tourist lodge and, lastly, the structure of everyday life of the workers and their families in their camps. This overall view of the research with its three-pronged approach allowed me to keep in focus the rationale for data collection and, at a later date, integrate the three research areas into a larger theoretical argument.

There was also an important personal side to this research, that I was mostly unaware of at the time, but has had the effect of changing me as a person. On the basis of these experiences at Whitewater Lake, I became less likely to take life's everyday 'trials and tribulations' for granted. When I am struggling with some aspect of my life, I think for a moment about how the Anishinaabe people living up in the bush country of northern Ontario also struggle, with fewer resources at their disposal than I have. They carry on their lives and their struggles with acceptance and dignity, rarely complaining about their lot in life.

It is true that my research in Whitewater Lake country involved some difficulties, but these were endured for only a relatively short period of time. I always had the option to leave this area if I wished, and had the means to do so. This was not much of an option for the Anishinaabe people themselves. Whatever hardships I might have suffered did not have to be tolerated for my whole life, as might have been the case with the northern Indigenous residents.

The trials that were a part of my research were for the most part taken pretty much for granted as part of a lifelong process for the Anishinaabe.

The hardships are many for these hardy people—planes crash, people are burnt in house fires, freeze in snow banks, are hit by trains, and live at an economic level that southern Ontario residents would hardly tolerate. I do not wish to sound smug in any way, but research in the northern bush country not only allows the fieldworker to begin to appreciate life on life's terms in the northern locale, but also to appreciate the benefits of living in the south as well. One should also add that such research is not for the faint of heart. Overall one might say that fieldwork engenders a better awareness of life in general because we are able to see our own life's path in a larger, more comparative perspective. These occurrences are the stuff of everyday life; the details, the background, and personalities that fill out our life's experiences, imbue them with meaning, however obscure, and serve to propel us forward in time.

Chapter Five
Wendell, the Hermit of Best Island

Solitude can feel like a prison to those who don't want it, while others deliberately seek to be alone in the hope of liberating themselves from noise and busyness. Many hermits across the ages can be seen to have chosen their isolation. However, as history tells us, the question of choice hasn't always been so clear-cut.

Kate Wilkinson (2018), *The Hermit Life from Medieval to Modern*

In 1992, French sailor Roger Lextrait agreed to live alone on the Palmyra Atoll for one year, but stayed for seven more. As he explained, the reason that he spent all those years alone on an isolated island was because "I wanted to get away from the unnecessary complication of modern life. I wanted to be close to nature and to have absolutely no human beings around me—just to see whether I could do It. It was like a challenge; I wanted to try something completely new."

This adventure started when the owner of the island approached him and asked if he would go out there and be the manager, because people had been going to the island without permission and then, if they had trouble, possibly suing him when they go back to Hawaii. In fairness, Lextrait was not entirely alone. One of the first things he did was go to an animal shelter and got a dog, a German Shepard, he named TouTou. For anyone who has spent time alone for long period, you will know that dogs can be the best companions. They always seem to be happy, ward off strangers, and, as the joke goes, never talk back.

Being alone all this time took some getting used to. Lextrait does mention that "Sometimes the loneliness would just attack me. The way I fight loneliness is to get busy," which sounds like good advice for all of us. He would also have the luxury of swimming with dolphins and diving every day. "Under the water," he said, "is like another world; it is so beautiful. That was one way I took my loneliness out."

This almost luxurious life of solitude described by Lextrait appears to be a very distant version of the hermit's life of Wendell Beckwith described in this chapter. Beckwith lived for almost twenty years in the Subarctic region of northern Ontario on Best Island in Whitewater Lake (see map of Whitewater Lake). Temperatures would plunge to -30°C, or colder, for weeks at a time. However, Wendell's goal was to seek isolation not for entertainment or to enjoy a holiday, but to engage in serious scientific research. This chapter describes his life in northern Ontario, the people he met, and some of the work that engaged him.

Eccentrics of Northern Ontario Wendell Beckwith at Whitewater Lake

The initial design for the ORG tourist lodge at Whitewater Lake was originally proposed by Wendell Beckwith a resident at Best Island on the far side of the Whitewater Lake. Wendell suggested that the lodge be built out of upright poles in the shape of a teepee with a covering of moose hides soaked in a water repellent solution. As it turned out, his design was not adopted because there were concerns about the durability of such a structure, and how it would ever hold the number of people necessary to make the lodge a money-making proposition.

There was no doubt that Wendell was an eccentric fellow, although well-liked by the Anishinaabe people in the area. He had a little museum of Indigenous crafts and other odds and ends that he used in support of his ideas which generally promoted the ingenuity of the Aboriginal inhabitants of the area. As Kate Wilkinson explains, "Society has often looked to hermits for the insight they are presumed to have gained through solitude. While in some cultures hermits have embraced the role of wise man or healer, others would rather be left alone." Though hermits throughout the ages have adopted different roles in the public imagination, they all face the question of how to live completely and radically alone. For many, Wilkinson explains, this state has had huge mental challenges, and in some cases the dangers of being alone have proved deadly. But for those who genuinely seek it, the solitude of the hermit life can have its rewards.

In *Robinson Crusoe and the Morality of Solitude*, Barbara Taylor (2018) suggests that 'loneliness' as we know it today is a modern concept, dating from the 19th century. In earlier centuries, the manner in which it was described then are very different from the way solitude is understood today. Loneliness, as a modern concept, is regarded in a sympathetic manner and attempts are consequently made to alleviate the lonely person's isolation. In today's world, people who choose the solitary life are respected for their choice, but in the past there were very negative views of solitude.[41]

In this context, Robinson Crusoe has become an icon of solitude and probably is the most dominant depiction of seclusion in Western literature. Yet, Crusoe does not succumb to his aloneness and go insane, rather he rarely complains but seems to embrace the experience. There are times, which are rare enough, when Crusoe does despair at his lack of companions, as we would expect that most people would, being the gregarious creatures that we are. However, as with many people who aspire to the solitary life, they often do not regard themselves as alone in life, thinking that they have divine companionship.

For some reason, northern Ontario has been a magnet for eccentrics who find their way there when they might not find acceptance in more southerly environments. As an example, when I was a boy there was a fellow who used to come and visit my father's garage in Nipigon. I never knew what his real name was but the residents of the town called him 'Birch-bark Alex' because of his home-made cowboy hats made out of birch bark which he was always trying to sell to anyone who would listen. Alex had all these quirky ideas about such phenomenon as, for example, sunspots (aliens were able to cool certain sections of the sun), eclipses (unknown forces used magnetism to align celestial bodies), or any other topic that you wished to raise. People generally accepted him and his theories because he was fun to talk to—he was so serious about these farfetched ideas as to be almost humorous. One of Alex's favorite topics was the large whale that he claimed once lived on his property. Now this tale really got people riled up because of the very absurd nature of it.

People at times thought that Alex was making fun of them and that he presumed to be smarter than everyone else. Which was the case until for some unknown reason a contingent of archaeologists and other scientists from the Royal Ontario Museum arrived to investigate Alex's claims. Now he was telling everyone, "See, told you so!" Apparently there were whale bones found on Alex's property and, no, he did not drag them there as everyone thought. The explanation went like this: at a time after the last ice age the water levels of the Great Lakes were much shallower than they are now.

During this prehistoric time period whales were able to swim from the Atlantic Ocean up the St. Lawrence River into the Ottawa River and from there into Lake Superior. One of these whales found its way right onto Alex's property and became stranded there, was the official explanation from the ROM experts. The reason that whales can no longer make the journey up to Alex's property is because of something called 'isostatic rebound', which is to say, after the massive ice sheet melted the suppressed land around the North Bay outlet into Lake Nipissing rose about fifteen meters which effectively blocked off further connections to the ocean. Eventually this phenomenon caused a massive plumbing back-up with the Great Lakes finally flowing over Niagara Falls.[42]

The problem with these eccentrics is that their stories and theories have enough factual evidence hidden in them to be almost believable. Most people, though, were cautious about believing these tales in case someone was 'pulling their leg' or otherwise intent on making fools of them. Curiously, most of these eccentrics were males living the life of a hermit so people thought that their isolation was a contributing factor in their wild ideas.

Biographical Sketch

Wendell King Beckwith, in a curious case of convergent place names, was born in 1915 at Whitewater, Wisconsin, and died in 1980 at Whitewater Lake, Ontario. His father, Raymond Beckwith, was a design engineer and inventor. After finishing high-school, young Wendell went on to attend the University of Alabama, majoring in Botany, but dropped out after only one year, apparently because he was not permitted to take advance classes in electronics. As such, whatever knowledge he might have had about engineering and science was either learned from his father or self-taught. Nonetheless, Wendell found employment for a time as a draughtsman, and later in the 1930s to the 1950s was employed as a research engineer for the Milwaukee Electric Tool Co. He rose through this company eventually working as the company's chief development engineer and vice president where he designed and patented several pieces of equipment.

In about 1945, Wendell left this company to set up his own development lab in Whitewater, Wisconsin. He also worked until 1955 as a consultant for the Parker Pen Company; however, he did not invent the ball-point pen as has been suggested by some people, although he did receive four patents pertaining to writing apparatus and associated machinery. However, while at the Parker Pen Company he developed methods of making a ball for ballpoint pens using sapphires. Beckwith is credited with developing the 'T-Ball Jotter' pen, and has a number of patents in his name.[43] During the years 1955–1956 Beckwith left his wife and family of five children. In the following year (1957–1958), he began working for the Gravity Institute in New Boston located in New Hampshire where he analyzed submissions for funding. While there a United States government lab approached him to further their research on unidentified flying objects, but he refused because it would have involved working in groups, whereas he wanted to work alone. By the late 1950s, however, he was searching for a place of solitude in which to conduct his research. During the following three years Wendell spent time living at various locations in Northern Wisconsin and, in 1961, moved to Best Island on Whitewater Lake, Ontario.

In this remote area of northern Ontario, Wendell began to construct a cottage with the financial aid of an American businessman named Harry Wirth and to begin his scientific research. Until the end of the decade, that is until 1969, he spent the winters in Wisconsin and then lived during the summer months at his Whitewater Lake cottage. Entering the 1970s he began to live at Best Island year-round where he received various visitors from the local Anishinaabe population, members of the 'Outward Bound' group, as well as other friends. From 1971 to 1980, his friend Rose Chaltry of Minneapolis, Harry Wirth's former secretary, lived with him during the summer months.

Rose Chaltry (R) with Donald Patience
Photo: Edward Hedican

By the mid-1970s, Beckwith's funding agreement with his benefactor Harry Wirth began to deteriorate with the result that he had to begin depending on Rose Chaltry and other friends for supplies. He also had protracted issues with the Ministry of Natural Resources because he lacked landed immigrant status and refused to apply for a land use permit. When an immigration officer visited him in 1973, he remarked that "Beckwith's work appears to be connected with the magnetic and electrical forces of our galaxy and their effect on human migration through the past centuries. He is attempting to forecast the effect they will have on future population movements and trends and also on the effect on space travel and on interplanetary travelers themselves" (Nicholson 2011b).

Beckwith's research comprised most of his time. He was constantly making astronomical and meteorological observations, taking notes on whatever topic interested him at the time, and filing his note papers into binders and folders. In 1979, he agreed to bequeath his research notes, papers and various experimental apparatus to the government of Ontario on his death. These notes and written observations covered an eclectic range of topics such as astronomical forces of the galaxy, historic human migrations, studies of the Egyptian pyramids and Stonehenge in England. Wendell had a special interest in 'Pi' which is the ratio of the circumference of a circle to its diameter, which Edward Burger (2020) has called "The most important number in the universe."[44] Wendell was apparently intrigued by such numbers and how often they recurred in nature. He also was very interested in the connection between astronomical events and the migration of large groups of people. According to scholars who have examined his work there were certain notable deficiencies, such as his use of a 1930s version of high school mathematics and a preference for 'popular' information rather than more academic works for his evidence.

His various notes, binders, and correspondence are housed in the Thunder Bay Museum under 'The Wendell Beckwith Papers'. These papers not only include his correspondence and research notes but also sketches, plans, drawings of some of his inventions and buildings along with audio tapes. One of the problems that those compiling his various papers and other materials had been that Wendell appears to have abandoned the usual dating method and preferred instead to use a self-devised system whereby his materials are dated using numbers from the point in which he permanently moved to Whitewater Lake. Much of his material, though, remains undated. Another problem is that years after Beckwith's death, his material was gathered up in haste and placed in boxes in no particular order. Most of his notes are neatly written with color drawings, except for those of later years when he appears to have developed a notable shake. It does not appear that Beckwith ever intended that his work was to be prepared for publication (*Wendell Beckwith, 1963–1980*. www.thunderbaymuseum.com/wp-content).[45]

There are also various newspaper articles written decades after Beckwith's death, mostly in Thunder Bay's *Chronicle-Journal* which added further details on his life and research. As an example, one details "His Life of Pi,"

(Nicholson 2011a), another discusses the building of his various cabins (Nicholson 2001b), and a later one describes the details of his life on Best Island (Gunnell 2014). Toronto's *Globe and Mail* also published an article describing the deterioration of Beckwith's various buildings (Strauss 2005). Wendell Beckwith no doubt reached the pinnacle of his fame when an article about him appeared in *National Geographic*:

Recluse inventor Wendell Beckwith settled on Best Island near the southeast corner of Wabakimi's Whitewater Lake in 1961, where he'd spend the next two decades alone in the name of research. The precisely designed cabins he built still stand, some of which reflect the ideas he studied here in isolation. His so-called Snail cabin winds like the creature's shell, reflecting how pi is represented throughout the natural world, an idea he was particularly taken with. The structure defies architectural efficiency, said to produce so much heat in Northern Ontario's brutally chilly winters that Beckwith needed to spend only 10 minutes collecting wood each day. You can access Best Island with an outfitter, like Wilderness North, or by boat (Hannah Lott-Schwartz 1978).

Wendell's Cabins

In the case of Wendell Beckwith, I happened to visit him on various occasions during the research that I was conducting at Whitewater Lake, even spending a weekend with him during the month of January during a cold spell of -30° F. His property (I do not think he actually owned anything there, was just a squatter) consisted of several log cabins, a storage shed and a dock all constructed of logs that he had cut on Best Island, or had dragged from the Whitewater Lake shores during the winter. His cabins had an experimental aspect as well. One of these, called the 'Snail' was built into the edge of a sandbank. As Nicholson (2011b) notes in a Thunder Bay *Chronicle-Journal* article:

Wendell Beckwith's Cabin
Photo Courtesy of the Thunder Bay Museum

In 1977, Beckwith began constructing a new cabin, called the Snail, which in his words, was 'a new dimension in bush habitation'. He wanted to create an abode that would be easy to heat, use local materials, could be constructed by unskilled labor and completed in one building season. The Snail was constructed into a hillside using swamp spruce. It featured a unique spiral design with a skylight to allow the cabin to be naturally lit. Beckwith reportedly said that the Snail needed less energy than one eight-foot length of dead spruce per day to heat. Beckwith had hoped that he could construct more homes like the Snail and have other researchers come to Best Island to conduct their own experiments and research and be able to share ideas while having the benefit of solitude. His idea was not to be (Nicholson 2011b).

His main cabin, I remember, had several interesting gadgets which he had constructed suggesting that he was an intelligent man with some education. In his cabin were rows of note books in which he explained contained his 'scientific' observations over the years. He let me examine several of these and the various drawings and algebraic calculations in them were not comprehensible to me. I understand, though, that the ROM thought this material interesting enough to store permanently in their archives. As an example, there was an interesting reason why Wendell chose Best Island in the first place to conduct his experiments and jot down his observations. From what he explained to me, there were several significant vertical lines of longitude joining the north and south poles and his place was on one of these.

In those days without electricity, radio or television, there was a shortage of entertainment so I sat back and tried to follow Wendell's explanation. He started off, "the Meridian that runs through Greenwich, England, is internationally accredited as the line of 0°, or 'prime meridian'. The 'anti-meridian' is halfway around the world, at 180°. It is the basis for the international Date Line. Any point on the earth can be reckoned by calculating coordinates, the point where parallels (lines of latitude) and meridian intersect."

"So far so good," I thought, "but please get to your point."

Wendell Beckwith at Work
Photo Courtesy of the Thunder Bay Museum

He continued, "Coordinates are very useful for military engineering, rescue operations and all types of useful applications. At this point I wanted him to explain why the location of his cabin was significant. Wendell went on, "Because of the earth's location, there is a close connection between longitude and latitude. Comparing local time to an absolute measure of time allows longitude to be determined…"

At this point, I had enough. I never really received a comprehensible explanation. Later, when I had the opportunity to look at a map of the region, I determined that his cabin was just west of 89° longitude and near 51° latitude. None of this information unfortunately was of any use to me in determining the significance that Wendell attached to his cabin's location.

The Viking Sword Mystery

I tried to change the subject, "Well how about the famous Beardmore sword," Wendell, "what about this, any ideas?" Wendell wanted me to refresh him on the details, which, if the reader is interested, has been published in Douglas Hunter's *Beardmore: The Viking Hoax that Rewrote History*, 2018. The short version of the story is that in the 1930s a prospector, Eddy Dodd, claimed to have found a purported Viking sword and other relics on his mining claim near the town of Beardmore where I was born incidentally situated near the western shore of Lake Nipigon in northwestern Ontario. This news prompted an almost immediate investigation by experts at the Royal Ontario Museum.

At the time, the ROM, needing to increase its visitor circulation to avoid bankruptcy, displayed the sword and other associated materials at its entrance, accompanied by numerous newspaper articles speculating how the Vikings could have made it to far flung Beardmore. For over two decades, the relics remained on display. Their significance of course was that the finding of a Viking sword, which was never in dispute, challenged all the existing theories of the time frame when Europeans first reached North America.

By the 1950s, scholars in Europe and elsewhere in North America began to question the legitimacy of the archaeological finds, some claiming that the sword represented a well-thought out hoax. ROM's director, Charles Trick Currelly unfortunate name?, had staked his reputation on the find's authenticity which also tarnished the reputation of the Museum. Although

Scandinavian experts verified that the sword was indeed of Viking origin, there were questions about how the sword had arrived in Eddy Dodd's hands. Further investigation revealed that Mr. Dodd had owned several buildings in Thunder Bay that he used as rental accommodations. According to one story, a Norwegian tenant had skipped out on his rent, leaving the sword hidden in the basement. Dodd apparently found the sword and reconstructed a supposed Viking burial site which included the sword. ROM investigators actually arrived at the site, conducted a superficial investigation, and were pressed into verifying the graves authenticity. Not long after, however, anthropologist Edmund Carpenter, who launched a crusade against the find's authenticity, eventually convinced scholars that the grave was a fraud. Dodd's motive, some suggested, was to advertise his mining site with the hope of realizing a handsome profit on its sale.

The controversy, however, continues to this day. The evidence against the find is based more than anything else on speculation about Eddy Dodd's motives than on any factual evidence which discredited the Viking grave. According to European scholars, the Viking sword is authentic, and because of its style and other metallurgical characteristics also fits into the right time frame for a North American discovery.

This was the time to stop this exposition and ask if Wendell had any thoughts on the matter. He was bristling with nervousness, and was indeed ready to formulate a theory which I had never heard before. Wendell got up from his chair and went to his cupboard, withdrawing a glass into which he poured some water. He kept pouring water into the glass, drop by drop practically, until there was a noticeable 'bulge' of water actually rising above the rim of the glass. "This," he explained, "is a convex meniscus curve. This will keep certain light objects afloat because of the surface tension of the water. Ever see a water strider move along atop the surface of the water without sinking? Same principle."

Wendell then took out a small needle from a leather pouch in which he kept sowing materials. He then bent down so his eyes were close to the top of the glass and deftly slid the needle onto the top of the water. It actually floated on the surface with small lines radiating out. The needle slowly spun around for a few seconds and then settled in about the center of the water. Wendell then rooted through his equipment and pulled out a small compass, setting it near the needle. "See," he exclaimed, "the needle is aligned in a direct north-south direction. It's the pull of the magnetic north that aligns the needle in this direction."

"Ok," I was thinking, "thanks for the physics lesson, but what about the Vikings?"

"I'm getting to that," he insisted. "There seems to be a fair amount of archaeological evidence that the Vikings maintained settlements in Newfoundland (L'Anse aux Meadows, I thought). If they had travelled all that way from Scandinavia exploring Iceland and Greenland as well, there is no reason to believe that they would not have travelled down the St. Lawrence River. If this was the case, then the Vikings would have keep going along the old fur trade routes leading into the Ottawa River, across Lake Nipissing and then into Lake Superior at Sault St. Marie. From there, it is a relatively easy route, since their boats were made for ocean travel, to sail along the north shore of Lake Superior, eventually reaching Nipigon Bay at the uppermost reaches of Lake Superior. Entering this bay, they would then travel directly north up the Nipigon River into Lake Nipigon."

"Probably what the Vikings were attempting is to find a route into James and Hudson Bay from which they could travel back home to Scandinavia. From Lake Nipigon to James Bay, the route is complicated. Your goal would be to reach the Albany River and from there it's easy sailing to the coast, but reaching the Albany from Lake Nipigon involved a number of portages. The entry point is Ombabika Bay which is situated on the northeast area of Lake Nipigon. This is a very large bay, with a relatively narrow entrance. From there, one goes up the Ombabika River, then connect with the Ogoki River, eventually reaching the Albany River at the present day communities of Ogoki and Marten Falls. Perhaps there was a storm happening, of which Lake Nipigon is famous, and the Vikings I believe made a mistake and took shelter in a bay south of Ombabika. However, thinking they were in Ombabika they became confused, and travelled up a smaller river near Beardmore, eventually becoming ever more disorganized. They never made it to their destination but became lost and scattered about like the Franklin Expedition."

At this point, when Wendell stopped to take a breath, I quickly asked, "Well, what about this needle demonstration of yours, what does that have to do with the Viking story?"

"I was just getting to that," Wendell said. "So here's my theory," he continued. "The Viking ships use a specific type of ballast as a counterweight to keep their ships upright called 'meteoric iron'. This type of iron is derived from meteors descended from outer space which, during their fall to earth and the intense heat involved, become purified. Before modern smelting, this was the only source of pure iron in the world. If a Viking ship with its ballast of meteoric iron were set still in relatively calm water, the ship would behave like the needle that I just showed you—the ship would align itself in a north-south direction because of the pull of the magnetic north pole. Thus the Viking's had in their ships a natural compass."

There was a lot to take in here, I thought, but his explanation made sense to me. It was also a reasonable explanation for Beardmore's Viking sword that I had not heard of before. Also interesting is that in Hunter's book on the 'Viking hoax' there is not any mention of a theory similar to the one Wendell proposed, even though it was hard to believe that others had not thought of Wendell's explanation as well. The fact that Wendell was able put this explanation of a long standing archaeological mystery together so quickly amazed me.

Wendell's Other Innovations

When day light came, Wendell took me on a tour of his cabins showing me a few of his innovations. Near the front door was a slice of a large log with a sizeable crack in it. According to Wendell this was his 'humidity indicator'. In the center of this log slice was a nail to which was attached a piece of wire. There were markings inscribed on this log. As Wendell explained, as the humidity increased, the crack in the log began to close up as the log absorbed moisture, thus moving the nail in one direction or another.

Inside his cabin were other interesting features. His bed had a crank mechanism attached to it so that he could roll it up during the day to make more room. In the center of his cabin was a box-like structure also with a crank attached. He flipped open the top of this box, wound up the crank and a tray appeared from beneath his cabin. "My refrigerator," he exclaimed. Outside he showed me a new cabin that he was constructing. It was built into the side of a sandy hill. The idea was to save energy by using sand as an insulating material. The front, he said, would be open with glass windows to optimize the sun's rays and trap more energy. In addition, as he took me to the top of the hill, there was a long shoot. Logs were sent down this shoot, much like loading a gun's magazine. "Then I don't have to carry all these logs around to the front of my cabin," was his explanation. There were probably other such innovations that he did not have time to show me.

Wendell in the News

Through the years Wendell's notoriety eventually made it into the news. He was not one of those eccentric hermits who shunned civilization, chasing people away with a shot gun. Instead, Wendell was gregarious, always willing to talk with strangers, show them his cabins and discuss his scientific theories. As a result, Best Island became a regular stop for passing canoeists, fishermen and other adventurous people.

One newspaper article was entitled "Hermit's Former Home in Dire Straits: Beckwith Home was a Regular Tour Stop" (Lyzun, K. www.tbsource.com 2 December 2005). The article begins with: "Wendell Beckwith was considered by many to be a strange yet brilliant man who chose Whitewater Lake as the center of the universe, and his own private place of solitude and study." It explains that since his death in 1980 Wendell's log cabins have fallen into decay and a tug-of-war has developed over who is actually responsible for the upkeep and what should be done with the property.

Various interested parties were involved in the dispute from a rich American (Harry Wirth), provincial government officials, such as the Ministry of Natural Resources, and Anishinaabe residents of the area. As the story goes, Beckwith was a former American engineer who claimed to be an inventor of the ballpoint pen who was robbed, he claims, by employees of an unscrupulous patent company. In 1961, Wendell left his job, his wife, and five children behind in Whitewater, Wisconsin, to pursue scientific research in the Canadian north at a lake with the same name as the place he left in the United States. According to documents that were left behind after his death, Wendell believed that Whitewater Lake was an important place for celestial occurrences. His scientific notes detail his fascination with concepts of magnetism and astronomical forces of the galaxy, with Stonehenge, and the number 'Pi'.

At Best Island, Beckwith found the perfect location to carry out his research in an undisturbed manner. For the next several years, Wendell travelled to Whitewater Lake every summer, constructing his buildings and carrying on his studies until he decided to move there permanently in 1969.

Indigenous people took an interest in this peculiar 'shaganash' or white man. As Arlene Slipperjack, a resident of Collins whose family had their trap line in the Whitewater Lake area, related in 2005, "Wendell was our first 'guest', before him we hardly saw anyone but prospectors camping on the lake. Then he just came out of the blue on an airplane," she recounted. "When he arrived, we didn't know what to make of him. My mother told us, 'remember when you used to play and sing songs about a bearded man and that was going to come and getcha? Well he's here, so you'd better go and make friends!'"

In an interview, Ms. Slipperjack indicated that her family helped Wendell build his cabins since he was not capable of lifting the heavy logs. She said that he did not even know how to put wood in the stove and that he would have frozen to death without their help that first winter. Wendell also became like a grandfather playing with them and taking the children on canoe trips. Her relatives showed him how to make sleds, snowshoes and canoes. Arlene's mother made beaded mittens and a leather cap for him. Many of these items are now ostensibly displayed at the Thunder Bay Historical Museum.

The Anishinaabe of Whitewater Lake found it odd that people referred to Wendell as a hermit because he was such an easy going man. He had many visitors and was always friendly with those who dropped by. Some of the visitors were other scientists interested in his astronomical research or eco-tourism groups such as those belonging to Outward Bound. One of these visitors, Bruce Hyer, said that he was invited by Wendell for a visit. As Hyer related, "Wendell invited me up for Christmas. It was 60 miles from my place to his, and I skied the whole way. It took me three days. When I got there, Wendell was gone, and there was just a note: 'Sorry Bruce, I had to get my teeth fixed,' after which he had to ski all the way back again." He also related that it was his opinion that Wendell 'was a fascinating man. Part genius, part charlatan, part nut case'.

What most people did not realize was that Wendell had an American benefactor who paid for his expenses, which later became a problem because Wendell had promised his home and contents to the Province of Ontario. Later, when Wendell died this benefactor, named Harry Wirth, arrived he was furious over the promise Wendell made. Consequently, a big controversy developed over the ownership of both the land and Beckwith's collected artifacts. Wirth indicated that he agreed to fund Beckwith's scientific ventures as long as he would agree to maintain the Best Island cabins as Wirth's summer retreat, which on this basis Wirth claimed ownership rights in the property. According to Bruce Hyer, "In 1980, Wirth headed up to see Wendell because he heard that Wendell had bequeathed all his stuff to the government. He felt that Wendell had sold him out. They had heated arguments on the beach because Wendell came to believe that he had done all the work himself, and on that based claimed ownership."

Not only that, but Wendell was an illegal alien who had made his home on what was Crown Land. It was part of his quirkiness that he refused to apply for landed immigrant status because he regarded himself as a 'citizen of the world'. So after he died, there was a big bureaucratic mess to clean up. He was just 65 when he died which set in motion a battle that he probably never imagined or would have ever wanted. Just before he died, Wendell formally agreed to leave his research and collected artifacts to the Ontario Government. Partly this agreement was the result of the fallout with Wirth, and partly because Wendell was trying to negotiate his immigration status with the government. An agreement was eventually reached in which Beckwith was granted 'ministerial permission' to stay in the province because of his work with the Anishinaabe of Whitewater Lake. Apart from his refusal to apply for landed immigrant status in Canada, Wendell also refused to apply for a land permit. It was as a result of these legal entanglements that Beckwith agreed to leave his cabins to the province upon his death.

In 1980, after Wendell died, Wirth returned to northern Ontario and began a heated battle with the province in a widely publicized law suit. Wirth's position was that the cabins were his property because he had spent hundreds of thousands of dollars to build the cabins. Wirth felt that the Ontario Government had unjustly taken the property and he demanded compensation in the range of $3 million. Eventually he lost the case in the long run. Many people in the area had fond memories of Wendell and came to regard Wirth as a wealthy American jerk who was just trying to throw his weight around.

Wendell's cabins have now fallen into disrepair and if nobody does anything soon there will be nothing left in a few years. Some people wish the province would step in to preserve his heritage as a tourism site, while others think that the whole place should be left to return to nature. Those who remained in contact with Wendell in his elder years said that he suffered physical ailments that made winter living tough for almost anyone in this remote area of northern Ontario. Don Plumridge, a charter plane pilot, would stop in at Wendell's place once and a while to check up on him. As Plumridge says, "Well, Wendell had cataracts in the last years and had stopped going to the ice hole in the lake for water in the winter." Adding that he feared that Beckwith would have an accident walking around Whitewater Lake and might fall through the ice. "Despite his age," the pilot added, "Beckwith always seemed to have a 'youthful inquisitiveness' about him. He always had a 'wonderment' about him. He always wanted to know about you and what you did, not really talking about what he did."

The Thunder Bay Historical Museum Society was the beneficiary of most of Wendell's artifacts and research. Scientists who have examined the material, which I heard in a radio interview, claim that they have had a great deal of trouble deciphering Wendell's notes. In 1983, Wendell's wife sent a letter to the Ontario Ministry of Citizenship and Culture asking that copies of his work be sent to his children. "He never wrote to them," she said, "so they don't even have a letter. It is almost as if he disappeared from their lives." However, according to Arlene Slipperjack, Wendell's children had come to visit him quite often despite his wife's claims. She also added that it was quite a shame that the cabins had fallen into such disrepair. "Maybe ten or twelve years ago we could have kept up the cabins, but were forbidden from doing so. My brothers and cousins built them. They could have been repaired easily, but the province doesn't want us to do anything. It's weird that they're not putting any money into it, just letting it all fall down."

According to pilot Plumridge, "perhaps it was the way Beckwith wanted it after all. I don't think he would have minded letting the buildings go back to nature. In fact, I think he would have been upset to see people trying to rebuild and replace it. It wouldn't be the same."

Lessons Learned

As with many people who travelled around the Whitewater Lake area in the mid-1970s I have my own memories of Wendell Beckwith. He had his quirky ways, but we can all say that he was a friendly fellow, to say the least. As I mentioned before, for whatever reason, various eccentric people have ended up in northern Ontario. Maybe they go there because local people have some sympathy for the oddballs of life, or maybe they can attract attention in ways that are not possible in the southern urban centers. In any event, I never heard of anyone of these so-called hermits who had made the impact that Wendell did. He was also a charming man, always ready with a smile, and a giggle. As far as his scientific research was concerned, it is difficult for me to say, and so I will leave this topic for the experts. As far as I am able to determine, even to this day, there has never been a report made of his scientific findings, even though experts have examined his research materials.

I have a background, not very extensive to be sure, in differential calculus. Wendell did let me examine his notes on several occasions but I hardly knew even where to begin—"All Greek to me," as the saying goes. We were all sorry to hear about the way Wendell was treated in his later years. It must have been hard living in the wilds of Whitewater Lake with the -60°tempratures, all alone, with the howl of the wind and wolves as your only friends, and no way of communicating with his fellow man. As mentioned, though, probably this was the way he wanted it, while this was not the everyday life for most of us.

Conclusion

During their ethnographic research anthropologists occasionally encounter people such as Wendell Beckwith who are, one might say, in and out of their own culture at the same time. Wendell became an endearing person to the Anishinaabe people of Whitewater Lake because without their help it was obvious that he would not survive very long. The Slipperjack family whose trap line was situated in this area helped Wendell build his cabins and donated leather crafts and artifacts to his make-shift museum.

As far as my own research was concerned, Wendell was a valuable source of information because he had interactions with Indigenous people in the area that others did not have. He was an endearing person in many ways, first because of his apparent helplessness, but also because of his enigmatic theories on so many topics. I was glad to have known Wendell Beckwith for the short period of time that I was conducting research in the Whitewater Lake area because he was able to give me insights into the area that I would otherwise not have access to, especially in terms of his interrelationships with the Anishinaabe people of northern Ontario.

Many of the people like Wendell often are unable to cope in 'mainstream' society —for a variety of possible reasons. But, they find refuge and eventually friends and family in First Nations communities, communities that are often more accepting of eccentric people, including those with various disabilities than, say, cities such as Toronto, Vancouver, or maybe even Thunder Bay. This is less about them trying to bring attention to themselves and more about finding a caring community that will accept their differences, which are sometimes mental, physical, or even legal. Wendell Beckwith died of a heart attack on his beloved island in 1980 at age 65. The account that I was told when I was up at Whitewater Lake, which I cannot verify one way or another, is that he was having an argument with some Ministry of Natural Resources officials about the fate of his cabins. The quarrel became heated, I was told, so Wendell took a breather from the controversy and went down to his dock to get some fresh air and it was there that he died. He was a man who loved his solitude and distained human conflict. It is doubtful that northern Ontario will ever see the likes of Wendell Beckwith again.

Chapter Six
Emotional Experience in Fieldwork

Experience is not what happens to a man. It is what a man does with what happens to him.

Aldous Huxley, *Texts and Pretexts* (1932)

As scientific understanding has grown, so our world has become dehumanized. Man feels himself isolated in the cosmos, because he is no longer involved in nature and has lost his emotion 'unconscious identity' with natural phenomenon.

Carl Jung, *Man and His Symbols* (1964: 85)

Human beings are complex creatures. The number of identifiable emotions that one can experience is so varied as to defy definition and calculation, ranging from anger and anxiety on one side to xenophobia on the other, with hundreds in-between. Emotional experiences may pose a problem for community-based researchers, especially those who are prone to think of themselves as social scientists with objective, value-free methodologies. It is an interesting facet of anthropological research that so little attention has been given to the role of emotional experiences in fieldwork.[46]

The fact of the matter is that long term fieldwork is apt to evoke a variety of responses, both emotional and otherwise, emanating from the community members with whom one is immersed. To deny or ignore these responses is to also disregard an important source of information. After all, if we are a community-based researcher and we feel sorrow, for example, there is a reason for this response that should be examined if for no other reason than these responses allow us to get to know ourselves better. Is there something in our own background that elicits certain emotional responses or does the source emanate from the community members themselves?

Examining emotional experience in anthropological fieldwork could be seen as an example of what now is being called 'autoethnography'. Autoethnography can be defined as "an ethnographic method in which the ethnographer attempts to understand another culture through a description and analysis of their own fieldwork experience" (Ferraro, Andreatta, and Holdsworth 2018: 113). This approach changes the focus of research, at least for the time being, on ethnographers themselves, rather than on community members. As Ferraro et al. explain, "the purpose of doing so is to gain insights into the culture being studied as well as the influence of one's own emotions on the conduct of fieldwork and the generation of anthropological knowledge" (2018: 113). In addition, the written account of this experience often takes the form of a narrative which describes the events that the ethnographer experiences and an analysis of what this experiences means, which is to say, the impact that experiences have on researchers themselves (Ellis 1991; Ellis and Bochner 2000).

This chapter focuses on the emotional responses that I experienced during the course of my fieldwork when a young man of the Collins community named Elijah Yellowhead was killed when he was hit by a train. As it happens, I knew Elijah long before I ever began my fieldwork since we were both tree planters working for a company from Thunder Bay when I was still an undergraduate student at Lakehead University. In other words, Elijah was not just an 'informant' in the community but also a personal friend of mine. When the time came for his funeral, I felt a number of ambivalent emotions. For one thing, I felt that our prior friendship removed him from the manner in which I would deal with other people in the community. On this basis, I did not want to engage in his funeral as a research opportunity and so did not attend it. This was an example, as I thought about it more, when research opportunities and personal relationships should be kept separate. Not everyone would necessarily agree with my interpretation, but at the time this made sense to me.

Fieldwork Experience and Epistemology

The term 'epistemological relativism' can be defined as "the doctrine that all knowledge is relative, context dependent, situated, and culturally constructed" (Sidky 2004: 424). It also concerns the nature and sources of human knowledge; the manner in which people gain understanding through their various experiences in life. Of course there is a cultural basis for gaining knowledge since what one already knows, or thinks they know, has a determining effect on the manner in which new knowledge is interpreted and stored. In the view of most anthropologists, at least, there is no absolute, totally objective view of reality. Everything that we see and everything that happens to us in life is experienced through a shroud of linguistic, social and cultural lenses.

Even from the viewpoint of science, knowledge is regarded as tentative and provisionally accepted. In this light, objectivity is understood to occur in relationship to human experience, which implies certain variabilities in the manner in which the universe is seen to operate as to its underlying principles. One of the problems with fieldwork, then, concerns the fact that we never seem to have as much control over what is going on around us as we would sometimes wish. Human beings can be contradictory; occasionally acting unreasonably, or in irrational ways.

To use the words of Margaret Mead, which sum up the point that I am attempting to make here about experience as an epistemological factor in fieldwork, "The fieldworker is wholly and helplessly dependent on what happens…one must be continually prepared for anything, everything—and perhaps most devastating—for nothing" (1975: 25). During my fieldwork in the Anishinaabe community of Collins there was not much that happened which I did not find interesting in one manner or another. This does not mean that I tried to force all my experience into the mold of my dominant political-economic research theme, but I contemplated situations long enough in my mind to see if I could take advantage of them in some way for my research purposes. I never forgot that I needed material, as Mead reminds us, otherwise we would unfortunately have nothing to say and our field trip would be wasted along with the funds that were required to send us there.

As such, fieldworkers need particular events and situations so that they can be studied, analyzed, and placed in a larger context. As Hortense Powdermaker has explained, ethnographers "write out of their immersion and participation in a particular situation...the particular illuminates the human condition" (1966: 296). On occasion, these 'particulars' come to us, unannounced, on our doorstep, but mostly, we have to go out and seek them, to reach out, even though we might feel shy or retiring. I now believe that I have some understanding of what Clifford Geertz meant when he talked about ethnography becoming 'imprisoned in the immediacy of its own detail' (1973: 24). In social anthropology, there are many grand theories attempting to explain human behavior and interaction, but 'on the ground level' of everyday life we can only perceive the particulars, the details, of people's activities and the manner in which they live their lives in various social and cultural contexts of existence.

Geertz's idea of ethnography becoming 'imprisoned' suggests that it is almost as if time becomes crystallized at certain points in our fieldwork journey, such that some events attain added meaning or significance because they stand out in such sharp relief to the other mundane situations that happen in the ordinary course of everyday life. It is only with the aid of hindsight that we learn from our experiences in fieldwork, however a certain period of reflection is necessary at times to consider the direction our fieldwork is heading and what we should be doing to keep it on track. The people, places, and things within which we become 'encased', or 'imprisoned' in Geertz's terms, are not often what we would have predicted or maybe even preferred.

We really have no choice but to play the ethnographic cards, as it were, that are dealt to us. It is up to us to make of them what we can. It is the everyday events, the everyday stuff of life—the details, background, and personalities—that fill out our life's experiences, imbue them with meaning, however, at times, obscure, and serve to propel us forward in time. Time does not stand still in our fieldwork, and it does not await our reflections and musing about what is happening. Everyday life goes on whether or not we can keep up with the pace of it or not, suggesting that the metaphor of being 'imprisoned' is somewhat misplaced. We are not shackled in any way, but forced to keep up a steady pace as time speeds along before our eyes. The time possible for introspection is necessarily short; it awaits a rare period of calm when we can collect our thoughts and try to place the occurrences in our lives, the at times chaotic turmoil of everyday happenings, in some kind of systematic order.

The course of everyday events allows the ethnographer only rare periods to engage in a certain amount of self-reflection. During these diurnal pauses, when we are capable of devoting thought to it, fieldwork is capable of facilitating an understanding of who we are as people and, in a wider sense, the cultural milieu that has spawned the ethnographer. Elvi Wittaker raised a similar point about this self-reflective endeavor: "What is particularly intriguing for them self-reflective researchers is experience, the turning inward, in order then to turn outward. They concentrate on the individuals, on person and on self" (1992: 191). Such a discussion of ethnography as a context for self-reflective introspection is also at the heart of our attempts to understand emotional experiences when conducting fieldwork.

An emotional experience is understood in the framework of other such feelings—attempts at understanding are virtually inseparable from the then, and now, as historian Joan Scott commented when she told us, "Experience is at once already an interpretation and in need of interpretation" (1991: 779). Emotional experiences, then, are what 'we feel', but they are also what we have learned to feel, as "an arbitrary imposition of meaning on the flow of memory," suggests Bruner (1986: 7). In this context, memory needs structure to organize our thoughts and feelings, and experience is the content that fills the void in memory's structural organization.

One could summarize, then, that there is a cultural and social context to emotional experiences in fieldwork that can become highly personalized, as lived experiences relate the 'personal to the cultural' (Denzen and Lincoln 2000: 931). As a methodological approach, Ellis explained that "Resurrecting introspection...as a systematic sociological technique will allow sociologists to examine emotion as a product of the individual processing of meaning as well as socially shared cognitions" (1991: 23). There is a question here, however, concerning how one examines or comprehends, emotional experience and then translates this comprehension into some meaningful form which is intelligible in a cross-cultural perspective. These 'socially shared cognitions' to which Ellis refers probably have some empirical validity within a particular culture, but one suspects that they would be difficult to identify across cultural boundaries.

Of course, this is not to say that there does not exist universal human emotional responses involving death, grief, or loss of loved ones; it is just that these responses are tempered, or contextualized, within specific cultural norms and values. Perhaps, then, this helps to explain my reticence about involving myself in the funeral process. I had not yet acquired that 'intimate familiarity within the group', to use Hanyano's (1979: 100) term and therefore felt uncomfortable about engaging in the emotional sharing that becoming involved in the funeral would have entailed. This sort of emotional sharing of a deeply felt experience was something that I was not prepared to deal with, even though my presence would probably have been accepted by those involved because of my long-term residence in the community. As such, it is not so much the length of time spent living in a community that prepares one for dealing with emotional experiences, it is more the capacity to sort out what are appropriate emotional responses in different settings, and a knowledge about what a suitable response should be in a proper manner.

When you think about it, appropriate responses are partly personal, in the sense of the experience acquired, and partly acquired through one's training as an ethnographer (see Bernard 2006; Robben and Sluka 2006). In this context, lessons learned during fieldwork are as much about ourselves as they are about answering our particular research questions. "In the end," Tanya Lurmann wisely suggests "the more you know about yourself, the way you learn, and the way those tendencies are distributed among human beings, the more wisely you will gauge the way your own experience will inform you about the experience of others and about what and how they learn. But it is always worthwhile to pay attention to your experience" (2010: 235).[47]

Another important question pertains to the reasons researchers are apt to under report the emotions that they experience during their fieldwork. Spencer and Davies (2010) suggest that one consideration is that emotions are often linked with irrationality, and so discussing such matters might tend to suggest a negative aspect to their research. They suggest though that denying one's emotions altogether does not necessarily lead to better research. "While the traditional empiricists asserted that methods essentially restrained sentiment," they commented, "they were less ready to admit that these very same methods could *evoke emotions of a different order* emphasis in orig." (2010: 8).

The suggestion, then, is that the methods used in fieldwork cannot function independently from the persons who employ them. In Spencer and Davies' (2010) study, they argue that emotions are not antithetical to thought or reason, but could, instead, be a source of untapped sources of insights that can complement more traditional methods of anthropological research. Similarly, works such as Jean-Guy Goulet and Bruce Miller (2007) show how 'extraordinary' field experiences, such as visons, dreams, and illusions can be epistemologically informative. And in another instance, Lynne Hume and Jane Mulcock's (2004) volume shows with impressive clarity how ethnographic discomfort and awkwardness can also be sources of insight and revelation. In addition, Ruth Behr (1996) and Gina Ulysse (2002) demonstrate the manner in which experience-based fieldwork narratives give credence to the emotions and experiences that inform understanding.

In another related study, Helena Nassif asks the question "How is 'the field' shaped by the emotional" (2017: 49). In this paper, she explores how the impact of emotions, especially fearful experiences, are reflected on both the research and the researcher in Egypt. As she states further, "I start from my fieldwork experience of living through complex emotions, the most imposing and visceral of which was fear, to discern its effects on my ethnography. I contend that there is an analytical value to attending the rarely reported and investigated fear of the ethnographer in the field. Emotions are not only useful but also necessary to generating a complex understanding of the empirical experience" (2017: 50; see also Hage 2009; Jamar and Chappuis 2016). Fieldworkers also occasionally suffer from panic attacks. As Ashleigh McKinzie describes in her essay on the topic of fieldwork emotions and the influence on research, "Panic was a new friend who didn't go away. I would panic over panicking and then panic over the quality of data I was collecting…I had these racing thoughts despite good news about my accomplishments" (2017: 492). It is evident, then, that the topic of emotional issues in ethnographic fieldwork is a growing field of considerable scholarly interest in anthropology and a variety of other associated disciplines.[48]

Reflexivity and Emotional Experience

The emotional aspects of fieldwork begin almost immediately. Sometimes the experience is described as 'culture shock',[49] which really involves two sets of feelings. On the one hand, there is the feeling of disassociation—of experiencing a notion of being disconnected from one's own culture and all that is familiar. There is almost the realization that one has to begin operating in a cultural domain in which one is unfamiliar with the behavioral norms and expectations. Jean Briggs, in an account of her research experiences among a small group of Inuit, attempts to describe her initial experience when conducting fieldwork in the Canadian Arctic whom she first met by being flown to their camp in a single engine plane that the government chartered to service the remote camps and villages of the north:

It was only as the hum of the motor faded into the snow-heavy clouds that I fully realized where I was. Realization came in the form of a peculiar sense not of loneliness but of separateness, of having no context for my experience...no bond of language, of understanding, or of shared experience linked me with the silent Eskimo behind me (1970: 23).

As such, building on several related themes discussed above in the academic literature on emotional experience in anthropology, this chapter explores the experiential aspects of ethnographic fieldwork, especially in terms of the fieldworker's emotional responses to the hardships faced by local people in the anthropologist's research community. An ethnographic example is discussed concerning fieldwork in a northern Canadian Indigenous village that evoked an intense emotional reaction to the incident described in the following pages. Then, an exploration is explored in the context of the epistemological implications of emotional experience in qualitative research. The learning experience that resulted from this exploration is that introspection is a necessary yet understudied component of exploring subjectivity in ethnographic fieldwork. As Ulin (1984: xi) cogently suggests, "Fieldwork or participant observation has led many anthropologists to struggle with epistemological problems related to understanding other cultures as part of a dialectical process of self-understanding."

The focus on this chapter is based on my fieldwork in northern Ontario in an Anishinaabe community in which a young man, Elijah Yellowhead, was killed by a Canadian National Railway passenger train. Elijah was a friend of mine even before this fieldwork as we had worked together in the Thunder Bay area while I was still an undergraduate student at Lakehead University. When I started my fieldwork in Collins, we subsequently renewed our friendship. This sorrowful experience filled me with feelings of intense sadness and remorse but my academic training left me largely unprepared to deal with the emotional consequences of this event. At the time of Elijah's death, I was emotionally torn between attending his funeral and gathering ethnographic data, or not attending to respect the family's privacy in a sensitive situation even though I was probably expected to attend the church service because of our friendship.[50]

Eventually, after much introspection and soul-searching, I decided that not to attend was a methodological or ethical issue in fieldwork. When I reflected on the incident further, I came to realize that one source of my reticence was my lack of control over events and how the emotional conflict that I experienced influenced my research. My lesson learned in this incident is that a study of our inner, emotional selves should become a necessary aspect of our methodological inquiry. Such emotional introspection is also apt to reveal much about how emotional states influence the researcher's ability to process information in the field (Hedican 2006).

The main thesis argued in this chapter is that emotional work is part of the epistemology of ethnographic methods. Since epistemology has to do with the creation of knowledge, then it needs to be understood that emotional experience is not only a state of being but also a process by which knowledge is a product of our processing of information as individuals. In the social sciences, there is a tendency to focus only on overt behavior, as if this were the only significant aspect of the research endeavor. The suggestion in this chapter is that an examination of our inner experiences, especially in terms of our attempts at emotional introspection, is an equally important aspect of anthropological enquiry.

Perhaps a study of one's emotional experience has been a neglected or understudied phenomenon in ethnographic methodology because of its complex and sometimes ambiguous nature. As human beings, the fieldworker in ethnographic research is a feeling, self-examining individual, yet it is difficult at times to decide what we feel, especially when conflicting and ambiguous emotions 'flood over us'. As several more recent ethnographic studies suggest, a study of our inner emotional selves should become a necessary aspect of anthropology's research methodology. The reason for this suggestion is that such emotional introspection is apt to reveal much about how emotional states influence the researcher's processing of information in the field. In turn, we could also learn more about how we process meaning during the course of our anthropological studies, thus adding to our understanding concerning the epistemological process of knowledge acquisition itself.

There is no doubt that the study of emotional experience is difficult work, as are most attempts to gain a measure of self-awareness. Most of us are trained to be detached, objective observers. We may be told as graduate students that such techniques as participant-observer is difficult to describe because one is only partly an observer, and, in turn, only partly a participant. We are not allowed to become full participants in another society for fear that we will lose our objectivity. Overt behavior is seen as all that matters, whereas a person's inner experience is either ignored all together, or regarded as not particularly significant.

One of the purposes of this chapter, then, is to suggest that from my own experience as a fieldworker that the study of emotions be brought into the anthropological study of behavior, along with other social, economic, and political research considerations. One of the problems is that we currently lack the methodological techniques to study feelings, especially in terms of any depth. Perhaps the reason for this lacuna is that we tend to regard ourselves as social scientists, with an emphasis on the objective, readily observable aspects of behavior. The Durkheimian approach, whereby one seeks 'social facts', The first and most fundamental rule is: *Consider social facts as things* (1938 1895: 14) is apt to lead one away from a search for the richness of subjective experiences that are involved in ethnographic research if only they were sought.[51] Researchers are not just situated on the margins of the community life that is studied; they are also an integral component of the knowledge that is gained and processed. As such, the researcher's inner experience of this endeavor is a salient facet of how it is that we come to understand understandings not our own, to paraphrase Clifford Geertz (1973).

Experiencing Our Everyday Lives

As a social science, anthropology is unique in many regards but one of the most important of these are the relationships that one forms with the members of the adopted community in which one lives. The experience of living day in and day out, of experiencing the everyday lives of peoples who usually live in isolated, remote places, and the bonds that are formed with our so-called 'informants' (people who provide information to the anthropologist who is conducting field research), is rarely one shared with the member of other academic disciplines. It does not take long for one to forsake the idea of community members as objects of study in an objective sense. Anthropologists form bonds with the other people among whom he or she lives, and important aspect of these bonds are the shared emotional experiences that develop over the course of time.

Elijah Yellowhead was a young man with whom I had developed a friendship with long before my anthropological training. I remember him as a shy man, with long stringy black hair who looked away when you spoke to him. As such, I already knew Elijah, and several other young fellows when I started to conduct my research in northern Ontario and I believe that we all trusted one another in a way that social bonds are formed among those in the same work environment, especially if there are some hardships involved. You begin to admire the other persons in your work crews for their endurance and for a shared sense of mutual stamina. It was for this reason that Elijah's death affected me in a very profound way, yet my academic training left me largely unprepared to deal with the emotional consequences of such an event.

In terms of the existing scholarly literature in the area of contemporary ethnography, various authors have shown a considerable concern with the personal experiential aspects of qualitative research. One of the characteristics of this literature in particular is that a multiplicity of terms has been used to describe this phenomenon, such as reflexive ethnography, autoethnography, or personal narrative (Davies 1999; Davies and Spencer 2010; Ellis and Bochner 2000; Hedican 2001, 2006; Macbeth 2001; and Reed-Danahay 1997). Taken as a whole this body of research demonstrates that the ethnographer's experience has become a matter of particular interest across a variety of academic disciplines, in particular, anthropology, sociology, and psychology.

Although it might be concluded that descriptions of the various dimensions of the field research experience have become more plentiful over the last several decades, an analysis of the core aspects underlying and shaping researchers' experiences have only begun to receive specific attention. Furthermore, it is an interesting matter that despite the importance of the role of experience in fieldwork, there nonetheless is a dearth of critical or analytical discussions of it in the literature, aside from the various descriptive accounts of this phenomenon. This would suggest that the importance of experience as an epistemological factor in qualitative research should be a matter of greater concern in the literature of fieldwork methodology. Of course we should also add that experiential aspects of fieldwork are furthermore an essential facet of the ethnographer's everyday life experiences during the course of community research.

Experiences in the conduct of ethnographic research comprise a complex and varied mixture of feelings and emotions, reactions, and personal demands so there is much to think about in everyday fieldwork, aside from our stated theoretical goals. These reflexive[52] understandings accumulate and are transformed over time the more they are thought about in the context of the continued social interaction with the people in the field of study. There is also the complex process of organizing the ethnographer's thoughts, putting them down on paper (or your laptop), rethinking them in the context of future events and situations, and then eventually drawing conclusions in the form of the final ethnographic account. As we work our way through this complex mix of thoughts and feelings we begin to realize that fieldwork is akin to psychoanalysis. By processing the events and experiences that our fieldwork entails, we also become more adept or capable at facilitating an understanding of who we are as a person. In addition, in a wider sense, we also become better able to assess the cultural milieu in which we work and live our lives.

It has been noted, for example, that "Fieldwork…has led many anthropologists to struggle with…our understanding of other cultures as part of a dialectical process of self-understanding" (Ulim 1984: xi). In turn, this observation is reinforced by Chiseri-Strater and Sunstein's comment that fieldwork makes us:

Consider your everyday experiences in new ways…but most of all helps you understand why you react and respond in the ways you do—based on your assumptions. It will encourage you not only to watch others but also to watch yourself as you watch them-consciously (1997: 2).

These comments tend to remind one (well, me at least) of R.D. Laing's cryptic and at times enigmatic treatise entitled *The Politics of Experience* (1967) in which he postulates that "We can see other people's behavior, but not their experience…I cannot experience your experience. You cannot experience my experience. We are both invisible men…The relation between experience and behavior is the stone that the builders will reject at their peril" (1967: 17–18).[53] Or, if one might paraphrase further, "I cannot experience you, and you cannot experience me. All we can do is experience each other experiencing ourselves." As such, if autoethnography describes studies and procedures that connect the personal to the cultural, then a noteworthy aspect of the introspection process that would serve to illuminate more fully the ethnographer's personal experience would be to focus on the emotive aspects of fieldwork. As Ellis has explained, "Systematic sociological introspection provides a way to look at the lived experience of emotions, but it requires that we...study our own emotions" (1991: 45).

Funeral for a Friend

It did not come as a complete surprise, but a shock nonetheless, when we had learned that Elijah had been struck by a passenger train and killed. A Thunder Bay newspaper carried an article of this tragedy and I remember reading that the accident has occurred in a rock cut. The engineer tried to stop the train as quickly as he could, but the railway cars would have skidded down the track for a considerable distance. When the engineer had finally halted the long length of railway cars, he then had to trudge back to the horrible scene and view the gruesome sight of Elijah's mangled body. It goes without saying that the passengers on the train were justifiably horrified to witness such a dreadful sight. The newspaper recounted that there was apparently a small group of men engaged in an overnight drinking party close to the railway tracks about half way between the villages of Armstrong and Collins.

Details of the incident in the newspaper story were quite sketchy which was not surprising considering the strong possibility that most of the men were probably inebriated and the night was partially dark. From one account, it was said that Elijah had wondered away from the group and was sitting on the railway tracks when the accident occurred. One would think that the sound of the oncoming train would be loud enough to arouse one even if intoxicated, but this is not always the case as there could have been a strong wind that night which might have masked the noise of the oncoming train. In any event, many moose whose hearing must be more acute than that possessed by humans are killed on the railway tracks every year. Apparently some even charge the train thinking that the locomotive might be an oncoming rival. In any event, a story began to circulate around Collins and Armstrong that the other members of the drinking party were old enemies of Elijah's family and that Elijah had been pushed out onto the tracks in retribution or retaliation for some past incident or familial grudge (none of these accusations were ever proven in court).

As appears to happen in such events in northern Ontario away from the more focused scrutiny of city life, there was not much of an investigation, certainly not enough evidence to charge any member of the party with a criminal offense, and in a few days there was hardly any mention of it. Curiously, even in Collins where I was conducting my fieldwork, I do not recall much of a call to action by his own family; there was more a sense of resignation to what had happened. When I was apt to ponder the reasons for this muted response, what came to mind was a stabbing involving Elijah and his sister-in-law. Elijah, who was in his mid-20s at the time, had never married. He lived in Collins with his married brother, Adam, in the home of Adam's wife, Harriet. Now you have to remember that these log cabins in the village usually consisted of only one room with people bumping into each other all the time, especially at night because there was no electricity.

From what I gathered at the time in terms of the village gossip, Harriet considered her brother in-law to be a bit of a 'lay about'. Granted, jobs in Collins were difficult to secure, even hunting around the village tended not to be very productive. As a result, marriage prospects for Elijah were rather slim, or none existent, all of which would have been a sore point for Harriet who had her own children to look after and on that account would have come to resent Elijah eating at their table and taking up sleeping space in her cabin. One could surmise, then, that Elijah would be considered on the periphery of the village social order.

There was an event which I still recollect today, when a knock on my cabin door revealed Elijah standing outside with his hand tucked behind him. At first, I paid no attention to this, but soon saw as he pulled his arm out in front of him a crudely bandaged hand soaked with blood. It was an ugly sight and my immediate thought was that this injury would surely become infected in short order. I grabbed him by the elbow, "Come in, quickly," I said. "Who did this to you?" I asked.

"Can't you guess," Elijah replied. "She came after me with a butcher knife, I stepped back to avoid the blow, but the knife struck me in the hand. I thought if I came to you that you wouldn't be blabbering this all over. I don't want any trouble about this, especially from the OPP in Armstrong," he said.

"Ok, let's have a look at the damage," I said. "Sit down here, on the bench," I instructed. First, I went over and lit my two burner gas stove and placed a sauce pan of water on it to heat. "Now, let's look," I said. Slowly I unwrapped the crudely bandaged hand. His hand was dirty, I noticed, and needed immediate attention but I had no antiseptics here. (Shouldn't all anthropologists carry a first aid kit into the field?) "I'll try my best," I told

Elijah, "but I don't have anything to stop the infections except to wash this wound," I said. After the water heated, I placed it in a wash basin. "It's pretty hot," I said, "but you need to soak your hand in hot water for a while. Just try to bear the heat, the hotter the better," I suggested.

Elijah began to place his hand in the water, but quickly withdrew it. "Ouch," he yelled, "this is way too hot."

"Ok, let's wait a bit, and then you can try again," I replied. After a few minutes, he tried again and gingerly placed his hand in the basin of hot water. "Keep it in there for ten minutes." I instructed, "then wash it with soap." His hand came out pretty clean, the bloody crusts had washed away, and so I began to bandage it up with strips of an old pillowcase I had. "Keep these other strips to replace the old ones when you can," I said.

"I heard you were a doctor," Elijah asked.

"I'm not a medical doctor, no, you're wrong there," I replied. I did not want to give the impression that I was available for medical treatment in the village—I'm no Paul Farmer, I thought. Soon after, Elijah was on his way. I thought of how easy it would be here to become infected with something. Access to hot water was difficult to obtain. Washing your hands was probably not a common practice. I knew many people in the village thought that white people were unduly obsessed with cleanliness.

Family Dynamics

As Elijah walked away from my cabin, I could see in a direct line of sight the small railway section house of his cousin, Mike Yellowhead, who was a relatively prosperous foreman for the CNR—what a contrast I thought, as Elijah made his way down the trail away from my cabin, between the two fellows. The Yellowhead family was one of the core centers of population in Collins. Its members originally came from Fort Hope on the Albany River and like so many others in this area, began to drift down toward the CNR line after World War II. Two brothers eventually settled in Collins. One, Joel (1908–1974), died in a house fire while I lived in Collins. He left two adult sons, Elijah and Adam, and four older daughters. The other brother was married to the former Alice Drake, who died the same year as her brother-in-law Joel. Alice had two sons, Mike and Luke, and a daughter, Sally.

As foreman of the CNR section crew, Mike was one of the most successful men in Collins. He drank a little but not too much. Remember my previous account when he ended up on my cabin floor one evening after his wife Nancy, a religious woman and regular attendee at the Anglican church, kicked him out one evening when he came home intoxicated. As I write this I began to wonder why people came to me occasionally when they were in some sort of trouble— "I need to think about this more," was my thought. Anthropologists are outsiders, yet members of the village nonetheless, and are apt to keep their mouths shut about gossip, maybe that was the answer, but the idea deserves more thought later.

Mike's position with the CNR makes him one of the most successful men in Collins. He commands considerable respect in the village, as he controls access to one of the only sources of full-time employment in the community. His income allows him a standard of living that is quite a bit above the norm, although the CNR house that he and his family live in is not particularly conspicuous. Of course everyone is aware of preventing jealously by others in the village. Mike's brother, Luke, in contrast to Mike's favorable position in community affairs, has led a troubled life. Luke has been plagued with psychological problems of undetermined origin, which led him to have all sorts of delusions, and has resulted on occasion with his placement in the Thunder Bay Psychiatric Hospital. Many people in the village fear him, thinking that he is possessed in some way with dangerous spirits.[54] When his mother (Alice) died, he lost his home base and has tended to just wander around the village late at night, which added to people's sense of apprehension.

Elijah, Luke's cousin, has shared a similar position on the periphery of the village social order. At the time of my fieldwork, Elijah was in his mid-20s, had never married, and lived as I mentioned with his married brother Adam, in the home of Adam's wife, Harriet Kwandibens. There was a constant state of trouble between Elijah and Harriet, which added, no doubt, to Elijah's sense of being an unwanted outsider, living as he did with his brother's in-laws. From Harriet's perspective, she would be expected to show a certain amount of civility toward her husband's brother, yet probably also felt resentful of Elijah's 'mooching' on their limited food supply and finances. On the other hand, Harriet's family, the Kwandibens, are also a fairly large family in Collins and Harriet's cousin, Peter works for the CNR. Nonetheless, Adam's situation in which he lives in his wife's house places him in a disadvantaged position since people would regard him as subservient to his wife and her family. As far as Elijah is concerned, his position as Adam's brother would place him in an even more underprivileged situation with regard to people's opinion of him.

The point here is that there are certain family dynamics involved in people's opinions of each other, in their patterns of interaction, and the social hierarchy of the village. From an anthropological position, these are all matters that would not be revealed except for a fairly long tenancy in the village—it takes time to learn all these various patterns of family connections which play such a significant role in residents' treatment of each other. Certainly I would say that it took me at least three months of residence in the village before I began to learn very much beyond the most insignificant and transitory details of village life. Of course, these patterns of interaction were the basis for most behavioral patterns in the village so a knowledge of the structure of family relations was a crucial aspect to understanding interaction patterns in Collins.

As time went on I began to see the Yellowhead family as somewhat typical of the large Indigenous (Anishinaabe) groupings that formed the core centers of population in places such as Collins. Such families have many diversified kinship links tying its members together and also provide a series of connections through marriage with other such 'clans' in the Collins area as well as 'back home' at Fort Hope. As with many such families in the northern bush country of Ontario, they have many unfortunate deaths at relatively early ages, caused by such accidents as house fires or other occurrences of suspected foul play or death 'by misadventure'.

In Elijah's case, details of his death were quite indeterminate. As mentioned previously, his death was apparently linked to a small group of men engaged in an overnight drinking party. One of the members of this party indicated that Elijah had left the group and was sitting on the railway tracks when the accident occurred. One wonders, if this was the case, why this observer did not do something to summon other members of the party to help remove Elijah from such a dangerous situation. The rumor circulating at the time that members of this drinking party were old enemies of the Yellowhead family and that Elijah had been pushed onto the tracks in retribution for some past grievance which then begs the question of what Elijah was doing with such a crowd in the first place.

Peter, the Métis storekeeper, had once told me that it was his theory that the numerous deaths on the railway tracks were really the result of a covert suicide cult. I thought this explanation a bit preposterous, however he went on with his explanation, "The diesel engine represents the power and destruction of the outside world over which the Anishinaabe have no control. As an act of defiance, they give themselves up to the monster, as they are not willing to live another day under its oppression." For those who might be familiar with the history of Indonesia, this story reminds me of the nobility of the island of Bali who, while being shot to death by the advancing Dutch soldiers, defiantly threw their jewels at their oppressors. In this light, Elijah was a courageous warrior, taking a stand against the indomitable Goliath. My first thought when hearing Peter's account was that I would doubt that other members of the Collins' community would agree with his interpretation.

Elijah's Homecoming

Peter and I waited for several nights in a row for Elijah's body to be returned by train to the Collins community. There was a lot of confusion concerning the whereabouts of Elijah's body, as we were not next of kin, and there was a rumor that Elijah's body had become mix-up with someone else at a funeral home in Thunder Bay. It took about a week, but eventually Elijah came home. I remember that it was a pitch black night. His casket was hurriedly hauled from the train and hoisted onto the men's shoulders, and a strange procession then wound its way through the trail in the bush leading away from the railway tracks. From a distance, it looked like a long snake carrying a box, with flashlights beaming this way and that as the casket was carried down to the Catholic church. There was no clergy in town, so the people conducted their own service, combining I was told both Christian and Anishinaabe spiritual elements, led by one of the village elders.

In my mind, I can still picture the eerie cavalcade of figures carrying Elijah's casket along the bush trail from the railway tracks. I can also remember my own feelings of ambivalence—the fieldworker part of me felt that I should get involved in the procession in some manner to gather information, whereas the side of me who was Elijah's friend felt that this was a solemn event and that the family's privacy should be respected in their time of grief. In fact, Peter, sensing my reticence about becoming involved in the procession, pushed me forward: "This might be your only chance to witness this sort of Native ceremony, what are you waiting for, if not to bear witness to such events?" he asked. I had no response to his urging. I felt the pull to move forward, but my feet would not carry me. As a result, I have spent many hours over the years reflecting on the meaning of this sense of ambivalence and what it meant to my fieldwork experience. The only answer that I have ever been able to come up with is that there are times when the research priorities of an anthropologist should take a back seat to the human tragedy occurring in one's midst.

There was something else that I needed to process, not so much as an anthropologist, but as a person whose friend has just died. It was almost as if this incident was one of those tests of judgment, or character, which was bound to occur sometime during one's research. As it was, Peter urged me at the most crucial moment to go along and attend the service, as if, as a leading member in the community, he was giving me permission to throw off my anthropological cloak and assume the role of an ordinary citizen of planet earth who is willing to show empathy to others in distress. Peter advised me to go forward because he nonetheless acknowledged what I knew in my heart, which was that I would lose the opportunity to learn something significant.

Later, when we had an opportunity to reflect on this episode in the following days, Peter pointed out to me that my main objection for not participating in the ceremony; namely, that I wanted to respect the Yellowhead family's privacy, was not well founded, as the people probably expected me, since I was both Elijah's friend as well as the ever-prying anthropologist, to attend the 'service' in any event. Peter also informed me that a (non-Aboriginal) New Zealand engineer, who was employed during the summer on the tourist lodge construction project, was also participating in the procession, crying and apparently caught up in the intense emotion of the event. As Peter also pointed out, nobody in the Yellowhead family ever censored him for his participation. When I asked Peter, in turn, why he did not attend the service, he replied that he was not a member of their family. However, this was not exactly true, since his wife Dorothy, and Mike Yellowhead's wife Nancy were sisters, making Peter a sort of in-law of the Yellowheads through his wife's family connections.

Even to this day, after reflecting on and off over numerous instances over the years since Elijah's burial, I still have not come to any firm conclusion on this matter of social propriety and involvement. When Elijah died, I was caught up in a personal dilemma about becoming involved in what I saw as essentially a private family mater, that is, Elijah's funeral should be left to his own family and their grieving process. I saw this partly as a moral or ethical issue in fieldwork, and partly as a methodological one concerning the participant-observer technique.

There is no doubt that I did not feel the same emotion as the New Zealand engineer, even though I had known Elijah for quite a few years longer. In retrospect, this is probably one of those classical fieldwork dilemmas, to get involved in the private affairs of informants or not. In this case, my main regret was that my reticence about getting involved in private matters got the better of me and prevented me from becoming involved in something that could have given me considerable private insight into the Collins community. This might seem odd to say, after all this forgoing discussion, but even after all these years if I had to do it all over again I am still not sure what I would do in this instance. In other words, reflecting on my ambivalence has really done nothing to resolve the issue of involvement in my mind.[55]

Lessons Learned

First of all, do not ignore your emotional experiences. Community-based researchers are not robots and if emotions are not recognized and dealt with they will surely rear their ugly head and cause trouble somewhere in the future. Second, it is all right to feel ambivalence about becoming involved in the social affairs of community members. We do not come equipped with a manual that instructs us on how to behave in all situations. We have to use our own better judgement, and hope for the best. Experience in these matters may help, but not necessarily so. Each situation tends to be unique in its own right, and the circumstance of situations changes with time and the social changes occurring in the community.

It is these sorts of experiences gained during the course of fieldwork that would suggest the subtle nature of gaining information. Learning and applying a kit bag of research techniques is one matter, but under the surface there is a myriad of ethical and methodological issues that have a propensity to emerge quite unexpectedly in day-to-day events that require a thorough thinking through. In my mind, these issues are important ones, not only at a personal level but also in terms of the broader sphere of the 'philosophy of science' and the methodological context of information management, use, and control.

Ultimately, there are probably no right and wrong answers to the various ethical and personal matters that emerge in anthropological fieldwork. Nonetheless, we still have to make decisions and hope that under the circumstance they are the ones that will cause the least harm. Sometimes we are best left to observe, and at other times participation is called for, but there are no hard and fast rules that will guide us in any given circumstance except for time-honored common sense.

And finally, as most ethnographers are probably aware, we never seem to have as much control over what is going on around us as we would sometimes prefer. With certain methodologies, such as structured interviews which I suspect most anthropologists would hardly use in their fieldwork, there would at least be the appearance of some measure of control, but when it comes to most of the research techniques available to the ethnographer, such as participant observation, we are forced for the most part to go along with the flow of events around us. In the end, a lesson that is hopefully learned is that fieldwork is largely a matter of how much we would like to shape events to suite our objectives, and how much we are willing to let events shape us, for if we are to live and learn in our discipline it is necessary to loosen up on the reins and let our experiences mold us in certain unanticipated ways.

Conclusion

One of the main conclusions that one could make in this chapter is that introspection, as a conscious attempt to understand our awareness through self-examination, could be made more explicit or systematic as a sociological technique, alongside such favorites as participant observation. Neglecting to examine our emotions, from an epistemological point of view, is almost certainly a grave error. If the pretense is made to understand the depth of social "reality," then it is necessary to know more about how the social and private inner experiences of the researcher affect the interpretation of human behavior, how emotions are processed in fieldwork, and what sorts of emotions are felt by a person conducting a field of study. Of course, there is a wide range of emotions possible to just about any situation, so identifying which ones we should identify for further introspections is not always an easy matter.

It would be useful to read about other ethnographer's struggles with dealing with emotional experience, as a process of self-dialogue and as a process of the living experience of emotions. Emotions are not just disembodied feelings that other human beings have; they are feelings that we share or hold in common with others. If one attempts to hide their reactions to fieldwork situations under the guise of 'scientific techniques', then there are certainly some problems here when using one's self as a subject of study, such as attempting to eliminate bias or overgeneralizing on the basis of the researcher's experience. Nonetheless, self-introspection has the potential to give us knowledge about the research endeavor that can be gained in no other way, through an examination of the manner in which we react to situations and the people around us.

In this chapter, I have attempted to relate an ethnographic account of the death of a young Anishinaabe man in a relatively isolated northern Canadian community and have endeavored to assess my emotional response to this distressing and tragic episode. From my analysis of this incident, an argument emerges that emotional responses in ethnographic fieldwork tends to involve some very complex epistemological issues that should be more adequately addressed in anthropological research.

One of these issues involves a feeling of ambiguity in certain fieldwork situations and how to respond appropriately to them. From my own personal perspective, I would suggest that our training in university methods classes does not provide sufficient sensitivity to circumstances in which there is an ethical or moral dilemma. Of course, we cannot expect hard and fast guidelines for all fieldwork situations since much of our knowledge is gained through experience. On the topic of experience, and its role in research, there are a few aphorisms that would appear useful, such as Socrates' view that "the unexamined life is not worth living," anthropologist Irving Hallowell's view that "human experience...must be thoroughly explored in all their ramifications and given more explicit formulation" (1955: viii) and Henry Ford's well-known view that "experience is not only the best teacher, it is the only teacher."

Thus, the experience that I remember most about Elijah's tragic death, in my own personal case, is of course losing a friend but also the intense conflict that I felt between the desire to gather information regardless of the sensitivity of the situation, on the one hand, and my feelings of empathy with the grieving village residents on the other. It is possible that other fieldworkers might have handled this situation differently than I did and not seen in it the ambiguity that

I perceived. They might also conceivably choose a different tactic to gather information, such as not becoming directly involved but staying more aloof from the community pain that was swirling around them, and interviewing participants afterward.

One can understand the rationale for taking this stance, thinking that they were there to do a job, which is to say, providing an objective view of community events. Becoming emotionally involved with the village residents and their problems in life might only hinder their efforts. One could therefore conclude that discussions of such sensitive subjects and a sharing of introspective accounts of emotional experiences in fieldwork can only serve to deepen our understanding of important methodological and epistemological issues in ethnographic research. In all, anthropology can only benefit from such efforts in the long term. My hope is that a discussion of this incident, and my emotional reaction to it, will further initiate dialogue on this perplexing matter of responding to grief and personal introspection in anthropological fieldwork.

Chapter Seven
The Anthropologist as
Land Claims Facilitator

Armstrong is a small town about 30 kilometers east of Collins on the CN rail line consisting of about 200 permanent residents, but growing during the summer tourist season to sometimes two times this population. There are also about 400 residents of the Whitesand First Nation reserve nearby. There is a main street through Armstrong comprising various businesses, such as the King George Hotel, colloquially known as the K-G. I stayed there once during the 1980s in a room situated over the raucous bar below which kept me awake for most of the night. The very first thing that I saw when I opened the door was a water heated radiator with a stout coil of rope attached to its' base. As I looked out the window I realized that this was the fire escape, meaning that in the case of fire one was expected to fling the rope out of the second story window and climb down. I wondered how many people would be capable of the athleticism required of this feat—not many I presumed, especially those in an inebriated state.

There is also a large (for the size of the town) Ontario Provincial Police (OPP) detachment on the main street, which I noticed was kept rather busy, especially in the summer. At the other end of the main street opposite the K-G was an abandoned American NORAD (North American Aerospace Defense Command) base, a relic of the 1950's nuclear paranoia. The buildings were all that was left of the base, which was converted into a motel, gas station, and restaurant, all closed in 1993. There was a windshield-shattering gravel road, now since paved, leading out of town, traversing a spruce treed wilderness of about 230 kilometers (145 miles) on Highway 527 to Thunder Bay. Just on the edge of town were several businesses catering to the fly-in fishing crowd, comprising mostly Americans from the upper Great Lakes such as Chicago and Milwaukee. My opinion of the Armstrong population was that it was a rough-and-tumble crowd of bush hardened people. I suspect that most of the town's population would not be averse to this description.

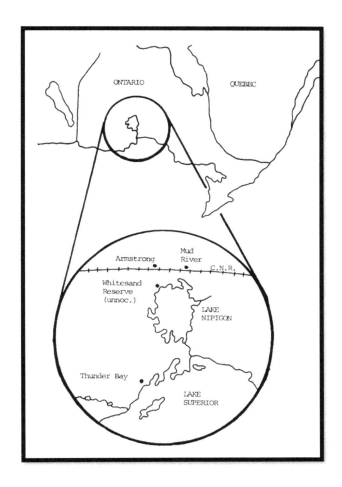

Location of the Whitesand Area

Getting Started

Not long after I was hired by the University of Guelph I was asked to join a committee called the Rural Development Outreach Program (RDOP) comprising professors from the across the various disciplines in the university. RDOP had recently completed a project in the James Bay area called the 'Moose Factory Servicing Project' which involved installing a water treatment plant for the hospital on Moose Factory Island. Then, shortly after my arrival, the Department of Indian Affairs in Thunder Bay asked RDOP if they had anyone on its committee who would be willing to assist in facilitating an Indigenous resettlement program in the Armstrong area pertaining to the Whitesand Band.

"That's your area, isn't it, Ed?" asked one of the members. "Know anything about the Whitesand Band?"

"Sure," I replied, "I just came back from the Armstrong area and heard that band members were trying to consolidate their population and move to a new reserve," I explained.

"Well, I guess you're our man then, do you want to get involved?" the RDOP Director asked, "we'll pay your expenses and buy you out of two of your courses, can you start this summer?" he asked.

"Two of our RDOP members will join you. You will work with the band Chief and other members of the band council in an attempt to reach a decision about which area they want to locate to; apparently there are several options," Tony, the Director, explained.

The original parameters of my role were set out as follows:

1. Assist the band council in determining band priorities;
2. Assist the band council in accessing information and developing skills;
3. Assist the band council and band membership to build greater self-reliance and self-determination through which their need for assistance would progressively diminish;
4. Evaluate the role of an independent community assistance agent in the process of building band self-determination.

As this project began to evolve, I soon found out that there were multiple parties involved, each with their own goals and objectives. In other words, this was not all just a matter of RDOP helping to choose a site in the Armstrong area for a new reserve. Little did we know at the time that Indian Affairs personnel in Thunder Bay had hired a consulting firm, without any consultation and then discussion with the Whitesand Band council, whose objectives were divergent in some important respects from the band council itself. When I started to assess the situation, I began to realize that my role was not simply to assist the band council in their decision-making, but also to coordinate their response, and develop a strategy, in relationship to the other parties involved.

When one attempted to look at the project as a whole, these various parties were the University of Guelph's RDOP committee and several of their personnel who were assigned to the project (a professor and graduate student from the Geography department), the Department of Indian Affairs in Thunder Bay, members of an external consulting firm, as well as myself. Upon arriving in Armstrong, it also became evident that a major player in the decision-making had not even been initially considered, which was the local branch of the Ministry of Natural resources. Personnel from this Ministry set out the alternatives for the site locations from which the Band were allowed to choose.

Thus, as it turned out, RDOP's attempt to fulfill their objectives (listed above) were greatly influence by a number of unanticipated or unforeseen factors, not the least of which was a tendency for conflicts to emerge when things appeared to be going well. In other words, it did not take me long to realize that the resolution of possible conflict among all the parties involved was a major pre-condition for the achievement for the wider objectives concerning Whitesand community development. This meant that RDOP, and consequently myself, was frequently called upon to act in an intermediary capacity in an attempt to reconcile the diverse objectives of the different parties involved. This was not, then, a coordinated effort to achieve one goal, but a matter of different parties with their own goals and objectives, some of which were at odds with those of the other parties.

Historical Background

Ever since the departure of the last ice age there have been three major river systems draining eastern North America. One of these, the Mississippi River, empties into the Gulf of Mexico, and another, the St. Lawrence system, drains the Great Lakes into the Atlantic Ocean. In northern Ontario, the Albany River drains into James Bay in a west to east direction. Travelling inland by canoe from Fort Albany, one paddles directly west until reaching the Ogoki River which sharply turns directly south and then into the north end of Lake Nipigon, the tenth largest fresh water lake in the world, at Ombabika Bay. From there, the route leads one across Lake Nipigon into the Nipigon River, and from there arriving at the town of Nipigon, touted to be the most northerly point on Lake Superior, and hence, into the Ottawa and St. Lawrence Rivers.

All of these routes were no doubt well known to the Indigenous people of the continent who passed this information along to the early European explorers and fur traders. So, when the Hudson's Bay Company, founded in 1670, began to build its factories as they were called on Hudson and James Bay its directors used this information to plot the location of possible interior posts. By 1682, the English had built four of these factories on the Nelson, Albany, Moose and Rupert Rivers which drew most of the fur trade wealth to the Hudson and James Bay coasts from the interior Anishinaabe and Cree. However, there were fur trade merchants situated in Montreal and Quebec City who were eyeing this trade wealth as well. Travelling up the St. Lawrence, then into Lake Superior, they made their way into Lake Nipigon, which had become the nexus of travel connecting James Bay to the St. Lawrence River. It was on the shores of this lake that the Quebec merchants attempted to circumvent trade from the interior of North America to Hudson and James Bay.

Fort Nipigon, situated at the south end of the Nipigon River that empties into Lake Superior, was the first of these posts, built in1679, and at the north end of Lake Nipigon, Nipigon House was constructed in 1792. Thus, the merchants from Quebec effectively controlled the north-south fur trade traffic from Fort Albany to Lake Superior. Farther down the coast of Lake Superior, at a place called the Grand Portage (now Thunder Bay) Fort Kaministikwia was built in 1679 to circumvent the western trade into the Lake of the Woods area. In a counter move, the Hudson's Bay Company was forced to build costlier posts in the interior, as trade to the coastal posts was beginning to dwindle.

By the early 1800s, prospectors began to move into the Canadian Shield north of Lake Superior. Violence erupted at a mining site in the 1840s near Sault St. Marie, which precipitated negotiations for a treaty in the area. Eventually, in 1850, a major treaty, the Robinson-Superior Treaty, was signed with the Indigenous occupants which encompassed all lands draining into Lake Superior from the Height of Land, just to the north of Lake Nipigon. The Robinson-Superior Treaty, along with the Robinson-Huron Treaty also of 1850, set a precedent for future negotiations such that subsequent treaties involved relatively large tracts of surrendered land, annuity payments, the establishment of reserves, and usually, a reference to hunting and fishing rights for the Indigenous inhabitants (Hedican 2013: 61–65). As we can well imagine, the Cree and Anishinaabe peoples of the Lake Nipigon area from the early fur trade on played a pivotal role because of their central position in influencing the fur trade of northern Ontario.[56]

The Whitesand Band

The Whitesand Band of Anishinaabe people in northern Ontario has waited a long time for a plot of land to call their own. Even though it had been over 130 years since the Whitesand people signed the Robinson-Treaty of 1850 with the British colonial government, whose responsibility had been taken over by the Canadian Government at the time of Confederation in 1867, band members were still negotiating on and off for a reserve on which to live for over a century. Pulp and paper companies, usually owned by American and British interests, the Canadian National Railway, and a multitude of tourist operators now owned or held long term leases on most of the available land formerly occupied by Whitesand people. In this case, the Anishinaabes' ability to make sound plans for the future were severely restricted by a decreasing opportunity to participate in the economic and social growth of the region.

By the early 1980s, Whitesand Band members were beginning to adopt a sense of urgency with the emergence of a new, younger generation who were more politically active than their parents and grandparents had been. Part of this political emergence was due to their skills in the English language that previous generations did not possess, as well as a general understanding of Canadian society. In addition, many members of the Whitesand Band were now engaged in wage employment, mainly for the CN railway and as guides for tourist operators, rather than as trappers which was characteristic of the previous generation.

This younger generation was also able to see that as the years went by they would have less opportunity to choose a reserve site that was suitable for them because of the rapid growth of governmental and resource company interests of the area during the previous decades. They also perceived that Whitesand Band members would have less good land to choose from each year, motivating band members to attempt a settlement with the government as soon as was expediously possible. All of these factors stimulated a sense of confidence among band members that they could now pursue their goal of obtaining from the Canadian Government a new reserve location on which to settle.

The Whitesand First Nation

Older Cabins

Newer Housing

There were others among the Whitesand Band population, comprised of more elderly members, who were suspicious of making hasty decisions feeling that if hurried decisions were made then only outsiders would gain. Given the consequences for future generations of Whitesand Band members, they argued, more time should be spent on thoroughly assessing any government offer. To complicate matters, conflicts began to emerge between a consulting firm that had been hired by the Indian Affairs office in Thunder Bay and band members over which potential sites for the new reserve could reasonably provide the means to earn an adequate living.

The people now known as the Whitesand Band were not always called by that name. When the Robinson-Superior Treaty was signed in 1850, all of the Indigenous people around Lake Nipigon were grouped together under the rubric 'Nipigon Band', and only one reserve was established at that time (Gull Bay, on the west coast of Lake Nipigon). Evidently the idea was that other reserves would be set aside for the other Anishinaabe of Lake Nipigon when they decided to settle in more permanent village communities in the future after the fur trading economy had run its course. One group, forerunners of the Whitesand Band, lived seasonally on Jackfish Island which was situated in the more southerly area of Lake Nipigon. After the signing of the 1850 Robinson-Superior Treaty, members of this band began to send petitions to the Canadian Government in the 1890s asking about the status of the reserve which they believed had been promised to them by this treaty.[57]

For whatever reason, their petition was either ignored by the Canadian Government or not received at all. In any event, members of the Jackfish Island band renewed their efforts on this matter about twenty years later. In 1907, the chiefs of the Jackfish Island band wrote to the Deputy Superintendent of Indian Affairs in the following letter:

We the Indians want to know definitely whether Jackfish Island is an Indian Reserve. We do affirm to your Department that our Indian Agents, particularly the present one does not attend to our affairs, nor will he answer a letter. He promised us that he would pay all the Indians at this reserve, he failed to do this. On that account, Indians do not like to come here (Letter dated 17 July, 1907, from chiefs Wegwans, Kwisises, and Bouchard, Gull Bay, Ontario).

It was not until seven years later, in 1914, that Jackfish Island was confirmed as a reserve by the Province of Ontario, but only 363 acres were allotted, which was considerably fewer than the 1000 or so acres originally requested by the band. This did not matter much in any event since by that time most of the Jackfish Island population had given up waiting for a response from the Indian Affair Department in Ottawa and had moved to the north end of Lake Nipigon, which gave them much closer access to the new (in 1911) Canadian National rail line by this time. This new site was located on either side of the Whitesand River; hence, their new name which corresponded to their new location.

Then, three years later, in 1917, the Indian Agent in Port Arthur (now Thunder Bay) wrote to the Secretary of Indian Affairs stating that:

Chief James and all the Indians who previously resided on Jackfish Island Reserve are very anxious to surrender this Reserve and have a new reserve set aside on the north bank of the Whitesand River. The Indians who live on the Reserve can find no employment there on Jackfish Island and could not find a market for berries or fish. At least, 1000 acres should be secured as fully forty families would reside there (Letter dated 18 September, 1917, from W.R. Brown, Indian Agent, Port Arthur Thunder Bay).

This information was then sent to the Deputy Minister of Lands and Forests not Indian Affairs, whose response for a reserve change was evidently less than enthusiastic:

It would appear that the Indians have now all the land they are entitled on Lake Nipigon, and it does not seem advisable that the shores of this lake should be further cut up by setting apart Indian lands. I would suggest to you that if your application was amended and that you would apply for, say, from one to two hundred acres of land, that a License of occupation to your Department on behalf of these people might be given consideration (Letter dated 25 August, 1917, to A. Grigg, Deputy Minister of Lands and Forests from J.B. McLean, Assistant Deputy Minister of Indian Affairs).

It was in response to this letter that the Port Arthur Indian Agent (for DIAND) wrote to his superiors in Ottawa complaining that such a small parcel of land, "when there are millions of acres of land surrounding this lake," would not provide a sufficient basis for the people to make a living. Indian Agent Brown also pointed out that he "found Chief James to be a good level-headed Indian and I consider that he knows what he is doing when he asks for the transfer" of a larger tract of land.

The issue of the land transfers subsequently generated further controversy when Chief Fire Ranger McLeod submitted his report: "In looking at it from the Forest Reserve standpoint, it would make another scar on the shores of the

Lake, and to me, old Lake Nipigon is the most beautiful lake in the world." Included in this correspondence was also the response on one Indigenous person name not indicated who expressed the sarcastic opinion that "the Ontario Government should bring in a law to shoot all Indians so that the moose and fish would not be molested." Antagonisms were clearly emerging among the various interest groups—Indigenous people, forestry officials, DIAND officials, railway concerns, tourists, among others—early on in this area of the Province of Ontario.

There are several matters apparent here. First, the land in question on Lake Nipigon belongs to the Province of Ontario, and is thus a provincial responsibility, administered by the Department of Lands and Forests. Second, The Department of Indian Affairs is a federal agency and does not have jurisdiction over provincial lands. Consequently, in this situation, the provincial government has the final say in the matter which explains the Lands and Forest Department's somewhat condescending or patronizing response to the request. In addition, the Jackfish Island people are a federal responsibility as set out in the Indian Act. Obviously provisions should have been originally set aside in the 1850 Robinson-Superior Treaty for an allocation of lands to the unsettled Indigenous population. Finally, a so-called 'License of Occupation' is no more than a leased property, still under provincial jurisdiction, and not federal property characteristic of other reserves administered by the Department of Indian Affairs, a situation that was never revealed to band members. The Indigenous people of Lake Nipigon had signed this treaty in good faith, relinquishing their ancestral rights to all the land in the treaty boundary, yet were now the victims of inter-departmental and federal-provincial wrangling.

As might be expected, the Indian Agent in Port Arthur was incensed with the Deputy Minister's response, and immediately wrote to his superiors in Ottawa:

There are millions of acres of land surrounding this lake Nipigon and I cannot understand why the Ontario government officials are averse to giving these people enough land to live on in a locality where they can earn a living (Indian Agent W.R. Brown, Port Arthur Thunder Bay).

In the meantime, Chief Tommy James was also growing impatient and wrote to Indian Affairs asking for two square miles on the Whitesand River, with a two-mile frontage on Lake Nipigon. A surveyor arrived a few months later and laid out a plot containing just 553 acres.

One can only imagine the sense of betrayal that Chief James and his other fellow band members would have felt at this turn of events. The surveyor subsequently wrote to Indian Affairs indicating that, "I told the chief that I would lay out 500 acres for him in the required shape wherever he wished to have it and he could fight for the remaining acres it afterward." As might be expected, the band objected to receiving so little. The Ontario Government, acting on the recommendation of the Chief Ranger in the area, further reduced this amount. In 1919, the Province of Ontario granted a License of Occupation on just 276 acres of the poorer land on the site, and with a smaller lake frontage than the band had originally requested, at the nominal fee of $10.00 per annum to be paid by the Government of Canada to the province of Ontario.

The Indian Agent in Port Arthur could have sent this information to Chief James himself. The fact that he asked officials in Ottawa to convey the bad news to the band would appear to indicate that there was some reluctance on his part to relay this report. In any case, a letter was sent to Chief James, setting out the conditions which the chief would *"please be very careful to comply with"*my emphasis. There was little that the band could do about this decision since it came directly from the Indian Affairs Department, and there was no higher authority to which they could appeal. Possibly Chief James might have expected such a response since the Government of Canada was beginning to reveal their duplicity toward the Indigenous peoples of this country.

Over the next forty years there was a steady decline in the permanent Anishinaabe occupation of the Whitesand lands. In the early 1940s, flooding appears to have occurred in part of the Whitesand allocation, probably due to Ontario Hydro's water diversion and dam construction program on the southern part of Lake Nipigon at Cameron Falls and Pine Portage for hydroelectric development.[58] This was a situation for which the Province of Ontario would not take any responsibility, blaming the flooding on 'seasonal rainfall' or some other spurious happenstance. Then, in 1951, the Whitesand Band was further impacted, as were many other bands in Canada, by Section 74 of the Indian Act governing band elections; namely, that only those residing on reserves could vote for the positions of Chief and band council.

By this time, it appears that there was no longer any members of the Whitesand band still residing on the Whitesand River property after the flooding; moreover, the band did not have legal status as a reserve although few people seem to have known this because under the License of Occupation the provincial government continued to retain ownership in the property. Under normal circumstance, the Department of Indian Affairs, as a federal government agency, would hold such property 'in trust, for the use and benefit of a band'. Thus, it is apparent that the Canadian Government in this case had abrogated its responsibility, when Canadian lands were transferred to Canada from the British under the terms of Confederation. Such 'technicalities' now appeared to matter little when dealing with the Indigenous population.

The band was not heard from again until 1967, when one of its members wrote to the Department of Indian Affairs inquiring about possible compensation for the flooding and clarification of the status of the Whitesand land: "It's getting worse there now," the letter indicated, "all the old houses were washed out. That's why the Indians don't stay on the Whitesand Reserve anymore." The Department of Indian Affairs refused to consider compensation for the Band's losses at Whitesand. Without even consulting with the band, which did not have a proper council at the time in any event, the Department of Indian Affairs cancelled the License of Occupation of Whitesand land in 1970, apparently considering it not worth the effort to continue to pay the $10.00 per year occupation fee for the property. The Whitesand people were now entirely homeless.

The Whitesand Band Coalesces

My initial contact with the Whitesand people occurred during 1974–1975 when I was conducting a one-year field investigation into the socio-political organization of non-reserve Anishinaabe people along the CN rail line (Hedican 1986). I soon found that many of these communities had shared characteristics. Most were the former summer meeting places of Indigenous people from large northern bands, most notably Fort Hope on the Albany River, who had come to the rail line to fish, trade furs, renew acquaintances, and generally just sojourn after the long winter months. With large numbers of northern Anishinaabe already more-or-less permanently established along the rail line by the end of the war years, the Whitesand retreat from Lake Nipigon in the 1940s meant a relegation to minority status in these emergent rail line villages. For example, in Collins during my research in 1974–1975 Fort Hope people represented 65.0% of the local population, members of the Nipigon House band comprised 18.1%, and Whitesand band members 12.1%, with the remaining 4.8% from a diversity of locations in northern Ontario such as Lac Seul, Cat Lake, and Osnaburgh House (Hedican 1986a: 37, Table 4). Thus, Whitesand people, because of their relatively small numbers in relationship to other Indigenous groups, were not able to effectively participate in the social and political life of either a reserve or non-reserve community. They had become marginalized in terms of their influence along the CN rail line.

Rail line villages on the north end of Lake Nipigon, such as Auden, Allenwater Bridge, Collins and Ferland, are dominated economically and politically by members of the Fort Hope Band. Many Whitesand people also live in these communities, but tend not to be part of the local leadership structure because of their minority status. Also, since the Whitesand Band's Reserve legal status only encompassed Jackfish Island, and since the Whitesand land was not a reserve under the federal stipulations of the Indian Act, the band was effectively blocked from electing a chief and council to transact its business. These conditions hardly engendered a sense of unity among Whitesand people. However, with a new generation of younger people wanting more political influence in determining the fate of the Whitesand people, the situation began to change remarkably in the late 1970s, leading to some of the first genuine attempts to resolve the Whitesand dilemma in several generations.

The outside political structure was an added factor which encouraged political mobilization among the Whitesand people. For example, the Minister of Indian Affairs repealed Section 74 of the Indian Act in 1977 which prohibited band elections for Indigenous people without a legal reserve which was the case with the Whitesand people. As such, the Whitesand people were able to hold band elections for chief and council for the first time in many years, leading to a relatively rapid change of political circumstance for band members regarding their search for new reserve lands. After holding a meeting of the members, the Whitesand Band established some basic election rules and elected its first council in recent memory. The very first Band Council Resolution appeared in August, 1977: "The first priority of this council is to regain reserve land for the Whitesand Band." The Union of Ontario Indians (which represents Indigenous people in Ontario with status under the Indian Act) was then requested to make representations on their behalf.[59]

By the following summer, the Band had identified a number of preferred areas for a new reserve (since the Whitesand River location was never a designated reserve under the provisions of the Indian Act), and had approached Indian Affair's regional planner with a request for a feasibility study. Minutes of Band meetings at the time indicated that by 1979 three potential sites had support—the old Band area on the Whitesand River, and two sites close to the CN rail road near Armstrong. In a vote on site selection, each of the possibilities received about a third of the votes cast. The Band further indicated a desire for approximately 640 acres as a reserve. The Ministry of Natural Resources indicated a preference for the sites near the railroad, each of which comprised about 400 acres.[60]

The Anthropologist Arrives

It was not long after that the Indian Affairs office in Thunder Bay contacted the University of Guelph's RDOP committee which I had only joined in the previous several months. Just after I had submitted my final grades for the winter semester, arrangements were made for me to travel to Armstrong. This involved flying into the airport at Thunder Bay, renting an automobile, and making the three or four hour drive up to Armstrong. After renting a room at a local motel, I then made contact the next day with a young man from the Whitesand Band executive who had been assigned to join me on a tour of the new reserve alternatives. It was only when I arrived that it became evident that there were emerging conflicts between the various parties involved in the negotiations. As such, this chapter describes some of the perils and advantages of conducting applied research in anthropology under such volatile conditions.

To reiterate, my initial involvement with the Whitesand Band was as a university sponsored coordinator—someone to aid the band administrators in sorting out issues and implement decisions. However, as events changed, this role was augmented by my attempts to mediate or at least act as a 'go-between' amongst a variety of conflicting interest groups. I do not believe that any of these groups were intentionally becoming more combative, it was just that each of the various groups had their own agenda that they were trying to advance, and each had their own set of priorities and objectives. It is also possible that each of these various groups were not entirely aware that their own individual interests might not be entirely compatible with those of the other groups. It was only when I began to discuss the Whitesand settlement issue with the members of each of these group that I became aware myself of the potential for conflict that was bound to emerge at one point in time or another.

At other times, as my stay in Armstrong progressed, additional roles, which I could loosely describe as 'animator' and 'facilitator' were also employed with varying degrees of success. It should be pointed out from the outset that I was not quick to identify any of these roles as there was very little in the anthropological literature that I could consult with regards to role playing by anthropologists under similar conditions. Actually I was surprised, when I attempted to find information on new roles for anthropologists, at the paucity of virtually any description in the academic literature on the situation that I was in, or anything even remotely similar. I do not intend to embark on a full-scale review of literature at this point, nor do I feel as if I was acting as a naïve neophyte, yet nonetheless I felt as if I was engaging in a role playing endeavor for which I was ill-trained and mostly unprepared for.[61]

My experience with the Whitesand band relocation issue, then, suggests that applied researchers who find themselves in situations that could be seen to be similar as my own should be prepared to actively explore new uses for themselves and the products of their research, especially as these roles relate to a mediating capacity. In addition to documenting a variety of role types, I will endeavor to indicate some of the ostensible impacts of mediated communication on Indigenous communities and, in turn, on academics engaged in applied research.

The Mediator Role

Within weeks of my arrival among the Whitesand people in the mid-1980s, events occurred which determined the course of the following summer's activities. In May, for example, two members of a Toronto-based consulting firm arrived to give band members a summary report of a land use study of one of the proposed sites, called JoJo Lake. This site has certain advantages, in that it is close to the railway but smaller, at 400 acres, than the band had hoped. However, this site did have the backing of many Whitesand people, fluctuating I would think from about 40 to 60 percent of the population, and the personnel at the Ministry of Natural Resources.

Two days after the consultant's arrival, a physical planner and a construction manager from the Department of Indian Affairs office in Toronto drove up to the Whitesand area. Their intention was to call a band meeting in order they indicated to discuss the consultant's report and to prepare for the summer's construction work. I found this development particularly distressful since the Whitesand band members had not as yet seen all of the proposed sites, nor did they have an opportunity to discuss among themselves what their preferences were. It was as if a decision had already been made by Indian Affairs to get this whole deal over with as expeditiously as possible, and implying also by their actions that the input of band members themselves was not important enough to take into consideration. In my own mind, I found myself becoming an adversary of this "rush job" and an ally of the band, as opposed to a neutral observer. I was aware after reading the letters from the past and the extent to which the Whitesand Band had been lied to about the License of Occupation, that one could expect duplicitous intentions by government officials and those they hired 'on behalf of the band'.

The meeting with the consultants took place in a vacated garage, a setting that I found condescending given the availability of proper meeting rooms in the vicinity. Seating was limited and the people appeared crammed together. One thought that crossed my mind was that you could never get away with such a venue if Indian Affairs officials were present. The consultants stood at the front with their shirts, ties and freshly pressed pants. The contrast with the Whitesand band members was disquieting. In the front of the room were several flip charts as if the presentation was going to be made with Bay Street professionals. The consultants were fast-talking, slick, as if they were selling property. They spoke volubly with their land-use terminology.

I looked at the back of the room where a number of elders sat, women with their large head scarves and billowing skirts, as would have been worn several generations ago. They squinted at the charts, mumbled to each other—it was evident that they hardly knew what was happening and probably knew only a modicum of English words. Later, when band members asked questions about the presentation, they were (privately) criticized. The implication was that the band was disorganized and not really prepared to make a decision, as if to cover up the nebulous, and virtually incomprehensible drawings, maps and other paraphernalia. As an example, one of the consultants made a point of indicating the convenient location for the building housing the washer and dryers.

Apparently the consultants were oblivious to the fact that there were Whitesand band members currently living in log cabins without running water. In my mind, there was such a disconnect between the consultants and the Indigenous people in the audience.

The consultants showed very little sensitivity to the cultural and linguistic differences involved, or to the fact that the Whitesand people did not all have degrees in urban planning or a land-resource science. Even the charts depicting the possible layout of the community also seemed too utopian for a bush environment. The consultants beamed away with the central, easy access laundromat, when in reality most people probably grew up washing their clothes in the lake.

Having come from a stint of fieldwork in Collins several years before, where people lived in log cabins and heated their abodes with wood, which was in relative abundance in the area, I was puzzled about where the community members would acquire the fuel necessary to heat their houses. Then one of the consultants indicated that the proposed site was situated in a very sandy area "so of course, no one can cut down any of the tress or else everything will end up blowing away." Even if people would not have wood to heat their houses, from what material would they build them in the first place. I wondered, was DIAND going to build their houses for them? There was never any mention of this suggestion. The whole process of this 'consultation' meeting left me mystified and I wondered what I was doing here in the first place since 'assisting the band' to arrive at a decision regarding their new reserve was the least of the band members' problems.

It was becoming increasingly evident that the pace of developments had quickened for reasons which I could not determine other than to think that it was in the interest of Indian Affairs to solve an uncomfortable situation and put it behind the department. The band manager then approached me. He indicated that the Council was very confused because its members thought that the consultants would spend the summer preparing a feasibility study, which would then give the band time over the winter months to discuss the report and to arrive at decisions. Instead, it was becoming increasingly evident that the consultants, in conjunction with Indian Affairs, would press the Whitesand band for a decision on site selection almost immediately, even possibly after the meeting with the consultants. Band members were practically in a panic situation. Here they had waited decades for a chance to choose a new reserve and now it was apparent that they would be forced to make a decision with little consultation or time to talk the matter over. To see this state of affairs, unfold day by day, or even hour by hour, was a very disconcerting matter to witness.

As the Band Manager explained to me, there were no members of the Band Council who had agreed to the accelerated submission of the report, yet everyone (meaning the consultants and DIAND) was acting as if all the preliminaries had been settled. When this matter was raised with DIAND's planner, the response was that it would be in the band's best interest to move quickly this summer since there were other Indigenous communities in the Thunder Bay District making urgent requests for land use studies. The implication was clear; by holding to the terms originally agreed upon between DIAND and the band the Whitesand Band risked being bypassed in favor of more compliant Indigenous settlements. This not so veiled threat astonished me, to tell the truth. Who could not see the paternalistic attitudes involved—I was embarrassed for the Whitesand people that they still had to endure such a treatment by professionals who should know better in this day and age.

The Whitesand Band members came to the conclusion that DIAND, in concert with the consultants, were trying to rush the Whitesand people through a difficult negotiation process. From DIAND's perspective, band members were not making the best use of their time and, as a result, the band was consequently not prepared for visits from DIAND staff. By the end of this first week, communication had broken off between band members and their visitors. Despite this turmoil, however, some semblance of band solidarity began to emerge around this resettlement issue. But before a way around the impasse was found, I was unwittingly tossed into the fracas myself.

The day the outsiders were to leave Armstrong, a breakfast was arranged for the parties involved at a restaurant across from the band office at the old radar base. I was one of the last to arrive, and as I walked into the room it was evident that an earnest discussion had been going on for some time. Before I could even pour a cup of coffee, one of the consultants began to take me to task for, in his words, 'agitating the band'. DIAND's planner then interceded, offering the opinion that it was RDOP personnel that had caused the impasse, by not acting as an effective intermediary, and not because of any inherent weakness in the relationship between DIAND and the Whitesand Band. The evening before I had given some thought to such a situation developing, reasoning that the consultants would not wish to blame their clients (DIAND and the Whitesand Band) for the deadlock.

Thus, RDOP was destined to play an 'easy victim' role, and over the next few hours I struggled to press my explanation of the problem—lack of Band-DIAND communication—on somewhat unwilling ears. Essentially my argument was that the Whitesand Band had never really had much contact with DIAND, or any other government officials for that matter. The fact that many Whitesand people speak only the Anishinaabe language, in conjunction with a general dispersal of the band as a whole, meant that DIAND would have to make special efforts to establish effective Band-DIAND dialogue. An aloof, authoritarian DIAND presence, I argued, would only serve to further isolate, and antagonize, the Whitesand people. I also thought that DIAND's strategy of blaming RDOP for the impasse in communications was a disingenuous tactic to shift blame to a more neutral party, and therefore alleviate any blame that might come their way for the problem.

Despite the acrimonious nature of this breakfast meeting, the discussion did serve several useful purposes. First, most of the contentious issues were openly discussed for the first time and, while they were not solved immediately, a consensus began to emerge on which problems needed to be addressed before others if the project was to proceed. Second, because the meeting was so heated it was brought to the attention of DIAND's Planning Director for Ontario, who attempted to ameliorate the crisis by enacting the following course of action: (1) a letter was sent to the Whitesand Band indicating that the time frame for the band's response to the consultant's report had been extended; (2) the consultant's association with the Whitesand Band was terminated; (3) a new District Superintendent for Indian affairs (a local Indigenous person who belonged to the Thunder Bay Reserve) was appointed; (4) a plan was initiated to fill the planner's position in the Thunder Bay Office so that there would be little need for the band to deal directly with DIAND's Toronto office; (5) and finally, the Planning Director saw much of the problem stemming from communication difficulties between the band and DIAND, especially at the district level.

The steps that he took to strengthen RDOP's position, that a continued lack of effective communication between the band and outside interests, would have a negative impact on the band's attempt to access information and develop planning skills. Needless to say, I personally felt a certain measure of vindication regarding the accusation that had been levelled at me in my role as a conduit of information to the Whitesand Band. In this sense, the mandate initially outlining RDOP objectives, especially the second one, to wit: "To assist Band Council in accessing information and developing skills" had been achieved.

The role of the anthropologist in this situation, I must admit, was a troubling one. While there were several positive results of the consultant's meeting, these results were mostly not consciously intentional ones. The ad hoc nature of the anthropologist's role still brings into question what the most appropriate role should be in such situations of social involvement. There is the possibility, then, that a combination of roles would have the most beneficial effect.

The Facilitator Role

The intervention of the Planning Director, and the appointment of an Indigenous person as District Superintendent, were moves that made the Whitesand people feel that some hope still existed for their land claims and resettlement program. They now had access to positions of power within the Department of Indian Affairs, but for the most part they were not sure how to benefit their position through the use of these new channels. One benefit, though, did accrue to them almost immediately—more time for reassessment of the Whitesand relocation program. As with people on the brink of signing something which they did not fully understand, but feeling compelled to sign anyway in order to save face, the band now began to search for a more comprehensive understanding of their predicament. What the Whitesand people thought they needed was a wider perspective on local issues concerning such matters as land tenure and access to resources.

By mid-summer, new questions were being raised: "Where can we find out about all the treaties that have been signed?" They were interested in historical situations pertaining to the James Bay Agreement in Quebec (1975) and the Mackenzie Valley Pipeline debate, or Berger Inquiry (1977), among a host of others. "Were there films and books on these topics?" they asked. I was quick to inform them that, yes, there was much information on these topics and that their position at the bargaining table would be enhanced if they knew about how other Indigenous groups leveraged their position to their advantage. For starters, we then began an examination of the three volume set of *Canada: Indian Treaties and Surrenders* (Canada 1891, Coles Reprint 1971), which provided useful information on amounts of land reserved for other bands in the Robinson-Superior treaty limits that the Whitesand Band members could use for comparative purposes.

In all, one cannot be sure that the specific details of the land claims, treaties, or agreements that we examined were of immediate use to the Whitesand Band. What they did learn nonetheless would probably be more help in the band's long term planning. That is, land settlements must be carefully prepared, the spoken work carries little credibility in a court of law, and finally, avoid 'selling short' under external pressure. What the band had yet to determine at this time was how to strengthen their bargaining position by an aggressive interaction with outside agents, which in large part stemmed from a lack of confidence on the part of band members in their dealings with the larger Euro-Canadian society. This lack of confidence was most evident during the Band-DIAND conflict discussed earlier. In situations of external conflict, band members tended to withdraw into a form of passive resistance, rather than actively demanding an explanation for the questionable treatment band members had received from various governmental agencies.

Whitesand First Nation Band Office

One of the main reasons for the band's withdrawal in situations of external controversy, besides feelings of powerlessness when confronted by outsiders, is a confusion over how to act in order to achieve the results they want. Greater experience in Indigenous-Euro-Canadian negotiations would go a long way in solving this problem, but in the meantime an exposure to the literature can illustrate examples of how other Indigenous communities have successfully handled problems similar to those faced by the Whitesand Band. In addition, a person who can act as an intermediary, or 'facilitator' between the Indigenous community and outside sources of information can therefore serve a useful function—to expand on possible alternative courses of action which might be open or closed to the community. By the end of the summer, the Whitesand band members could visualize different paths to the achievement of their goals which, it was hoped, would result in more effective planning in the future.

The Animator Role

Now that Whitesand people began to realize the extent to which outside sources of information could be useful in local problem solving, or at least in suggesting alternative ways by which problems could be handled, they began to inquire about ways to gather their own information. Thus, 'information management' has come to be seen as a crucial part of the band's development. As such, RDOP had an important role to play in accessing information and developing skills, that is, in 'animating' band aspirations for more knowledge. A number of examples can be used to illustrate the specifics of this role performance, such as assisting the Band Council in (1) developing a usable inventory of information on the band itself, its activities, skill sets, education and other possible areas of useful knowledge; (2) identifying training and skill requirements; (3) developing appropriate methods of consulting with band members, and (4) identifying sources of assistance, including provincial and federal social service programs.

Progress in achieving these objectives was made on a number of fronts. As an example, 'The Whitesand Band Human Resource Inventory', prepared with RDOP's assistance, served the Band Council when decisions needed to be made on the abilities and needs of families likely to move to the new reserve, as well as on the development of a skills training program. In addition, the Band Council was able to implement a plan to conduct mini-workshops for the

Whitesand people living in the scattered settlements along the CN railway. The purpose of these gatherings was to inform the more isolated band members of recent developments concerning such matters as the consultant's land use report, and the progress of the land settlement program with DIAND's and the Ministry of Natural Resources assistance. Another purpose was to gather feedback from band members in a more structured format that existed at the time in regular band meetings. In what may be taken as an encouraging sign in attempts to build greater self-reliance, which was one of RDOP's more salient objectives, the band decided that DIAND and RDOP would not be represented at the workshops, since it was felt that band members themselves would be more comfortable expressing their opinions about the proposed reserve without outside observers, and for the more elderly members, without having to use English to express their ideas.

Both the Human Resource Inventory and the workshops are examples of results that can be obtained when an appropriate 'animator' is able to stimulate local participation in information gathering. The next step would be to provide assistance on how to utilize its own assessment of the findings, and to use these findings to guide policy objectives. When band members are able to refine these abilities, it can be expected that they will also have a sharpened sense of band objectives and priorities regarding community development needs. In sum, the 'animator' role has the potential to help the band realize its capacity for undertaking progressively more complex activities in the future.

Summary

One conclusion that can be drawn from the foregoing discussion is that the main barrier to Whitesand resettlement has been a faulty passage of information among the main parties to the dispute. Historically, Indian agents and forestry officials have failed to give the Whitesand people the pertinent facts, and it is evident that at times an attempt was made to conceal or even to disguise information that would benefit the band.

Lack of consultation with the band was a related problem, such as when the License of Occupation was issued without informing band members that the Whitesand location was actually not a reserve at all, but merely a rented piece of property. In another instance, the actions of Ontario Hydro either caused, or was a contributing factor to the flooding of Lake Nipigon in the

1940s which resulted in the band members having to relocate to other locations along the CN rail line. Even today there appears to be little contact between the band and outside officials. When I interviewed DIAND's District Superintendent in Thunder Bay, I learned after a lengthy wait in the lobby, that he had never visited the Whitesand Band and appeared to know very little about who the people were, where they lived, or the names of the chief and council members. I subsequently learned that the Band chief, or one of the councilors, occasionally paid a call at the District office to file reports or attend to other bureaucratic business but would rarely meet with the District Superintendent. Band members tend to be reticent about initiating contacts that, if pursued vigorously, might have more effectively served their negotiating interests with non-Indigenous people.

Over time there were developments underway that were relevant to a settlement of the Whitesand land claims. Overall, DIAND appeared more responsive to the Whitesand objectives when its officials actually took the time to know the names of the band chief and council members. A First Nation person now fills the position of DIAND's District Superintendent, and overall it appears that DIAND has now accepted 'self-determination' as an accepted Indigenous goal, and as a result more resources than before are being committed to resettling Whitesand people. The planning position in DIAND's Thunder Bay office is now staffed with an energetic individual who is more objectively critical of the consultant's land use study than had been the case previously. Band members have also become more responsive now that they have the funds to conduct workshops and other forms of inter-band communication. Faced with what they thought was complete intransigence on the part of outside officials, there presently exists a new feeling of solidarity among band members than they ever had before.

The Whitesand Band did eventually agree to accept an offer of 249 acres of property for a reserve near the town of Armstrong in 1984 (see www.whitesandfirstnation.com). However, although the band said that it would accept the offer its leaders later changed their mind when a deeper issue arose. As Chief Douglas Sinoway explained, "We began to realize that there was something wrong. All around us there was development occurring and we still had a very high unemployment rate among band members. We ran into all kinds of private interest in property around us when we were looking for a reserve site. We wanted a partnership in its development."

The band subsequently developed a new attitude toward its relationship to the larger society. Chief Sinoway, for example, indicated that they did not want to own the property in question because, "We have to look at a different approach here with land claims. If there is a settlement, the term 'settlement' implies a debt is settled. We want to have a mutual agreement for the future" (all quotes from J. McGrath, 1989).

The Whitesand Band then became caught up in a much larger dispute over the initial Robinson-Superior Treaty of 1850 in which various bands in the region contended that they were not represented when the treaty was signed. The bands wanted more control over the mineral and timber-rich territory stretching from Thunder Bay to the Pukaskwa National Park near Marathon, on the north shore of Lake Superior, and up north to the Atlantic-Arctic watershed. This is a vast area that includes the rich Hemlo gold fields, forestry industry woodlands, and several small towns and villages.

When all of this claim went into litigation, the Ontario Court of Appeals at one point ruled, however, that even if a band had not signed the treaty, their ancestors lived in the area covered by the treaty and received its benefits and were therefore considered treaty Indians. The director of DIAND's specific-claims office further said that the First Nations bands themselves must share the blame for the long drawn out disputes over these claims. DIAND's Director Klein then concluded that "Indian organizations waste time and effort when they know the policies we are working under, and they still ask for more. We're trying to deal with matters 100 years old or older. If it takes another year or two to arrive at a settlement, that would seem insignificant."

Nonetheless, given the long-standing climate of distrust that had permeated the negotiations between the parties over the years, such a prediction may have been overly optimistic. There are potentially many years ahead for involvement by land-claims researchers and social scientists, including anthropologists, before any definitive settlement can be reached between the government and the increasingly politically active Indigenous groups. The challenge for the social scientists of the future is how to participate in this settlement process in an effective and meaningful manner.

Lessons Learned

Probably the most important lesson learned from the Whitesand settlement episode is that there is a considerable potential for controversy that one should be aware of and that it would be worth trying to learn more about the circumstances that are likely to lead to such situations. Fieldwork in anthropology frequently involves the participation of various parties who are apt to hold different views and perceptions about the role of the anthropologist. As such, it is important to try to anticipate those areas where there is potential conflict and attempt to prepare beforehand ways to accommodate the views and aspirations of the participants in a project. In many ways, the future of anthropologists as 'cultural brokers' hinges on abilities to see various sides to a problem and help to develop novel ways of countering these difficulties.

To use the Whitesand land settlement as an example of a learning experience, I believe that it was predictable that the band would seek to protect their own interests and saw those interests as essentially at odds with those of DIAND which is ironic of course since DIAND personnel are charged with protecting the interests of Indigenous people. Of course other interested parties, such as the Ministry of Natural Resources, have their own interests to protect and these are not always aligned with those of Indigenous people, so there is potential here as well for conflict between the two parties. As far as the interests of the anthropologists are concerned, these are not well defined and they do not have a stake, or power base, to secure with the result that they are apt to become the focal point for any hostility because they could be blamed with impunity.

In the Whitesand case, I felt that it was in the best interest of the band to learn as much as its members could about other land claims so that they could be prepared as much as they could for their negotiations with DIAND and Natural Resources personnel. In other words, my 'go slow and learn' approach was at odds with DIAND and their hired consultants who were more interested in resolving this land claim problem as expeditiously as possible because it was largely an embarrassment to the Federal Government. It was for this reason that DIAND began to suggest that I was not fulfilling my mandate with RDOP which they understood was to move the band's decision-making process along more quickly so that the new reserve could be built without any more wasted time. It is also possible, of course, that DIAND viewed RDOP as working for them and as such the anthropologist that RDOP engaged was a de facto DIAND employee and consequently should support their interests. DIAND and the consultants did not share my view that members of the Whitesand Band should be given all the time they needed even if it meant greater expense. My rationale was that the Whitesand people would have to live with the results for many generations to come—a point which was seen as much less crucial by DIAND and the consultants.

Conclusion

The conventional role for anthropologists is to engage in ethnographic research which they write up as an ethnography and thereby advance the knowledge in their discipline. On occasion, they are asked to participate in what might be termed 'unconventional' projects that involve Indigenous people and the members of various governmental agencies who are attempting to solve certain problems. While the role of the ethnographer is a fairly well defined one, whatever role that the anthropologist adopts in these new, unconventional settings is apt to be fraught with certain difficulties. In my own case, I have attempted to analytically define at least three of these roles— facilitator, animator, and mediator—however there could be further possibilities. In such cases as the one that I was involved in, it is important to document how these various roles played out in terms of their efficacy and problems so that others might learn from this experience.

The emerging situation today is one in which anthropologists enact various new roles, aside from the conventional one of an ethnographer. This new trend suggests a movement away from an older tendency to sidestep the effects and repercussions of an anthropologist's involvement in local affairs. As time goes on and anthropologists attempt to increase their relevancy in the modern world they are apt to find their positions to be one fraught with potential difficulties such as stress, tension, resentment, and hostility on the part of various parties since their position might be regarded as a threat to the other's interests and political agendas.

The stress that a modern anthropologist might feel is based on a multiplicity of factors such as their psychological temperament, political, or moral persuasion, as well as local factions and group interests. With increasing regularity, anthropologists are finding themselves caught up in such situations as the Whitesand affair, and to the extent that the members of the discipline are able, they can no longer afford to ignore the various dilemmas and ramifications of fieldwork conducted in modern settings of this world we live in. We should also remember that while land claims are not usually part of your everyday life, for the members of many Indigenous communities there can be no greater focus to their lives.

Chapter Eight
The Ipperwash Tragedy and
Settler Colonialism

No matter whether the dimension is time, place, or social class, racism has been endemic in Canada...the degree, scope, and persistence of the phenomenon leads to a single conclusion: racism in Canada has been institutionalized.

Stanley R. Barrett, *Is God a Racist?* (1987: 307)[62]

This sense of entitlement, this expression of white privilege, has a long history, manifesting itself in a national narrative.

Hirschfelder and Molin (2018:1)

There can be no doubt that the settlers in North America, especially those of European decent, live a privileged life. Their lives, to a large extent, are based on privileges that have been unearned because they have taken over lands that they have never originally owned. In addition, a self-justifying mythology, which one could term *narratives of disentitlement,* has been espoused by the settlers which denies ownership of the land by the nation's Indigenous population.

The Ipperwash Tragedy

On 6 September, 1995, Dudley George of the Stony Point First Nation[63] was shot and killed by Ontario Provincial Police (OPP) officer Kenneth Deane. George had been participating in a peaceful protest over land claims in Ipperwash Provincial Park, which had been expropriated from the Anishinaabe after the Second World War. The reason for the protest at the provincial park, which had been closed after the Labor Day weekend of that year, was the result of Ontario's Premier Mike Harris ordering the OPP's Emergency Response Team to use all necessary force to disband the protesters. The protesting group was engaged in something akin to a 'sit-in' as it was composed of families on a camping trip. There were never any weapons found that could be associated with the Ipperwash protesters. As a result of George's death and the grievous mishandling of the protest it took almost two decades for an inquiry to be held, after Mike Harris's Conservative government had been defeated by the provincial Liberal party.

The roots of this protest extend back almost two centuries when settlers, former soldiers, and land speculators began to secure land from the British government after the War of 1812.The Anishinaabe (or Chippewa as they were known at the time) originally ceded title to over two million acres of land to the British Crown under the terms of the Huron Tract Treaty of 1827. The Anishinaabe, with this treaty, relinquished 99 percent of their traditional territory and as such retained only one percent of their ancestral hunting grounds. At that time in 1827, all of the signatories to the Huron Tract Treaty—Walpole Island, Sarnia, Kettle Point, and Stony Point—were treated as one large band. Eventually, in 1919, the Kettle and Stony Point Band was created and separated from the Sarnia and Walpole Island bands.

Location of Ipperwash Provincial Park

Just after the turn of the twentieth century, beginning in 1912, the band's Indian Agent began to pressure the Kettle and Stony people to surrender their beachfront property at the Kettle Point Reserve. The logic presented by the Indian Agent was that the members of this reserve would eventually need land for agricultural development and, as such, the sale of the beachfront property would serve to purchase more economically necessary land. In those days, the Indian Agent had considerable powers. As a consequence of the 1885 confrontations, the Department of Indian Affairs (DIAND) became more centralized, which resulted in the department assuming greater control over the lives of Canada's First Nations people. As an example, Indian Agents presided over band council meetings and could, in effect, direct the political life of reserve communities. DIAND officials were empowered as well to lease reserve lands without a band's consent. In 1911, an amendment was made to the Indian Act which allowed for the expropriation of reserve lands for public purposes (see Leslie and Maguire 1978; Hedican 2008b, 2013: 4, 30–33).

The Kettle Point reserve members lost their beachfront property in 1927 when a local land developer purchased the property from the Department of Indian Affairs, despite objections from First Nation residents. Then, in 1928, additional beachfront property at the Stony Point Reserve was sold to another real estate developer and Sarnia politician. This politician later 'flipped' some of the lots for $10,000 a piece, thus realizing a considerable profit. Later, in 1936, the Ipperwash Provincial Park was created from additional reserve lands. The chief and council of Kettle and Stony Point Band then notified DIAND that there were burial sites located at the park, however there was never any action taken by the Ontario government to preserve or otherwise protect these burials.

More reserve lands were further expropriated without the permission of the Kettle and Stony Point members in 1942, under the War Measures Act,[64] in order to construct ofa military base for army cadets (see Lindsay 2014). The Department of Defense promised to return the land after the Second World War, yet, despite repeated requests by the original Aboriginal residents, the property was not returned as promised after the war.[65] As a result of the increasing frustration of band members, they decided to occupy Ipperwash Provincial Park on Labor Day Monday in September 1995 as an act of protest. It was during this protest that Dudley George was killed by OPP officer Kenneth 'Tex' Deane. Officer Deane was subsequently asked to resign from the OPP but refused, claiming that Dudley George was seen carrying a gun and as such he acted in self-defense. In a later hearing, there was never any evidence presented demonstrating that George was carrying a gun, just a large stick, and as a result Deane was found guilty of criminal negligence causing death. Deane was then given a suspended sentence and community service as punishment for killing the unarmed protester.[66]

Dudley George

The Conservative government of Mike Harris refused to call an inquiry into the events surrounding the protest which ended under such tragic circumstances. Eventually the Harris government was defeated and in November 2003, with a change in government, an inquiry was initiated under Commissioner Sidney Linden whose report was released in 2007. The *Report of the Ipperwash Inquiry* (https://www.ontario.ca/page/Ipperwash-inquiry-report) contains many disturbing details. As an example, in a cabinet meeting just prior to the OPP's assault on Ipperwash Park, it was revealed in sworn testimony by Ontario's Attorney General Charles Harnick that Premier Harris had used profanity in reference to the park protesters.

At this meeting, the claim was made that Mike Harris said, "I want the fucking Indians out of the park." Harris later admitted to saying this phrase but denied using the 'f' word as a racist trope. Yet, one is left to wonder, then, why his own attorney general would lie about such a matter, especially given the fact that his testimony was given under oath. Harnick indicated that he found Premier Harris's remark 'insensitive and inappropriate' (*CBC News*, 14 February 2006; Peterson 2008).

The issue over Premier Harris's denial once again became an object of public attention in February 2006, when CTV aired a television movie called

One Dead Indian which was based on a book by journalist Peter Edwards (Edwards 2003). When the Ipperwash Inquiry Report was released to the public, Mike Harris referred to the Harnick's allegations as 'malicious and petty' (*CBC News*, 31 May 2007).

Unfortunately, Mike Harris was not the only person in power who used profanity in reference to the First Nations residents. There were several OPP officers as well, not realizing that their conversations were being tape recorded at the time, who used egregious vulgarity when describing the Indigenous occupants of Ipperwash Park.[67] There is no doubt that a general perception among the residents of Canada is that their country is home to tolerant people who are among the most unprejudiced and respectful people in the world. The Ipperwash report, unfortunately, reveals that our elected officials and police officers are just as capable as those whom Canadians regard as repressive regimes to engage in racially oppressive acts. It is also disappointing to learn about the manner in which dissent, especially among those living in racial minorities, is dealt with. Are we not guaranteed under the Charter of Rights and Freedoms the right of peaceful protest? It seems that the most hateful brutality is directed toward Canada's Indigenous citizens by the very persons whom we would assume are the bastions of respect and justice in this country.[68]

In Canada, we commonly view on television the brutal manner by which dissent of peaceful protesters is dealt with by government-sponsored violence in Russia, Syria, or China, among others. Many would hold smug attitudes about how much better behaved their own police are toward its citizens. Canadians may regard themselves as living in a civilized society in which its citizens are not pummeled into submission simply because their political views differ from those in power, especially among subjugated people who have little access to the institutionalized mechanisms of power to resolve their disputes with government.

As an example, in James Tully's monograph he discusses the relationship between power and governance. He writes, "From the perspective of the governed, the exercise of power always opens up a diverse field of potential ways of thinking and acting in response," and then adds, "in confrontations of this kind (such as struggles of direct action, liberation, decolonization, revolt, revolution, or globalization), the relations of governance are disrupted and the relatively stable interplay of partners in a practice of governance gives way to the different logic of relations of confrontation among adversaries in strategies of struggle" (2008: 23-3-24).

In such confrontations and struggles, the goal of the governed is to attempt to implement new relations of governance and new practices of freedom. Similarly, in *Culture Meets Power*, Stanley Barrett argues that "power and conflict are twins", just as "power and resistance are twins" (2002: 72–73). He then cites Michael Mann's (1993: 315) argument that "When people in the West today complain of the growing power of the state, they cannot be referring sensibly to the despotic powers of the state elite itself, for if anything these are still declining...But the complaint is more justly levelled against the state's encroachments. The powers are now immense...The state today penetrates ever day life more than did any historical state." As far as civil disobedience is concerned, Burstein (2008: 375–376) comments on "any type of conduct where the offender has intentionally broken the law for the purpose of trying to affect positive social change." In this context, civil disobedience "presents a unique challenge for the justice system, as it involves the actions of normally law-abiding citizens seeking to change public policy by illegal means or, worse, by interfering with the lawful interests of other citizens." In this context, it is quite evident that the Ipperwash protesters never intentionally set out to break the law or that they wanted to change public policy 'by illegal means'.

One is led to wonder, as the Ipperwash protest illustrates, the reasons why Indigenous protests over treaty rights and land claims almost always seems to involve the police (see Hedican 2008b, 2012b). Aboriginal leaders assume that they have the legitimate right to protest inequities in the justice system when treaty rights are abrogated. However, when elected officials meet such protesters with demonstrable force, this move shifts the balance of power away from the legitimate right of dissent. As Christie (2007: 156) argues, Indigenous protesters have a "right to free expression which is grounded in a conception of liberal democracy, and of the conditions necessary for the promotion of values and ideals highly esteemed by those living in and through a liberal democratic structure." Indeed, one may suggest that Indigenous protesters are exercising their right to peaceful assembly and free speech which is protected by our constitution.

The question, then, is "what is the appropriate nature of police activity in the face of Indigenous dissent?" In the Ipperwash case it is obvious that the leadership at the very apex of Ontario's government made a fateful decision to suppress dissent by the inappropriate and inequitable use of force. With regards such situations, Christie argues that "inappropriate police activity in relation to the Aboriginal protest may lead to questions about the relationship between the police and the government in power (especially…if it appears the government inappropriately directed the police in this matter)" (2007: 155).

A related matter concerns the suppression of the facts in the Ipperwash protest, which is to say, the obvious attempt by Premier Mike Harris to cover up his government's complicity in the death of Dudley George. As Beare (2008: 19) explains, "One can trace, for example, the refusal of the Conservative party in Ontario to hold an inquiry into the shooting of Dudley George at Ipperwash and the campaign promise made by the Liberal party that culminated in an inquiry after their election." Thus, one can perceive a certain tension in the case of the Ipperwash Inquiry between social scientific perspectives on the one hand, and the more restricted legalistic view of the events on the other. Social scientists such as criminologists are apt to be more interested in the 'working relationship' between the police and government, while lawyers would be prone to point to case law as an interpretation.

Then there is the more general view of the so-called 'Indian problem' (Dyck 1991). Anyone who is in my profession soon comes to realize that there are various points of view held by Canadian citizens. Once, when I was conducting my fieldwork in Collins during the 1970s, I was taking the CNR passenger train from Armstrong. As I was standing near the doorway waiting to disembark, the conductor approached me, asking in apparent disbelief: "You getting off here?" When I said that I was, he looked at me with a puzzled look, "But why?" he asked, again with a quizzical expression. "Well, I work here," I said. "Really?" he responded. Then, as if to confide in me, in the sense that because we were both white men that we might share similar views of the Indigenous people, he stood back in a self-protective stance and shouted, "Well, I'll tell you what I would do to solve the Indian problem. I'd drop off a case of wine and a box of hunting knives, and that would be the end of your problem!" Then he laughed a bit, as if he suddenly realized that because I was getting off at Collins I might not share his racist views.

Anytime I'm on a bus and sit down beside a fellow traveler, I never know where a conversation might lead. As soon as my seat mate finds out that I'm an anthropologist with an interest in Indigenous issues, many people have questions which they often ask in a very serious manner. "Why are these Natives protesting all the time, can't they just leave the past in the past and move on to the modern society?" is a favorite question I frequently hear. When I try to explain that there are treaties which bind the Canadian government, and as such the population at large, to certain legal commitments, their eyes sort of gloss over in disinterest. They have their misanthropic views and quite possibly hoped that I might validate them with some scholastic argument. When that does not happen, they tend to lose interest in our conversation rather quickly.

Institutional Racism

As a working definition, "institutional racism means racism that is intrinsic to the structures of society. It may be overt or covert, expressed formally in the laws of the land, or less visibly in patterns of employment and the content of school textbooks" (Barrett 1987: 307–308). Using a quote from forty years ago, Valentine (1980: 47) pointed out, as a result of successive government strategies to dominate and control Indigenous people, they "have the lowest incomes, the poorest health, and the highest rates of unemployment of any single group in the country." All these years later, similar statistics still prevail, so, what one might ask has changed? Once a phenomenon becomes institutionalized, once it becomes an integral part of a society's structural organization, it becomes virtually permanently imbedded. Thus, we find that even the Premier of Ontario, considered one of Canada's enlightened provinces, was prone to racist rhetoric. From there, racism filters down through the various layers of society, through the educational, judicial and political systems, whether its citizens wish to admit it or not, perpetuating itself through time.

The Ipperwash protest illustrates the manner in which a governmental body, such as Ontario Premier Mike Harris's coterie of like-minded politicians, can quickly mobilize the police force at its command to quell dissent. Of course this is a common practice in the repressive political regimes that the Canadian government is so quick to criticize, yet little is apparently said when such an egregious use of force is used against its own citizens. Thus, policing is an important area of concern as it relates to discrimination and institutional racism. Holbert and Rose (2004), as an example, suggest that the harsh treatment of Indigenous and racial minorities is a result of the overt racial prejudices of the individual police officers themselves. In addition, Gumbhir (2007: 55) concludes that "institutional racism and associated discriminatory practices are generally embedded in the laws, rules, policies, norms, and standard practices of an institution, and can manifest itself in discrimination in a number of ways."

Police have the prerogative to arbitrarily use their discretionary power in a prejudicial manner when it comes to arresting or detaining for questioning members of racial minorities. In Toronto, OPP Commissioner Fantano was issued a warning by the provincial government to deal with the issue of racial profiling among his police officers (*Toronto Star*, 11 December 2003). Aboriginal people express their frustration with the police prerogative of detaining people for "reasonable suspicion." There is a suspicion that there exists a police bias because such authorities are much quicker to detain or arrest Aboriginal persons suspected of committing a crime than non-Aboriginals exhibiting similar behavior. As Whyte (2008: 116) explains: "Beyond the issue of the level of the formal police practices of detaining and charging, Aboriginal people complain about being treated disrespectfully and, at times, abusively; they complain about being under constant suspicion; and they complain that police do not conduct serious and thorough investigations of crimes committed against them."

From the perspective of police officers, they complain that their role in Aboriginal land claims protests places them in an obtrusive, untenable or even dangerous position. They point out that police officers are frequently thrust into situations that are conflict-ridden in the first place, or whose parameters and ground rules are inherently ambiguous, such as Aboriginal acts of civil disobedience, with little in the way of guidelines according to which they might conduct themselves.

The Ipperwash confrontation is an example of the dangers faced by the police when the Premier of the province forces the police into a potentially dangerous situation. The OPP were told to enter Ipperwash Park as evening was setting, and they were told that a member of the Stony Point First Nation had told the OPP commander that protesters were armed with AK-47s and other firearms. However, as stated in the Ipperwash Report, "a fundamental problem was that the information about guns was not fully authenticated or verified by OPP intelligence officers" (Linden 2007: 56). In addition to the false firearms report, there was also other misinformation reported to the OPP that damage had been done to a car by a group of park occupiers. A rumor had also been started that the occupiers had smashed the windshield of a vehicle belonging to a female driver using a baseball bat. The Ipperwash Report, though, found all of this information false and misleading, as indicated by a transcript of the testimony of Detective Constable Dew derived from his comments before the Inquiry on 19 September, 2007.

There is no denying, though, the hardened racist attitudes apparently held by OPP Sergeant Stan Korosec, who was in charge of the Emergency Response Team at Ipperwash. On a recording of the incident, Officer Korosec is heard saying, "We want to amass a fucking army. A real fucking army and do this. Do these Fuckers big-time" (Linden 2007: 27). On the evening prior to the killing of Dudley George (5 September, 1995), three OPP cruisers approached the Ipperwash parking lot, and one of them rammed into one of the picnic tables on which several Anishinaabe people were sitting, causing it to break up under the impact of the collision. Stony Point protesters then flung the broken table onto the hood of the cruiser amid much yelling and commotion.

During the subsequent altercation Aboriginal witnesses to the Linden Inquiry testified that several OPP officers made racist comments, during the incident, referring to the protesters as 'wagon burners' and 'wahoos'. One of the OPP officers is said to have pointed at Dudley George and said, "Come on out, Dudley. You're going to be the first" (Linen 2007: 27). On the day of Dudley George's funeral (11 September, 1995), his sister Pam George discovered that mugs and T-shirts with the OPP insignia, mixed mockingly with Native symbols, were being sold in a local convenience store. The Ipperwash Report commented on this incident, noting that "The use of the broken arrow imagery targeted a distinct group of people by their race through the use of violent imagery. It is a negative, stereotypical symbol of the Aboriginal people in the context of the ERT Emergency Response Teams exercising their power over the occupiers" (Linden 2007: 30).

It was also noted in the Linden Report that one of the major contributing factors in the killing of Dudley George was that the directives given to the OPP officers by the Harris cabinet were comprised of members who appeared to be acting with excessive haste. The OPP officers claim, as indicated in the Linden Report, that they were not prepared in any way for a possible armed confrontation with the Ipperwash protesters, especially in an evening setting. It would appear, then, that the chain of command from the Premier's office to the OPP officers 'on the ground' was flawed and subject to misinformation. As Commissioner Linden (2007: 49) stated in his summary of the situation:

In my view, Premier Harris's comments in the dining room where the cabinet meeting was held, and generally the speed at which he wished to end the occupation of Ipperwash Park, created an atmosphere that unduly narrowed the scope of the government's response to the Aboriginal occupation. The Premier's determination to seek a quick resolution closed off many options.

Another complicating matter was that conversations between OPP officers were recorded, unknown to them, which indicated some members of the police force were flawed by racist inclinations. It is also apparent that Sergeant Ken Deane's shooting of Dudley George was a spontaneous act, although because of the impending darkness occurred under mitigating circumstances. It is important to note, however, the heightened emotions of the moment and the premeditated racist attitudes of some OPP officers. Take, as an example, a revealing seventeen-minute tape which emerged during the Inquiry which involved a conversation between OPP Inspector Ronald Fox, who had attended the 'dining room meeting' with Premier Harris at Queen's Park, and Inspector John Carson, the commander overseeing the standoff at Ipperwash Park.

Recorded on this tape is a discussion of Premier Harris's view that the government has "tried to pacify and pander to these First Nations people far too long" and that the use of "swift affirmative action" was needed to remove the protestors from the park. Officer Fox then left the meeting frustrated with the comments made by Premier Harris, and then phoned the Incident Commander at Ipperwash, Inspector Carson, to explain to him what had happened at the meeting:

"John, we're dealing with a real redneck government. They're fucking barrel suckers; they just are in love with guns, there's no question they couldn't give a shit less about the Indians (Linden 2007: 50)." Obviously this sense of urgency, whether truly reflective of the Premier's wishes or not, place particular pressure on any attempts to negotiate an end to the confrontation.

On 1 April, 1996, Dudley George's family filed a wrongful death lawsuit in which Premier Harris was named as one of the accused, based on allegations that Harris initiated and ordered the raid that killed Dudley George. When he testified at the eventual trial on 21 November 2001, Mike Harris denied that he had ordered the OPP to conduct the raid on the protesters. Then, the following year, on 19 February 2002, Mike Harris launched a $15 million libel suit against the *Globe and Mail* based on an article the newspaper published which implied that he took part in a homicide. Harris continued to deny that he ever ordered the use of force in the Ipperwash incident. However, the George family did settle a civil law suit against former Premier Harris in 2003, and accepted a $100,000 settlement from the Ontario Provincial Police plus undetermined legal costs. At the time that the Ipperwash Inquiry was called in 2007 under Premiere Dalton McGuinty, Harris referred to the allegations that he and his government were responsible was based on "false and politically motivated accusations" (*CBC News*, 31 May 2007).

Racism in Canada

Experts on racism in Canada, such as Henry and Tator (1985: 322), offer a trenchant commentary on Canada's treatment of the Indigenous population which would appear to be indicative of the handling years later of the Ipperwash protesters:

No group has suffered more seriously from racism than our native people, and Canada's discriminatory treatment of them has been widely documented. The history of the relationship between native and white Canadians has been characterized by exploitation and the denial of the most fundamental rights and freedoms, including the annihilation of native people's culture, land, and sovereignty.

When there is media attention on Indigenous issues in Canada, such as occurred during the Oka crisis or the Ipperwash protest, the federal government engages in what one researcher has called 'mock change'. As Barrett (1984: 190) reiterates:

Governmental programs set up to instill a sense of independence and self-reliance among Native people are discontinued just when it appears that they might be successful. The government makes a show of consulting with Native peoples, thus putting them momentarily off guard, but introduces legislation exactly the opposite of what was requested by Native peoples.

This is exactly what happened in 1964 when the Minister of Indian Affairs in the Trudeau government, Arthur Laing, commissioned a review of the social, educational and economic situation of the Indigenous people of Canada and to offer recommendations. When the so-called "Hawthorn Report" was released in 1966–1967, suggesting in one of its recommendations that the

Indigenous people of Canada should be regarded as 'Citizens Plus', the Trudeau government, in 1969, then presented an inexplicable proposal that was almost the exact opposite of this recommendation, suggesting that the entire Indian Affairs bureaucracy should be disbanded in the resulting White Paper, rather than a strengthening of Indigenous rights which was the expectation.

In another government tactic, during a time of crisis, a Royal commission is apt to be instituted, as was the case with the Royal Commission on Aboriginal Peoples after Oka in 1990. Millions of tax payers' dollars were subsequently paid to high flying executives and politicians for consultation fees, but little trickled down to the reserves that desperately require funding for housing and employment programs.

Canadians might succumb to a whip-lash trying to follow the federal government's inconsistent approaches to Indigenous issues. In 2007, as an example, Canada refused to ratify the United Nations Declaration on Indigenous Rights, but the following year, in 2008, Prime Minister Harper held a media friendly news conference to deliver his apparent heartfelt apology in which he "asks the forgiveness of the aboriginal peoples of this country for failing them so profoundly" (Harper 2008). It is difficult to decide what the true feelings of the politicians actually are, as they vacillate from one polar policy decision to another throughout Canadian history. It is one matter to apologize for the harm done by past administrations, but when the ostensible grief is not followed up by measures which redress this harm one could be excused for doubting the politicians' sincerity. The message conveyed when there is little in the way of supplemental actions after a crisis is that Indigenous issues in Canada are essentially trivial matters, not worth the politicians' efforts or time to examine, and not to be taken seriously.

Narratives of Disentitlement

From the moment they encountered Indigenous people in the Western hemisphere, Krech (2010: online) explains, "Europeans classified them in order to make them sensible. They made the exotic comprehensible with familiar categories. In the process, they reduced men and women to stereotypes, to caricatures, noble or ignoble, benign or malignant, rational or irrational, human or cannibal—savages all." Thus, European settlers engaged in demeaning narratives of the Indigenous people they encountered, and since

227

these people were characterized in a negative manner, an opportunity was afforded the Europeans to disenfranchise them and in the process divest them of their lands and heritage.

In Canada, the litigation over land claims has become polarized because many in the country's settler population has little interest in recognizing Indigenous rights. While there have been some court settlements, there is nonetheless a strong tendency, epitomized by Tom Flanagan (2000), to disparage the concept of Aboriginal rights. Those who support Flanagan's anti-Indigenous views, as in a number of *National Post* articles (Chwialkowska 2002; Kay 2001), suggest that government funding for reserve programs "create perverse incentives for people where there is no future." In this article, Flanagan is cited for promoting the view that the federal government should expurgate its funding for Aboriginal people's legal research and litigation of land claims. It also suggests that Ottawa cease funding for self-government programs because of its high cost and that it does little to change the appalling living conditions on some reserves.

Another supporter of Flanagan's views is Jonathan Kay (2001) who makes a neo-conservative case for the assimilation of First Nations people into the Euro-Canadian mainstream society. Of course, the assimilationist arguments have been around for a long time on the Canadian political scene. The Trudeau government's White Paper in 1969 is just one example of attempts to terminate Ottawa's responsibilities toward Indigenous people, codified in various treaties and other agreements. While a number of examples could be used to illustrate the point that various governments have attempted to suppress, or eliminate entirely, Indigenous cultures, one might point to the 1884 legislation to outlaw the potlatch, a central political and economic institution in Northwest Coast societies. In addition, a revision to the Indian Act in 1927 was a determined attempt to deny Indigenous people the right to lobby for rights and to organize themselves.

This restriction prohibited the formation of Aboriginal political groups beyond the community levels of government, with the result that national-level organizations did not begin to emerge until the 1960s. The residential school debacle was another insidious attempt to purge Indigenous culture from susceptible school children, a move which was also strongly supported by various religious bodies who saw these educational facilities as an easier path to religious conversion than proselytizing alone. In Kay's (2001) *National Post* article entitled 'A Case for Native Assimilation', he suggested the only way to eliminate Aboriginal poverty on reserves is for First Nations people to abandon their culture and adopt the values of the larger Euro-Canadian society.

What is often ignored in such diatribes is that Aboriginal status is entrenched in the Canadian Constitution Act and the Charter of Rights and Freedoms of 1982:

The guarantee in this Charter of certain rights and freedoms shall not be construed so as to abrogate or derogate from any aboriginal, treaty or other rights or freedoms that pertain to the aboriginal peoples of Canada.

The existing aboriginal and treaty rights of the aboriginal peoples of Canada are hereby recognized and affirmed. In this Act, 'aboriginal peoples of Canada' includes the Indian, Inuit and Metis peoples of Canada.

Those who would deny the significance of the federal governments' constitutional responsibilities to Aboriginal peoples commonly refer to the so-called 'Indian problem'. As an example, Noel Dyck asks in the title to his book, *What is the Indian 'Problem'* (1991). Dyck concludes that, "Although the difficulties that Indians, like all human beings, suffer are many and various, the 'problem' that has dictated their lives for so long and with such sad consequences has resulted from the usually well-intentioned by, nonetheless, coercive and arbitrary tutelage to which they have been subjected." While I would generally agree with his summation, Dyck's use of the term 'well-intentioned' is not entirely accurate, since there has been a concerted effort for most of Canada's history to subjugate the Indigenous population of the country to the best interests of the settler population.

As such, the history of the Williams Treaties among the Mississaugas is an example of the manner in which European settlers divested the Indigenous population of their lands through a process of disentitlement. In Canada, the processes of 'settler colonialism' and 'Indigenous erasure' have been going on almost from the very foundations of this country. If one examines the history of Toronto, for example, a week-long celebration occurred in 1884 with the commemoration of the city's fiftieth anniversary. In effect, this celebration was in reality a commemoration of Toronto's relationship to British colonialism and imperialism, rather than its Indigenous roots. On the first day of this event, a parade displayed Toronto's British heritage; there were speeches by Daniel Wilson, President of University College, and Chief Samson Green of the Tyendinaga Mohawks. Sadly, the event really turned out to be a celebration of the erasure of the area's Indigenous past, and celebrated instead its European future. An idealized portrayal of the Indigenous-settler partnership was on display which ignored the role of local settlers in the dispossession of the Mississauga. The 1884 commemoration marked the founding of the Toronto settlement in 1793, considered the city's 'founding moment'.

The deed by which the British settlers acquired the territory from the Mississauga in the Toronto Purchase of 1787 was deemed not even relevant enough to be mentioned, however the 1834 Act of Incorporation became 'the symbolic deed to Toronto's modernity'. Who were the Mississauga? Where did they go? They were just erased from Toronto's colonial history, as if they never existed in the first place, whereas the British allies, the Mohawks who were late comers to Ontario and certainly not one of the province's 'Indigenous' populations, were given a conspicuous seat at the podium to mark the event (Freeman 2010).

In another example, in Jeffrey Denis's (2020) *Canada at a Crossroads*, he draws on settler colonial studies to illustrate the various social and psychological barriers which exist in transforming white settler ideology toward decolonization. In particular, he finds one of the main barriers is the settlers' sense of group superiority and entitlement in the ongoing colonial process. In his book, Denis illustrates how contemporary Indigenous and settler residents relate to one another, and the manner in which they differ or maintain conflicting perspectives on such topics as treaties, history and cultural issues. However, such commonly proposed solutions—intergroup contact, apologies, and collective action—have their pitfalls as well as promises. Ultimately, Denis contends, genuine reconciliation will only come about with a radically restriction of Canadian society especially in terms of fulfilling historical treaty responsibilities.

As far as the fulfillment of treaty responsibilities is concerned, one of the main reasons that Indigenous people are speaking out against the erosion of their traditional territories by an ever-expanding Euro-Canadian population is that the settlers have an apparent voracious appetite for land. Many businesses in Canada have begun to post notices recognizing that they are situated on Indigenous land. In Guelph, Ontario, for example, the former Bookshelf Café has recently changed its name to the Miijidaa Café in recognition of the area's Indigenous heritage (*miijidaa* in Anishinaabe means 'let's eat', according to the café's website at https://miijidaa.ca).

In addition, two Indigenous leaders have spoken out as advocates for Aboriginal rights in Canada. In *Unsettling Canada* (2015), Arthur Manuel and Grand Chief Ron Derrikson build on a unique collaboration between two First Nation leaders. Both men have served as chiefs of their bands in the British Columbia interior and in the process have established international reputations. It is interesting that their backgrounds are so diverse. Grand Chief Ron Derrikson is one of the most successful Indigenous business men in the country, while Arthur Manuel has been a longtime advocate for Aboriginal title who has spoken forcefully against settler colonial attitudes that are at the root of the dispossession of Indigenous lands because of expropriations and other unjust practices that have taken place throughout Canada's history. In particular, both leaders have attempted to bring fresh perspectives and new ideas to the unfinished business of Canadian Confederation which is the place of Indigenous peoples in the country's political and economic space. In the final chapters of their book, they set out a plan for a new sustainable Indigenous economy and the various processes that could lead to their goal.

White Privilege and Settler Colonialism

'White privilege', Cousins (2014: 1385) asserts:
describes unearned advantages afforded to people who are assumed, based largely on complexion and specific physical features, to be of European, especially western European, ancestry...it favors people who are, or are presumed to be, white by enabling political and economic systems and corresponding power structures to grant only these people unmerited and simultaneously unacknowledged advantages.

The concept of white privilege is also used to understand the mechanisms of social ascendency and power. "White privilege," Stanley (2017: 149) suggests, "indicates that a person who is recognized as 'white' by the broader society is better positioned to reap advantages *owing to their whiteness*...thus they are more likely to benefit from additional layers of protective cushions such as personal failings, alcohol or drug addiction"(see also Rothenberg 2002). In addition, there are other scholars who link concepts of white privilege with processes of settler colonialism. Bonds and Inwood (2016: 715), for example, state that "We situate white supremacy...as the foundation for the continuous unfolding of practices of race and racism within settler states."

Bonds and Inwood also distinguish between colonialism, in the larger context, and settler colonialism within the parameters of these larger structures. "Settler colonialism," as such, "focuses on the *permanent* occupation of a territory and removal of indigenous people with the express purpose of building an ethically distinct national community."

As such, "settler colonialism is theoretically, politically, and geographically distinct from colonialism which is to say the imperial expansion by militaristic or economic purposes." However, settler colonialism is not conceptually divergent from the larger sphere of colonialism itself because it is essentially concerned with "the exploitation of marginalized peoples in a system of capitalism established, by and reinforced through racism" (ibid: 715). However, while these authors conceptually distinguish between the larger sphere of colonialism, and its subcategory of settler colonialism, these two processes are nonetheless linked historically. As in the Canadian case, the British government established its grip on northern Canada with the Hudson's Bay Company as an important commercial arm of its Imperial expansion, and in time its focus nevertheless moved outward as a center of population growth.

Further support for the premise that settler colonialism is founded on notions of white privilege and, furthermore, that these processes and attitudes while originating in the historical past, nonetheless find expression in the modern world. Today, Elkins and Pederson (2005: 1) suggest, the "legacies of settler colonialism are everywhere to be seen." As such, then, settler colonialism "is not in the past…but rather the foundational governing ethic of the 'new world' state" (ibid: 3). This proposition—that settler colonialism continues today as a basis for the modern world—finds further expression in the writings of Patrick Wolfe (1998, 2006) who notes that settler colonialism cannot be seen as an essentially fleeting stage but must be understood as the persistent defining characteristic of this new world settler society. Speaking of Australia, another former British colony, he succinctly states that "the determination 'settler-colonial state' is Australian society's primary structural characteristic rather than merely a statement about its origins…invasion is a structure not an event" (1998: 163).

It follows then, according to the proposition that racist attitudes toward Indigenous people begin with the assertion of white privilege, that settler colonial structures are essentially built on discriminatory structures of white entitlement and dispossession. Accordingly, the development of modernity across the world is based historically on "the emergence of white racial identities as an integral component" of the inequitable structures that are found in today's world that form the basis of unequal racial relationships in government, economy and social orders. "Indeed, it is my contention," Bonnett (2016: 2) asserts that "one cannot grasp the development of the modern world, and more especially the notion of what is modern and what is not, without an appreciation of the racialized nature of modernity, and, more particularly, of its association with a European identified white race." This would suggest, then, that Canada's issues of white privilege have their origins in a British Imperialist colonial strategy that begins initially with the Hudson's Bay Company as the vanguard of colonial capitalism, and then emerges later, as in the case of the Red River Colony, in the form of settler colonialism based on Indigenous territorial dispossession (Bumsted and Smyth 2019).

It is also evident that similar processes linking white privilege and settler expansionist strategies occurred in the United States as well. In Hixson's (2013) *American Settler Colonialism,* he explains that settler colonialism:

ultimately overwhelmed ambivalence and ambiguity. Indians, who had used and changed the land for centuries, proved willing to share land with the new comers but not simply to give it up to the settlers. The Euro-Americans, however, were on a mission to take command over colonial space. A process that entailed demarcation and control, boundaries, maps, surveys, treaties, seizures, and the commodification of the land (2013: viii; see also Harris 2004).

The topic of 'settler colonialism' has become an increasingly important discussion point in the literature concerning Indigenous people in the modern world. While various definitions of settler colonialism have been proposed in recent years, several characteristic themes have emerged in the academic literature concerning Indigenous issues in North America. As an example, Alicia Cox (2017) suggests that "Settler colonialism is an ongoing system of power that perpetuates the genocide and repression of indigenous peoples and cultures." She further suggests that settler colonialism "normalizes the continuous settler occupation, exploiting lands and resources to which indigenous peoples have genealogical relationships." This evolving field of settler colonialism focuses on the spread of Eurocentric values which suggests that the settlers have a moral superiority as a justification to occupy Indigenous lands. This type of colonialism, it is pointed out, is not a thing of the past because in many countries, such as Canada, the United States and Australia, Indigenous people continue today to be subjected to ongoing systems of domination.

This process of settlement by colonial occupiers is not simply a system of exploitation but one whereby Indigenous people are displaced from their original territories usually because of economic interests. As Zahedieh (2010: 392–393) notes, all forms of colonization revolved around the expansion of British trade. Thus, the term 'settler colonialism' can be understood to mean a form of colonialism in which the goal is to ultimately displace an Indigenous population of a colonized territory and replace them with a new society of settlers. This strategy is based on a form of exogenous domination which is usually initiated, organized, and supported by an imperial authority. The processes of domination are all-encompassing, such that "different expressions of imperialism cover all forms of colonization, including white settler nations, extractive and commodity colonies, and protectorates of strategic locations" (Kennedy 2017: 6).

Narratives of Inequality

The term 'narratives of inequality' has in recent years joined the works on Indigenous disentitlement along with such now familiar phrases as 'Indigenous erasure', 'settler colonialism', 'colonial capitalism', 'laissez-faire racism', 'post-colonial criticism', among others. In Melissa Kennedy's study, she notes that, "The crash of 2008 challenged the discourses of modernity, progress, and development that were touted as the prerequisites for worldwide improvement in standards of living and popular conceptions of wealth and poverty, by revealing at once worrying immiseration in the world's richest countries" (2017: 5–6). One of the primary reasons for this 'immiseration' is a recognition that the world's people are economically divided, as in the developing terminology, such as First and Third Worlds, 'West and the Rest', the Global North and South, and so on.

What is pertinent to the present discussion concerns the methods used by colonial powers to "winnow out the indigenous and migrant losers from the winners of capitalism" (Kennedy 2017: 17). In other words, poverty and disentitlement are 'built into' the mechanisms of colonialism in such a way as to create these 'narratives of inequality'. It is the structures of inequality that are instituted in new colonies which tend to marginalize the local Indigenous people through resource extraction, land privatization, and the labor exploitation of local populations in the interest of profit maximization in acts of collusion between resident settlers and the imperial powers.

This process of marginalization, or even 'erasure' in some terminology, is aided by the narratives created by settler populations which perpetuates in the colonies such unequal social relations and discriminatory attitudes toward the colonized. In turn, these discriminatory attitudes tend to become ingrained in settler attitudes, expressed as racism, and continues into the present day and in the cultural practices of the colonizers today. "Structures and mechanisms of capitalist inequality," Melissa Kennedy suggests, "instituted in early settlement have long-lasting repercussions, continuing today in the disproportionate poverty of indigenous peoples within nations states" (2017: 60).

Indigenous Erasure

One definition of 'Indigenous erasure' is the process "whereby settler societies discount and eliminate the presence of American Indian peoples, cultures and polities. This erasure is part of a larger imperative to diminish the existence of American Indians in order to access land and resources. One method of erasure is to narrowly define who might be an American Indian" (Orr, Sharratt and Iqbal 2019: 2078). In fact, this process of elimination has been occurring in Canada for a very long time. When treaties were signed with the various Indigenous peoples, a list was made of the signatories to these treaties. Various disputes arose because some Indigenous people were unable to attend the treaty signing ceremony and were therefore not included in the band's roll.

As time went on other Indigenous people were eliminated, such as Indigenous women who married those not regarded as 'treaty Indians'. These people then became relegated to a 'non-status' population and were denied residence on their original reserves. While the original intentions may have been to eliminate sexual discrimination in the Indian Act, Bill C-31[69] also created many new problems as well because it failed to solve the problem of 'Indian erasure' in Canadian federal legislation (see Asch, Borrows, and Tully

2018; Morgensen 2012: 2–22; King 2016). In the Trudeau-Chrétien era, with their 1969 White Paper proposal which sought to terminate the special status for First Nations people, Assembly of First National Chief Phil Fontaine commented that, "The attempts to erase our identities hurt us deeply. But it also hurt all Canadians and impoverished the character of our nation" (*CBC News*, 11 June 2008). Apparently ingrained negative attitudes toward Indigenous peoples by the larger Canadian population are not so easily erased.

Lessons Learned

In the small town in northern Ontario where I grew up, discrimination was a sensitive issue. There were two relatively large reserves in the vicinity so that proportionately the Aboriginal population was much larger than would be the case for many larger southern Ontario communities. This demographic factor meant that the people of the 'settler' population were in much more regular contact with Aboriginal people than might occur in other areas of the province.

It would be difficult to say whether or not this population balance was a factor in increasing or decreasing discriminatory acts, since one might argue the situation both ways. However, when discussing education as a factor in diminishing discrimination, which is to say, is a person less likely to discriminate against others if they are more educated? Surprisingly, in Barrett's study of right-wing extremism in Canada, he found that increased education may actually increase discriminatory tendencies:

As far as education is concerned…we are in for a surprise. Often the right wing—especially the extreme right—is dismissed as the gathering ground for the ignorant and uneducated with the assumption that if only we could get them back to school, they would see the error of their ways. Yet 62 per cent of the ninety-three radical-right cases analyzed in this study had attended university, college, or technical school (1987: 35–35).

In fact, he suggests that the percentage is probably higher because "often they remain anonymous *because* they are well-educated, economically secure, and don't want to jeopardize their positions" (ibid). One conclusion, as a matter of policy is concerned, is that increasing "education attainment per se as the panacea for the crippling problems brought on by racism is simplistic and superficial" (1987: 37). The 6 January 2021 attack on the White House would appear to bear this conclusion out as many of the protesters appeared to have solid careers as lawyers, real estate agents, nurses, managers as well as veterans of the military or police forces. In another surprising conclusion, Barrett found that increasing contact between the members of different races may actually also increase racist and anti-Semitic attitudes.

Of course one may scour the available literature on racism in society and write volumes on the topic without ever finding out why people behave the way they do or hold the misanthropic beliefs that they hold. Therefore, there is a danger here of promoting superficial ideas and lending support to faulty policies. As an anthropologist, however, I am drawn back to the basic idea that people behave and think the way they do because they learn these matters from their peers and in their upbringing which are subsequently passed down through the generations. Racist ideas are therefore difficult to change, no matter how much education a person has or how much money they earn. As such, there does not seems to be any single factor that can explain racist attitudes and beliefs.

In the family that I grew up in, my father told us on a fairly regular basis that "if you can't say anything good about another person, then don't say anything at all." Then my mother, who grew up in southern Ontario during the 1930s, would relate the discriminatory behavior that was inflicted upon her family because they belonged to the Catholic faith. On my father's side of the family, whose relative came from Ireland, he had his own stories to relate about anti-Irish attitudes. As my own life turned out, I met an Anishinaabe woman and we had four children together. They often attend Aboriginal events, especially during the summer, such as sweat lodges, pow-wows, Native dances and teaching by elders. My children then also realize the benefits of cultural understanding. My son moved to northern Ontario and married an Aboriginal woman and they live on a reserve with their two daughters. One of my daughters won the Tom Longboat award as Canada's Indigenous athlete of the year. I never planned my life this way; you can call us biracial if you want but we all just try to be supportive of each other and stick to the positive matters in life, as my father suggested.

Conclusion

If Canada is regarded by others as one of the most tolerant nations in the world, then this is unfortunately for the most part an inaccurate characterization. The Indigenous people of this country have suffered through a continual history of discriminatory acts from the very pinnacle of our political system, in terms of repressive government policies, almost since the very beginning of European settlement in Canada. Their land was often taken away from them by force, or other schemes, which reduced their population through disease and policy measures which diminished their ability to make a satisfactory living. Treaties were made, and then inexplicably broken. Protests were held on many occasions by members of the Indigenous population, but these were at times met with deadly force. Assimilationist policies were forced upon them, such as the residential school system, by the members of religious bodies under the guise of charitable acts. How the Indigenous people were able to survive to any degree at all under such repressive political, economic and social systems is a major miracle in itself.

The Ipperwash protest of September, 1995, by the Stony and Kettle Point Indigenous people further illustrates as much as any other incident the depth to which racist attitudes exist in Ontario. The Anishinaabe people signed a treaty with the British government in 1827 ceding millions of acres of their territory for very minimal considerations. Then, through insidious means by agents of the Indian Affairs Department, the small amount of land that the Indigenous people were given in return was removed from their possession, against their will, by a collusion of government employees, politicians and greedy real estate agents for private gain in order to create Ipperwash Provincial Park. Furthermore, during the Second World War a further erosion of their land base occurred when the War Measures Act was used to remove additional Indigenous lands to create Camp Ipperwash.

Since they had no other recourse, the Stony and Kettle Point residents began a protest against these measures by occupying Ipperwash Park with unarmed men, women, and children. This protest was met with the most egregious use of force imaginable when the Premier of Ontario sent in a highly armed tactical force of OPP officers. The use of racially motivated profanity in reference to the Indigenous protesters was used by both the Premier, Mike Harris, and the OPP leader of the tactical response team. An OPP sergeant,

Kenneth Deane, showed little in the way of caution by shooting protester Dudley George for no apparent reason other than he was carrying a walking stick. This incident illustrates the hardened racist attitudes which continue to be exhibited today and which permeate the governmental and law enforcement agencies.

Chapter Nine
Anthropology in the Courtroom

The government of Canada sincerely apologizes and asks the forgiveness of the aboriginal peoples of this country for failing them so profoundly.

Prime Minister Stephen Harper, 11 June 2008

Canadian politicians are fond of talking about restorative justice, reconciliation and forgiveness, especially when on the campaign trail before elections. Unfortunately, after their speech is over they return to their regular business of suppressing Aboriginal rights in the courts. Does anyone really know, as an example, how much of the Canadian tax payers' money is used to litigate indigenous land claims?

The Cost of Litigating Indigenous Land Claims

APTN (Aboriginal People's Television Network) ran a news report with the title 'Despite Promise of Reconciliation, Trudeau Spent Nearly $100 million Fighting First Nations in Court in his First Years in Power' (18 December 2020, https://www.aptnnews.ca). The claim is made that the Liberals under Justin Trudeau spent more than Stephen Harper's government over a similar three-year time period.

If the claim is correct, the amount of money spent by the Trudeau government litigating Indigenous land claims in Canada is nothing short of astounding. CIRNAC (Crown-Indigenous Relations and Northern Affairs Canada) spent $58 million on legal services in the last fiscal year (2019) which is two times more than that spent by the RCMP or the Defense Department respectively, and more than any federal department other than the Canadian Revenue Agency, APTN claims, based on their research into existing public records.

All in all, CIRNAC was involved in 366 active court cases, with another 764 'dormant' ones, in 2019, amounting to $6.6 billion in legal liabilities. Its overall potential legal liabilities rose to $22.4 billion with land claims and other special claims factored in. To put this all-in perspective, this figure amounted to 85 percent of the entire federal government's total contingent financial liability(seehttps://www.rcaanccirnac.ca/eng/1577108612523/157777108888 864#chp5). What this means is that CIRNAC is the most sued and most legally exposed federal department in the Canadian government. To put this all in perspective, the Justice Department alone incurred $3.2 million in court costs fighting survivors of St. Anne's Indian Residential School since 2013.

Prime Minister Trudeau spent slightly more cash on Indigenous lawsuits through his first three years in power than Harper did in his last three years when the department was known as Indian and Northern Affairs Canada (INAC). Under former Prime Minister Stephen Harper, INAC spent $92.4 million on litigation between 2012 and 2015. Under Trudeau, the department spent $95.9 million—$3.5 million more—between 2015 and 2018.

After winning power five years ago, Trudeau promised to reject the 'adversarial', 'ineffective', and 'profoundly damaging' approaches of the past. "It is time for a renewed, nation-to-nation relationship with First Nations peoples, one that understands that the constitutionally guaranteed rights of First Nations in Canada are not an inconvenience but rather a sacred obligation," he told the Assembly of First Nations delegates in 2015. Since that time, the former INAC complex—now split into CIRNAC and Indigenous Services Canada—has spent $346.9 million on legal services. For the most part, all of these legal battles and the money spent goes on outside of the public eye.

Prime Minister Justin Trudeau at the Assembly of First Nations Special Chiefs Assembly in 2015. Photo: APTN

The Anthropologist as Expert Witness

In the early months of 2015, I began a series of telephone conversations with Mr. Peter W. Hutchins, an attorney specializing in Canadian Aboriginal law, whose company, Hutchins Legal Inc., is based in Montréal, Quebec. As a litigator, he has appeared before the Supreme Court of Canada, the Federal Court of Canada, as well as the courts of virtually of all of Canada's provinces and Northwest Territories. He has particularly been involved in negotiations concerning historical and contemporary treaties between First Nations and the Crown in right of Canada. Hutchins Legal Inc. provides further information on its webpage:

Our law firm continues to build its reputation for delivering effective, responsive, and creative solutions to the diverse legal matters faced by First Nations, Inuit and Métis peoples and communities. We are committed to building partnerships with our clients in order to best protect and promote their interests and needs (http://hutchinslegal.ca).

The purpose of the phone calls, Mr. Hutchins explained, was to ask if I would be willing to participate in an Indigenous land claim dispute as an expert witness in support of a number of First Nations who had initiated a land claims over the Williams Treaties of 1923 in southeastern Ontario. He indicated that he had previously made several phone calls around Ontario and eventually reached an Anishinaabe professor from an Aboriginal studies department, as well as discussing the matter with several other interested parties. This professor indicated that he did not feel confident to become involved in the land claims case himself because he had limited practice in such instances; however, he recommended me because of my experience in engaging with various Indigenous issues in the province.[70]

This attorney also said he learned that I had forty years' experience teaching Indigenous studies courses at the university level, was involved in previous land claims cases, and would have the expertise to help them out. As a starter, he said, the law firm wanted me to prepare an affidavit that would be used as evidence in a Federal Court of Canada hearing to take place in May of that year. This affidavit, he explained, would be used in support of the Plaintiffs, the Mississaugas of Alderville First Nation et al. in their claim pertaining to the Williams Treaties of 1923.[71] It was also probable, Mr. Hutchins indicated, that I would be subsequently called as an expert witness to give verbal testimony concerning an affidavit that I would be asked to prepare. My affidavit, it was explained, was to assess the credibility of another affidavit presented by the Crown, as defendants in the case, which had been prepared by Dr. Alexander von Gernet.

Alexander von Gernet's Affidavit

The affidavit in question had been prepared by Alexander von Gernet, an archaeologist by training, who was frequently brought forward by the Crown in their attempts to undermine the credibility of oral testimony given by Indigenous elders in various land claims cases. As an example, von Gernet testified on behalf of the Crown in the *Buffalo v. Canada* (2005) case which dealt with the treaty rights claims of the Samson Lake Cree of Alberta. As might be expected, von Gernet testified that oral evidence cannot stand alone, which is to say, it must be corroborated with other lines of evidence.[72] As such, in case after case, a central issue pertained to the emphasis that courts should place on oral traditions as a basis for Indigenous land claims in Canada, and Dr. von Gernet was usually the Crown's expert witness.

As Arthur Ray (2015) explained:

Normally courts only accept evidence from eyewitnesses because of the 'hearsay rule'. This rule precludes judges from receiving evidence from individuals who have obtained it 'second hand'. The problem in Aboriginal and treaty rights litigation is that the historical questions that inevitably arise call for the gathering of evidence from a time period that lies beyond the direct experiences of living people (i.e., the current generation).

Ray provides further clarification: "Oral evidence presented by Elders often poses the biggest challenge to the courts given that judges normally do not deal with this type of evidence, nor are they familiar with the Aboriginal protocols that are associated with it (see also Ray 2012)." Similarly, in a classic work on this topic, *Oral Tradition as History*, Jan. Vansina differentiated these two types of knowledge noting that oral histories are "reminiscences, hearsay, or eyewitness accounts about events and situations which are contemporary, that is, which occurred during the lifetime of the informants, but oral traditions are no longer contemporary. They have passed from mouth to mouth, for a period beyond the lifetime of the informants" (1985: 12–13). As such, oral traditions can be understood to extend across several generations.

The problem facing the courts in weighing the accuracy of Indigenous oral history arose prominently in a significant Aboriginal fishing case in British Columbia known as *Regina v. Van der Peet* (1996). In this case, the presiding judge appeared to diminish the importance of the oral evidence. However, when the case was appealed, the Supreme Court of Canada warned that:

A court should approach the rules of evidence, and interpret the evidence that exists, conscious of the special nature of aboriginal claims, and of the evidentiary difficulties in proving a right which originates in times where there were no written records of the practices, customs and traditions engaged in…The courts must not undervalue the evidence presented by aboriginal claimants simply because it does not conform to standards of evidence presented in other cases (*Regina v. Van der Peet,*1996, para. 9).[73]

These lines of reasoning resonate with Miller's (2011) discussion, in *Oral History on Trial,* regarding the usages of oral history as valid evidence in litigation. Miller suggests that the boundaries between oral history and oral tradition are nebulous at best, and therefore there is no clear demarcation between the two. The reasons that Miller gives for this situation is that the characteristics of oral traditions show considerable diversity in their narrative formats and internal structural composition. Oral traditions also serve different purposes from society to society, and are apt to be interpreted differently by the members of various generations.

In Ray's (2012) essay, he also points to similar difficulties, noting that:

Traditional knowledge and oral traditions history are crucial lines of evidence in Aboriginal claims litigation and alternative forms of resolution, most notably claims commissions. These lines of evidence pose numerous challenges in terms of how and where they can be presented, regarding who is qualified to present it, concerning the question of whether this evidence can stand on its own, and developing appropriate measures to protect it from inappropriate use by outsiders while not unduly restricting access by the traditional owners.

Thus, there are many reasons why Indigenous oral traditions do not mesh very well with the customary procedures of Euro-Canadian jurisprudence.

In yet another case (*Tsilhqot'in Nation v. British Columbia*, 2007[74]), Professor von Gernet again testified on behalf of the Crown in which his assessment focused on the use of oral history as an inadequate basis for establishing lines of evidence. In this case, von Gernet testified that oral history evidence could never stand on its own. Justice Vickers, however, rejected von Gernet's opinion as mere conjecture: "I was left with the impression that von Gernet would be inclined to give no weight to oral tradition evidence in the absence of some corroboration…His approach is not legally sound…if a court were to follow the path suggested by von Gernet, it would fall into legal error on the strength of the current jurisprudence" (2007, para. 154).

Bruce Miller has conducted a thorough review of von Gernet's experience as an expert witness and his views of oral traditions. According to Miller (2011: 9), von Gernet "creates a false dichotomy and implies a subordination of oral materials to written historical ones and of Aboriginal epistemology to that of North Atlantic sensibilities, a position in contradiction to that of the Supreme Court of Canada." In another case, *Benoit v. Canada*[75] (2003), Miller stated that:

"Benoit relied on Crown expert testimony that was highly suspect to anthropologists and Aboriginal scholars alike" (2011: 110). Napoleon's view was that "there are several other very troublesome parts to the Court of Appeal's judgment. The Court relied on the evidence of von Gernet, quoting him at great length about weighting oral history evidence" (Napoleon 2005: 136).

Thus, when the attorney for the Hutchins Legal firm presented me with an affidavit prepared by von Gernet, and asked for my written opinion, which would then be presented as evidence to the Federal Court of Canada in the Alderville et al. land claim, there was an expectation as to what to expect since a trail of discussion has followed him in the scholarly literature. Alexander von Gernet's affidavit that was presented to me appeared to differ hardly at all from that which he gave in the previous cases cited above. His basic point was that the oral testimony of Indigenous elders was not reliable as evidence, and that it was probably inferior, in his opinion, to that of written documents, which many of us would not regard by now as a hackneyed and clichéd point of view.

In my own affidavit to the Federal Court of Canada, sworn on 30 April 2015, I made the following statement in relationship to my perceived knowledge of von Gernet's credentials to pass an opinion on Indigenous oral testimony:

Whatever he might say about the previous research conducted into Indigenous oral traditions by Dr. Manitowabi, it would have very little academic, practical or professional merit. Of primary importance is that Dr. von Gernet's training has been in the field of archaeology and there is little indication that he has ever conducted first hand research in community settings using a grounded theory approach. As far as his publication and teaching record is concerned, again there is little indication that he knows much more about the topic than the average undergraduate student would have (Canada 2015).

I searched in vain for any evidence that he had conducted even a modicum of credible research into Indigenous oral traditions and could not find anything, except for a few obscure government reports. One wonders, then, on what basis he was forming his opinions. Certainly training as an archaeologist does not give one this sort of career preparation. And then, perhaps most importantly of all, there are implications of bias in his testimony because of the (alleged) substantial payments made to him by the Federal Government to testify against Indigenous interests.

As an example, Paul Barnsley, a reporter for the Indigenous *Windspeaker* newspaper, sought documents relating to von Gernet's payments by DIAND (Department of Indian Affairs and Northern Development) through an access to information request. It is curious that the name of the beneficiary of these payments was blacked out, however, Barnsley contends, with confidence, that the money was paid to von Gernet. He further proposed that von Garnet "has been paid more than $321,000.00 for a contract that began in July 10, 1999, and was to end on October 31." In addition, "pay-out for his services totaled $82,390.00, bringing his von Gernet's earnings to date to about $278,000.00."

Barnsley also noted that von Gernet had testified on behalf of the Crown in the Samson Cree Nation's oil and gas lawsuit. He contended that under the circumstance von Gernet would have hardly been in a position to provide unbiased expert testimony as he was in effect on the Crown's payroll. In other words, the implication is that von Gernet was paid specifically to delegitimize Indigenous interests in the Samson Cree Nation's oil and gas lawsuit:

Native leaders have long complained that DIAND pays huge sums of money to entice educated people to testify against Native claimants in court...They believe the large sums offered are a subtle inducement to see things the government's way (Barnsley 2002).

By comparison, in terms of my own involvement in the *Alderville et al.* case, the final invoice that I submitted to Hutchins Legal, which involved seven hours of cross-examination in Federal Court, travel back and forth from Guelph to Toronto, preparation of an affidavit, visiting a lawyer for commission of the affidavit, various phone calls, emails and review of numerous documents amounted to $1,415.00. I was well aware that it would be the Indigenous people who would be paying my expenses, whereas in the case of von Gernet his fees were paid in effect by the Canadian taxpayer for which there was little apparent accountability required.

Treaties of Southern Ontario

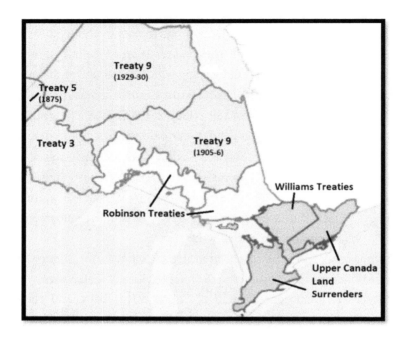

Treaties of Ontario
Courtesy of the Government of Ontario

In order to gain title to Indigenous land, Britain negotiated a series of treaties—known as the Upper Canada land surrenders—with the Mississauga, Chippewa and other First Nations residing near the St. Lawrence River and lower Great Lakes. Between 1781 and 1812, these land surrenders transferred ownership to the Crown in exchange for one-time payments and in some cases, hunting and fishing rights. Surrenders that occurred after 1818 were compensated with annuities (annual payments).

However, much of the land in the upper Ottawa River and Muskoka regions had not been surrendered. This was problematic because the Ontario government was already using that land for white settlement but without the relinquishment of Aboriginal Title. As Borrows and Coyle assert, "reflecting on the relationship between Canada and First Peoples raises fundamental questions about Canada's legitimacy as a state and of Canadians' claims to be entitled to live where they do" (2007: 3). Lack of a treaty meant that the

Chippewa and Mississauga inhabitants were not receiving anything in exchange for the use of their land, such as financial compensation or the guarantee of land rights. Additionally, the Johnson-Butler Purchase of 1787–1788 presumably surrendered a large tract of territory along the central north shore of Lake Ontario for settlement, but this was later disputed.[76] Indigenous calls for redress eventually resulted in a federal investigation.

Appointed by the minister of justice in 1916, Robert V. Sinclair began to investigate these matters. He confirmed that there were in fact many problems with the treaties' allotment of lands and that not all lands had been fully ceded. In 1923, the governments of Ontario and Canada appointed a three-man commission—known as the Williams Commission—to further investigate. It consisted of Robert V. Sinclair (the commission's federal negotiator), Uriah McFadden (a lawyer) and Angus S. Williams (the provincial negotiator). The commission's ensuing report affirmed Indigenous historic claims to large tracts of land in central and southern Ontario. Consequently, in 1923 the commissioners brokered two new treaties—known as the Williams Treaties—to extinguish Chippewa and Mississauga title to the lands in question.

The Williams Treaties, 1923

The Williams Treaties were signed in October and November, 1923, by the governments of Canada and Ontario, and by seven First Nations of the Chippewa of Lake Simcoe (Beau Soleil, Georgina Island and Rama) and the Mississauga of the north shore of Lake Ontario (Alderville, Curve Lake, Hiawatha and Scugog Island).

As the last historic land cession treaties in Canada, the Williams Treaties transferred over 20,000 km^2 of land in south central Ontario to the Crown; in exchange, Indigenous signatories received one-time cash payments. While Chippewa and Mississauga peoples argue that the Williams Treaties also guaranteed their right to hunt and fish on the territory, the federal and provincial governments have interpreted the treaty differently, resulting in legal disputes and negotiations between the three parties about land rights. In 2018, the Williams Treaties First Nations and the Governments of Ontario and Canada came to a final agreement, settling litigation about land surrenders and harvesting rights.

No negotiations preceded the signing of the Williams Treaties in 1923. Instead, government officials dictated the terms that Canada and Ontario had decided earlier that year to the First Nations signatories. The reason for the governments' haste may have had to do with the fact that Ontario was already using most of the territory in question, and therefore, officials were highly motivated to extinguish all remaining title to it. Historian Peggy Blair (2009) added that First Nations peoples may have been ready to take their grievances to the League of Nations and to British officials in London, England in that same year, perhaps prompting the federal government to move quickly with the treaties.

Federal representatives signed the first Williams Treaty between 31 October and 7 November 1923 with the Chippewa peoples of Rama, Christian Island and Georgina Island in the Lake Simcoe area. The second treaty, essentially identical to the first, was signed by the Mississauga peoples of Alderville, Scugog Lake, Mud Lake and Rice Lake between 15 and 21 November 1923. Signings occurred on band territory.

By signing the treaties, the Crown received three tracts of land: the first lay between the Etobicoke and Trent Rivers and was framed by Lake Ontario's northern shore, the second expanded north from the first to Lake Simcoe. Together, these tracts made up roughly 6,475 km^2. The third tract of land measured 45,584 km^2 and lay between the Ottawa River and Lake Huron. In exchange, the Mississauga and Chippewa peoples received a one-time payment of $25 for each band member. The Mississauga also received $233,425, while the Chippewa received $233,375 (both were one-time payments). From an Anishinaabe perspective, this money made up a fraction of their land's estimated value.

Interpretations and Perspectives

When compared to the Upper Canada land surrenders and Numbered Treaties, the Williams Treaties provided less favorable terms for the First Nations signatories. The Chippewa and Mississauga peoples, who had no legal representation at the treaty talks, received modest lump sum payments for large sections of land instead of annuity payments distributed in perpetuity. The Williams Treaties also surrendered hunting and fishing rights to off-reserve lands—a significant departure from what had become common practice in the

Robinson (Superior and Huron) and Numbered Treaties. The Williams Treaties were concluded between Canada, Ontario, and seven Chippewa and Mississauga First Nations. These Treaties provided for no annuities, no treaty rights, and no reserve lands. They marked the culmination of decades of injustice suffered by the Chippewa and Mississauga during which the Crown failed to respect the First Nations' Pre-Confederation Treaty rights and settled the First Nations' territories which had not been surrendered contrary to the Royal Proclamation[77].

There are various reasons as to why the Williams Treaties look different than other land cessions. In addition to the government's hastiness with the treaty proceedings, historian Peggy Blair (2009) argues that after the mid-1800s, the Ontario government, keen on facilitating white settlement, may have purposefully excluded certain Indigenous rights from the written text of the Williams Treaties. She also suggests that the Canadian courts caused a serious injustice by applying erroneous cultural assumptions in their interpretation of the evidence. In particular, they confused provincial government policy, which has historically favored public over special rights, with the understanding of the parties at the time. The signatories may not have realized that they were relinquishing these rights because in historic treaties they were usually retained. Land use rights in the territory covered by the Williams Treaties has been the subject of 20th- and 21st-century legal disputes between the descendants of Indigenous signatories and the federal and provincial governments.

Alderville Litigation and the 2018 Settlement

In 1992, the seven Williams Treaties First Nations filed a lawsuit against the federal government—*Alderville Indian Band et al v. Her Majesty the Queen et al*—seeking financial compensation for the 1923 land surrenders and harvesting rights. In May 2012, the trial entered the first stage in which profile witnesses, chosen by the community, testified on behalf of their community to the court. Stage two began on 29 October 2012 and involved the testimony of experts in subjects involving treaties and Canadian history. Based on the evidence presented, Canada and Ontario acknowledged limited off-reserve treaty harvesting rights, specifically in the Treaty 20 area, as well as other regions covered by certain pre-Confederation treaties.

In 2016–2017, the parties discussed ways to negotiate a settlement outside of the courts, and litigation was dropped in favor of ongoing negotiations. In March 2017, the Ontario government announced that the province, the federal government and the seven Williams Treaties First Nations had begun formal talks to resolve the issues identified in the Alderville litigation.

In 2018, the Williams Treaties First Nations together with the Governments of Ontario and Canada came to a final agreement, settling the litigation. The terms include financial compensation ($666 million by Canada and $444 million by Ontario), recognition of treaty harvesting rights, and the ability for each of the First Nations to add 4,452 ha. to their reserve. Additionally, the Governments of Ontario and Canada formerly apologized to the Williams Treaties First Nations. On 17 November 2018, in Rama, Ontario, the Honorable Carolyn Bennett, Minister of Crown-Indigenous Relations, apologized on behalf of the Government of Canada for the negative impacts of the 1923 Williams Treaties on the Williams Treaties First Nations (Borrows and Coyle 2017; Blair 2009; Hedican 2017; Surtees 2017; https://williamstreatiesfirstnations.ca/).

There is no way to undo the past, nor to fully atone for wrongs perpetuated over many decades. In concluding a negotiated settlement that includes compensation to address historic wrongs, the ability to expand your reserve land bases, and the recognition of your pre-Confederation treaty harvesting rights, I believe that we have the opportunity to open a new chapter. A chapter where trust can be rebuilt; Anishinaabe culture, language, and teachings are celebrated; treaty rights are respected; and our relationship is further strengthened for the benefit of the seven generations to come. We are committed to writing this next chapter together, in the spirit of reconciliation and partnership.

Thank you. Miigwetch.

Chief Kelly LaRocca, representing the Williams Treaties First Nations, then presented the following conciliatory statement:

After almost a century of our ancestors being denied access to their lands, their harvesting rights, their culture and their way of life, the Williams Treaties Settlement Agreement is a testament to the perseverance of our people. While no amount of compensation, financial or otherwise, can ever truly compensate or repair the intergenerational trauma or loss of cultural continuity that the seven First Nations signatory to the Williams Treaties have suffered, this settlement agreement marks the beginning of healing for our people. We look forward to a future that moves on from the legacy of 95 years of protesting, petitioning, litigating and finally negotiating to redress these historical injustices. Today we finally celebrate the just recognition of our existing constitutionally protected harvesting rights, ability to expand our lands, financial compensation and the formal apology from the governments of Canada and Ontario to our ancestors and all of our people. Today marks the renewal of our Treaty relationship with one another.

However, *Anishinabek News* (21 November 2018), in an editorial entitled 'Williams Treaty Settlement Looks Huge in Headlines', presents a less salubrious view of the treaty settlement, "The $1.1 billion settlement amounts to $85 an acre for the land which the Crown claims was 'surrendered' by the terms of the Williams treaties, from the shore of Lake Ontario to Lake Nipissing in the north, from Lake Huron east to the Ottawa River. Property in that area currently sells for between $12,000 and $15,000 per acre."

Anthropology in the Courtroom

On 5 May 2015, the day that I was scheduled to be cross-examined by the Crown on my affidavit, I agreed to meet with Mr. Hutchins before the proceedings in a coffee shop across from the International Reporting room, 100 King St. N., Toronto, where the morning's proceedings were to take place. Since the proceedings were to take place beginning at about 1:00 pm, we did not have much time to discuss whatever strategy we might consider to adopt.

We got down to the matter at hand rather quickly. Mr. Hutchins' first question to me was "What approach do you think the Crown's attorney will take during your cross-examination?" I answered, in retrospect rather naively it turned out, "Well I expect that the attorney will try to find out my attitudes toward the Williams Treaties and how Professor von Gernet's affidavit addressed this issue."

"You would expect that would be the Crown's intention," Mr. Hutchins responded, "but most likely the approach will be to undermine your credibility, perhaps even in subtle ways that you might not expect, in order to suggest that your assessment of von Gernet's affidavit is not credible."

"You have to be aware," he continued, "that the Crown's lawyers are very clever people, so you will need your wits about you from the very beginning of the cross-examination. It will be slippery slope downhill for you if you are not prepared."

"Now," Mr. Hutchins asked, "have you given any thought to how you will approach the questions?" I mentioned that the last time that I had this much on the line in a cross-examination was at my PhD thesis defense which was many years ago. At this defense, I realized that there was a two-hour time limit, so when each question was asked of me I tried to become very verbose, continuing to talk even when the chair of the defense was tapping his watch vigorously. My thinking at the time was that as soon as I finished my response, another perhaps more challenging question would be coming my way, so I would be wise to continue with my answer as long as possible.

At this, Mr. Hutchins began to laugh: "Sorry to say, but this is more serious than a grad thesis defense, there is a lot on the line here, and your previous approach will only get you into trouble. The lawyers will cut you off quickly if they think that you are getting off track. Here's what I would suggest, try to keep your answers brief. The more you talk, the greater the possibility that the lawyers will find reasons to dig more deeply into your answers. So, it is best, I think, not to elaborate too much. Also, it is important to try to anticipate the direction of the lawyer's questions; ask yourself "where is he or she going with this line of questions?" So with this bit of advice, I suddenly grew apprehensive, but I kept reminding myself that I was supposed to be the expect here—try to keep a calm demeanor and do not get flustered.

The original transcript of the cross-examination (Canada 2015; Hedican 2015a) comprises over 80 pages so there is no need for a recounting here on all the details involved. However, in order to give some sense of the questioning and my responses, I have included for the reader's perusal the initial stages of the proceedings. The cross-examination began at 1:00 pm and for the next two hours I was questioned by the lawyer representing the Federal Government. After this, we had a 30-minute break which was followed by further questions by a lawyer representing the Government of Ontario.

FEDERAL COURT
OF CANADA
BETWEEN:

MISSISSAUGAS OF ALDERVILLE FIRST NATION ET AL.
Plaintiffs
and

HER MAJESTY THE QUEEN
Defendant
and

HER MAJESTY THE QUEEN IN RIGHT OF ONTARIO
Defendant

This is the cross-examination of **DR. EDWARD HEDICAN** on his affidavits sworn to on 30 April 2015, held on consent of the parties at the offices of International Reporting Inc., 100 King Street West, Toronto, Ontario on May 5, 2015.

Upon commencing on Tuesday, 5 May 2015 at 1:03 p.m.

COURT REPORTER: Please state your name for the record.

THE AFFIANT: My name is Edward Hedican.

CROSS-EXAMINATION BY MR. YOUNG:

Q. All right, Dr. Hedican. You swore or affirmed an affidavit on 30 April 2015.

A. That's correct.

Q. Your current academic or professional position is what?

A. I'm a full professor of anthropology at the University of Guelph.

Q. Do you have an academic specialty or an area of concentration within anthropology?

A. Yes, I would say that my area of specialization is in Aboriginal or Indigenous studies, especially with grounded field work, qualitative methods, and ethnography. I've conducted very extensive field research in northern Ontario.

Q. Okay. So help me understand when you say 'contemporary' meaning, what, specifically, that expression means to you in terms of defining your work and the area of your—the area within which you work.

A. We have a term in anthropology called the 'ethnographic present', meaning the present-day situation that research is being conducted in. So when I'm conducting research, it is occurring in the now time, as it were, the present.

Q. The time at which the research is being conducted? A. Right.

Q. So the term 'ethnographic present' would refer to the specific present during which that particular research was conducted, not research that was conducted on peoples living in the past.

Q. Or events of the past.

Q....a piece of information. There's a code of conduct, and since you're testifying, strictly speaking, you should bind yourself to it. So I'm going to provide it to you. It's a published thing. I'll give you an opportunity to read it, and ask whether you agree to abide by it in giving your—swearing your affidavit and in giving your testimony here.

This is from the Federal Court Rules. It's a schedule under Rule 52.2— you'll see this when you see it—called 'Schedule Code of Conduct for Expert Witnesses'.

And take a moment to read it. Please don't feel rushed.

Q. Now, I'd asked you about the code earlier, and I wanted to just get your guidance on the role of anthropologists in this kind of work that we're now faced with, we as people involved in a lawsuit.

And the book that you referred to, I think, even in your affidavit, is 'Applied Anthropology in Canada: Understanding Aboriginal Issues'?

A. Yes.

Q. It's the second edition?

A. Right.

Q. That's the most recent one?

A. Right.

Q. Published by University of Toronto Press?

Q. You probably didn't bring it with you, but I have a copy of a particular chapter I'd like you to look at, if you could. Chapter 3. Just have a look at this. It's called 'Research Strategies, Advocacy in Anthropology'. Do you see that? Is that from your book?

A. Yes.

Q. It's a reproduction of a chapter from your book?

A. Correct.

MR. YOUNG: Could we mark that reproduction of the chapter from his book as Exhibit Number 1, please?

EXHIBIT NO. 1:

Copy of Chapter 3 of 'Applied Anthropology in
Canada: Understanding Aboriginal Issues' by Dr. Hedican
MR. YOUNG: Thank you.

Q. Now, looking at Exhibit 1, if I could take you to your copy, page 62 of the book. There's a section called 'The Advocacy Question in Applied Anthropology'.

Q. I'm just going to read this short section to you to make sure we're on the same page, but two pages here:

"The basis of advocacy anthropology...Do you see that at the bottom of page 62?"

A. I do.

Q. "The basis of advocacy anthropology is the view that objectivity in the social sciences is, for the most part, an illusion. Furthermore, one's failure to push for the implementation of a goal represents a form of advocacy in itself. The reason objectivity is considered illusory is because personal and political biases frequently play a role in controlling the anthropologist's commitment to study one situation rather than another. To opt out, to refrain from action is, itself, a form of advocacy because one's interaction ensures that the actions of others will have a greater effect on the final outcome of a situation."

Is that something you wrote?

A. It's something I wrote, but it's a summary of the article by Marvin Harris in 1991.

Q. Is it a view that you adopted when you wrote it?

A. It's—as I mentioned, it's a summary of this particular person's point of view. It's not particularly my personal, say, persuasion.

Q. Do you have a different view about objectivity in anthropology than the one that's expressed here in your book?

Q. So is your persuasion different from what's expressed in this two pages from your book?

A. I would say probably, yes.

Q. In what way is it different?

A. I feel that taking sides limits a person's objectivity, so I'm not necessarily condoning it. And these are not—this is not a position I'm stating that I necessarily endorse. This chapter is about different points of view that anthropologists have on the basis of different types of research that have been conducted.

Q. So after reviewing these different points of view in your book, do you come to a place that I should be looking for where you would express your views on research strategies and advocacy in applied anthropology? Is there a place I'm going to find it in your book?

Q. My question is, if I look to the conclusion of this book, 'Anthropology in Canada', second edition, will I find your position on the advocacy question in applied anthropology?

A. Possibly. You'd have to point out a particular page or—

Q. So you can't tell me—it's your book. You're the author.

A. Right. I just told you what my position is.

Q. Yes. Your position is—

A. That advocacy tends to run counter to objectivity which, in turn, tends to undermine, I guess, an anthropologist's analysis of particular situations.

Q. That means they—the anthropologist should examine the entire record without intention, fear or concern about showing any bias.

A. It depends on what the entire record is that you're talking about.

Q. Well, the record that's available on a particular subject.

A. Are we talking about contemporary records, historical records?

This line of questioning concerning objectivity in anthropology and possible biases by the researcher continued for a considerable period of time. The questioning then eventually moved on to the role of the expert witness in litigation, which in this case concerned presenting evidence in land claims cases.

Q. You do understand that in litigation, experts testify for the Court.

A. Right.

Q. You've read the code of conduct.

A. Right.

Q. You do understand that experts typically respond to specific questions or are given terms of reference to guide their research.

A. Okay.

Q. You understand that practice, don't you?

A. Absolutely.

Q. It's not something you've had to do because you haven't been in cases, but at least you understand that that's an approach, which is to set terms of reference.

A. Correct. Maybe I haven't done it in a—a legal environment, but this type of approach is pervasive in the academic life in which I live. We submit articles for peer review, for example.

People assess the merits, the strengths, the weaknesses of different papers. So—

Q. Yes. I'm not asking about that.

A. So—

Q. I wasn't asking about that, but…other researchers' terms of reference.

A. Could you clarify the term 'terms of reference'?

Q. Well, that's what I'm asking about, Doctor. You haven't done a report for a lawsuit before; correct?

A. By 'terms of reference', do you mean a person's particular perspective, their particular political persuasion? I'm not—

Q. Let's deal with this—

A. —sure—

Q. —one question—

A. Well, I'm not sure what you're asking. That's all.

Q. That's fair. I'll try and make it clearer. But let's deal with it one question at a time.

I asked you if you had worked—you confirmed that you have not worked to prepare a report for litigation before.

A. Correct.

Q. You prepared an affidavit here.

A. There's always a first time.

Q. When you prepared the affidavit here, were you asked to address a particular subject?

Commentary

At this point, there was a short break in the proceedings and when everyone retuned the topic turned to the validity of Indigenous oral testimony in land claims cases. Eventually, near the end of the question period, the prosecuting attorney retuned once again to the conclusion, especially the final two pages, in my Applied Anthropology book (Hedican 2008a). The intent of these questions I suspected was to suggest that my testimony should be considered invalid because anthropologists are not objective enough in their points of view; that is to say, that anthropologists in their land claims testimony are too prone to side with the Indigenous perspectives on the matter.

I should also indicate that I had developed a strategy beforehand. One of the aspects of this strategy was to provide answers in a most minimal way, anticipating that the attorney for the Crown would be looking for evidence to invalidate my testimony. It surprised me that he had a copy of my Applied Anthropology book on hand and what I had written, perhaps years previous, should be entered as evidence. As best as I was able I tried to adhere to the position that just because a particular topic is mentioned in my writings should not necessarily lead to the conclusion that this was my opinion. Rather, I suggested, I was merely summarizing a number of viewpoints in anthropology.

I realized that the intent of the questioning would be to undermine my testimony, so in this sense anyone acting as an expert witness needs to be wary, or should we say, on guard, for the line of questions posed by the opposing attorney and where these are likely to lead. Remember, that while appearing as an expert witness in a land claims case may be a novel experience for some academics, the attorney for the Crown has been conducting this sort of litigation for many years, so be wary of pitfalls. See Federal Court—Aboriginal Law Liaison Committee for Aboriginal Litigation Practice Guides[78] and Ray (2012, 2015) for "battles over evidence in Indigenous rights litigation." One aspect of my participation in the court proceedings in the Williams Treaties case that surprised me was the combative and confrontational nature of the interrogation process.

I was especially surprised when the Crown's attorney mentioned a 'Code of Conduct for Expert Witnesses' which I had not, unfortunately, heard about before. The attorney handed a sheet of paper to me which outlined what my position as an expert witness should be:

1. An expert witness named to provide a report for use as evidence, or to testify in a proceeding, has an overriding duty to assist the Court impartially on matters relevant to his or her area of expertise.
2. This duty overrides any duty to a party to the proceeding, including the person retaining the expert witness. An expert is to be independent and objective. An expert is not an advocate for a party.

Under the Federal Court procedures, this is referred to as Rule 52.2 (Canada, 2021, *Code of Conduct for Expert Witnesses: Federal Court Rules.* Justice Laws Website: http://laws.justice.gc.ca/eng/regulations).

In what I thought was a clever move by the Crown attorney, he pulled out from under his table a copy of my book on *Applied Anthropology in Canada* (Hedican 2008a). As the testimony above indicates, the attorney asked me to go to page 62 in my book in which there is a discussion of 'The Advocacy Question in Applied Anthropology'. I knew right away where he was going, having just read the code of conduct stipulating that "an expert is not an advocate for a party." He would no doubt read sections of my book in an attempt to demonstrate that I was not a reliable witness because I was in effect acting as an advocate for the Indigenous position. I was determined that he was not going to pin this on me, and that he would not be successful in discrediting my testimony.

The attorney's approach was to 'cheery pick' certain lines from my book and then ask if I had written them. "Yes," I would reply, "but you are taking these quotes out of context." I could tell that he was getting frustrated with me, that I was not willing to be pulled along into a testimonial *cul de* sac in which I would be forced to admit that I was not an objective witness, that I was biased in favor of Indigenous causes. What I kept insisting was that the lines that he was quoting from my book were simply my attempts to illustrate the positions of various authors on the question of objectivity in anthropology, and that these lines did not necessarily represent my own position on the subject. Of course, when I made this comment I knew he would be forced to ask me "Then what is your position?" And in response, "That I was attempting to follow the Code of Conduct by not being an advocate for the First Nations involved in the Williams Treaties." At that, he tried to change his tactic, realizing no doubt that it was he himself who had become boxed into a corner. While the attorney shuffled through his papers, I tried to fortify myself against the next verbal onslaught. The whole experience was nerve wracking, to say the least, but I was determined not to fall into his legal leger-de-main and casuistic dead falls.

In academia, there are various types of interrogations, such as that which occur in a thesis defense for example, however these situations are rarely so vehemently contested. Ray (2003: 254) commented on this aspect of legal proceedings with his testimony as well which mirrored my own experience:

The opposing sides hotly contested all aspects of the plaintiff's and the province's history. As a result, I faced four days of stressful cross-examination by two teams of lawyers who represented the province and the federal government. They not only challenged the evidence I presented to the court but put my scholarly publication record on trial too.

For my own part, I had to keep reminding myself that the cross-examination was not necessarily intended to be a personal attack, but a search for evidence or 'truth', and that I should respond in a measured and controlled manner. "The adversarial nature of the process greatly enhances the challenges they face," Ray (2013: 272) notes, such that

In hotly contested cases, experts often find it difficult to avoid taking such challenges personally and becoming emotionally involved. From the beginning, the adversarial nature of the process frequently has had a divisive impact on the community of experts.

Land claims in particular has led to a polarization of positions that can be quite exhausting, as in Dinwoodie's assessment: "anthropological and ethnohistorical research on First Nations has polarized in accordance with roles assumed in land claims litigation" (2010: 31). He also states that "The overriding political issue of present-day Canada is not Quebec sovereignty but land claims" (ibid: 39). This 'initiative', according to Widdowson and Howard (2008: 83), "was largely a response to the policy vacuum that was created in the aftermath of the rejection of the Trudeau government's 1969 White Paper." Similarly, Miller (2004: 155–156) notes that Trudeau and his government was "battered by the First People's united and vehement rejection of the White

Paper of 1969, and thus were prepared to deal with Aboriginal land claims on a collective, systematic basis."

Another source of 'polarization' is that there are scholars who are critical of anthropologists who they regard as adopting an uncritical view of Indigenous land claims. As an example, Widdowson and Howard (2008), as Dinwoodie (2010: 33) suggests, are "predisposed against land claims and have a ideological antipathy for culturally based rights." Their argument is similar to one promulgated by Thomas Flanagan several decades ago in his controversial work *First Nations? Second Thoughts* (2000). The suggestion of these authors is that First Nations never formally held land and, as such, how could its members demonstrate a land claim? It is worth noting also that Tom Flanagan served as a key strategist to Stephen Harper during the 2004 election. However, when the Assembly of First Nations condemned Flanagan's views, Harper began to distance himself from Flanagan's controversial opinions and affirmed his commitment to Aboriginal rights (Warry 2007: 30, 129). Not surprisingly, Flanagan (2000: 157–162) draws on the opinions of Alexander von Gernet in support of his attempts to denigrate the value of Aboriginal oral traditions and to assert the superiority of European historical methods.

By contrast, John Borrows (2001, 2002) offers a compelling refutation of both Flanagan and von Gernet's views on Aboriginal oral history, suggesting instead that Aboriginal legal values can be utilized to develop new systems of law which better serve both Euro-Canadians and Indigenous peoples. As far as anthropologists' involvement in Indigenous land claims is concerned, in Widdowson and Howard's view, to use Dinwoodie's (2010: 44) words, they are nothing "but parasites—lobbyists who stand to benefit financially from distorting the facts regarding aboriginal culture and history." Again, not surprisingly, von Gernet has somehow evaded their wrath and scrutiny concerning his apparent magnanimous financial windfall.

Anthropologists Giving Expert Testimony

The idea that anthropologists acting as expert witnesses are nothing more than 'parasites' underlies a certain antagonism that some scholars in other disciplines hold for anthropology. There are probably good reasons why anthropologists are called to give expert testimony. As a starter, they often spend a long period of time conducting research among a particular group of people and in a specific area. In my own case, this period of time amounts to about five decades, with the results that one becomes very familiar with a population or community over several generations on a firsthand basis. The scholars in no other discipline that I know of can make a similar claim, so that it is no wonder that anthropologists are asked to give testimony based on their familiarity and professional knowledge of a specific population.

There are no other individuals in academic life who possess this depth of factual basis for their opinions on Indigenous rights. To call them parasites, one suspects, underlies a sort of professional jealously and insecurity that is no doubt unfortunate, what in the vernacular would be regarded as a 'cheap shot' and unbecoming a professionally trained academic. While some regard this opinion as self-serving, nonetheless, years of academic training, sustained periods of field research, and mastery of the tools of ethnography lend legitimacy to anthropological expertise (Carr 2010). In fact, "the appointment of anthropologists", Holden (2020a: 1) notes, "as country experts has become increasingly frequent…in specialized fields of law, such as native land titles and First Nations rights in America and Australia" (see also Holden 2020b; Rodriguez 2018).

In 'Adjudicating Indigeneity', Christopher Loperena (2020) discusses the use of anthropological testimony in the court of human rights. He argues that there are very good reasons why anthropologists are sought as expert witnesses: "Anthropologists are asked to participate as experts because courts understand our expertise as aligned with the positivist mandates upon which legal decisions are based. As experts, we must first detail from where we derive our expertise, outline our academic credentials, and describe the scientific means by which we gathered our ethnographic material" (2020: 598–599; see also Anders 2014; Good 2008). In other words, there is a scientific basis to the testimony offered by the anthropologist which is based on a scientific methodology, and not on hearsay or other speculative opinions. And, as Loperena further adds, "The highly structured nature of our work as experts makes it difficult to avoid the constraints placed on us by the law" (2020: 600).

In Lawrence Rosen's pioneering work in the anthropological domain of expert testimony, he writes that anthropologists:

have testified on everything from racial segregation, miscegenation laws, and child custody to the blood types of putative fathers, the nature of religious communities, and the cultural background of criminal defendants. However their predominant role has been in cases involving American Indians (1977: 556).

In his more recent work, Rosen (2020) presents a historical overview of contemporary issues when social scientists act as expert witnesses in legal proceedings. One of the main points he makes is that anthropologist's testimony has taken place in a variety of social settings and has involved the interaction of those from a diversity of cultural backgrounds. In this context, it is important to recognize the manner in which "expert claims affect the creation of legal facts and how vital it is that any historical or contemporaneous approach be seen in the large context of the cultural assumptions of the society at large" (2020: 125). As in my own situation in the Williams Treaty land claims case, the testimony was complicated by the fact that the veracity of Indigenous versions of oral traditions was being interpreted in the context of Europe standards of jurisprudence and a reliance on written documents. The anthropologist in such cases is forced to adopt an intercalary position between Indigenous and Europe views of acceptable versions of 'valid' evidence (see also Rosen 2006, 2018; Zenker 2016)

Another issue he identifies pertains to the ways in which the members of different cultures recognize the qualifications of experts. In the European tradition, one is apt to look for specific training or specialized knowledge recognized, for example, by university degrees. In an Indigenous culture, experience and familiarity with certain issues is important, thus a reliance on elders as repositories of cultural knowledge is apt to be relied upon. There is also the matter of procedures by which expert testimony achieves a recognized level of proof concerning dispositive evidence. He also discusses situations in which historians act as expert witnesses and how their testimony may differ from anthropologists. Archaeologists, as well, are commonly called to give testimony in Aboriginal rights cases. Hogg and Welch point to several difficulties that serve as limitations to the use of archaeological evidence. As an example, these limitations "include issues inherent in the particularism of archaeological data and difficulties of presenting to courts what are typically large volumes of facts not immediately relevant to essential questions courts must address" (2020: 234). Another important issue pertains to deficiencies in the education of lawyers and judges which could lead to misunderstandings and misinterpretations (Mason 2006).

An issue in this regard is how the testimony of the members of each of these disciplines may clash over their interpretation of the same historical documents. Also, experts may be regarded with greater skepticism is some cultures than in others. As an example, Freckelton (1985: 382) suggests that "An important difference between Australia and the United States is that experts are not held in the same regard. In the United States...there is not the same mystique when an expert is called into the witness box and, accordingly, there is not the same danger that improper weight will be given to his testimony." Thus, Rosen (2006: 92–93) observes that the creation of facts in legal systems is, at its core, a cultural process which allows for considerable flexibility in interpretation.

In a similar way, Renato Rosaldo argues that the job of the cultural anthropologist in studying oral narratives is to provide an account about the manner in which the Indigenous people themselves perceive their own history, rather than deny their version of how their lives have changed through different time periods. His argument is that history is none other than a 'cultural construct', which involves "plundering other people's narratives by sifting through them into degrees of facticity—true, probable, possible, false—risks misunderstanding their meanings" (1980: 91). Indigenous scholars, such as John Borrows (2001) and Val Napoleon (2005), none the less emphasize that in the end Indigenous thought processes are evaluated in European terms, which leaves open the possible problem of Indigenous and European understandings simply being incommensurable. Furthermore, as Borrows points out, oral histories are inherently controversial, not necessarily because of the format or form of a culture's oral traditions, but because of the content in which they are "encased." As he explains:

The mere presentation of Aboriginal oral evidence often questions the very core of the Canadian legal and constitutional structure...As such, oral tradition is controversial because it potentially undermines the law's claim to legitimacy throughout the country due to the illegality and/or unconstitutionality of past actions (2001: 10).

In another example, Richard Price, an anthropologist, provides a personal account of his role as an expert witness which offers further nuances to the legal adjudication process. He notes that as with many anthropologists his participation in legal cases "has been unexpected and dictated by unforeseeable circumstance" (2017: 416), as was my own participation in the Williams

Treaties land claim. As far as the issue of objectivity is concerned, which was a key point in my own cross-examination made by the Crown's attorney, Price is quite explicit in indicating that "there is no question of where our fellow anthropologist Sally Price's personal and professional loyalties lie. If we can assist the Saamaka People in any way, we consider it a privilege. And as anthropologists, we consider it part of our professional ethical responsibilities" (2017: 429). Thus, we might conclude that anthropologists who act as expert witnesses might also adopt a variety of roles and positions on the question of objectivity from those who act as consultants, mediators, or advocates (see Hedican 1986b). Additional issues pertain to Indigenous perspectives on the courtroom situation (Timperley 2020; Hart 2018; Hausler 2012; Ray 2015) as well as the larger problem of multidisciplinary perspectives on the adjudication of Indigenous rights (Henrard and Gilbert 2018; Miller and Menezes 2015; Ray 2011).

Anthropology in the Public Sphere

A central question emanating from this discussion of the anthropologist as expert witness concerns the future of anthropology. The traditional role of the cultural anthropologist as fieldwork ethnographer will probably not disappear any time soon, however one is led to wonder if the discipline is on the verge of a dramatic shift in direction, one in which new, non-traditional roles, will shape the future course of anthropology.

Several decades ago, in his presidential address to the American Anthropological Association, James Peacock delivered a speech entitled 'The Future of Anthropology'. A central point of this address was that "while sustaining the fundamentals, probing the deep mysteries of the human species and the human soul, we must press outward, mobilizing our work and ourselves to make a difference beyond the discipline and the academy" (1997:9)

In terms of the future course of anthropology, Peacock envisioned three possible scenarios. One of these is that the discipline of anthropology eventually becomes extinct due to the downsizing that has been occurring in colleges and universities, the "rationalizing" of curriculums with low enrollments, which could make anthropology a target for either outright elimination or a merger with larger departments. At present, anthropology is a vulnerable discipline because of its relatively small size compared to other disciplines in academia. Anthropologists of my age group will no doubt remember when anthropologists were often hired in sociology departments, and it was only decades later that stand-alone anthropology departments began to emerge. The danger today is a regression backward into possible oblivion in the university calendar.

A second possibility is that anthropologists continue to cling to university and museum settings, largely forgotten in a sort of intellectual backwater, writing their arcane papers on the couvade, the avunculate and other esoteric topics that are inscrutable, and are regarded as irrelevant, to most other human beings in the modern world. In this case, they will probably be seen as quaint leftovers of the bygone days of Franz Boas and Margaret Mead but without their intellectual stature.

Alternatively, a third course could involve anthropologists attempting to reinvent themselves, in order to prevent possible intellectual annihilation. Anthropologists could aim for new directions, infused with a new sense of mission, as a way of re-establishing itself. As Peacock perceives the future, anthropology could become:

Intriguing and creatively diverse, iconoclastic and breathtaking in its sweep and perception, profound in its scholarship, but would become integral and even leading in addressing the complex challenges of a transnational, yet grounded humanity. Society needs anthropology (1997: 9).

This chapter on anthropologists engaging as expert witnesses in the courts is one possible direction. Probably one could not stake an entire career on such a role, but it does suggest future possibilities that could profitably be explored further in the future.

Lessons Learned

When Peter Hutchins asked me to participate in the defense of the Indigenous peoples who were participants in the Williams Treaties, I must admit feeling a certain trepidation. After all, I thought, was I getting into something that would cause me a lot of trouble. I had not engaged before in litigation of Indigenous land claims and so wondered if I would do more harm than good. Mr. Hutchins reminded me of my history in anthropology researching Indigenous issues of various sorts. It is true that several decades before I was involved in the Whitesands land claim in northern Ontario. However, at that time there was little literature on anthropologists engaging in what might be called 'non-traditional role performance'.

What is the use, I asked myself, of my career if it is not to be useful in some sense? The idea of a 'practical' anthropology has a long history in the disciple going back to Malinowski's article of the same name published in 1929 [1970]. Malinowski's concern was with the colonial pressures on Indigenous populations involving land tenure, health, and demographic change. He suggested that British colonial administrators should leave Indigenous customs intact as far as possible in order to lessen the impact of colonial rule, even allowing self-rule in some areas.

His argument overall was that ethnographic information has 'practical' value in understanding the internal conflict that resulted from the external intrusions of colonial administrations on local social and cultural characteristics. His suggestion was that a separate field, called *practical anthropology*, be instituted which would focus on the more useful aspects of ethnographic fieldwork. Later, in the 1950s, Saul Tax's started an applied program called the Fox Project in which he used the term *action anthropology* (Tax 1958). Since then various other terms have been used, such as *applied anthropology* (Hedican 2008a), *activist anthropology* (Maskovsky 2013), and *public anthropology* (Hedican 2016), among other designations and role descriptions.

With this history in the discipline in mind, I felt that I needed to set my apprehensions aside and focus on becoming involved in the land claims process as a learning experience. We all have choices to make. I could choose either to see this request as a troubling situation to be avoided, or I could see it as an opportunity to be taken advantage of. The lesson that I learned is that I was capable of taking inspiration from my academic predecessors. If Malinowski, Tax, and others could find the courage to become involved in difficult public situations, then the question is "why can't I?"

There were several aspects of my testimony that I did not expect. The first of these was the Crown attorney's insistence that I be an 'objective' witness when I thought that it was rather obvious that I was appearing in defense of the Indigenous land claim. By the same token, when reading von Gernet's prepared document on his opinion of Indigenous oral traditions pertaining to the land claim, I almost thought that he was being facetious when he suggested that Indigenous oral traditions should be discounted because they were not as reliable as European written documents.

While his training was not as a cultural anthropologist, I nonetheless felt that archaeology was still an associated discipline of anthropology, and in this regard he should have showed more cultural sensitivity to his claims. In any event, his testimony was nothing less than a complete condemnation of Indigenous oral traditions which, if he was being held to the same objective standards that the Crown's attorney demanded that I do, then his testimony could be discounted on this basis. What I learned, then, was to expect disingenuous positions to be taken in the court room in which Indigenous land claims were being adjudicated—it appeared to me as a surprise that arriving at the 'truth' appeared to be a secondary goal to winning the case at all costs. Of course, one is reminded of Aeschylus's comment that "in war and apparently in legal proceedings, truth is the first casualty."

Conclusion

The most obvious conclusion that could be made concerning anthropologists acting as expert witnesses is that their prior training—in conducting fieldwork and as ethnographers—is insufficient training for engaging in the new roles that they find themselves. There is far too much of the "riding on the seat of your pants approach." While the above review of literature pertaining to the role of the anthropologist as expert witness is concerned, there is far too little discussion on how to prepare oneself for the testimony that they will be asked to deliver. There is also the issue of objectivity and how to avoid having one's testimony invalidated by a possible contravention of the 'code of conduct' in the court's rules. Of course, different countries probably have their own rules of conduct that may, or may not, be in congruence with each other.

One approach is to refocus the educational system in universities. At the University of Guelph, it was decided to design a new graduate program focused on issues in public anthropology. As a next step, one of our larger second-year undergraduate courses was designed to explicitly examine various public issues in society. In this way, students coming through the anthropology program have an opportunity to examine various social issues. Seminars are also conducted on topics of public concern, and professors with experience in public anthropology are routinely invited to lend their expertise to this emerging field. It is all a learning experience, however a decision has been made to make anthropology more accountable to society at large by lending the expertise of those trained in anthropology to provide useful, or 'practical', guidance (to use Malinowski's term) for those who are destined to be the leaders of the future.

In another attempt to bring public anthropology into the classroom, in my second-year undergraduate class on Aboriginal issues, the transcript of my testimony in the Williams Treaties land claim case was used to dramatize the event. Different students were given parts, as indicated in the transcript, and 'played out' the various roles line for line from the transcript before the class of about 200 students. Another group of students was then given the task of characterizing or analyzing the testimony. This sort of legal drama brought the land claims case into reality for the students, and illustrated the difficulties faced by the expert witness under cross-examination by a well-prepared attorney. In this way, public anthropology was demonstrated in a real-life situation, as opposed to some hypothetical event that one would read about in a text book. Only the future will tell if anthropology in the public sphere becomes the dominant direction of the discipline, yet continued discussion of this public role is no doubt a useful practice in sorting out the issues involved.

Chapter Ten
Back to the Future

This book is partly a memoir of a northern anthropologist, partly a history of anthropology in Canada, and partly a theoretical incursion into everyday life. It extends over a fifty-year period, from 1967 when I was working in an INCO mine in Thompson, Manitoba, then decided to take a chance at a career in academic life, up until I retired as a Professor Emeritus for the University of Guelph in 2020. This is not to mean that I have stopped being an anthropologist, on the contrary, even today I remain as interested in the subject as I ever have. So, what have I learned over these last five decades.

Well, for one thing, issues change with the times and so one has to try to keep up and not get stuck in some bygone era. It's a truism I know but life is, or should be, a learning experience. If you have not learned much in life, then in all probability you have been wasting your time. We make mistakes as well, but we keep on trying. When I made anthropology my major in 1968, I felt that I was making a commitment to follow certain ideals that were intrinsic to that disciple. Central to these ideals is the principle of respect, which I thought was embodied in the concept of cultural relativism; the idea that the way people in other cultures live their everyday lives should be given deference even though these lives may differ in significant ways from the standards and values of the anthropologist's own society. Yes, one could certainly debate the merits of this approach and find fault with its basic premise, but I thought for the time being at least it was a good philosophical place to start my new life.

Policies and Prospects

Although this book has focused on a roughly 50-year period, it is difficult to say if this discussion has been followed in a lineal fashion, or if there are circular occurrences happening. What I mean to say is that the discussion begins more or less with Prime Minister Pierre Elliot Trudeau and his 1969 White Paper which many people regarded, to use Harold Cardinal's words, as "a thinly disguised program of extermination through assimilation" (1969: 1). Ironically, five decades later, Indigenous leader Russ Diabo makes the same charge against his son, Prime Minister Justin Trudeau, that was made against his father when he states that Justin Trudeau's policies are:

A continuation of the 1969 White Paper of the Prime Minister Pierre Elliot Trudeau, which adopted the equality language of the civil rights movement but was intended to strip us of our treaties, nullify our legal and political status as collective rights holders and assimilate us into Canadian society (Russ Diabo, *The Tyee.ca*, 5 May 2020).

Thus, it is quite possible that the Hegelian dialectic is at play here with Indigenous policies in Canada moving in a circular fashion. Then there is Sally Weaver's prophetic statement in the last sentence of *The Hidden Agenda* in which she concludes that "The White Paper was an experiment for which both Indians and government will pay for many years to come" (1981: 204).[79] It is unfortunate that she did not live long enough to be able to assess the validity of her prognostication. Thus, it is evident that over the fifty-year period discussed in this book Indigenous policy in Canada has come virtually full circle; that we have come 'back to the future'.

During the latter part of the 1960s there was serious debate taking place in Canadian society about the place of Indigenous people and anthropologists were themselves beginning to play a significant role in developing policy initiatives (Cairns 1970). In 1966–1967, *A Survey of the Contemporary Indians of Canada* had just been published by Harry Hawthorn at the University of British Columbia and Marc-Adélard Tremblay at Laval. The research that provided the foundation for this report was an enormous undertaking involving some fifty ethnologists and resulting in 150 recommendations concerning economic, political, and educational needs and policies. The most significant of these stated that:

Indians should be regarded as 'citizens plus'; in addition to the normal rights and duties of citizenship, Indians possess certain additional rights as charter members of the Canadian community (Hawthorn 1966–67: 13).

At the time, I remember feeling a heightened sense of optimism prevalent in the 1960s that significant changes were on the way concurrent with the Civil

Rights Movement in the United States and the persistent protests against the war in Vietnam.

Then, in 1969, there was the inexplicable White Paper of the Trudeau government which appeared to be an attempt to throw history backwards, to the oppressive policies of previous generations, such as the 1927 ban on Aboriginal political organizations, or the refusal to allow Indigenous people to vote in provincial or federal elections. As Sally Weaver (1981: 3–4) stated, under the guise of "an attempt at consultative democracy—the federal government released its White Paper in June 1969 that proposed a global termination of all special treatment of Indians, including the Indian Act." Even though many Indigenous people found fault with the Indian Act, it nonetheless enshrined some of their charter rights which had been granted prior to Confederation in 1867. This new policy by Prime Minister Trudeau, and his right hand man, Jean Chrétien, Minister of Indian Affairs, and later a Prime Minister himself, appeared to be a reversal of forward looking or enlightened policies such as that embodied in the 'Citizens Plus' statement just promulgated a year or so earlier.

As one might have predicted, this new policy caused shock and alarm not only among Indigenous people, but among many sympathetic observers as well. As Weaver (1981: 5) stated, "Social Scientists, especially anthropologists, were shocked by the White paper. They could not believe the government's intention of embarking on a policy that had proven so destructive to Indian communities in the United States during the 1950s." The term 'termination psychosis' was proposed to describe the fear and insecurity felt by the members of cultural systems whose communities were severely threatened (Josephy 1971).

Condemnation was quick to follow. As Cree Leader Harold Cardinal indicated, this new proposal could be viewed as "a thinly disguised program of extermination through assimilation. For the Indian to survive," Cardinal stated, "he must become a good little brown white man" (1969: 1). Shortly after, a counter-proposal, the Red Paper, was prepared by the Indian Chiefs of Alberta (1970). It was clear that Indigenous people in Canada wanted their special rights honored, not eliminated, even though there was widespread criticism of the Indian Act itself. They also sought to have their grievances over land and treaties recognized and dealt with in an equitable manner. The manner in which Indigenous affairs in Canada were being dealt with by

Trudeau's Liberal Government was hardly a case of 'consultative democracy' when Indigenous peoples themselves were denied any meaningful participation in the very policies that would determine their future. By the spring of 1971, the policy was formally withdrawn, but distrust of the Trudeau government's intentions involving termination initiatives lingered for many years, especially when Jean Chrétien himself became Canada's Prime Minister.

With the advent of the new decade of the 1970s, different issues began to predominate in the Indigenous news especially in the areas of resource extraction and the possible deleterious effects on Indigenous communities in northern areas of Canada. In Quebec, the Bourassa Government's plans to generated hydro-electric power by damming major river systems in *Nouveau Quebec* was met with alarm since the area under consideration have never even been ceded by treaties with the Indigenous population. However, as Gold and Tremblay explained, "without exception all the anthropological studies of Quebec communities of this period were to show how the changes in the 'Quiet Revolution' in Quebec were being reflected at the regional level…the issue of who controlled the Quebec economy preoccupied many anthropologists" (1983: 55). Thus, the controversy surrounding the James Bay hydro-electric project was seen less in the context of Aboriginal rights than it was of Quebec nationalism and economic independence from the rest of English-speaking North America. Nonetheless, it took the federal government another thirty-two years, until 2007, to reach a $1.4 billion settlement with the Cree over outstanding land claims.

At McGill University, Richard Salisbury initiated the Programme in the Anthropology of Development (PAD) in 1971which ushered in a period of consultant-oriented research, as shown by the program's first major work, *Development and James Bay* (Salisbury et al. 1972). Subsequent research was undertaken primarily for the Indians of Quebec Association and the Grand Council of the Cree. A wide range of reports were prepared under PAD's 'Brief Communications Series', such as research into subsistence resource use, income security, and the impact on hydro-electric development of the Cree trapping economy. This applied work on the northern Cree by anthropologists at McGill highlighted a focus on Indigenous studies with a practical application (Salisbury 1986; Silverman 2004).

These studies by McGill anthropologists led to a greater emphasis on the more applied aspects of the discipline, as research leading to the James Bay Agreement (1975) was seen "as a laboratory for applied anthropology under pressure of the plans to develop dams in northern Quebec" (Price 1987: 3). Furthermore, as Salisbury explained, the Quebec studies emphasized the important relationship between application and theory: "the present high international status accorded to Canadian applied anthropology can be related to its strong emphasis on theory…and to the mutual trust that has developed in Canada between researchers and policy-makers" (1979: 229).

Indeed, by the 1980s the applied emphasis became more solidified with the formation of the Society of Applied Anthropology in Canada (SAAC) in 1981 (Hedican 2008a). This organization served to introduce a new generation of applied anthropologists to expanded research opportunities. Most prominently, the anthropological research of Sally Weaver (1981, 1986, 1990) was particularly noteworthy during this period as she focused on the development of governmental policy and its effect on Indigenous affairs. Weaver's examination of the Department of Indian Affairs in *Making Canadian Indian Policy* (1981) was an especially important publication during this period as it established the significance of anthropological research in the study of power elites and the manner in which they create policy priories and set political agendas.[80]

In 1985, the first significant amendment to the Indian Act occurred since 1951 with the passing of Bill C-31. The intent of this bill was to eliminate a discriminatory piece of legislation whereby Indigenous women and their children could lose their status under the Indian Act upon marriage to non-Indian persons (as defined in the Indian Act). On the other hand, marriage by status men to non-status women did not result in a loss of status for the Indian man; instead, the non-status women that he might marry actually gained status even though they might not have any Indigenous heritage at all. According to the terms of Bill C-31 no persons would henceforth either lose or gain Indian status through marriage.

The legislation sounded straight forward enough. One applied for status by filling out a form, submitted the appropriate documents and then waited for a decision. However, a number of complications emerged. Many people were not able to identify their grandparents, or lacked appropriate documentation and their applications were rejected. Another issue was that Bill C-31 inadvertently created different categories of status Indians. As an example, those who originally had status but lost it could apply for reinstatement under section 6 (1) of the Indian Act. Those who would have obtained status from a parent who lost it needed to apply under section 6 (2). These different sections of registrants had an effect on who, and under which conditions, a person could pass down their Indian status to subsequent generations.

As one might expect, under these circumstances the success rate for applicants was not very high. There were 42,000 applications for reinstatement of Indian status by 1985, yet only 1,605 were accepted. By 2001, when the application process ceased, just over 105,000 individuals had been added to the status Indian population. For the year 2001, the total status Indian population of about 623,000 persons therefore consisted of nearly one-seventh of the registered Indian population of reinstated persons (Hedican 2008a: 229).

Here is a personal note to give some context to the issues involved. I was the spouse of a woman who was formerly a member of the Fort Hope Band (Eabamatoong Indian Band on the Albany River). She subsequently had lost her Indian status as a young child when her mother coincidently lost her status because she married a non-status male. Since both the mother and child were born with Indian status they both had their status reinstated (under section 6-1). We afterward had four children, all of whom eventually received Indian status under the 'one-generation rule' (those born with status can pass their status down one generation, however those in the other section 6-2 category cannot). In this particular case, my son married a woman with status and so their two daughters have status and can pass it down to their children. My eldest daughter, however, married a man without status and so her two boys were denied status. She subsequently has been fighting this provision of Bill C-31 and now has been successful in gaining status for one of her sons (the eldest), but the youngest has not gained status thus far. As such, even in the same family, two children have quite different circumstances.

There are those who fought their case through the courts for many years, the most famous of which has probably been that of Lynn Gehl's court challenge. Lynn Gehl is an Anishinaabe First Nations woman whose application for Indian status was denied in 1995 because she did not know the name of her maternal grandfather. As she explained, "They made the assumption that this unknown grandfather was a non-Indian man, and through the process of that assumption I was denied Indian status registration" (*CTV*

News 2013). Pamela Palmeter, a First Nations lawyer, claimed that despite Bill C-31 discrimination against Indian women and children continues. As she clarifies, "Imagine if Canadians had to worry about losing their Canadian citizenship or the right to live in their home province based on who they married or their gender." Palmeter estimates that nearly 50,000 children of First Nations women have been denied status because of the way Aboriginal Affairs now assumes the unnamed father on their birth certificate is non-Aboriginal (*CTV News* 2013). In Gehl's case, a decision of Ontario's Court of Appeal granted her Indian status on 20 April 2017, yet these are the sorts of struggles with which Indigenous people in Canada often have to contend in their everyday lives.

Gehl's court challenge which started in the 1980s continued for over three decades. By the 1990s when most people were beginning to forget about the repercussions of Bill C-31, much more serious incidents were beginning to occur. This new decade hardly had begun when, on 11 July, 1990, the Canadian Government under the pretense of the so-called War Measures Act sent an armed contingent to quell a protest at Oka, Quebec. The initial cause of the protest appeared innocent enough—a prosed expansion of a golf course onto disputed Mohawk lands—but the result was deadly. The Mohawk Warrior Society met the Quebec Provincial Police and army reservists head on, shot were fired, and during a barrage of bullets 31-year-old Corporal Marcel Lemay was shot and killed. Later, in the middle of August, a contingent of RCMP officers intervened in the dispute and in one exchange of hostilities fourteen officers were sent to hospital.

The Oka 'Standoff' of 1990

The decision to bring in the Canadian army cost Canadian taxpayers nearly $83 million and, altogether, the expenditure for the province of Quebec amounted to $112 million (*CBC* News, 10 July 2000; Hedican 2013: 112–113). As a result of the so-called Oka Crisis and long-standing Indigenous issues, the Canadian Government established an investigation referred to as the Royal Commission of Aboriginal Peoples (RCAP) which lasted for five years (1991–1996). The final RCAP report comprised five volumes of more than 3,500 pages in total. RCAP turned out to be the most expensive Royal Commission in Canadian history, costing $63 million.

In all, the RCAP report made more than four hundred recommendations, such as the establishment of a special Aboriginal parliament, called 'the House of First Peoples', and many more recommendations that would have cost the Canadian tax payer billions of dollars if they were ever implemented. Given such an expensive initiative one would think that the federal government would show a strong interest. In fact, there was a virtual lack of a substantial response which must have been disheartening to many given the cost and effort involved. As RCAP co-chair George Erasmus warned, "If the reality is that once more Indigenous peoples' hopes have been dashed, and that this was all for nothing, then what we say is that the people will resort to other things" (Hedican 2013: 30).

One of these 'other things', surely not anticipated by Erasmus would no doubt include the deadly protest at Ipperwash Provincial Park on 4 September, 1995, in which protester Dudley George was shot and killed by Ontario Police Officer Kenneth Deane (Hedican 2008b, 2013). On that deadly day, the OPP responded to what was essentially a land claims protest, under the direction of Ontario's Mike Harris. The OPP officer responsible for Dudley George's death was subsequently found guilty of criminal negligence causing death, but was given a suspended sentence and community service, thus avoiding any jail time for what many regarded as a case of manslaughter. However, Acting Sergeant Deane died in a car accident shortly before he was scheduled to testify at the Ipperwash Inquiry. It took until November 2003, with a change of government, for an inquiry to be initiated under Commissioner Sidney Linden. The Ipperwash Inquiry did not corroborate Sergeant Deane's version of events— that Dudley George shouldered a rifle in a half-crouched position and was prepared to fire on the sergeant. The Inquiry concluded unequivocally that "Dudley George did not have a rifle or firearm in the confrontation with the police on the night of September 6, 1995" (Linden 2007: 72). The Ipperwash Inquiry also reiterated an important point:

Nearly all of the lands and inland waters in Ontario are subject to treaties between First Nations and the British and Canadian governments. They are living agreements, and the understandings on which they are based continue to have the full force of law in Canada today (2007: 80).

As with RCAP, this commission was an expensive proposition. And as with Oka, the War Measures Act was also used as a vehicle of suppression, in this case utilized in 1942 to expropriate lands belonging to the Stoney point people under the Huron Tract Treaty of 1827. The Ipperwash Inquiry cost $13.3 million, a relatively low price tag compared to RCAP, and made 100 recommendations. Together, both RCAP and the Ipperwash Inquiry cost the Canadian Government $73.3 million, and since probably very few Canadian would even remember these inquiries, let alone indicate any of the 500 recommendations made between them, one wonders if the money could have been better spent on, say, improving on-reserve housing, school buildings, roads or other infrastructural requirements.

The idea that much of this funding was gobbled up by commissioners and their witnesses for plane fares, car rental, hotel accommodations and restaurant meals now seems particularly offensive. One might suspect that such commissions only purpose to give governments a certain amount of breathing room in times of crisis and to deflect criticism away from them in the intervening years between the event and the publication of a commission's recommendations which are hardly ever acted upon anyway. In a somewhat sardonic note, anthropologist Regna Darnell has observed that "Royal Commissions provide politicians with space to avoid confrontation and conflict. Extremists on both right and left are wont to mutter about the 'anesthetic' quality of the always numerous and broad-ranging recommendations" (2000: 171).

The 20th century ended when the map of Canada changed for the first time in fifty years (since Newfoundland joined Confederation in 1949) with the creation of a new territory called Nunavut on 1 April 1999. It was Prime Minister Jean Chrétien, in an ironic historical twist, who presided over the inauguration of Nunavut. Remember that it was Chrétien who was the Minister of Indian Affairs in the Pierre Trudeau government when the White Paper of

1969 proposed to terminate the federal government's responsibilities for Indigenous Affairs. As Jean Chrétien reminisced in his speech:

It is personally very important for me because when I started as Minister of Indian and Northern Affairs in 1968, we were discussing at that time to establish responsible government in the Yukon and Northwest Territories. For me, to be associated with this great step for the Eastern Arctic is extremely important (Ohler, *National Post,* 1999).

Premier Paul Okalik, a thirty-four-year-old Inuit lawyer, also appeared optimistic about the future of Nunavut. In delivering his oath of office, he pronounced that "Today the people of Nunavut formally join Canada. Today we stand strong and we welcome the changes Nunavut brings." In addition, an Inuit elder commented that "When we had our historical election of February fifteenth 1999, heaven smiled on us. Heaven is smiling again today" (Mahoney, *Globe and Mail,* 1999). The Inuit people of the Canadian north, after centuries of relative isolation compared to the Indigenous people in the rest of Canada, are only now beginning the process of building their own society. The Inuit are engaged in a process of redefining themselves in terms of who they are and what their relationship is to be with the rest of Canada.

For other Indigenous people in Canada, the advent of the new millennia did not begin with such a propitious beginning. To the disappointment of many in this country, the federal Conservative government came under heavy criticism in 2007 when Canada voted against the United Nations Declaration on the Rights of Indigenous People (*Toronto Star*, 13 September 2007). Grand Chief of the Assembly of First Nations Phil Fontaine declared, "This is a stain on the country's international reputation. It is disappointing to see this government vote against recognizing the basic rights of Canada's First Peoples." According to the Minister of Indian Affairs Chuck Strahl, "It's the UN Declaration inconsistent with the Canadian Constitution, with Supreme Court decisions and with our own treaty negotiations and obligations." He further added that the Declaration should only be passed with the prior consent of the 650 or so First Nations of Canada.

It was in this context that Prime Minister Stephen Harper's apology to Indigenous people in the House of Commons on 11 June 2008 appeared to have a disingenuous tinge to it. The apology was meant to ask forgiveness of the Indigenous people of Canada for the harm done to the former students of Indian residential schools. The text of this speech declared that:

The government of Canada regrets the harm done to Aboriginal peoples through its past policies. The government now recognizes that the consequences of the Indian residential schools' policy were profoundly negative and that this policy has had a lasting and damaging impact on Aboriginal culture, heritage and language. The government of Canada sincerely apologizes and asks the forgiveness of the Aboriginal peoples of this country for failing them so profoundly. We are sorry (Harper 2008).

It is interesting that less than a year earlier, the Conservative Government's Minister of Indian Affairs, Chuck Stahl, indicated that, "For First Nations people in Canada, I think we've seen too many empty promises."

It would probably be correct to assume that Indigenous leaders in Canada would approve of Harper's statement at least to the extent that Canada has finally begun to take responsibility for its past actions and injustices toward the country's First Nations. The question remains nonetheless about whether the Canadian government would now act to institute new policies to replace the older negative ones of assimilation and paternalism? It is almost as if there are two levels of activities going on in this country with a disconnect between the two of them. At one level, the federal level, we have a prime minister, supposedly speaking on behalf of the country as a whole, asking for forgiveness for past wrongs and injustices that the Canadian population has perpetuated against the Indigenous people of the country.

Then, at another level, there is the actual business of the courts where concrete laws and policies are put into action. As one could see in my testimony at the Williams Treaties settlement how vigorously the lawyers for the Crown, both at the federal and provincial levels, argue against the Indigenous position on treaties and land claims. There is no doubt that making amends for past wrongs is also an important step in restoring such high ideals as justice and decency, but these gilded words also need to resonate in the courts as well where legal decisions really matter.

It would appear inevitable, then, that politics would enter into most facets of government policy involving Indigenous people and state structures. As Peter Hutchins (the lawyer who defended the Mississaugas in the Williams Treaty claim) argued:

Power and principle frame the portrait of State-Indigenous relations— irrespective of era, irrespective of place. With this portrait, Western courts have struggled for a century and a half. Aboriginal litigation of course has one prominent characteristic—almost inevitably it involves the state as plaintiff or defendant. Politics is introduced into the brew, principle is often siphoned off (2010: 215).

We could conclude, then, that confrontation and disrespect are bred by combative relationships, usually initiated by the injustices that one party perceives have placed it at a disadvantage. Government initiatives need long term commitments to succeed, not vague and unsubstantiated promises.

The beginning of this discussion started with a focus on the Trudeau-Chrétien era of the late 1960s which saw a reversal of the previous assimilationist policies of former governments which attempted to integrate Indigenous people in Canada into the larger Canadian society. The Hawthorn Report of 1966–1967 clearly stated that assimilationist policies do not work, and in its place an emphasis on 'citizens plus' should be the new attitude of government administrators and policy makers. Indigenous people not only have inherent privileges as Canadian citizens with the right to vote, but also because of their 'original' status, as written into treaties, they had rights beyond those possessed by members of the settler population. Then, inexplicably, the Trudeau government introduced its White Paper in 1969 which was soundly rejected by First Nation leaders, especially in western Canada.

From then on, the Trudeau government appeared to withdraw from any involvement in Indigenous issues, even though treaties, the Indian Act, and reserves are a federal responsibility. This reticence was particularly evident in the 1970s with the negotiations over the James Agreement of 1975 which made it abundantly clear that the federal government had no appetite for engaging in the fray between Quebec and the Cree. It was not until the mid-1980s, as a result of the egregious treatment of Indigenous women in the Indian Act that any initiative at all was shown by the federal government to correct long-standing inequities in its federal legislation. However, even then, Bill C-31 showed a complete lack of foresight when the changes were made.

The resulting reinstatement of over a hundred thousand Indigenous people increased the band rolls by twenty percent, however little thought was apparently given to the consequences of the changes. As an example, would such people be allowed to return to their original reserves, and if so, where would the funding come from for the necessary increases in housing and employment that would be necessary to support so many returnees? In an ironic twist, since Bill C-31 was supposedly initiated to end discrimination of

Indigenous women in the Indian Act, it actually tended to increase the existing inequities because the changes inadvertently caused two classes of status Indians.

Further policy quagmires awaited the federal government into the 1990s. The Oka debacle of 1990 in which an army corporal was killed, and the Ipperwash protest of 1995 during which Dudley George was fatally wounded by an OPP officer, resulted in the federal government spending almost $200 million of tax payers' money, and proposing five hundred recommendations, most of which were largely ignored. The inauguration of Nunavut at the end of the decade offered Jean Chrétien an opportunity for some measure of redemption after the 1969 White Paper caused so many Indigenous people to turn against him, however there were probably many non-Inuit people who were left wondering why they themselves did not also receive such favorable treatment from the federal government.

The next two decades, between 2000 and 2020, once again illustrated the federal government's ineptitude in managing Indigenous affairs when an inexcusable decision was made in 2007, for whatever reason, not to ratify the UN Declaration on the Rights of Indigenous peoples. This political blunder tended to blunt what was supposed to be a heart-felt apology by Prime Minister Harper in 2008 for the Canadian government's complicity in the residential school system and previous assimilationist policies. Finally, in 2010, under intense pressure, the federal government eventually became a signatory to the agreement, however skepticism remained over the federal government's apparent sincerity in dealing with extant Indigenous issues.

There were further challenges ahead for the remainder of the decade. One of these was the 'Idle no More' protest movement of 2012 which tended to amalgamate Indigenous groups and environmental activists over Bill C-45, referred to as an 'omnibus bill', which was regarded as a threat to the apparent removal of protections for forests and waterways. As far as First Nations people were concerned, the process of deregulating waterways was a direct challenge to their treaty rights, and a possible contributor to the diminished protection of northern wilderness areas (Coates 2015). A further problem developed when a rift occurred between the Idle No More (INM) supporters and the leaders of the Assembly of First Nations (AFN). The AFN was initially a supporter of the INM protests, however the latter's founders emphasized their intention to remain a grassroots movement, indicating that "we have been given a clear mandate…to work outside the systems of government" (*National Post* 2013; *Globe and Mail* 2013).

On a more positive note, the Indian Residential Schools' Truth and Reconciliation Commission (TRC), which was established on 2 June 2008 (www.trc-cvr.ca), was generally considered to be a positive step in promoting restorative justice as a result of the acts of cultural genocide inflicted on Aboriginal peoples in Canada. Restorative justice is an approach that seeks to heal, or "restore," the relationships between offenders, community members, and the victims of the offenses that have taken place over many generations. As Niezen stated, "Public apologies and truth and reconciliation commissions have become like confessionals for the states" (2010: 179; see also Henderson and Wakeham 2013; Niezen 2013).

One could also suggest that the TRC is an example Indigenous peoples attempts to buttress neo-colonial trends. As an example, in Bonita Lawrence's (2013) insightful study called *Fractured Homeland*, she focuses on the Algonquins of Pikwakanaga and the comprehensive land claim they originally launched in 1992, during which it was discovered that two-thirds of the Indigenous population had never been recognized as possessing status under the Indian Act. As her book's title indicates, the Algonquin have suffered from a 'fractured' identity because of the neo-colonial pressures asserted over them and their traditional lands as a result of the imposition of a provincial boundary, which divided the population across two provinces, and the Indian Act, which denied federal recognition for many of the members of this First Nation.

In a similar fashion, Glen Coulthard (2014), in his work subtitled *Rejecting the Colonial Politics of Recognition*, suggests that at the heart of colonial relationships between Indigenous peoples and the nation-state is the false promise of recognition. He argues further that "this orientation of liberal politics to the reconciliation of Indigenous nationhood with state sovereignty is still *colonial* insofar as it remains structurally committed to the dispossession of Indigenous peoples of our lands and self-determining authority" (2014: 152).

Thus, there are also those who would suggest that the recognition of a separate Indigenous identity in Canada is impeded by a conservative sector of the Canadian population who oppose the 'liberalization of society'. As an example, Kymlicka refers to the 'patriarchal cultural conservatives' who not only oppose liberalizing reforms, but equally seem to oppose principles of multiculturalism and Indigenous rights. As such, Kymlicka's conclusion is that in Canada "there has not been (and is not now) any significant level of public support for any of these forms of multiculturalism among cultural conservatives" (2007: 105). On this basis, Kymlicka's suggestion would provide a reasonable explanation for the federal government's resistance to the hundreds of reasonable recommendations which were proposed in the 1996 RCAP Report, as well as those of the Ipperwash Inquiry in 2007, in addition to Canada's 2007 vote against Indigenous Rights in the United Nations Declaration. Therefore, it would appear that in the decades ahead, there will emerge again contentious political strife between the so-called settlement population of Canada and their resistance to furthering the cause of the rights of Aboriginal peoples, as has already occurred for most of this country's historical past.

The Anti-Indigenous Agenda

Fifty years is a long time to watch what is essentially a play with different actors outfitted in the same costumes, repeating much of the same lines, with only slight variations in the overall themes. The saying "*plus ça change, plus c'est la même chose*" of course comes to mind regarding Canada's often repetitious, mood-swinging policies toward Indigenous people.

Conrad Black, certainly no stranger to controversy, has written an opinion piece in the *National Post* in which he suggests that: "It is shocking and dangerous that the final report of the Truth and Reconciliation Commission of Canada, published in 2015, has been so widely accepted as a full accounting of Native grievances and the basis for policy changes and reparations to accommodate those grievances" (20 March 2021). For those who have been around for a while, one wonders at Black's interest in his continuing anti-Indigenous put-downs. I can count at least another half-dozen of his anti-Indigenous diatribes of his in the *National Post* alone.

Black promises more 'analysis' to come in the following weeks even as I write this. As far as the present article is concerned, John A. Macdonald is praised for passing the Indian Act of 1876 which "aimed to protect natives from dishonest whites and to assist them in becoming educated and self-sufficient farmers with a stable, post-nomadic residential livelihood." The residential school system, which Black admits did cause 'real harm to many people', nonetheless was not 'the malign plans of evil men'. As one might expect, an extensive amount of space is allotted to conservative political scientist Tom Flanagan in what could be termed one of the founding pieces of the 'anti-Indigenous industry' in his *First Nations, Second Thoughts*:

Canada will be redefined as a multinational state embracing an archipelago of Aboriginal nations that own a third of Canada's land mass, are immune from federal and provincial taxation, are supported by transfer payments from citizens who do pay taxes, are able to opt out of federal and provincial legislation and engage in 'nation to nation' diplomacy with whatever is left of Canada (2000: 5).

One can only assume that Conrad Black included Flanagan's quote in his article because he agrees with this antagonistic stance toward Indigenous people. There are so many inaccuracies in this quote, especially those concerning taxation, that another book would be required to refute them. The article ends with a vaguely disguised threat, "The sooner Canada stops shadow-boxing with it conscience and get to grips with the implications of what is afoot, the better." Contemporary media commentators are apt to call this sort of reporting "a dog whistle—red meat for the neo-conservative right wing." Black is obviously using white Canadian suspicions of Indigenous policies in an attempt to drum up support for the *Post*, but adds nothing new or innovative to the debate.

As far as the conservative media's contention that the Indigenous people of North America were composed of primitive, uncivilized tribes compared to their superior European counterparts is concerned scholarly research in anthropology, archaeology and history paints a different picture. When Cortez entered the Aztec city of Tenochtitlan in 1519, there were over 60,000 dwellings and more than 300,000 people in the main city (perhaps even a million people spread out into many suburbs). The citizens were described to be being well dressed wearing fine clothes, wore necklaces of gold and jewels, and had an abundance of delicious food, many artisans, and their shops displayed a wide variety of luxury goods for the aristocracy (Willey 1966: 156–162). According to anthropologist Brian Fagan, "Merchants from hundreds of miles around converged on both cities Tenochtitlan and Teotihuacan, where every conceivable kind of merchandise was sold and distributed in the great markets" (1984: 30). At this time, "the city was considered the best provisioned city in the world," according to multiple sources (1984: 82).[81] Then, in a surge of unimaginable savagery, Cortez "massacred the assembled nobles in the temple precinct, killing some four or five thousand Indians, then looting the city" (1984: 271). Remember also that at the point of contact, European explorers caused pandemics in the Americas that decimated Indigenous populations.

By contrast, in the capital cities of Europe, such as Paris and London, the population never rose above 50–60,000 people during this period. For the most part, the citizens lived-in rat-infested squalor with plagues ravishing the population every few years. Starvation and food shortages were common as most people lived in veritable filth. People commonly begged in the streets with rotten rags dripping for their bodies. The stench was said to be so unbearable that the aristocrats needed to cover their faces with perfumed cloths that they held to their face. In Canada, Jesuit Paul Le Jeune described the Iroquois people that he came into contact with in 1634 as more intelligent than ordinary European peasants. Now compare this version with Black's outdated and inaccurate description of Native Americans.

A follow up to Black's article appeared shortly after. Historian Tylor Noakes contends that Conrad Black has purposely ignored 'inconvenient truths' (26 March 2021). "Europeans no more brought civilization to the Americas than they discovered it," Noakes asserts. Black's description of Indigenous North Americans is not based on recent scholarship, but rather on "antiquated nineteenth-century historical narratives…Black's understanding of Indigenous history isn't revisionist so much as it is retrograde," Noakes says. Black plays up to what the average Canadian thinks they know about Indigenous history rather than attempt to inform the public about recent scholarship. Such a task would not fit his political purposes, since he attempts to demean Canada's Indigenous people for his own conservative agenda. Noakes concludes that Black's "assertions are contradicted by the historical record and archaeological evidence."

If nothing else, Black's commentary is not much more than a continuation of the anti-Indigenous conservative right wing push back that gained momentum with Flanagan's book. By now, the outline of the neo-conservative agenda is particularly clear: Indigenous peoples do not deserve 'special status', we are all equal Canadians; stop spending enormous amounts of tax-payers' hard earned dollars fighting Indigenous land claims, they are relics of the past and should be left there; abolish reserves, they are doing more harm than good in isolating Indigenous people, who be better off 'integrated' into mainstream Euro-Canadian society; and, among other proposals, do away with the Indian Affairs bureaucracy and the Indian Act, both of which cause considerable damage because they keep Indigenous people in a continual state of poverty and isolation.

Indigenous people have grown weary of this continual barrage of disparaging literary commentary from the conservative rightwing. Joe Dion, Chairman and CEO of Frog Lake Energy Resources Corp., says that he takes "issue with his Black's high-handed put-down of my people's history and their economic and cultural contribution to this country." Dion further indicates that:

It's unhelpful in the present environment for Black to diminish my people's contribution as not measuring up to the achievements of the European settlers who landed here. It's divisive to treat our people as 'others', distinct from the rest of Canadians. We are your friends, but that friendship cannot be abused. And it's disrespectful to consider us as 'nomads' in our own land, as if we deserved the rigors of colonization foisted upon us, once dispossessed of our lands (14 August 2017).

It should be further noted that Black appears oblivious to many facts that do not fit neatly into his right-wing perspective, such as the Indigenous 'land rights' that are protected by the Canadian Constitution, as well as the nearly 250 Supreme Court rulings in favor of Aboriginal rights in the resource sector.

Unfortunately, Conrad Black is not the only one promoting an anti-Indigenous agenda. One of the most prolific writers promoting anti-Indigenous tropes is Frances Widdowson of Winnipeg's Frontier Centre for Public Policy (FCPP). One of the main activities of this 'think tank' is to promote climate change denial. In September 2018, the Frontier Center ran a radio ad claiming to debunk myths about the Indian residential school system that resulted in the deaths of 6000 Indigenous children. The Assembly of First Nations National Chief, Perry Bellegarde denounced the ad because it "knowingly turned its back on the facts" (*CBC News* 24 September 2018). The ad begins with the question: "are Canadians being told the whole truth about residential schools?" A professor at the University of Regina, James Daschuk, comments that "I honestly do not understand why they would devalue their own brand by coming out with an advertisement that's so egregiously wrong." A spokesperson for the FCPP attempted to distance itself from the ad by saying that it had 'no editorial control' over the piece.

Frances Widdowson is listed as a Senior Fellow with the FCPP who uses a political economy perspective in her research on aboriginal policy, as well as the politics of religion. She is known for several controversial books on Indigenous issues, such as *Disrobing the Aboriginal Industry: The Deception Behind Cultural Preservation* (2008, with husband Albert Howard). The main point of the book, according to its publication blurb, is "to expose the industry that has grown up around land claims settlements, showing that aboriginal policy development over the last thirty years has been manipulated by non-aboriginal lawyers and consultants." The authors single out the clergy, consultants, lawyers, and anthropologists who "have used the plight of aboriginal peoples to justify a self-serving agenda" (2008: 9). Within an Indigenous community, "Privileged leaders live in luxury and are paid huge salaries, while most aboriginal people rely of social assistance...The vanity and arrogance of an unprincipled native leadership is supported by…the bureaucrats and academics whose careers would be jeopardized by exposing the non-performance of current aboriginal policies…The result is a squandering of billions of dollars each year" (ibid: 9–10).

In a book review, well-known political scientist Peter H. Russell, professor emeritus of the University of Toronto, concludes that:

The first thing to be said about the book is that it is not based on well-researched empirical political science. Most of the evidence for their thesis is anecdotal. Careful empirical research of any first nation community, on or off reserve is totally lacking. Broad historical propositions are advanced that distort history and provide an ill-informed basis for appraising current policy in relation to Aboriginal peoples (2010: 785).

In addition, he "profoundly disagrees with the assumptions of these authors and their empirical characterizations of Aboriginal people's culture and capacities past and present" (ibid: 786).

In another review, Daniel Salée (2010) notes that "the very existence of Indigenous peoples disrupts the liberal image mainstream Canadians have of themselves and their country. It forces them into a rather uncomfortable reassessment of the foundational notions of state and nation they hold dear, of the core values by which they define themselves" (2010: 315). He further suggests that Indigenous people got in the way of European settlers' plans, such that "no effort was spared to dismiss their socio-political relevance, infantilize them, and even obliterate them, both symbolically and physically" (ibid: 316). Furthermore, the present book has unleashed 'a howl of indignation within anti-colonialist…circles'. In the end though, *Disrobing the Aboriginal Industry* "errs in so many ways as to discredit their own argument and discourage any engagement with it… the book falls seriously short of providing the much needed dispassionate ground for a cold-headed discussion of the challenges and issues faced by Aboriginal communities in Canada today" (ibid: 322).

As with several other reviews of *Disrobing*, Lemelin (2009: 357) points to the unwarranted divisiveness promoted by Widdowson and Howard:

If we are to address the narratives of the victims and survivors in aboriginal society, while celebrating healers and success cases, we will need to move away from confrontational and divisive dialogues and promote forums where difficult issues like some of those outlined in this book can be addressed in an environment of mutual respect and tolerance.

There can be little doubt that many people would agree that it is an easy matter to criticize and plant the seeds of discord between Indigenous people and Euro-Canadian as Widdowson and Howard attempt to do, however it is an entirely different matter to conduct serious research into today's social problems and seek equitable solutions.

Widdowson's later work plays on similar themes. In *Separate but Unequal* (2019), the theme of 'parallelism', which is to say, the view that Indigenous cultures and the wider Canadian society should exist separately from one another in a 'nation-to-nation' relationship, is the subject of an in-depth critique. Her view is that 'parallelism' will not result in a more equitable relationship between Indigenous and non-Indigenous people, rather such an approach will only isolate the Indigenous population further.

To solve the issue of Indigenous dependency, Widdowson invokes the long abandoned assimilationist approach, of which we have not heard much about since Trudeau's 1969 White Paper. There is a bit of a slight of hand used here since Widdowson clarifies that it is not assimilation that she is recommending but 'integration'. As she explains, the term 'assimilation' is not used by her in order avoid "some of the negative aspects of the latter assimilation by recognizing that certain cultural features are beneficial if they facilitate participation in the wider society. In fact, integration assumes that the best aspects of different cultures will be kept and enable a more complex and socially beneficial civilization to exist" (2019: 46). The fact that she feels the need to hide such an important discussion away in an obscure footnote raises a myriad of questions. One of the most important of these is: who decides what are 'the best aspects of different cultures' to be integrated? By disguising an old bogey-man in more acceptable clothing does little to hide an odorous and unworkable concept that has been vehemently opposed by Indigenous people for the last fifty years.

Widdowson's (2021) most recent critique of the Truth and Reconciliation Commission's findings is called *Indigenizing the University*. She begins by examining the suggestion that the poor educational levels of many Indigenous people could be improved by 'Indigenizing the university'. Her intention in this volume stems from a "lack of critical thinking about Indigenization…there is resistance to listening to differing points of view or engaging in any kind of critical analysis" (2021: 2). She calls this issue a matter of 'Groupthink' which Widdowson defines as "a psychological phenomenon that happens in collectives when the desire for social harmony results in irrational decision-making" (ibid: 3). In addition, she contends that "Criticism of Indigenization need to be heard, and a more comprehensive understanding should not be stymied because supporters of this initiative are politically opposed to having their ideas scrutinized" (ibid: 6).

My own view, based on an involvement with the Indigenous Resource Center at the University of Guelph for nearly four decades, would suggest that Widdowson is beginning with a false premise. What she is suggesting is that we take a critical view of Indigenous perspectives in the university and then decide if this is a way to proceed or not. Such issues were decided decades ago, and there is evidently wide support for including both Aboriginal students and Indigenous points of view in the university curriculum. The University of Guelph also has an Office of Intercultural Affairs which supports the participation of students from racially diverse backgrounds which includes various faith perspectives. As well, the university has an Indigenous Student Society which is a club accredited through the Central Student Association. As well, there is a President's Advisory Committee on Aboriginal Initiates (PACAI) which works to advance reconciliation and decolonization initiatives at the university. All of these groups, initiatives and curriculum developments which encompass Indigenous perspectives serve to counteract the sorts of xenophobic attitudes espoused by Frances Widdowson and others who support her anti-Indigenous agenda of cultural and racial intolerance.

So here is a further question to ponder, are Frances Widdowson's views to be considered 'hate speech', or more simply 'tough critique'? This is the issue discussed by Alexandra Shimo in a *Maclean's* article (2009). The scene was a heated verbal exchange between Widdowson and several participants at a meeting of the Canadian Political Science Association. Although Widdowson indicated that "Everyone's against the promotion of hatred," one participant claimed that she implied that the Indigenous population was composed of "backward people wandering aimlessly through the woods." According to Barbara Arneil, a UBC professor, "What's at stake is more important than merely the right to say contentious things. The right to free speech isn't about the right to say 'anything', but the right to say what's respectful. It's okay to speak your mind in academia, if what you say doesn't offend anyone."

There were professors though who came to Widdowson's defense, such as those who support the First Amendment to the U.S. Constitution. There were also those who wanted the Ontario and Canadian human rights commissions to provide written assurance that there would be no interference 'with legitimate academic discourse'. Each reader needs to think through this issue themselves. My opinion is that bad ideas do not stand the test of time; ask anybody who did not believe in the law of gravity how jumping off a tall building worked out for them.

The Justin Trudeau Era

As far as the Justin Trudeau era is concerned, Indigenous affairs in Canada was not ushered in with much fanfare or aspirations of dramatic change for the better. By this time, Indigenous people had become weary of the old promises, and the seemingly inevitable betrayals. The same old assurances are made at election time, after which the Indigenous agenda is once again put on the back burner. Indigenous protests, born out of frustration for the unfulfilled hollow promises of the past, are apt to be met with brutal suppression, rather than conciliatory understanding. Protests are followed by the inevitable Royal commission, costing millions of dollars, coupled with an abundance of thoughtful recommendations, which are seldom acted upon, and the cycle repeats itself through history in a cyclical pattern.

A *Toronto Star* (11 January 2021) article echoes this consumer fatigue: "Is Justin Trudeau's plan for Indigenous rights a step in the right direction, or just another hollow promise from Ottawa?" There is every reason to ask this most pertinent question. During the COVID-19 era the Liberal government has initiated direct negotiations with band councils, through Zoom calls, over matters relating to land and self-government. Apparently there are over 80 ongoing negotiations happening with almost 400 First Nations, Métis, and Inuit communities.

There is apprehension that such Zoom-style 'negotiations' are subject to less scrutiny than might otherwise be the case with reporters or other media present. A main concern is that the Trudeau government will accede to the resource companies' strategy to gain access to Indigenous lands. No one is forgetting that this government has deemed resource extraction industries 'essential', suggesting that these companies have been given tacit approval, such as probably is the case with the Trans-Mountain expansion. The suggestion is that the consultations are 'jointly designed', however the government negotiators have discretionary power over which decisions are able to be forwarded to various cabinets for approval. Of course, one is reminded that in early 2018 the Liberal government tried a *légere de main* maneuver when Justin Trudeau outlined his plans for reconciliation when he promised to finally honor Indigenous rights and turn a page on their harmful suppression.

In public, there were fine sounding words delivered in speeches, but details of the government's plans were clouded over with abstract rhetoric—a sense of *déjà vu* all over began, inevitably, begins to settle in. Proposals trickled out. Apparently there might be plans for a municipal-style government for First Nations reserves. Does anybody remember the *Sechelt* case of 1986 which held such promise (see Etkin 1988)?

The Municipal Model of Self-Government: Pros and Cons

Using a municipal model of self-government, as in the Sechelt case, has been discussed off and on for the last fifty years. In the 1960s, the Hawthorn Report provided a fairly comprehensive overview of issues, advantages, and problems with the municipal incorporation of Indigenous communities (1966–67: 285–311). As a starter, the Hawthorn Report notes that the British North America Act (BNA) gives the provinces exclusive rights to make laws dealing with the 'municipal institutions of the province' (section 92–8), which covers such areas as taxation and the maintenance of various institutions such as hospitals and schools, as in 'generally all matters of a merely local or private nature in the province'.

The powers of local levels of government to provide services has been growing in importance over time. Part of the reason is that there has been a certain measure of integration of local and provincial governments, and a more distant relationship with the federal government. However, one consequence of this growing provincial involvement has been a diminished power in the local communities to regulate its own activities in matters of local importance. There is a fear that if this situation continues then the local community government would become not much more than a local administrative apparatus through which various provincial government departments could apply their policies and regulations at the local level. Local governments as autonomous decision-making bodies could suffer a decline with increased provincial involvement in the application of policies and regulations.

As far as Indigenous communities are concerned, the advancement of self-government at the local-level presents community members with a stark choice: firstly, do they wish to continue within the existing structure of the Indian Act and Indigenous Affairs bureaucracy; or secondly, would it be better for them to situate their communities within the framework of local governments as conceived by the provinces for their non-Indigenous residents? The option is not one of simply establishing more self-government responsibilities, but of establishing these more fully within the provincial-municipal framework. At the same time, it would not seem feasible for Indigenous First Nations to operate independently of the provinces and simultaneously maintain their more direct relationship with the federal government.

The decision of the Sechelt band in British Columbia to adopt a municipal framework was a very important occurrence because of its experimental situation. This move was the first concrete attempt in Canada to counteract the long-standing trend whereby the development of Indigenous self-government was seen to take place only within the rather narrow confines of the Indian Act. The Hawthorn Report also suggested that any change in this direction toward municipal incorporation could also serve to reduce existing discriminatory practices currently applied to Indigenous communities:

This principle that Indigenous bands are to be treated as municipalities would be a reversal of the present discriminatory situation in which Indian bands are generally excluded except where special provision has been made for their inclusion. The present situation is completely unsatisfactory for it rests on the unacceptable proposition that the possession of the special community status implied on the reserve system justifies exclusion of Indian communities from access to services and benefits routinely provided to non-Indian communities (Hawthorn 1966–67: 305).

The *Sechelt Indian Band Self-Government Act*, which was passed in 1986, was the first formal Aboriginal self-government arrangement in Canada. The Sechelt Constitution, which also came into effect in 1986, included provisions on voting rights and the qualifications for running in band elections, which were consistent with similar Indian Act provisions at the time. Specifically, the Indian Act provisions limited voting rights to those members who were ordinarily on-reserve residents and denied voting rights to those who were not.

The Indian Act provisions were subsequently found to be inconsistent with equality rights under the *Canadian Charter of Rights and Freedoms* in *Corbiere v. Canada (Minister of Indian and Northern Affairs)*, 1999 2 S.C.R. 203. Following the Corbiere decision, section 77 of the *Indian Act* has been rewritten to exclude the words 'ordinarily resident on the reserve' to make it Charter-compliant, but the Constitution was not similarly amended.[82]

Thus, the Sechelt band became the first band in Canada to develop its own constitution and withdraw its reserve lands from Indian Act jurisdiction. This decision by the Sechelt band, in effect, set a precedent by creating a new level of government for Indigenous communities. Rather than have reserve lands held by the Crown 'in trust', Indigenous people now apparently have the opportunity to move beyond usufructuary title to 'fee simple' ownership. With this move, technically speaking, Indigenous people would then have the opportunity, previously denied to them, to mortgage, surrender, transfer or inherit property on their reserves. The advantages to this move are evident, at least on the surface. Clear title to Indigenous lands would serve to overcome or remove some of the current impediments to economic development which are now restrained by the Indian Act.

It needs to be specified, however, that Sechelt lands still remain as a reserve under the Constitution Act of 1867. It remains registered with the Reserve Land Register. Thus, provincial laws apply to Sechelt lands only to a limited degree, and yet the band council has significant powers beyond those of conventional municipalities:

The Sechelt Act sets out as its primary purpose to…enable the Sechelt Indian Band to establish and maintain self-government for itself and its members on Sechelt lands and to obtain control over the administration of the resources and services available to its members (Etkin 1988: 87–89).

One of the special features of the Sechelt Act is the right of the band council to tax non-Indigenous residents on the land, within constraints imposed by provincial statutes. In addition, large portions of the Sechelt land have been developed and leased to approximately 500 non-Indigenous residents, and this revenue now forms a substantial part of the band's economic base. This is the situation with my own summer cottage on the Saugeen Reserve in Ontario. In fact, an article in the *Saugeen Times* (22 February 2021) indicates that the Saugeen First Nation has been leasing land since 1947. As the article indicates, returning Indigenous war veterans were also given lots in recognition of their service. Obviously the whole situation of reserve land in Canada needs a more thorough future investigation, however in the Sechelt case the band has the right to acquire and hold property and presumably to sell or otherwise dispose of that property, a provision not normally allowed for under the Indian Act.

The Sechelt case was decided by a special act of parliament, and therefore it holds considerable promise as a way that other Indigenous communities would be able to break out of the legislative constraints of the Indian Act. The powers exercised by the Sechelt band are analogous to current Canadian municipal powers and give the band control over all essential services and land developments. Given what would appear to be some significant advantages of adopting a municipal model for Indigenous reserves, one wonders why there has not been a rush by other bands to adopt this approach.

Soon after the Sechelt Act was passed in 1986, an article appeared questioning whether or not the concept of Indigenous self-government was an 'instrument of autonomy or assimilation' (Bolt and Long 1988). As an example, the Assembly of First Nations was quick to condemn the Sechelt proposal, indicating that the Sechelt Act was just one step above the Indian Act and should be not be regarded as self-government, since the act is seen as a legislative solution that betrays their aims for sovereignty. Previously, in 1983, the Penner Report (Canada 1983), concerning the Special Committee on Indian Self-Government, also supported the Assembly of First Nations' criticism of the 'legislative solution' to self-government, noting that such a proposal fails to take account of the origins and rights of Indian First Nations in Canada. A major objection is that permission to opt in would be a favor granted to bands that the Minister of Indian Affairs, or her discretion, deemed to be sufficiently 'advanced'. Therefore, the paternalistic role of the Department would be maintained under such a proposal, according to Etkin (1988: 98). The Union of British Columbia Indians also opposed the Sechelt plan, and was supported by most other Indian bands in the province. These moves caused the Sechelt Band to eventually resign from the various provincial and national organization of which it had formerly been a member.

The opposition to the Sechelt plan concerns a wider issue: how to achieve Indigenous self-government. Opponents of the Sechelt municipal government plan are critical of the idea of achieving self-government through federal legislation which would allow the federal government to veto local proposals it opposes, which the critics do not see as self-government at all, but government within a colonial regime. In other words, there is concern that the municipal model is too much of a 'Eurocentric' (see Hedican 2014) political model to follow. The Assembly of First Nations was also insisting that the federal government formulate a comprehensive claims policy to settle Indigenous disputes, as opposed to the Sechelt case which is seen as taking a piecemeal approach. It is also a difficult matter to determine if the Sechelt approach would be a useful solution for other Indigenous communities seeking self-government. Some see the Sechelt Act as just another form of 'institutional assimilation':

The Sechelt initiatives are designed to remove gradually the exclusive unilateral ties with the federal government and incorporated Indian collectivities into provincial government structures and federal line departments. Canada's Indian policy of institutional assimilation is so deeply entrenched and has such a momentum that emerging Indian self-government is sure to be profoundly shaped by it (Bolt and Long 1988: 49).

All in all, there are characteristics of the Sechelt band which tend to make it a special case. The most obvious fact is that it is situated near the large urban center of Vancouver such that Sechelt is already part of a municipal structure on a *de facto* basis even if not officially so. In this respect, it differs considerably from the more rural, northern bands with their small populations and isolated influences. It is just as important to study governmental initiatives in these more remote locations, even though these communities may lack the publicity accorded the Sechelt case.

One of the issues that later emerged was that the Sechelt Indian Band Constitution previously did not comply with the equality rights relating to voting and running for office in Sechelt elections protected by section 15 of the *Canadian Charter of Rights and Freedoms*.

Amendments to the Sechelt Constitution were required to allow Sechelt (Shíshálh) members who are not resident on Sechelt Lands to vote and run for office in the next band elections, which were scheduled for March 2020, thereby making it compliant with the Charter.

In another example, the formation of Nunavut in 1999 provided a different model of self-government. The governing body in this case is responsible for one large land mass in which the population comprises both Indigenous and non-Indigenous persons in a territorial-style government. Although the Inuit comprise a majority of the Nunavut population (about 84 percent), they must still form a government that comprises competent, non-indigenous points of view and areas of interest.

Back to the Future

So now, we project ourselves over three decades into the future, and see in an article posted on the *APTN National News* (Diablo 2020) offering the opinion that Justin "Trudeau's policies…threaten Indigenous Rights which Quietly Aims at Assimilation." As such, it appears as if time has stood still in the Indigenous rights debate over self-government. The issue of assimilation was certainly an issue fifty years ago when then Prime Minister Pierre E. Trudeau put forward the policy proposal commonly known as the White Paper back in 1969.

It is certainly an interesting historical matter that a charge of promoting assimilationist policies should be leveled at both the father and son, both Canadian Prime Ministers during different time periods over a period of five decades. It is evident, then, that concerns over government policies aimed at assimilating Canada's Indigenous population never seem to go away, becoming both Canada's past and future simultaneously. Diabo, a former contender for the position of National Chief of the Assembly of First Nations, argues that the agenda of our present Prime Minister, Justin Trudeau, is none other than "a continuation of the 1969 White Paper of then Prime Minister Pierre Elliot Trudeau…which intended to strip us of our treaties, nullify our legal and political status as collective rights holders and assimilate us into Canadian society" (5 May 2020). Exactly fifty-one years earlier, Cree leader Harold Cardinal exclaimed that "The new Indian policy promulgated by Prime Minister Pierre Elliot Trudeau's government…is a thinly disguised program of extermination through assimilation" (1969: 1). Five decades later even the wording appears the same. Has nothing changed over this time period? Diablo's quote could have been written in 1970, and Cardinal's statement in 2020!

Back in the days of the Hawthorn Report (1966–67) because of the 'Citizens Plus' recommendation, the philosophy of special status for First Nations people in Canada was an idea that was becoming generally accepted among Indigenous peoples themselves, social scientists, and the news media (*Globe and Mail*, 22 February 1967; Mortimore 1967). This was especially the case with the notion that Indigenous people should have a greater choice of lifestyle, whether it meant staying in their own communities or outside them (Weaver 1981: 21). Above all, "Indians can and should retain the special privileges of their status while enjoying full participation as provincial and federal citizens" (Hawthorn 1966–1967: 7). It follows then that the question of assimilation should be a matter of choice for Indigenous people to decide, a decision not made for them by the government or anybody else. Furthermore, it is up to the federal government to ensure that the delivery of services to Indigenous people is continued. As the Hawthorn Report asserted, it is up to the federal government to protect their special status within Canadian society and "act as a national conscience to see that social and economic equality is achieved between Indians and Whites" (1966–1967: 13).

This is not to suggest that the Hawthorn Report was not the subject of controversy. There were those who felt that the Report should have been more critical of the Indian Affairs bureaucracy. For anthropologist R.W. Dunning of the University of Toronto, who had conducted first hand ethnographic fieldwork in the First Nations community of Pekangekum in northwestern Ontario during the mid-1950s, the Report was negligent in not challenging the paternalistic role of Indian Affairs sufficiently. Dunning was not critical of any of the 151 specific recommendations *per se*, and lauded the research conducted by his anthropological and other social scientific colleagues. Nonetheless he thought that the Report was 'worthy of 1867' because it failed to question the legitimacy and monopoly of the Indian Affairs Branch's control over Indigenous people (1967: 52).

Dunning, along with others, had anticipated that the Report would have made recommendations that were more far-reaching in changing the structure of Indian administration. As Dunning indicated in his ethnography of the Pekangekum community, "Its political sovereignty is attenuated if not controlled ultimately by the Indian Affairs administration…It is possible that Pekangekum may in this respect be representative of a large number of similarly placed northern woodland groups who have suffered both economically and socially almost overwhelming and revolutionary culture contact" (1959: 20). The Indian Affairs Branch, one may assume by Dunning's characterization, was not just another benign governmental structure, but was responsible for widespread 'suffering' among indigenous people. Dunning (1969, 1971) continued his criticism of the Canadian government's policies toward the Indigenous people into the 1970s (see also Hedican 1982, 1987).

In all, Dunning's dissatisfaction with the Report was that it had not recommended the dissolution of the Indian Affairs Branch, although researchers who had contributed to the Report had considered such a recommendation but eventually rejected it (1966–1967: 8, 387–400). Aside from the 'custodial care' role of the Department, it could also be pointed out that criticism of the Report also concerned the lack of proposals that would allow for any meaningful involvement of Indigenous people themselves in planning their own future, and in the virtual lack of their involvement in an advisory capacity in formulating the recommendations (see Weaver 1976, 1981: 84–86). As noted by Walter Rudnicki, a senior Indian Affairs Branch official, who echoed anthropologist Dunning's (1967, 1969) previous criticism in the *Canadian Forum*, "it is relevant to note that none of Hawthorn's recommendations have ever been referred to Indian leaders and spokesmen for comments or discussion. The Indians were simply by standers in a scene where experts had a conversation among themselves and arrived at their own consensus" (in Weaver 1981: 86).

Yet, even nearly forty years later, in 2005, the Hawthorn Report with its emphasis on 'Citizens Plus' has been touted as not so much a model of assimilation but one of 'integration'. In a *Globe and Mail* article by columnist Jeffrey Simpson, 'integration' is put forward as 'a third way' or alternative to assimilation and self-determination. In this dialogue, the distinctions begin to become blurred:

Rather than assimilation or self-determination, the 'citizen plus' model seeks to integrate aboriginals to a certain extent in mainstream society, without forcing them to become like the rest of us. In mainstream society, they learn modern skills. They work there. They hold on to their heritage. They negotiate, as do many citizens, between their specific identity and the broader, Canadian one (*Globe and Mail*, 26 November 2005).

Of the very puzzling matters raised by this quote, one wonders what Simpson meant by 'like the rest of us', implying that Canadians are a homogenous group, or does he mean 'like Whites'? In a chapter on 'the new assimilation arguments', Warry suggests that Jeffrey Simpson's view is certainly 'paternalistic' because it 'gives the impression that Aboriginal people can only be successful if they leave the reserve', which is described in a stereotypical manner such that "reserves equal outmoded culture and traditions; cities equal assimilation and integration" (2007: 47).

There are further issues sullying Justin Trudeau's relationship with Indigenous people, especially as these relate to the petroleum industry. Once again debates involve resource and development issues as they did in the 1970s, such as the Mackenzie Valley Pipeline Inquiry in the Northwest Territories. After a lengthy investigation, Chief Justice Thomas Berger produced a report, *Northern Frontier, Northern Homeland* (1977) that generated considerable controversy at the time. The inquiry heard from people in communities all along the Mackenzie corridor, as well as Indigenous studies specialists such as Richard Salisbury (1977b) and Michael Asch (1982, 1983). The results of the Berger Inquiry were accepted by the government, which stipulated a moratorium of ten years on future gas and oil development in the Mackenzie District until such time as Indigenous land claims and environmental impact problems were resolved.[83]

One of these environmental problems concerned the possible impact that a pipeline could have on Indigenous country food gathering such as hunting, trapping, and fishing. As Berger indicated in his report, "there has always been a traditional renewable resource sector in the North, but instead of trying to strengthen it, we had, for a decade or more, followed policies by which it could only be weakened or even destroyed" (1983: 366–377). The fact of the matter is that the renewable resource industry of hunting and fishing is an important economic factor in northern Indigenous life, which sustains northern residents with nutritious food at a price much less than would be available in local grocery stores in the south (Hedican 1985, 1991b). If Indigenous people in northern areas of Canada would be required to remove country food production from their communities because of some unforeseen environmental disaster, then the resulting hardships would be incalculable.

The stakes as far as the larger Canadian economy is concerned are very high, with difficult decisions to be made on both sides. One of the issues concerns how the northern economy is portrayed. As an example, Berger notes that "people who tried to earn a living by hunting, trapping, and fishing had often been regarded as unemployed" (1983: 367). Indigenous economies are often portrayed as 'backward' because they exploit traditional resources. They are at times portrayed as being antithetical to 'modernization'. The narrative promulgated by vested interests in the resource exploitation sector, or those wishing to promote an assimilationist program, contrasts 'modern-backward', or 'modern-traditional'. There is also the suggestion that the traditional Indigenous economy of the north is in rapid decline, and will likely disappear altogether in the near future. Of course all of these prognostications are not based on credible research.

It is evident, then, there has occurred a polarization in the debate over resource development in the Canadian north. As such, there has also been a polarization concerning perceptions about 'development' and how it is to be defined and on whose terms. Commenting on the Mackenzie Valley Pipeline debate, as an example, Asch has taken particular exception to the view that, as time goes on, "the inherent superiority of the rational industrial economy is such that it will inevitably replace the backward and irrational one" (1982: 4). Thus, such a characterization lends credibility to the view that there exists an inherent competition between the wage economy on the one hand and the non-wage, traditional sector of the northern economy on the other. In reality, and I have found this to be true in my own research in northern Ontario, there is a certain complementarity between the two sectors of hunting and wage work. Berger has referred, then, to the 'mixed economy', suggesting that "In the north today, the lives of many native families are based on an intricate economic mix. At certain times of the year, they hunt and fish; at other times they work for wages" (Berger 1977: 122).

We can therefore surmise from the preceding discussion that the manner in which Justin Trudeau is presently criticized, as in the *New York Times* article (10 March 2020) in which the Liberals are accused of "consistently picking oil interests over the rights of Indigenous people," is based on a faulty dichotomy. It is not as if Indigenous people are necessarily against 'development', since they could benefit through wage opportunities, but their dissatisfaction is with the possibility of environmental disasters, such as the Exxon Valdez oil spill in Alaska, that could destroy their traditional economies. Of course, there are many people, both Indigenous and non-Indigenous, who regard the fossil fuel industry as declining in the future as renewable forms of energy become ever more prominent.

In any event, one wonders if history is moving backward, or forward, or both ways at the same time, since the issues facing father Trudeau and his son do not appear to be appreciably different over a fifty-year time span. All of which suggests, as far as the Indigenous rights debate is concerned, that we are back and forth between the future and the past in an interminable loop from which there does appears to be no perceptible escape.

Conclusion

This book roughly covers a 50-year period (1970–2020) of anthropology and Indigenous studies in Canada. It begins in the 1960s, a period which I have characterized in my mind as 'the age of Margaret Mead'. We were the Boomer generation, we came in large numbers, and were trying to throw off the past of World War II and the greasers of the 1950s with their duck tail hair style and silly pom-poms hanging from their car windshields. We loved the Beetles, wore long hair to the angst of our parents, and donned raggedy bell-bottom jeans.

Margaret Mead was our hero because she had the boldness to speak out against racism and sexism. She supported the youth of the 1960s and our quest for identity. She was a grandmother we all wish we had—bold, daring and carrying her quirky forked staff. When I started university in 1968, I took my first anthropology course, not really knowing what the subject matter was about because it was not taught in high school. As I mentioned before, my father asked Mom, "Can't Eddie take something that we can pronounce?" What was appealing to me about anthropology was its global perspective and philosophical stance of cultural relativism. The people who in previous generations were called 'primitive' now had intelligent things to say. They were the survivors who would probably outlast the militaristic, nuclear age of a decadent Western society.

As we moved into the 1970s we left behind a difficult period in Canada with its conflicting messages. On the one hand, a large group of anthropologists wrote the Hawthorn Report with its 'Citizens Plus' recommendation which we took to recognize Indigenous rights. Pierre Elliot Trudeau, the Prime Minister, astounded everyone with the termination (do away with the Indian Act, reserves, DIAND) proposal of the White Paper of 1969, but what would be left? Into the 1970s, the Quebec government under

Premier Robert Bourassa announced that the province intended to dam the major rivers emptying into James Bay in order to construct a gigantic hydroelectric project. Premier Bourassa completely ignored the fact that *Nouveau Quebec*, comprising some 410 thousand square miles (1,066,000 square kilometers) of territory had never been ceded by a treaty with the Indigenous groups of the area.

A bitter court battle ensued led by the Grand Council of the Cree and regional Inuit groups on one side and the Quebec government on the other. Out of McGill University a group of anthropologists, mostly comprising graduate students associated with the Programme in the Anthropology of Development headed by Richard Salisbury, volunteered their time to write a variety of impact assessment reports. These reports portrayed a disastrous future for the Cree and Inuit if the project was allowed to proceed. Eventually an agreement was reached in 1975 after an injunction on the project was granted by Judge Malouf which was suspended a week later. The James Bay and Northern Quebec Agreement (1975) was regarded by some as the first modern Indigenous claims settlement in Canada because it left the Cree and Inuit with substantial control over their territory. Programs were created for hunter income support, environmental protection and wildlife management. Financial compensation amounted to over $230 million spread out over 20 years.

Contracts for hydroelectric power, however, did not materialize as an alliance of the Sierra Club and the Cree lobbied in New York state to have the project terminated, resulting in the cancellation of two large contracts for electric supply valued at about $17 billion. Nevertheless, the Quebec government continued to build dams and divert water supplies, most notably on the Eastmain River which was completed in 2006. This was followed in 2007 when the Cree signed an agreement with the federal government for an additional $1.4 billion over 20 years in compensation.

The 1980s saw the Constitution Act of 1982 which recognized 'existing' Aboriginal rights, although the term was not defined. The Charter of Rights and Freedoms (1982) did make explicit mention of Aboriginal and treaty rights which were 'hereby recognized and affirmed'. In 1983, the so-called Penner Report urged that Indigenous people in Canada should be allowed to form their own level of government, with an eventual phasing out of the Indian Act and the Department of Indian Affairs. An attempt to eliminate the discrimination of Indigenous women in the Indian Act resulted in the passage of Bill C-31 in1985, however there were various problems with registration and the adjudication of applications for reinstatement, as well as different categories of 'status Indians' emerging with some having less advantageous status than another. By 2001, just over 105,000 individuals were successfully added to the status Indian population which represented an increase of nearly one-seventh of the registered Indian population. However, there were various court contests ongoing into the future, such as the Lynn Gehl challenge which resulted in her successful granting of Indian status in 2017.

In other developments, the Sechelt Band near Vancouver in British Columbia was granted a form of self-government in 1986 with a version of municipal status. Other First Nations, after the Assembly of First Nations criticized this move, shied away from following the Sechelt path. The formation of Nunavut in 1999 provided a different model of self-government which comprised a combination of Indigenous and non-Indigenous people. The Royal Commission on Aboriginal Peoples (RCAP) was released in 1996 putting forward more than 400 recommendations. Prime Minister Harper subsequently declined an invitation to discuss the recommendations at an all-chiefs conference, a response described as 'disturbing and astonishing' by Indigenous leaders (Cairns 2000: 5).

The new millennium saw the release of the Ipperwash Report in 2007, instituted as a result primarily because of the shooting death of protester Dudley George, but the resulting 100 recommendation were similarly ignored. Also in 2007, the United Nations Declaration on Indigenous Rights was passed easily on a worldwide basis, except for the Stephen Harper government, which finally relented in 2010 under intense public criticism. When Prime Minister Stephen Harper issued an apology in 2008 on behalf of Canadians over the harmful effects on Indigenous people who were involved in the Residential School system, it tended to lack the sincerity that was intended because of his previous refusal to ratify the UN Human Rights Declaration.

In the present era of the Justin Trudeau government, observers are still assessing the effects on Indigenous people before and during this present pandemic period. What is unnerving to many is the vast amounts of money that his Liberal government is expending in an attempt to counteract Indigenous rights. As an example, between 2015 and 2018 the Trudeau government has spent almost $100 million litigating First Nations land claims in the courts. On the other hand, Justin Trudeau promises a program of reconciliation. "It is time for a renewed nation-to-nation relationship with First Nations," he told the Assembly of First Nations delegates in 2015, "one that understands that the constitutionality guaranteed rights of First Nations are not an inconvenience but rather a sacred obligation" (*APTN News*, 18 December 2020).

All in all, an important question remains: "Can an understanding of the past lead to a better comprehension of the future?" Indigenous people in Canada may hope for a better future, but hope needs to be supported by concrete program for change that are not just renewed forms of duplicity. As a *New York Times* (10 March 2020) article indicated:

When Justin Trudeau became prime minister of Canada in 2015, he promised a new relationship with Indigenous people, "built on respect, rights and a commitment to end the status quo." He promised funding for Indigenous cultural activities and education. He called for recognition of aboriginal land rights…So among activists there appears to be just as much skepticism as hope…about whether Native political authority over their old territories in Canada will finally be realized or remain a thin formality, a veneer of legitimacy for ongoing colonialism.

As far as anthropology in Canada is concerned, there is a realization that over the last fifty-year period, fluctuations in government policy toward Indigenous people do not appear to progress in a linear fashion, but back and forth in a sort of dialectical dance, each party moving forward, then backward, through time. However, whether we like it or not, we must all move on to the next fifty years (2020–2070) of anthropology in Canada, leaving the past behind as new challenges engage our imagination. For beyond the beaten path lies many more interesting possibilities than most of us are capable of perceiving.

Epilogue: 10 Lessons Learned

First of all, let me make it clear that I have no intention of telling anyone what to do with their life or how to live it. These are simply some of my own observations and experiences that may or may not be of any value to anyone else.

1. Treasure the opportunities that come your way in life. If you ignore your opportunities, you will not get very far. Above all, do not let fear get in the way of achieving your goals.

2. Learn to listen, and listen to learn. Most of us do not learn very much when we are talking. Try to resist the urge to talk most of the time in a conversation. Ask questions, then stay quiet and listen.

3. It's alright to make mistakes. When things are going well in our lives, we do not learn very much, its only when we get into troubling situations that we need to make changes in our lives that eventually benefit us, otherwise we tend to keep making the same mistakes over and over again.

4. Life is shorter than you think, so get going. Try not to waste your time in non-productive ways. If you do not set goals for yourself, how can you ever expect to achieve them?

5. Keep in touch. After I left Collins, I kept in touch with people in the community. At first, they were just people that I met doing my fieldwork, then they became life-long friends. Many of the older people have now passed away, and those that were just babies then are now parents and even grandparents. Today we keep in touch by Facebook and Messenger. The younger people especially are looking for old photographs of the people they never knew. They are also interested in various family connections and what certain people were

like. In certain ways, as incongruous as this may sound, I've become one of their elders.

6. Try not to control what is happening around you. Let life 'flow' the way it was meant to happen; don't get in the way. We all have our plans, but circumstances change so we should too.

7. Let people come to you. Stay on the sidelines for a while. Soon people will get curious about who you are.

8. Be yourself, and not somebody that you aren't. Nobody likes a phony, a braggart or a bully. Learn to love yourself, you are unique in the universe, there will never be another 'you' so appreciate who you are.

9. Try to do more by doing less. Many people today rush all over the place and hardly get anything done. Then, what they do is too superficial, lacks depth. In the morning, try to think of just a few things that you would like to accomplish that day, then stick with the plan.

10. Above all realize that life is a gift, so treat it with respect. Today is called the present because that's what it is, a gift, it will never come around again.

Postscript

5 April 2021

I had a dream last night.

I was getting ready to go into my last class at the university when my eldest daughter knocked on the door and burst in. More and more she is acting more like a parent than a daughter. For some reason, she pulled a cloth out of her back pocket and began to dust me off as if I was a card board cutout that she had hauled out of the basement. Then she said, "Dad, I want you to try to remember to stick to your lecture today. Nobody wants to hear about those days when you lived in those log cabins up north and it was 50 below."

So my last class was finishing and I wished the students good luck on their final exam. One of the students got up and began to clap. Soon he was joined by several others around him and this began to spread out to the rest of the class. I felt a warm glow envelop me.

Then I walked over to the doorway as another class was starting to come in. A young professor walked through the door wearing the same sort of dark

310

beard that I had many years before. He went over to me and said that this was his first class and that he was so scared that he had forgot his lecture. I watched in disbelief as he stood on the podium and began to talk about his recent research trip to northern Ontario where he lived in log cabins and it was 50 below.

References

Abu-Lughod, L. 1991. Writing Against Culture. In R.G. Fox, ed., *Recapturing Anthropology*, pp. 37–62. Santa Fe, NM: School of American Research, University of Washington Press.

Acoose, J. 1995. *Iskwewak.Kah'Ki Yah Ni Wahkomakanak: Neither Indian Princess nor Easy Squaw.* Toronto: Women's Press.

Agar, M.H. 1980. *The Professional Stranger: An Informal Introduction to Ethnography.* New York: Academic Press.

American Anthropological Association. 1999. Declaration on Anthropology and Human Rights. (http://humanrights.americananthro.org/1999-statement-on-human-rights/).

Amit, V. 2000. *Constructing the Field: Ethnographic Fieldwork in the Contemporary World.* New York: Routledge.

Anders, G. 2014. Contesting Expertise: Anthropologists at the Special Court for Sierra Leone. *Journal of the Royal Anthropological Institute* 20 (3):426–444.

Anderson, K. 2000. *A Recognition of Being: Reconstructing Native Womanhood.* Toronto: Sumach Press.

Anishinabek News. 2018. Williams Treaty Settlement Looks Huge in Headlines. 21 November.

Anthropology News. 1973. P.J. Epling Obituary, 14 (7): 4.

APTN National News. 2020. Despite Promise of Reconciliation, Trudeau Spent Nearly $100M Fighting First Nations in Court During First Years in Power. 18 December (https://www.aptnnews.ca).

Aron, A. and S. Corne, eds. 1994. *Writings for a Liberation Psychology*. Cambridge, Mass.: Harvard University Press.

Asch, M. 1982. Capital and Economic Development: A Critical Appraisal of the Recommendations of the Mackenzie Valley Pipeline Commission. *Culture* 2 (3): 3–9.

—2014. *On Being Here to Stay: Treaties and Aboriginal Rights in Canada*. Toronto: University of Toronto Press.

Asch, M., J. Borrows and J. Tully. 2018. *Resurgence and Reconciliation: Indigenous-Settler Relations and Earth Teachings*. Toronto: University of Toronto Press.

Ashland Daily News (Wisconsin, USA). 1893. Ed Hedican Shot: A Desperate Gambler Held for Trying to Shoot an Officer. 30 March.

Ashland Daily Press (Wisconsin, USA). 1893. Hedican's Death: The Sad Calamity Which Befell the Officer Greatly Regretted. 30 March.

Bailey, F.G. 1969. *Stratagems and Spoils: A Social Anthropology of Politics*. New York: Schoken.

Balduk, J. 2008. On Liminality. Conceptualizing 'in between-ness'. Unpublished Master's Thesis. Radboud University.

Baldwin, W.W. 1957. Social Problems of the Ojibwa Indians in the Collins Area in Northwestern Ontario. *Anthropologica* 5: 51–123.

Barley, N. 1986. *The Innocent Anthropologist: Notes from a Mud Hut*. Harmondsworth: Penguin Books.

Barnsley, P. 2002. Transparency and Accountability Spurned: DIAND Department of Indian Affairs and Northern Development Blacks Out Critical Information in Expert Witness Payment. *Windspeaker* 20 (6). (http://windspeaker.com)

Barrett, S.R. 1976. Social Anthropologist: Marginal Academic. *Canadian Review of Sociology and Anthropology* 16: 161–181.

—1984. *The Rebirth of Anthropological Theory.* Toronto: University of Toronto Press.

—1987. *Is God a Racist? The Right Wing in Canada.* Toronto: University of Toronto Press.

—2002. *Culture Meets Power.* Westport, CN: Praeger.

—2009. *Anthropology: A Guide to Theory and Method.* 2nd ed. Toronto: University of Toronto Press.

Bataille, G. and C. Silet. 1981. *The Pretend Indians: Images of Native Americans in the Movies.* Iowa City: The University of Iowa Press.

Battiste, M., ed. 2000. *Reclaiming Indigenous Voices and Vision.* Vancouver: University of British Columbia Press.

Battiste, M., and S. Youngblood Henderson. 2011. Eurocentrism and the European Ethnographic Tradition. In M.J. Cannon and L. Sunseri, eds., *Racism, Colonialism, and Indigeneity in Canada*, pp. 11–19. Don Mills: Oxford University Press.

Beare, M.E. 2008. Shouting Innocence from the Highest Rooftop. In *Honoring Social Justice*, M.E. Beare, ed. Toronto: University of Toronto Press.

Beech, N. 2011. Liminality and the Practices of Identity Reconstruction. *Human Organization* 62 (2): 285–302.

Behar, Ruth. 1998. *The Vulnerable Observer: Anthropology That Breaks Your Heart*. Boston: Beacon Press.

Bell, R. 1870. Report on the Geology of the Northwest Side of Lake Superior and of the Nipigon District. *Geological Survey Department of Canada* 74: 345–403.

Benoit v. Canada. 2003. 242 F.T.R. 159, 2003 FCA 236.

Berger, P. L. and T. Luckman. 1966. *The Social Construction of Reality: A Treatise in the Sociology of Knowledge*. Garden City, NY: Doubleday.

Berger, T.R. 1977. *Northern Frontier, Northern Homeland: Report of the Mackenzie Valley Pipeline Inquiry*. Ottawa: Supply and Services Canada.

—1983. Native Rights and Self-Determination. *Canadian Journal of Native Studies* 3 (2): 363–375.

Berkhofer, R. 1978. *The White Man's Indian: Images of the American Indian from Columbus to the Present*. New York: Knopf.

Bernard, H.R. 2006. *Research Methods in Anthropology: Qualitative and Quantitative Approaches*. New York: Altamira Press.

Bishop, C.A.1974. *The Northern Ojibwa and the Fur Trade: An Historical and Ecological Study*. Toronto: Holt, Rinehart, and Winston.

Black, C. 2021. The Truth about Truth and Reconciliation. *National Post*, 20 March.

Blair, P.J. 2009. *Lament for a First Nation: The Williams Treaties of Southern Ontario*. Vancouver: UBC Press.

Boas, F. 1888.*The Central Eskimo*. Report of the Bureau of Ethnology, 1884–1885. Washington, DC: Smithsonian Institution.

—1940. *Race, Language, and Culture*. New York: Macmillan.

Boellstorff, T. 2008. *Coming of Age in Second Life: An Anthropologist Explores the Virtually Human*. Princeton, NJ: Princeton University Press.

Boggs, C. 1976. *Gamsci's Marxism*. London: Pluto Press.

Bolt, M., and J.A. Long. 1988. Native Indian Self-Government: Instrument of Autonomy or Assimilation. In J.A. Long and M. Bolt, eds. *Governments in Conflict? Provinces and Indian Nations in Canada*. Toronto: University of Toronto Press.

Bonds, A. and J. Inwood. 2016. Beyond White Privilege: Geographies of White Supremacy and Settler Colonialism. *Progress in Human Geography* 40 (6): 715–733.

Bonnett, A. 2016. *White Identities: An Historical and International Introduction*. London: Prentice-Hall.

Borneman, J. and A. Hammoudi, eds. 2009. *Being There: The Fieldwork Encounter and the Making of Truth*: Berkeley, CA: University of California Press.

Borrows, J. 2001. Listening for a Change: The Courts and Oral Tradition. *Osgoode Hall Law Journal* 39: 1–38.

—2002. *Recovering Canada: The Resurgence of Indigenous Law*. Toronto: University of Toronto Press.

Borrows, J. and M. Coyle, eds. 2017. *The Right Relationship: Reimagining the Implementation of Historical Treaties*. Toronto: University of Toronto Press.

Bradwin, E.W. 1928. *The Bunkhouse Man: A Study of Work and Play in the Camps of Canada, 1903–1914*. New York: Columbia University Press.

Briggs, J. 1970. *Never in Anger*. Cambridge: Harvard University Press.

Brinkmann, S. 2012. *Qualitative Inquiry in Everyday Life: Working with Everyday Life Materials.* London: Sage Publications.

Brown, J.S.H.1976. Changing Views of Fur Trade Marriage and Domesticity: James Hargrave, His Colleagues, and the 'Sex'. *Western Canadian Journal of Anthropology* 6 (3): 92–105.

—1980. *Strangers in Blood: Fur Trade Company Families in Indian Country.* Vancouver: University of British Columbia Press.

Brumann, C. 1999. Writing for Culture: Why a Successful Concept Should not be Discarded. *Current Anthropology* 40: S1–S27.

Bruner, E.M. 1986. Experience and its Expression. In V.W. Turner and E.M. Bruner, eds., *The Anthropology of Experience,* pp. 3–30. Urbana: University of Illinois Press.

Buffalo v. Canada. 2005. FC 1622.

(http://decisions.fct-cf.gc.ca/fccf/decisions/en/item/46344/index.do)

Bumsted, J.M. and J. Smyth. 2019. Red River Colony. In *Canadian Encyclopedia.* Toronto: Historical Canada (Retrieved from: https://search-proquestcom.subzero.lib.uoguelph.ca/docview/2316370537?pqorigsite=primo, accessed 28 April 2020).

Burger, E. B. 2020. Pi: The Most Important Number in the Universe (http://www.thegreatcoursesdaily.com, accessed 14 April 2021).

Burstein, P. 2008. Sentencing Acts of Civil Disobedience: Separating Villains and Heroes. In *Honoring Social Justice*, M.E. Beare, ed. Toronto: University of Toronto Press.

Butterly, J.R. and J. Shepard. 2010. *Hunger: The Biology and Politics of Starvation.* Lebanon, NH: University Press of New England.

Cairns, A.C. 2000. *Citizen's Plus: Aboriginal Peoples and the Canadian State.* Vancouver: University of British Columbia Press.

Canada. 1891. *Indian Treaties and Surrenders.* Ottawa: Queen's Printer (Coles Reprint 1971).

—1983. *Indian Self-Government in Canada: Report of the Special Committee* (The Penner Report). Ottawa: Queen's Printer.

—1986. *Sechelt Indian Band Self-Government Act.* Ottawa (https://laws-lois.justice,gc.ca/eng/acts).

—2012. *Aboriginal Peoples Survey (APS).* Ottawa: Statistics Canada (https://www150.statcan.gc.ca/n1/en/catalogue/89–653-X).

—2015. Federal Court of Canada. Mississaugas of Alderville First Nation et al. v. Her Majesty the Queen, concerning the cross-examination of Dr. Edward Hedican.

—2019. *Reclaiming Power and Place: The Final Report of the National Inquiry into Missing and Murdered Indigenous Women and Girls. June 3* (http://www.mmiwg-ffada.ca/).

—2021. *Code of Conduct for Expert Witnesses: Federal Court Rules.* Ottawa (Justice Laws Website, https://laws.justice.gc.ca/eng/regulations/SOR-98-106).

Cannon, M. J. and L. Suneri, eds. 2011. *Racism, Colonialism, and Indigeneity in Canada.* Oxford: Oxford University Press.

Cardinal, H. 1969. *The Unjust Society: The Tragedy of Canada's Indians.* Edmonton: M.G. Hurtig.

Carr, E.S. 2010. Enactments of Expertise. *Annual Review of Anthropology* 39: 17–32.

Carter, S. 1997. *Capturing Women: The Manipulation of Cultural Imagery in Canada's Prairie West.* Montreal: McGill-Queen's University Press.

Casey, E. and Martens, L., eds. 2007. *Gender and Consumption: Material Culture and the Commercialization of Everyday life.* Aldershot: Ashgate.

CBC News. 2000. Oka Crisis Ottawa's Fault: Ciaccia. 10 July.

—2006. Harris Denies Using Profanity over Native Protest. 14 February.

—2007. George Family Braces for Ipperwash Inquiry Report. 31 May.

—2007. Ipperwash Allegations 'Malicious and Petty,' Harris says. 31 May.

—2007. Ipperwash Inquiry Spreads Blame for George's Death. 31 May.

—2014. Lynn Gehl Challenges Indian Status Denial in Ontario Court. 20 October.

—2018. Radio Ad Claiming to Debunk "Myths" of Residential Schools Draws Criticism. 24 September.

Cerwonka, A. and L. Malkki. 2007. *Improvising Theory: Process and Temporality in Ethnographic Fieldwork.* Chicago: University of Chicago Press.

Chwialkowska, L. 2002. Bands Must Make Audits Public. *National Post*, 15 June.

Chiseri-Strater, E. and B.S. Sunstein. 1997. *Fieldworking: Reading and Writing Culture.* Upper Saddle River, NJ: Prentice-Hall.

Christie, G. 2007. Police-Government Relations in the Context of State-Aboriginal Relations. In *Police and Government Relations: Who's Calling the Shots?* M.E. Beare and T. Murry, eds. Toronto: University of Toronto Press.

Churchill, W. 2001. *Fantasies of the Master Race: Literature, Cinema, and the Colonization of American Indians*. Monroe, Main: Common Courage Press.

—2007. *Pacifism as Pathology: Reflections on the Role of Armed Struggle in North America*. Oakland, CA: Arbeiter Ring Publishers (AK Press).

—2020. Comments in: *Media Smarts: Common Portrayals of Aboriginal People* (https://mediasmarts.ca/diversity-media/aboriginal-people/common-portrayals-aboriginal-people?gclid=EAIaIQobChMIiIfN-jq6AIVr__jBx0UQAudEAAYASAAEgIRnPD_BwE).

Classen, C. and D. Howes. 2006. The Museum as Sensescape: Western Sensibilities and Indigenous Artifacts. In E. Edwards, C. Gosden and R. Philips, eds., *Sensible Objects: Colonialism, Museums and Material Culture*, pp. 199–222. Oxford: Berg.

Clifford, J. and G.E. Marcus, eds. 1986. *Writing Culture*. Berkeley: University of California Press.

Coates, K. *#Idle No More: And the Remaking of Canada*. Regina: University of Regina Press.

Collins, W.H. 1906. On Surveys Along the National Continental Railway Location between Lake Nipigon and Lac Seul. *Geological Survey Department of Canada, Sessional Paper* 26: 103–109.

Corbiere v. Canada (Minister of Indian and Northern Affairs), 1999 2 S.C.R. 203.

Coulthard, G.S. 2014. *Red Skins, White Mask: Rejecting the Colonial Politics of Recognition*. Minneapolis, Minn.: University of Minnesota Press.

Cousins, L.H. ed. 2014. White Privilege. *Encyclopedia of Human Services and Diversity*. Western Michigan University, Thousand, Oaks, CA: Sage Publications.

Cox, A. 2017. Settler Colonialism. *Oxford Bibliographies* (https://www.oxfordbibliographies.com/view/document/obo-9780190221911/obo-9780190221911-0029.xml).

Crapanzano, V. 2003. *Imaginative Horizons: An Essay in Literary-Philosophical Anthropology*. Chicago: University of Chicago Press.

CTV News. 2013. Idle No More Co-Founder Supports Spence, not Blockades. 13 January.

Culhane, D. 1998. *The Pleasure of the Crown: Anthropology, Law, and First Nations*. Vancouver: Talonbooks.

—2003. Their Spirits Live with Us. *American Indian Quarterly* 27 (3): 593–606.

Daly, R. 2005. *Our Box Was Full: An Ethnography for the Delgamuukw Plaintiffs.* Vancouver: UBC Press.

Darnell, R. 2000. Canadian Anthropologists, the First Nations, and Canada's Self-Image at the Millennium. *Anthropologica* 42 (2): 165–174.

Davies, C.A. 1999. *Reflexive Ethnography: A Guide to Researching Selves and Others.* New York: Routledge.

Davies, J. and D. Spencer. 2010. *Emotions in the Field: The Psychology and Anthropology of Fieldwork Experience.* Stanford, CA: Stanford University Press.

de Certeau, M. 1984. *The Practice of Everyday Life*. Berkeley, CA: University of California Press.

Deflem, M. 1991. Ritual, Anti-Structure and Religion: A Discussion of Victor Turner's Processual Symbolic Analysis. *Journal of the Scientific Study of Religion* 30 (13): 1–35.

Deloria, P.J. 1998. *Playing Indian.* New Haven, CT: Yale University Press.

Denis, J.S. 2020. *Canada at a Crossroads: Boundaries, Bridges, and Laissez-Faire Racism in Indigenous-Settler Relations.* Toronto: University of Toronto Press.

Denzen, N.K. and Y.S. Lincoln, eds. 2000. *Handbook of Qualitative Research.* Thousand Oaks, CA: Sage Publications.

Diablo, R. 2020. Trudeau's 'Zombie Policies' Threaten Indigenous Rights. *The Tyee News*, 5 May (The Tyee.ca).

Dinwoodie, D.W. 2010. The Canadian Anthropological Tradition and Land Claims. *Histories of Anthropology Annual* 6: 31–47.

Dion, J. 2017. Conrad Black's Put-Down of Indigenous People Unhelpful in Current Climate. *National Post* 14 August.

Dreier, O. 2008. *Psychotherapy in Everyday Life.* Cambridge: Cambridge University Press.

Driben, P. 1986. *Aroland is Our Home.* New York: AMS Press.

Driben, P. and Trudeau, R.S. 1983. *When Freedom is Lost: The Dark Side of the Relationship between Government and the Fort Hope Band.* Toronto: University of Toronto Press.

Dunning, R.W. 1958. Some Implications of Economic Change in Northern Ojibwa Social Structure. *Canadian Journal of Economics and Political Science* 24 (4): 562–566.

—1959. *Social and Economic Change Among the Northern Ojibwa.* Toronto: University of Toronto Press.

—1967. The Hawthorn Report. *The Canadian Forum* (June): 52–53.

—1969. Indian Policy—A Proposal for Autonomy. *The Canadian Forum* (December): 206–207.

—1971. The Indian Situation: A Canadian Governmental Dilemma. *International Journal of Comparative Sociology* 12:128–134.

Durkheim, É.1938 1895. *The Rules of Sociological Method.* Chicago: University of Chicago Press.

Dyck, N. 1991. *What is the Indian 'Problem': Tutelage and Resistance in Canadian Indian Administration.* St. John's, NFLD: Memorial University of Newfoundland Social and Economic Studies, No. 46).

Edwards, P. 2003. *One Dead Indian: The Premier, the Police and the Ipperwash Crisis.* Toronto: Stoddard.

Edwards, E., C. Gosden, and R.B. Philips. 2006. *Sensible Objects.* Oxford: Berg.

Elias, N. 1988. On the Concept of Everyday Life. *In* J. Goudsblom and S. Mennell, eds., *The Norbert Elias Reader.* Oxford: Blackwell.

Elkins, C. and S. Pederson, eds. 2005. *Settler Colonialism in the Twentieth Century: Projects, Practices and Legacies.* New York: Routledge.

Ellis, C. 1991. Sociological Introspection and Emotional Experience. *Symbolic Interaction*14 (1): 23–50.

Ellis, C. and A.P. Bochner. 2000. Autoethnography, Personal Narrative, Reflexivity: Researcher as Subject. In *The Handbook of Qualitative Research*, pp. 733–768. N.K. Denzin and Y.S. Lincoln, eds. Thousand Oaks, CA: Sage Publications.

Epling, P.J., J. Kirk, and J.P. Boyd. 1973. Genetic Relations of Polynesian Sibling Terminologies. *American anthropologist* 75 (1): 1596–1625.

Epstein, A.L., ed. 1967. *The Craft of Social Anthropology.* London: Tavistock.

Etkin, C.E. 1988. The Sechelt Indian Band: An Analysis of a New Form of Native Self-Government. *Canadian Journal of Native Studies* 8 (1): 73–105.

Fagan, B.M. 1984. *The Aztecs.* New York: W.H. Freeman Co.

Feagin, J. R. 2010. *Racist American: Roots, Current Realities, and Future Reparations.* 2nd ed. New York: Rutledge.

Federal Court-Aboriginal Law Bar Liaison Committee. 2012, October 16. Aboriginal Litigation Practice Guidelines. (http://cas-ncr-nter03.cas-satj.gc.ca/fctcf/pdf/PracticeGuidelines%20Phase%20I%20and%20II%2016-10-2012%20ENG%20final.pdf).

Fergus County Argus. Montana, March 25, 1903.

Ferguson, H. 2009. *Self-Identity and Everyday Life.* Abingdon: Routledge.

Ferraro, G., S. Andreatta, and C. Holdsworth. 2018. *Cultural Anthropology: An Applied Perspective.* Toronto, ON: Nelson Education Ltd.

Flanagan, T. 2000. *First Nations? Second Thoughts.* Montreal: McGill-Queen's University Press.

Fleming, W.C. 2006. Myths and Stereotypes about Native Americans. *Phi Delta Kappan* 88 (3): 213–217 (https://www.questia.com/library/journal/1G1-154514926/myths-and-stereotypes-about-native-americans-most, accessed 23 April 2020).

Fortier, C. 2017. *Unsettling the Commons: Social Movements Within, Against, and Beyond Settler Colonialism.* Winnipeg, Man.: Arbeiter Ring Publishing (ARP Books).

Francis, D. and T. Morantz. 1983. *Partners in Fur: A History of the Fur Trade in Eastern James Bay, 1600–1870.* Montreal: McGill-Queen's University Press.

Freckelton, I. 1985. The Anthropologist on Trial. *Melbourne University Law Review* 15: 360–386.

Freeman, D. 1983. *Margaret Mead and Samoa: The Making and Unmaking of an Anthropological Myth.* Cambridge, MA: Harvard University Press.

Freeman, V. 2010. 'Toronto Has No History!' Indigeneity, Settler Colonialism, and Historical Memory in Canada's Largest City. *Urban History Review* 38 (2): 21–35.

Furtado, M. 2016. Dismantling White Privilege: Indigenous Erasure. *Out Front Magazine*, July 18.
(https://www.outfrontmagazine.com/perspectives/dismantling-white-privilege-indigenous-erasure).

Galbraith, J.S. 1957. *The Hudson's Bay Company as an Imperial Factor, 1821–1869.* Berkeley, Calif.: University of California Press.

Gardiner, M. 2000. *Critiques of Everyday Life.* London: Routledge.

—2009. Book Review: *Philosophizing the Everyday: Revolutionary Praxis and the Fate of Cultural Theory*, John Roberts (2006). London: Pluto.

Garrick, R. 2010. Marten Falls, Webequie Set Up Blockade in Ring of Fire. *Wawatay News,* 4 February.

Geertz, C. 1973. *The Interpretation of Cultures: Selected Essays.* New York: Basic Books.

—1983. *Local Knowledge: Further Essays in Interpretive Anthropology.* New York: Basic Books.

Geertz, C., R.A. Shweder, and B. Good. 2005. *Clifford Geertz and His Colleagues.* Chicago: University of Chicago Press.

Globe and Mail, Toronto. 1967. Vast Aid Urged to Enable Indians to Move from Depressed Reserves. 22 February.

—2005. Aboriginals are Voting with Their Feet for a Third Way. 26 November.

—2013a. Bob Rae Jumps into the Ring of Fire. 24 June.

—2013b. Idle No More Protests beyond Control of Chiefs. 1 January.

Goffman, I. 1959. *The Presentation of Self in Everyday Life.* New York: The Overlook Press.

Gold, G.L. and M.A. Tremblay. 1983. Steps Toward an Anthropology of Quebec, 1960–1980. In F. Manning, ed., *Consciousness and Inquiry: Ethnology and Canadian Realities.* Ottawa: Canadian Ethnology Service.

Golde, P. 1986. *Women in the Field: Anthropological Experiences.* 2nd ed. Berkeley, Calif.: University of California Press.

Good, A. 2008. Cultural Evidence in Courts of Law. *Journal of the Royal Anthropological Institute* 14 (SI): S47-60.

Gordon, T.H. 1996. Trial Date Set for Stoney Point Members Charged in Defense of traditional Territory. *Prison News Service* 54 (Spring).

Gorshon, W.S., ed. 2009. *The Collaborative Turn: Working Together in Qualitative Research.* Rotterdam, The Netherlands: Sense Publishers.

Gottlieb, A. 2012. *The Restless Anthropologist: New Fieldsites, New Visions.* Chicago: University of Chicago Press.

Goulet, J. and B.G. Miller. 2007. *Extraordinary Anthropology: Transformations in the Field.* Nebraska: University of Nebraska Press.

Green, R. 1984. The Pocahontas Perplex: The Image of the American Indian Woman in American Culture. *Sweetgrass* (July-August): 17–23.

—1992. *Women in American Indian Society.* New York: Chelsea House.

Griffin, J.H. 1962. *Black Like Me*. New York: Penguin Books.

Grunnell, A. 2014. Beckwith was a Character to Remember. *Chronicle-Journal* (Thunder Bay), 30 March.

Gumbhir, V.K. 2007. *But is it Racial Profiling? Policing, Pretext Stops, and the Color of Suspicion*. New York: LFB Scholarly Publishing.

Hage, G. 2009. Hating Israel in the Field: On Ethnography and Political Emotions. *Anthropological Theory* 9 (1): 59–79.

Hall, T., Lashua, B. and Coffey, A. 2008. Sound and the Everyday in Qualitative Research. *Qualitative Inquiry* 14: 1019–1040.

Hallowell, A.I. 1955. *Culture and Experience*. Philadelphia: University of Pennsylvania Press.

—1992. *The Ojibwa of Barrens River, Manitoba*. New York: Holt, Rinehart, and Winston.

Hamilton, J. 1998. Ipperwash Protesters Sent to Jail, Natives Angered over Injustice. *London Free Press*, 4 April.

Hanyano, D.M. 1990. *Road Through the Rain Forest: Living Anthropology in Highland Papua New Guinea*. Prospect Heights, IL: Waveland Press.

Harper, S. 2008. *Text of Prime Minister Harper's Apology*. 11 June (www.aine-inac.gc.ca; www.fns.bc.ca).

Harris, C. 2004. How Did Colonialism Dispossess? Comments from the Edge of Empire. *Annals of the Association of American Geographers* 94 (1): 165–182.

Harris, M. 1966. The Cultural Ecology of India's Sacred Cattle. *Current Anthropology* 7: 51–66.

—1968. *The Rise of Anthropological Theory*. New York: Crowell.

Harrison, F. 1995. The Persistent Power of 'Race' in the Cultural and Political Economy of Racism. *Annual Review of Anthropology* 24: 47–74.

Hart, E.R. 2018. *American Indian History on Trial: Historical Expertise in Tribal Litigation*. Salt Lake City: The University of Utah Press.

Hastrup, K. 1993. Native Anthropology: A Contradiction in Terms? *Folk* 35: 147–161.

Hauler, K. 2012. Indigenous Perspectives in the Courtroom. *The International Journal of Human Rights* 16 (1): 51–72.

Hawthorn, H.B. 1966–1967. *A Survey of the Contemporary Indians of Canada: Economic, Political, Educational Needs and Politices.* 2 Vols. Ottawa: Queen's Printer.

Hedican, E.J. 1982. Governmental Indian Policy, Administration, and Economic Planning in the Eastern Subarctic. *Culture* 2 (3): 25–36.

—1985. Modern Economic Trends among the Northern Ojibwa. *Man in the Northeast* 30 (FALL): 1–25.

—1986a. *The Ogoki River Guides: Emergent Leadership among the Northern Ojibwa*. Waterloo, ON: Wilfrid Laurier University Press.

—1986b. Sibling Terminology and Information Theory: An Hypothesis Concerning the Growth of Folk Taxonomy. *Ethnology* 25 (4): 229–239.

—1986c. Anthropologists and Social Involvement: Some Issues and Problems. *The Canadian Review of Sociology and Anthropology* 23 (4): 544–558.

—1986d. Some Issues in the Anthropology of Transaction and Exchange. *The Canadian Review of Sociology and Anthropology* 23 (1): 97–117.

—1987. The land Base Problem among Canadian Native People. *The Rural Sociologist* 7 (5): 459–464.

—1990a. Richard Salisbury's Anthropology: A Personal Account. *Culture* X (1) 14–18.

—1990b. On the Rail-Line in Northwestern Ontario: Non-Reserve Housing and Community Change. *The Canadian Journal of Native Studies* 10 (1): 15–32.

—1990c. The Economics of Northern Native Food Production. In J.I. (Hans) Bakker (ed.), *The World Food Crisis: Food Security in Comparative Perspective,* pp. 281–300. Toronto: Scholars' Press.

—1991a. On the Ethno-Politics of Canadian Native Leadership and Identity. *Ethnic Groups* 9 (1): 1–15.

—1994. Epistemological Implication of Anthropological Fieldwork, with Notes from Northern Ontario. *Anthropologica* 36: 205–224.

—2001a. *Up in Nipigon Country: Anthropology as a Personal Experience.* Halifax, NS: Fernwood Books.

—2001b. Spirituality, the Hidden Reality: Living and Learning in Anishinaabe Country. *The Canadian Journal of Native Studies* 21 (1) 27–43.

—2006. Understanding Emotional Experience in Fieldwork: Responding to Grief in a Northern Aboriginal Village. *International Journal of Qualitative Methods* 5 (1): 1–8.

—2008a. *Applied Anthropology in Canada: Understanding Aboriginal and Issues.* Toronto: University. University of Toronto Press. Revised 2nd edition.

—2008b. The Ipperwash Inquiry and the Tragic Death of Dudley George. *Canadian Journal of Native Studies* 28 (1): 159–173.

—2008c. Empathy. pp. 251–253, *Encyclopedia of Qualitative Research Methods*, Lisa M. Givens (editor), Thousand Oaks, Calif.: SAGE Publications.

—2012a. *Social Anthropology: Canadian Perspectives on Culture and Society.*

—2012b. Policing Aboriginal Protests and Confrontations: Some Policy Recommendations. *The International Indigenous Policy Journal* 3 (2): 1–17.

—2013. *Ipperwash: The Tragic Failure of Canada's Aboriginal Policy.* Toronto: University of Toronto Press.

—2014. Eurocentrism in Aboriginal Studies: A Review of Issues and Conceptual Problems. *Canadian Journal of Native Studies* 34 (1): 87–109.

—2015a. Affidavit of Dr. Edward Hedican, Sworn on 30 April 2015, by Commissioner of Oaths in the Province of Ontario, File No. T-195-92. Ottawa: Federal Court of Canada.

—2015b. Transcript of Cross-Examination of Dr. Edward Hedican on his Affidavits, Sworn to on 30 April 2015, held on 5 May 2015, File No. T-195-92, DOJ File No. 3545648. Ottawa: Federal Court of Canada.

—2016. *Public Anthropology: Engaging Social Issues in the Modern World.* Toronto: University of Toronto Press.

—2017a *The First Nations of Ontario: Social and Economic Transitions.* Toronto: Canadian Scholars' Press.

—2017b. Review of: Grounded Authority: The Algonquins of Barriere Lake Against the State. *Canadian Journal of Native Studies* 37 (2): 211–213.

Hegeman, S. 1989a. History, Ethnography, Myth: Some Notes on the 'Indian-Centered' Narrative. *Social Text* 23: 144–160.

—1989b. Native American 'Texts' and the Problem of Authenticity. *American Quarterly* 41 (2): 265–283.

Henderson, J., and P. Wakeham, eds. 2013. *Reconciling Canada: Critical Perspectives on the Culture of Redress.* Toronto: University of Toronto Press.

Henrard, K. and J. Gilbert. 2018. Introducing Multidisciplinary Perspectives to the Adjudication of Indigenous Rights. *Erasmus Law Review* 11 (1): 1–5.

Henry, F. and C. Tator. 1985. Racism in Canada: Social Myths and Strategies for Change. In *Ethnicity and Ethnic Relations in Canada*, R. M. Bienvenue and J. E. Goldstein eds. Toronto: Butterworths.

Hickerson, H.1973. Fur Trade Colonialism and the North American Indians. *Journal of Ethnic Studies* 1 (2): 15–44.

Highmore, B. 2001. Wild Things: The Material Culture of Everyday Life. *Journal of Design History* 14 (3): 248–250.

—2002. *Everyday Life and Cultural Theory*. London: Routledge.

Hirschfelder, A. and P.F. Molin. 2018. I is for Ignoble: Stereotyping Native Americans, Ferris State University, Jim Crow Museum of Racist Memorabilia (https://www.ferris.edu/HTMLS/news/jimcrow/native/homepage.htm).

Hixson, W.L. 2013. *American Settler Colonialism.* New York: Palgrave: Macmillan.

Hogg, E.A. and J.R. Welch. 2020. Aboriginal Rights and Title for Archaeologists. A History of Archaeological Evidence in Canadian Litigation. *Journal of Social Archaeology* 20 (2): 214–241.

Holbert, S., and L. Rose. 2004. *The Color of Guilt and Innocence: Racial Profiling and Police Practices in America.* San Ramon, CA: Page Marque.

Holden, L. 2020a. *Cultural Expertise: An Emergent Concept and Evolving Practice*. Baset, Switzerland: MDPI.

—2020b. Cultural Expertise and Law: An Historical Overview. *Law and History Review* 38: 1–18.

Horgan, J. 2010. Margaret Mead's Bashers Owe Her an Apology. *Scientific American*. October 25.

Howes, D. 1991. *The Varieties of Sensory Experience: A Sourcebook in the Anthropology of the Senses*. Toronto: University of Toronto Press.

—2003. *Sensing Culture: Engaging the Senses in Culture and Social Theory*. Ann Arbor, MI: University of Michigan Press.

Hubbard, P., Kitchin, R. and Velentine, G. 2004. *Key Thinkers on Space and Place*. London: Sage Publications.

Hume, L. and L. Mulcock, eds. 2004. *Anthropologists in the Field: Cases in Participant Observation*. New York: Columbia University Press.

Hunter, D. 2018. *Beardmore: The Viking Hoax that Rewrote History*. Montreal: McGill-Queen's University Press.

Hutchins, P.W. 2010. Power and Principle: State-Indigenous Relations Across Time and Space. In L.A. Knafla and H. Westra, eds., *Aboriginal Title and Indigenous Peoples*. Vancouver: University of British Columbia Press.

Huxley, A. 1932. *Texts and Pretexts*. London: Catto and Windus.

Ince, O.U. 2018. *Colonial Capitalism and the Dilemmas of Liberalism*. Oxford: Oxford University Press.

Indian Chiefs of Alberta. 1970. *Citizens Plus* The Red Paper. A Presentation by the Indian Chiefs of Alberta to the Right Honorable P.E. Trudeau, June 1970. Edmonton: Indian Association of Alberta.

Ingold, T. 2000. *The Perception of the Environment*. London: Routledge.

—2011. *Being Alive: Essays on Movement, Knowledge and Description*. London: Routledge.

Jacobson, M.H. 2009. The Everyday: An Introduction. *In* M.H. Jacobson, ed., *Encountering the Everyday: An Introduction to the Sociologies of the Unnoticed*. Basingstoke: Palgrave Macmillan.

Jamar, A. and F. Chappuis. 2016. Conventions of Silence: Emotions and Knowledge Production in War-Affected Research Environments. *Parcours Anthropologiques* 11: 99–117.

Jorgensen, D. 1992. Review of: *Victor Turner and the Construction of Cultural Criticism: Between Literature and Anthropology,* K.M. Ashley (ed.). *American Anthropologist* 94 (1): 196–197.

Josephy, A.M. 1971. *Red Power*. New York: American Heritage Press.
Jung, C. G. 1964. *Man and His Symbols*. New York: Anchor Books, Doubleday.

Kahn, M. 2011. *Tahiti Beyond the Postcard: Power, Place, and Everyday Life*. Seattle: University of Washington Press.

Kay, J. 2001. A Case for Native Assimilation. *The National Post*, 8 December.

Kennedy, M. 2017. *Narratives of Inequality: Postcolonial Literary Economics*. Cham, Switzerland: Palgrave Macmillan.

King, C.R. 2016. *Redskins: Insult and Brand*. Lincoln: University of Nebraska Press.

Kleinman, A. and R. Desjariais. 1995. Violence, Culture and the Politics of Trauma. In A. Kleinman, ed., *Writing at the Margin: Discourse Between Anthropology and Medicine*, pp. 173–189. Berkeley, Calif.: University of California Press.

Kluckhohn, C. 1957 1949. *Mirror for Man*. New York: McGraw-Hill.

Koehler, H.P. 1996. Stoney Point Peoples Support. 26 March. (www.execulink.com/hkoehler/stonsups.html.)

Krech, S. 2010. American Indians as the 'First Ecologists'. *The Encyclopedia of Religion and Nature.*
(https://www-oxfordreference-com.subzero.lib.uoguelph.ca/view/10.1093/acref/9780199754670.001.0001/acref-9780199754670-e-25?rskey=d6F9q9&result=3).

Kuhn, T.S. 1970 1962). *The Structure of Scientific Revolutions*. Chicago: University of Chicago Press.

Kuznar, L.A. 1997. *Reclaiming a Scientific Anthropology*. Walnut Creek, Calif.: AltaMira.

Kymlicka, W. 2007. *Multicultural Odysseys: Navigating the New International Politics of Diversity* New York: Oxford University Press.

Laing, R.D. 1967. *The Politics of Experience.* New York: Pantheon Books.

Landes, R.1937. *Ojibwa Sociology.* New York: Columbia University Press.

Lane, R.B. 1981. Chilcotin. In J. Helm, ed., *Handbook of North American Indians, Subarctic,* Vol. 6: 402–412. Wash.: Smithsonian Institution.

Lassiter, L. 2005. *The Chicago Guide to Collaborative Anthropology.* Chicago: University of Chicago Press.

Lawrence, B. 2011. Rewriting Histories of the Land: Colonization and Indigenous Resistance in Canada. In M.J. Cannon and L. Sunseri, eds., *Racism, Colonialism, and Indigeneity in* Canada, pp.68–80. Don Mill, ON: Oxford University Press.

—2013. *Fractured Homeland: Federal Recognition and Algonquin Identity in Ontario.* Vancouver: University of British Columbia Press.

Lawrence, B. and E. Dua. 2011. Decolonizing Antiracism. In M.J. Cannon and L. Sunseri, eds., *Racism, Colonialism, and Indigeneity in Canada,* pp. 19–27. Don Mill, ON: Oxford University Press.

Lefebvre, H. 1968. *Everyday Life in the Modern World.* London: Penguin.

Lemelin, R.H. 2009. Review of: *Disrobing the Aboriginal Industry: The Deception Behind Indigenous Cultural Preservation* (2008), *Arctic* 62 (3): 356–357.

Leslie, J.E. and R. Maguire. 1978. *The Historical Development of the Indian Act.* Ottawa: Indian and Northern Affairs.

Lett, J. 1987. *The Human Enterprise: A Critical Introduction to Anthropological Theory.* Boulder: Westview Press.

Lextrait, R. 2020. Last Private Resident and Caretaker of Palmyra Atoll. *THINK Newsletter* 31 December. (www.nbcnews.com/think/opinion)

Linden, S. B. 2007. *Report of the Ipperwash Inquiry.* Toronto: Publications Canada. (https://www.ontario.ca/page/Ipperwash-inquiry-report)

Lindsay, J. 2014. The Power to React: Review and Discussion of Canada's Emergency Measures Legislation. *The International Journal of Human Rights* 18 (2): 159–77.

Loperena, C.A. 2020. Adjudicating Indigeneity: Anthropological Testimony in the Inter-American Court of Human Rights. *American Anthropologist* 122 (3): 595–605.

Lott-Schwartz, H. 1978. Get Wild in the Stunning Nature of Ontario, Canada. *National Geographic* (www.national geographic.com/adventure).

Luhrmann, T. 2010. What Counts as Data? In J. Davies and D. Spence, eds., pp. 212–238. *Emotions in the Field: The Psychology and Anthropology of Fieldwork Experience.* Stanford, CA: Stanford University Press.

Lyzun, K. 2005. Hermit's Former Home in Dire Straits. (www.tbsource.com 2 December)

Macbeth, D. 2001. On 'Reflexivity' in Qualitative Research: Two Readings and a Third. *Qualitative Inquiry* 7 (1): 35–68.

MacCharles, T. 2014. Supreme Court Grants Land Title to B.C. First Nation in Landmark Case. *Toronto Star.* 26 June.

Mackay, Y. C. 2006. The Red Hat Society: Exploring the Role of Play, Liminality, and Communitas in Older Women's Lives. *Journal of Women Aging* 18 (3): 51–73.

Mackey, E. 2016. *Unsettled Expectations: Uncertainty, Land and Settler Decolonization.* Halifax, NS: Fernwood Publishers.

Madge, C. and O'Connor, H. 2005. Mothers in the Making? Exploring Liminality in the Cyber/Space. *Transactions of the Institute of British Geographers* 30 (1):83–97.

Maffesoli, M. 1989. The Everyday Perspective. *Current Sociology* 37: v-vi.

McGrath, J. 1989. Years of Deadlock: Land Rights Mired in Claims, Counter Claims. *The Guelph Mercury*, 5 December (orig. *Times-News*, Thunder Bay).

Mahoney, J. 1999. On a Frosty Northern Night, Nunavut is Born. *Globe and Mail*, 1 April.

Malinowski, B. 1922. *Argonauts of the Western Pacific.* New York: E.P. Dutton.

—1967. *A Diary in the Strict Sense of the Term.* New York: Harcourt, Brace and World.

—1970 [1929]. Practical Anthropology. In J.A. Clifton, ed., *Applied Anthropology*, pp. 12–25. Boston, MA: Houghton Mifflin.

Manuel, A. and Grand Chief R.M. Derrikson. 2015.*Unsettling Canada: A National Wake-Up Call.* Toronto: Between the lines.

Mann, M. 1993. The Autonomous Power of the State. In M.E. Olsen and M.N. Marger, eds., *Power in Modern Societies*, pp. 314–327. Boulder, CO: Westview Press.

Manyoni, J.R. 1983. Eager Visitor, Reluctant Host: The Anthropologist as Stranger. *Anthropologica* 25: 221–249.

Marcus, G.E. and M.J. Fischer. 1986. *Anthropology as Cultural Critique.* Chicago: University of Chicago Press.

Maskovsky, J. 2013. Protest Anthropology in a Moment of Global Unrest. *American Anthropologist* 115 (1): 126–129.

Mason, R.J. 2006. *Inconsistent Companions: Archaeology and North American Indian Oral Traditions.* Tuscaloosa: University of Alabama Press.

McGuire, S. and Georges, J. 2003. Variables Advances Undocumentedness and Liminality as Health Variables *Advances in Nursing Sciences* 26 (3): 185–195.

McKinzie, A. E. Scared to Death: Reflections on Panic and Anxiety in the Field. *Symbolic Interaction* 40 (4): 483–497.

Mead, M. 1928. *Coming of Age in Samoa.* New York: Mentor Press.

—1970. *Culture and Commitment: A Study of the Generation Gap.* New York: The Natural History Press.

—1977. *Letters from the Field, 1925–1975.*New York: Harper.

Merc, F. 1931. *Fur Trade and Empire.* Cambridge, Mass.: Harvard University Press.

Miller, B.G. 2011. *Oral History on Trial: Recognizing Aboriginal Narratives in the Courts.* Vancouver: University of British Columbia Press.

Miller, B.G. and G. Menezes. 2015. Anthropological Experts and the Legal System: Brazil and Canada. *American Indian Quarterly* 39 (4): 391–430.

Miller, J.R. 2004. *Reflections on Native-Newcomer Relations: Selected Essays.* Toronto, ON: University of Toronto Press.

Milton, K. 1996. *Environmentalism and Cultural Theory: Exploring the Role of Anthropology in Environmental Discourse.* London: Routledge.

Moran, J. 2005. *Reading the Everyday.* London: Routledge.

Morantz, T. 1982. Northern Algonquian Concepts of Status and Leadership Reviewed: A Case Study of the Eighteenth-Century Trading Captain System. *Canadian Review of Sociology and Anthropology* 19 (4): 482–501.

Morgensen, S.L. 2012. Theorizing Gender, Sexuality and Settler Colonialism: An Introduction. *Settler Colonial Studies* 2 (2): 2–22.

Mortimore, G.E. 1967. The Indians Were Here First: Treat them as 'Citizens Plus.' *Human Relations* (Ontario Human Rights Commission) 7 (15): 4–6.

Nadeau, D.M. 2020. *Unsettling Spirit: A Journey into Decolonization.* Montreal: McGill-Queen's University Press.

Napoleon, V. 2005. *Delgamuukw*: A Legal Straitjacket for Oral Histories? *Canadian Journal of Law and Society* 20 (2):123–155.

Nash, D. 1963. The Ethnologist as Stranger: An Essay in the Sociology of Knowledge. *Southwestern Journal of Anthropology* 19: 149–167.

National Post. 2013. Idle No More Founders Distance themselves from Chiefs. 1 January.

Nassif, H. 2017. To Fear and to Defy: Emotions in the Field. *Contemporary Levant* 2 (1): 49–54.

New York Times. 2020. Has Trudeau (Politely) Betrayed Native People Again? 10 March.

Nicholson. C. 2011a. Wendell K. Beckwith: His Life of Pi. *Chronicle-Journal* (Thunder Bay), 3 April.

—2011b. Beckwith Built Home for Research. *Chronicle-Journal* (Thunder Bay), 10 April.

Niezen, R. 2000. *Spirit Wars: Native North American Religions in the Age of Nation Building.* Berkeley, Calif.: University of California Press.

—2010. *Public Justice and the Anthropology of Law.* Cambridge: Cambridge University Press.

—2013.*Truth and Indignation: Canada's Truth and Reconciliation Commission on Indian Residential Schools.* Toronto: University of Toronto Press.

Nixon, R. 2011. *Slow Violence and the Environmentalism of the Poor.* Cambridge: Harvard University Press.

Noakes, T.C. 2021. A Reply to Conrad Black: On Indigenous History We Cannot Ignore Inconvenient Truths. *National Post*, 26 March.

Noblit, G.W. and Hare, R.D. 1988. *Meta-Ethnography: Synthesizing Qualitative Studies.* Newbury Park: CA: Sage Publications.

O'Connor, J. 2003. *Hollywood's Indian: The Portrayal of the Native American in Film.* Lexington: The University Press of Kentucky.

Ohler, S. 1999. Nunavut Born with High Hopes, Big Challenges. *National Post,* 1 April.

Oliphant, J. 2003. Taxation and Treaty Rights: *Benoit v Canada*'s Historical Context and Impact. *Manitoba Law Journal* 29 (3): 343–373.

Ontario. 1974. *The Northern Communities Act,* or *Bill 102, An Act to Provide for the Incorporation of Communities in Territory without Municipal Organization.* Toronto: Department of Treasury, Economics, and Inter-Governmental Affairs.

—2013.Ministry of Natural Resources. Far North Ontario: Community-Based Land Use Planning in the Far North Ontario.
(www.mnr.gov.on.ca/en/Business/Far/North)

—2014. Ministry of Indigenous Relations and Reconciliation. Land Claims.
(www.ontario.ca/ aboriginal/land-claims).

Orans, M. 1996. *Not Even Wrong: Margaret Mead, Derek Freeman, and the Samoans.* Novato, CA: Chandler and Sharp Publishers.

Orr, R., K. Sharratt and M. Iqbal. 2019. American Indian Erasure and the Logic of Elimination: An Experimental Study of Depiction and Support for Resources and Rights for Tribes. *Journal of Ethnic and Migration Studies* 45 (11): 2078–2099.

Palmeter, P. 2014. Indian Status: Why Lyn Gehl's Court Challenge Matters. *CBC News*, 20 October.

Parker, I. 1996. Discursive Complexes in Material Culture. *In* J. Haworth, ed., *Psychological Research: Innovative Methods and Strategies.* London: Routledge.

Pasternak, S. 2017. *Grounded Authority: The Algonquins of Barriere Lake Against the State.* Minneapolis, Minn.: University of Minnesota Press.

Peacock, J.I. 1997. The Future of Anthropology. *American Anthropologist* 99 (1): 9–17.

Peers, L. 2007. *Playing Ourselves: Interpreting Native Histories at Historic Reconstructions.* New York: Altamira Press.

—2016. A Token of Remembrance: The Gift of a Cree Hood, Red River Settlement, 1844. In J.S. Long and J.S.H. Brown, eds., *Together We Survive: Ethnographic Intuitions, Friendships, and Conversations*, pp. 107–129. Montreal: McGill-Queen's University Press.

Pels, P. 1997. The Anthropology of Colonialism: Culture, History, and the Emergence of Western Governmentality. *Annual Review of Anthropology* 26:163–213.

Pelto, P.J. 1970. *Anthropological Research.* New York: Harper & Row.

—1973. *The Snowmobile Revolution: Technology and Social Change in the Arctic.* Menlo Park, CA: Cummings Publishing Co.

Peterson, K. 2008. Land and Jail: Ipperwash, Official Racism and the Future of Ontario. 23 September (wwwdominionpaper.ca/articles).

Pink, S. 2012. *Situating Everyday Life: Practices and Places.* London: Sage Publications.

Powdermaker, H. 1966. *Stranger and Friend: The Way of an Anthropologist.* New York: W.W. Norton.

Practicing Anthropology. 1982. Applied Anthropology Formed in Canada 4 (1): 19.

Price, J.A. 1987. *Applied Anthropology: Canadian Perspectives.* Downsview, Ont.: Society of Applied Anthropology in Canada.

Price, R. 2017. The Anthropologist as Expert Witness: A Personal Account. In J.A.R. Nafziger, ed., *Comparative Law and Society*, pp.415–429. North Hampton, Mass.: Edward Elgar Publishing.

Quimby, G.I. 1960. *Indian Life in the Upper Great Lakes: 11,000 B.C. to A.D. 1800.* Chicago: University of Chicago Press.

Rabinow, P. 1977. *Reflections on Fieldwork in Morocco.* Berkeley, CA: University of California Press.

Ray, A. J. 1974. *Indians in the Fur Trade: Their Role as Trappers, Hunters, and Middlemen in the Lands Southwest of Hudson Bay, 1660–1870.* Toronto: University of Toronto Press.

—2003. Native History on Trial: Confessions of an Expert Witness. *Canadian Historical Review* 84 (2): 255–273.

—2011. Ethnohistorical Geography and Aboriginal Rights Litigation in Canada: Memoir of an Expert Witness. *The Canadian Geographer* 55 (4): 397–406.

—2012. *Telling it to the Judge: Taking Native History to Court.* Montreal: McGill-Queens University Press.

—2015. Traditional Knowledge and Social Science on Trial: Battles over Evidence in Indigenous Rights Litigation in Canada and Australia. *The International Indigenous Policy Journal* 6 (2). (Retrieved from: http://ir.lib.uwo.ca/iipj/vol6/iss2/5)

Ray, A.J and D.B. Freeman. 1978. *'Give Us Good Measure': An Economic Analysis of Relations Between the Indians and the Hudson's Bay Company Before 1763.* Toronto: University of Toronto Press.

Reed-Danahay, D. 1997. *Auto/Ethnography: Rewriting the Self and the Social.* Oxford, UK: Berg.

Regina v. Van der Peet. 1996. 2 S.C.R. 507.

Renner, E. 1984. On Geertz's Interpretive Theoretical Program. *Current Anthropology* 25 (4): 538–540.

Rich, E.E. 1967. *The Fur Trade and the Northwest to 1857.* Toronto: McClelland and Stewart.

Ridington, R. 1988. Knowledge, Power in the Individual in Subarctic Hunting Societies. *American Anthropologist* 90 (1): 98–110.

—1990. *Little Bit Know Something: Stories in a Language of Anthropology.* Vancouver, BC: Douglas & McIntyre.

Rifkin, M. 2017. *Beyond Settler Time: Temporal Sovereignty and Indigenous Self-Determination.* Durham: Duke University Press.

Robben, A.C. and J. Sluka. 2006. *Ethnographic Fieldwork: An Anthropological Reader.* London: Blackwell.

Robbins, R.H., M. Cummings, K. McGarry. 2017. *Sociocultural Anthropology: A Problem-Based Approach.* Toronto: Nelson education.

Rodriguez, L. 2018. Cultural Expert Testimony in American Legal Proceedings. *Cultural Expert Witnessing* 74: 1–10.

Rogers, 1962. *The Round Lake Ojibwa.* Toronto: Royal Ontario Museum.

—1965. Leadership Among the Indians of Eastern Subarctic Canada. *Anthropologica* 7: 263–284.

—1966. *Subsistence Areas of the Cree-Ojibwa of the Eastern Subarctic: A Preliminary Study*. Anthropological Series 70. Ottawa: National Museum of Canada, Bulletin 204: 59–99.

Rogers, E.S. and Black, M.J. 1976. Subsistence Strategy in the Fish and Hare Period, Northern Ontario: The Weagamow Ojibwa, 1880–1920. *Journal of Anthropological Research*32 (1): 1–43.

Rogers, E.S. and Taylor, J.G. 1981. Northern Ojibwa. In *Subarctic*, J. Helm, ed., Volume 6, *Handbook of North American Indians*, pp. 231–243. Washington, DC: Smithsonian Institution.

Rorty, R. 1991. Habermas and Lyotard on Postmodernity. *In* R. Rorty, ed., *Essays on Heidegger and Others: Philosophical Paper, Volume 2*. Cambridge: Cambridge University Press.

Rosaldo, R. 1980. Doing Oral History. *Social Analysis* 489–99.

Rosen, L. 1977. The Anthropologists as Expert Witness. *American Anthropologist* 79 (3): 555–578.

—2006. *Law as Culture: An Invitation*. Princeton: Princeton University Press.

—2018. Leave it to the Experts? The Anthropologist as Expert Witness. In L. Rosen, ed., *The Judgement of Culture: Cultural Assumption in American Law*, pp.57–93. London: Routledge.

—2020. Expert Testimony in the Social Sciences: A Historical Overview of Contemporary Issues. *Law and History Review* 38 (1): 123–142.

Rothenberg, P.S., ed. 2002. *White Privilege: Essential Readings on the Other Side of Racism*. New York: Worth Publisher.

Rumelili, B. 2003. Liminality and the Perpetuation of Conflicts: Turkish-Greek Relations in the Context of Community-Building by the EU. *European Journal of International Relations* (2):213–248.

Russell, P. H. 2010. Review of: F. Widdowson and A. Howard, *Disrobing the Aboriginal Industry: The Deception Behind Indigenous Cultural Preservation* (2008), *Canadian Journal of Political Science* 43 (3): 785–787.

Salée, D. 2010. Review of: F. Widdowson and A. Howard, *Disrobing the Aboriginal industry: The Deception Behind Indigenous Cultural Preservation* (2008), *International Journal of Canadian Studies* 41: 315–333.

Salisbury, R.F. 1962. *From Stone to Steel: Economic Consequences of Technological Change in New Guinea.* London: Cambridge University Press.

—1970. *Vunamami: Economic Transformation in a Traditional Society.* Berkeley: University of California Press.

—1973. Economic Anthropology. *Annual Review of Anthropology* 2: 85–94.

—1975. Policy Regarding Native Peoples: An Academic Social Scientist's Perspective. Paper Prepared for the National Social Science Conference, Ottawa.

—1976. The Anthropologist as Social Ombudsman. In D.C. Pitt, ed., *Development from Below*, pp. 255–265. The Hague: Mouton.

—1977a. Transactional Politics and Beyond. In M. Silverman, ed., *A House Divided? Anthropological Studies of Factionalism,* pp.111–127. St. John's, Newfoundland: Memorial University of Newfoundland, Institute of Social and Economic Research.

—1977b. The Berger Report: But is it Social Science? *Social Sciences in Canada* 5 (3): 10–12.

—1979. Application and Theory in Canadian Anthropology: The James Bay Agreement. *Transactions of the Royal Society of Canada* 17:221–241.

—1986. *A Homeland for the Cree: Regional Development in James Bay 1971–1981.*Montreal: McGill-Queen's University Press.

Salisbury, R. F. et al. 1972. *Development and James Bay: Some Implications of the Proposals for the Hydroelectric Scheme.* Montreal: McGill Programme in the Anthropology of Development.

Salzman, P.C. 1974. Tribal Chiefs as Middlemen: The Politics of Encapsulation in the Middle East. *Anthropological Quarterly* 47 (2): 203–210.

—1999. *The Anthropology of Real Life: Events in Human Experience.* Prospect Heights, Ill: Waveland Press.

—2001. *Understanding Culture: An Introduction to Anthropological Theory.* Long Grove, Ill.: Waveland Press.

—2008. *Culture and Conflict in the Middle East.* New York: Humanity Books.

Sanjek, R., ed. 1990. *Fieldnotes: The Making of Anthropology.* Ithaca: Cornell University Press.

Saugeen Times. 2021. Saugeen First Nation Has Been in the Business of Leasing Lots Since 1947. 22 February.

Schatzki, T., Knorr-Cetina, K., and von Savigny, E. 2001. *The Practice Turn in Contemporary Theory.* London: Routledge.

Schneider, H.K. 1974. *Economic Man: The Anthropology of Economics.* Salem, Wisc.: Sheffield Publishing.

Scholte, B. 1972. Toward a Reflexive and Critical Anthropology. In *Reinventing Anthropology,* D. Hymes, ed., pp. 430–457. New York: Pantheon Books.

—1984. On Geertz's Interpretive Theoretical Program. *Current Anthropology* 25 (4): 540–542.

Schwarz, M.T. 2013. *Fighting Colonialism with Hegemonic Culture: Native American Appropriation of Indian Stereotypes*. Albany, NY: State University of New York Press.

Scott, C. 1990. Some Thoughts on Regional Development and the Canadian North in the Work of Richard F. Salisbury. *Culture* X (1): 18–21.

Scott, J. 1991. The Evidence of Experience. *Critical Inquiry* 17: 773–779.

Scott, S. 2009. *Making Sense of Everyday Life*. Cambridge: Polity Press.

Sears, A. and J. Cairns. 2010. *A Good Book in Theory: Making Sense Through Inquiry*. Toronto: University of Toronto Press.

Seremetakis, N. 1994. *The Senses Still: Perceptions and Memory as Material Culture in Modernity*. Chicago, IL: University of Chicago Press.

Shankman, P. 2009. *The Trashing of Margaret Mead: Anatomy of an Anthropological Controversy*. Madison: University of Wisconsin Press.

Shannon, C. and W. Weaver. 1949. *The Mathematical Theory of Communication*. Urbana, Ill: University of Illinois Press.

Shaw, J. 2001. Derek Freeman, Who Challenged Margaret Mead on Samoa, Dies at 84. *The New York Times*, April 30.

Sherington, M. 2006. *Everyday Life: Theories and Practices from Surrealism to the Present*. Oxford: Oxford University Press.

Shimo, A. 2009. Tough Critique or Hate Speech? A Calgary Prof's Paper on the 'Aboriginal Industry' Starts a War. *Maclean's* 122 (7): 42, 2 March.

Shove, E., Watson, M., Ingram, J. and Hand, M. 2007. *The Design of Everyday Life*. Oxford: Berg.

Sidky, H. 2004. *Perspectives on Culture: A Critical Introduction to Theory in Cultural Anthropology.* Upper Saddle River, NJ: Pearson Prentice Hall.

Silverman, M, ed. 2004. *Ethnography and Development: The Work of Richard F. Salisbury.* Montreal: McGill University Libraries.

Singer, B. 2001. *Wiping the War Paint off the Lens: Native American Film and Video.* Minneapolis, Minn.: University of Minnesota Press.

Skinner, A. 1911. Notes on the Eastern Cree and Northern Saulteaux. *Anthropological Papers of the American Museum of Natural History* 9: 1–177.

Snelgrove, C. 2018. Review of: O.U. Ince, *Colonial Capitalism and the Dilemmas of Liberalism* (2018). *Canadian Journal of Political Science* 51 (4): 968–970.

Stanley, S.E., ed. 2017. *Confronting White Privilege.* New York: Oxford University Press.

Steckley, J.I. and B.D. Cummins. 2008. *Full Circle: Canada's First Nations.* Toronto: Pearson Education Canada.

St. John, G. (ed.). 2008. *Victor Turner and Contemporary Cultural Performance.* New York, Oxford: Berghahn Books.

Stove, D.C. 1982. *Popper and After: Four Modern Irrationalists.* Oxford: Pergamon Press.

Strauss, J. 2005. Odd Man's Odd Home Now Facing Extinction. *The Globe and Mail* (Toronto), 11 October.

Spiegel. A.D. 2011. Categorical Difference versus Continuum: Rethinking Turner's Liminal-Liminoid Distinction. *Anthropology Southern Africa* 3 (1–2): 11–20.

Spierenburgh, M. 2011. The Politics of the Liminal and the Liminoid in Transfrontier Conservation in South Africa. 34 (1–2): 81–88.

Stoller, P. 1989. *The Taste of Ethnographic Things: The Senses in Ethnography.* Philadelphia, PA: University of Pennsylvania Press.

—2009. *The Power of the Between: An Anthropological Odyssey.* Chicago: University of Chicago Press.

Surtees, R.J. 1986. *The Williams Treaties: Research Report.* Ottawa: Treaties and Historical Research Centre, Indigenous and Northern Affairs Canada.

Taylor, B. 2018. Robinson Crusoe and the Morality of Solitude. *Welcome Collection* 20 December. (https.wellcomecollection.org.articles).

Tax, S. 1958. The Fox Project. *Human Organization* 17 (1): 17–19.

Tempest, S. and Starkey, K. 2004. The Effects of Liminality on Individual and Organizational Learning. *Organization Studies* 25 (4): 507–527.

Thistle, J. 2017. *Kiskisiwin—Remembering: Challenging Indigenous Erasure in Canada's Public History Displays* (http://activehistory.ca/2017/07/kiskisiwin-remembering-challenging-indigenous-erasure-in-canadas-public-history-displays/ accessed 11 April 2020).

Thomassen, B. 2009. The Uses and Meanings of Liminality. *International Political Anthropology* 2 (1:5–28).

—Émile Durkheim between Gabriel Tarde and Arnold van Gennep: Founding Moments of Sociology and Anthropology. *Social Anthropology* 20 (3): 231–249.

Thunder Bay Museum. 2021. Wendell Beckwith, 1963–1980. (www.thunderbaymuseum.com/wp-content).

Timperley, C. 2020. Justice in Indigenous Land Claims: A Typology of Problems. *Politics, Groups and Identities* 8 (1):1–23.

Toronto Star. 2003. Province to Fantino: Deal with Profiling. 11 December.

—2007. Canada Votes Against Aboriginal Declaration. 13 September.
—2021. Is Justin Trudeau's Plan for Indigenous Rights a Step in the Right Direction, or Just Another Hollow Promise from Ottawa? 11 January.

Tsilhqot'in Nation v. British Columbia. 2007. BCSC 1700. (http://www.courts.gov.bc.ca/jbd-txt/sc/07/17/2007bcsc1700.pdf).

Tully, J. 2008. *Public Philosophy in a New Key: Democracy and Civil Freedom.* Cambridge: Cambridge University Press.

Turner, V. 1964. Betwixt and Between: The Liminal Period in *Rites de Passage. The Proceedings of the American Ethnological Society* 4–20.

—1967. *Forest of Symbols: Aspects of the Ndembu Ritual.* Ithaca, NY: Cornell University Press.

—1969. *The Ritual Process: Structure and Anti-Structure.* Chicago: Aldine.

—1974. *Dramas, Fields, and Metaphors: Symbolic Action in Human Society.* Ithaca, NY: Cornell University Press.

—1975. *Revelation and Divination in Ndembu Ritual.* Ithaca, NY: Cornell University Press.

Ulin, R.C. 1984. *Understanding Cultures.* Austin, TX: University of Texas Press.

Ulysse, G. 2002. Conquering Duppies in Kingston: Miss Tiny and Me, Fieldwork Conflicts, and Being Loved and Rescued. *Anthropology and Humanism* 27 (1): 10–26.

United Nations. 2007. *United Nations Declaration on the Rights of Indigenous Peoples*. (www.un.org/esa/socdev/ unpfii/documents/DRIPS_en.pdf).

Valentine, V. 1980. Native Peoples and Canadian Society: A Profile of Issues and Trends. In R. Breton, J. Reitz, and V. Valentine, eds., *Cultural Boundaries and the Cohesion of Canada*, pp. 45–135. Montreal: Institute for Research on Public Policy.

Vandermass, M. 2007. Canada at the Crossroads: The Ipperwash Legacy. Speech delivered at the Caledonia Lions Hall, 10 June.

van Gennep, A. 1960 [1909]. *The Rites of Passage*. Chicago: University of Chicago Press.

Vansina, J. 1965. *Oral Tradition as History: A Study in Historical Methodology*. Madison, Wisc.: The University of Wisconsin Press.

Veracini, L. 2010. *Settler Colonialism: A Theoretical Overview*. Palgrave: Macmillan.

—2011. Introducing Settler Colonial Studies. In *Special Issue: A Global Phenomenon. Settler Colonial Studies* 1 (1):1–12.

Visweswaren, K. 1998. Race and the Culture of Anthropology. *American Anthropologist* 100: 70–83.

Wabauskang First Nation. 2014. Supreme Court Confirms Ontario Must Respect Treaty Rights. Press release, 11 July. (http://www. chiefs-of-ontario.org/node/921).

Warry, W. 2007. *Ending Denial: Understanding Aboriginal Issues.* Peterborough, ON: Broadview Press.

Wasase, T.A. 2015. *Indigenous Pathways of Action and Freedom.* Toronto: University of Toronto Press.

Watson, C.W. 1999. *Being There: Fieldwork in Anthropology*. London: Pluto Press.

Weaver, S.M. 1976. The Role of Social Science in Formulating Canadian Indian Policy: A Preliminary History of the Hawthorn-Tremblay Report. In *The History of Canadian Anthropology, Proceedings No. 3, Canadian Ethnology Society,* J. Freedman, ed., pp. 50–97. Hamilton: McMaster University, Department of Anthropology.

—1981. *Making Canadian Indian Policy: The Hidden Agenda 1968– 1970.* Toronto: University of Toronto Press.

—1986. Indian Policy in the New Conservative Government: The Nielson Task Force of 1985. *Native Studies Review* 2 (1): 1–43.

—1990. A New Paradigm in Canadian Indian Policy for the 1990s. *Canadian Ethnic Studies* 22 (3): 8–18.

Weber, D. 1995. From Limen to Border: A Meditation on the Legacy of Victor Turner for American Cultural Studies. *American Quarterly* 47 (3): 525–536.

Wels, H., van der Waal, K., Spiegel, A., and Kamsteeg, F. 2011. Victor Turner and Liminality. *Anthropology Southern Africa* 34 (1–2): 1–4.

Whittaker, E. 1992. The Birth of the Anthropological Self and its Career. *Ethos* 20: 191–219.

Whyte, J.D. 2008. Developmental and Legal Perspectives on Aboriginal Justice Administration. In *Moving Toward Justice: Legal Traditions and Aboriginal Justice*, J.D. Whyte, ed. Saskatoon: Purich.

Widdowson, F. 2019. *Separate but Unequal: How Parallelist Ideology Conceals Indigenous Dependency.* Ottawa: University of Ottawa Press.

—2021. *Indigenizing the University: Diverse Perspectives.* Winnipeg: Frontier Centre for Public Policy.

Widdowson, F. and A. Howard. 2008. *Disrobing the Aboriginal Industry: The Deception behind Indigenous Cultural Preservation.* Montreal: McGill-Queen's University Press.

Wilkinson, K. 2018. The Hermit Life from Medieval to Modern. *Wellcome Collection.* 20 December. (https://wellcomecollection.org/articles)

Willett, J. and M. J. Deegan, 2001. Liminality and Disability: Rites of Passage and Community in Hypermodern Society. *Disability Studies Quarterly* 21 (3): 137–152.

Willey, G.R. 1966. *American Archaeology: North and Middle America.* Englewood Cliffs. NJ: Prentice-Hall.

Winch, P. 1958. *The Idea of a Social Science and its Relation to Philosophy.* London: Routledge & Kegan Paul.

Wolfe, P. 1998. *Settler Colonialism and the Transformation of Anthropology: The Politics and Poetics of an Ethnographic Event.* London: Cassell.

—2006. Settler Colonialism and the Elimination of the Native. *Journal of Genocide Research* 8 (4): 387–409.

Yang, G. 2000. The Liminal Effects of Social Movements: Red Guards and the Transformation of Identity. *Sociological Forum* 15 (3): 379–406.

York, G. 1990. *The Dispossessed: Life and Death in Native Canada.* Foreword by Tomson Highway. London: Vintage U.K.

Young, A.E. and D. Nadeau. 2005. Decolonizing the Body: Restoring Sacred Vitality. *Atlantis* 29 (2): 1–13.

Zahedieh, N. 2010. *The Capital and the Colonies: London and the Atlantic Economy, 1660–1700.* Cambridge: Cambridge university Press.

Zenker, O. 2016. Anthropology on Trial: Exploring the Laws of Anthropological Expertise. *International Journal of Law in Context* 12: 293–311.

Zittoun, T. and A. Gillespie, 2010. Using Diaries and Self-Writings as data in Psychological Research. *In* E. Abbey and S. Surgan, eds., *Developing Methods in Psychology*. New Brunswick, NJ: Transaction Publishers.

Notes

1. Introduction

[1] As one studies the ethnographic literature of the Indigenous people of the Subarctic it becomes apparent that significantly more research into the division of labor would make a substantial contribution to our understanding of these northern communities. Such research could start with Hallowell's (1955: 123) broad outline, as he describes such work: "men might be breaching a canoe containing the carcass of a deer or moose, evidence of a successful hunt, and over the lake possibly other figures bending from canoes to obtain fish from set nets…In another part of such an encampment the women were likely to be tanning skins, making moccasins, mending nets, or stitching with spruce roots the bark covers for the tipis. And it is still their duty to chop and haul wood. Babies, snugly strapped in their cradleboards were being carried over their mother's backs." Similarly, Robert Lane provides this description of the Chilcotin: "Women did camp work, prepared skins and clothing, wove baskets, and gathered plant foods and materials. Men hunted, fished, fought, and manufactured tools and equipment. Men and women often shared tasks of some individuals by preference engaged in tasks traditionally performed by the opposite sex" (1981:403-404).

[2] 'Field research in anthropology', or what is commonly known as fieldwork is the main technique used by anthropologists for studying the cultural phenomena in various societies. Related terms include participant observation which is the research technique involving living with the people of a particular community or culture over an extended period of time such that researchers immerse themselves in the day-to-day activities of the group under study, and ethnography which is a division of anthropology devoted to the descriptive

recording of cultures based on research techniques carried out through fieldwork (see Hedican 2012: 93-119).

[3] In anthropology, 'theoretical orientations' are a type of generalization which, in a scientific sense, could be defined as "general abstract propositions (theories) and specific propositions (hypotheses) that represent how and why reality is constituted" (Sidky 2004: 425). One may find different definitions of theory in the literature of anthropology. As an example, Barrett defines theory as "an explanation of a class of events, usually with an empirical referent, providing insights into how and what is going on, and sometimes explaining why phenomena exists." (2009: 41-42). A theory is also then a type of generalization because it organizes facts in a highly abstract manner, suggesting 'why—'—and not just 'how' or 'what—'—and a mode of explanation that informs us about why certain effects are brought about by certain causes. When theory works, we are presented with a view of the world that is systematic and orderly (see Hedican 2012:49-92).

[4] "Science," Lett (1987: 26) suggests, can be defined as "a systematic method of inquiry based on empirical observation that seeks to provide coherent, reliable, and testable explanations of empirical phenomena and that rejects all accounts, descriptions, and analyses that are either not falsifiable or that have been decisively falsified. In short, science is an attempt to acquire knowledge that is objectively valid." A related term, empiricism, has been defined by Barrett (2009: 33) as work "grounded in data, in facts, in the 'real' or concrete world." Positivism is a term also found in the anthropological literature which can be defined as "An approach to understanding the social and physical world based on a belief that reality is a concrete phenomenon discernible through observation and discoverable laws" (Hedican 2012: 277).

[5] When anthropologists conduct an ethnography, which is a descriptive study of a particular people, they write up their results as if they were still there, conducting their fieldwork, at that particular point in time. As such, the term ethnographic present refers to the time that the anthropologist was engaged in the conduct of his or her fieldwork, and not at some later point in time when the write-up takes place.

[6] Clifford Geertz (1926-2006) was an influential and controversial anthropologist of the last generation. For some, he was considered "for three decades…the single most influential cultural anthropologist in the United States" (Geertz, Shweder, and Good 2005). Yet, there are those who "find here

cryptic excuses for a vacuous paradigm and reparation for an ethnographer's failure to do a thorough job...'thick descriptions' are theoretically useless" (Sidky 2004: 332). While the controversial aspects of Geertz's work extend into many areas, such as his view that ethnographic reality does not exist apart from anthropologists' written versions of it, his approach to ethnography, which he termed 'thick description', is the source of much debate within anthropology. The appeal of Geertz's anthropology for many stems from his assertion that the important question about cultural phenomena is not about what they do, but what they mean.

[7] Postmodern anthropology was particularly prominent in the decades from about 1980-2000. It can be defined as an anti-science, subjective, literary perspective, which rejects the idea of universally valid objective knowledge and focuses on culture as open-ended negotiated meanings and stresses the examination of how ethnographies are written. During this postmodernist period, anthropologists saw science itself as artificial and not in touch with cultural realities, and some even regarded it as imperialistic and obscene (Hedican 2012:87-89). As Sidky (2004: 436) explains, postmodernist anthropologists "vehemently oppose science and scientific perspectives and instead advocate approaches based upon insights and the view of the social actors as individuals."

[8] The Algonquians (or Algonkians) are members of the largest Indigenous language family in Canada, which includes such First Nations as Cree, Blackfoot, Anishinaabe and Mi'kmaq. Its members are spread over the eastern part of North America, however its members eventually spread into the Plains area when horses became available through trade in the 1700's (Hedican 2017a: 7-10).

[9] Harold Innis's study The Fur Trade in Canada1970 [1930] is the classic work on the subject. In the 1970-1980 period there was a renewed interest in the fur trade, such as Ray and Freeman (1978), 'Give Us Good Measure', Bishop (1974), The Northern Ojibwa and the Fur Trade, Ray (1974), Indians in the Fur Trade, Francis and Morantz (1983), Partners in Furs, as well as earlier works of note, Galbraith (1957), The Hudson's Bay Company as an Imperial Factor,1821-1869, Merk (1931), Fur Trade and Empire, and Rich (1967), The Fur Trade and the Northwest to 1857.

[10] There is a tendency not only in the scholarly literature but in government reports as well to regard the northern wage and subsistence economies as if

these were separate entities. Probably this mistaken idea comes from those who have adopted an assimilationist attitude in which Indigenous people would eventually abandon their life in the bush and move into the predominantly Euro-Canadian towns and cities. However, for those who have conducted research in the Indigenous communities of northern Ontario, they soon become aware that most of these communities have a mix of the wage economy and income derived from subsistence production. Both of these sectors are apt to merge together so that they are variable phenomenon; at certain times of the year wage work is more prominent, and at others resources are derived from the bush environment. It is an entirely mistaken idea that one of these sectors will ultimately emerge as the only single most important facet of local northern economies.

[11] Again and again we come to the importance of gathering information on Indigenous communities through long-term, first-hand field work. It is hard to assess what is happening from 20 thousand feet, and who but anthropologists are willing to devote the time to actually live in an Indigenous community? Thus, there is much mistaken information circulating that is based only on second-hand observation or speculation, which is hardly the basis for building effective government policy.

[12] Despite this impressive body of research in northern Ontario it is now becoming quite dated as most of the ethnographers have either retired or passed away. For some reason there are fewer younger scholars taking up the task—the relatively harsh weather and environmental factors might be a significant factor in discouraging such research.

[13] The Ring of Fire is the name given to a vast region of mineral deposits in northern Ontario, situated about 400 kilometers northeast of Thunder Bay, in the James Bay Lowlands. The ring of Fire region was named after Johnny Cash's famous country and western ballad when Richard Nemis, founder and president of Noront Resources, first made significant mineral finds in the area (see Hedican 2017a: 143-146).

[14] Informants, as used in anthropology, refers to individuals who provide information to anthropologists during the conduct of fieldwork. Key informants are people who provide expert or specialized knowledge in their culture (see Hedican 2012: 272).

[15] As Barrett (2009: 248) explains "the burst of insight involves deep penetrations into the minute details of people's everyday lives, quick

perceptions that allow the fieldworker to understand their innermost motives. The burst of insight is comparable to shouting Eureka! When suddenly what was previously puzzling or only superficially understood makes sense."

[16] Participant observation is a research technique developed in social anthropology that involves living with the people of a particular culture or community over an extended period of time such that researchers attempt to immerse themselves in the day-to-day activities of the group under study (see Hedican 2012: 276).

[17] Ethnography is a division of anthropology devoted to the descriptive recording of cultures based on research techniques, such as participant observation, carried out through fieldwork (see Hedican 2012: 268-269).

[18] The idea of ethnography as fiction has been described by Sidky (2004: 425) as a "postmodern interpretivist jargon term applied to ethnographic writing…The postmodern interpretivists' usage of the term verges upon the definition of the world as false or unfactual. All ethnographic accounts are treated as fictions by interpretivists."

2. Our Academic Mentors

[19] On the subject of the extent to which our mentors or intellectual predecessors contribute to the development of our new knowledge base, it is worthwhile considering several points. Probably the most important of these is whether or not one considers the accumulation of knowledge a continuous process through time, or whether the accumulation of knowledge could be thought of as a discontinuous process which involves distinct breaks with the past. One of the main contributors to this debate is Thomas Kuhn who outlines in his book The Structure of Scientific Revolutions (1970 [1962]) the thesis that knowledge accumulation is a discontinuous process. He suggests that scientific enquiry takes place within a paradigm which he defines as a set of agreed upon conventions and assumptions that guide scientific research.

For a period of time, a paradigm directs research in a particular direction which he refers to as 'normal science'. Eventually the established paradigm encounters anomalies that it fails to solve. Eventually these anomalies accumulate resulting in a 'scientific revolution' and the adoption of a new paradigm which operates under different assumptions than the previous one (Kuhn 1970: 167-169). From Kuhn's perspective, each new paradigm is incommensurable with the previous one. The new paradigm explains what the previous one could not and offers a better understanding of the world. It offers a new beginning, yet there is no growth of knowledge or advances in scientific understanding, or so he suggests (Kuznar 1997: 57).

The contrary view is that scientific knowledge is cumulative and that paradigms are often commensurable. David Stove (1982: 3-4, 6) has offered a critique of Kuhn's perspective, noting that:

Much more is known now than was known fifty years ago, and much was known then than in 1580. So there has been a great accumulation or growth of knowledge in the last four hundred years...Kuhn would admit that normal science has solved a great many problems since 1580. Well, if it has solved these problems, then those problems have been solved haven't they?

We can therefore conclude, if we reject Kuhn's thesis, that mentors provide a valuable source of information that can be built up. Their experiences are worth listening to because then we might avoid the logical and practical pitfalls that they encountered during their careers.

[20] The critique of Margaret Mead's Samoan studies by Derek Freeman goes well beyond these two anthropologists and extends to American anthropology as a whole. As Sidky (2004: 159) explains:

The questions Freeman raised had serious implications for American anthropology. How could one of the most famous and well-respected anthropologists of her generation, one of the founding figures of the discipline, so to speak, be so mistaken. In Margret Mead and Samoa Freeman (1983) struck many in the American anthropological community like a bolt of lightning and set off a 'media feeding frenzy'. The debunker rose to prominence.

The wider issue not only concerned Mead and Freeman but the essential paradigm of American anthropology which is built on the idea that culture is not biologically determined. This wider issue is commonly referred to as the nature-nurture debate, which is to say that American anthropology was largely erected on the Boasian 'cultural determinist' paradigm, rather than on inherited biological characteristics. Another wider issue concerns the claim that anthropology is a science, as Sidky (2004: 160) notes, "if anthropology is a science, then how is it possible for Mead's work, which was so flawed, to stand unchallenged?" In a reply to this question, Orans (1996: 10) suggests that "Mead's work stood unchallenged even by reviewers who had a grasp of the most fundamental principle of science, which is that propositions must be verifiable and they must be accepted or rejected based upon how well they accord with empirical observations."

[21] Many important scientific discoveries are made by accident, such as:

Penicillin:

One of the biggest medicinal breakthroughs in history came about entirely by accident. Sir Alexander Fleming interrupted his experimentation with the influenza virus for a two-week holiday and when he returned he found that a mold had started to grow which deterred the virus. Penicillin was born and is now used to treat everything from pneumonia to a variety of infections and has saved millions of lives.

Strikable Matches:

John Walker, a British pharmacist, accidently got a lump of his fun mixture of antimony sulphide and potassium chlorate on the end of his mixing stick. When he tried to scratch it off it burst into flames, thus, at the end of an amazing series of events, an incredible breakthrough was made (see www.mynewlab.com, 'Ten Accidental Discoveries and Breakthroughs', accessed 8 April 2021).

[22] The transactional approach which Richard Salisbury advocated is discussed at length in his article 'Transactional Politics: Factions and Beyond' (Salisbury and Silverman 1977a:111-127). This approach was discussed previously by F.G. Bailey (1969) in his book Stratagems and Spoils: A Social Anthropology of Politics. In anthropology Bailey's work departed from previous studies which emphasized social structures and institutions and focused instead on people's decisions. From Bailey's perspective an important aspect of social relations concerns the transactions people make with one another, and the manner in which social relations are sometimes manipulated to achieve personal goals. As Barrett (2009: 102) explains, "In everyday life, Bailey observed, most of us, guided by self-interest, thread our way between the norms, seeking the most advantageous route."

[23] It is important to note the context in which this comment is made. In this paper Salisbury was discussing the 'ombudsman' role for anthropologist,

which is to say, acting as a mediator or ombudsman. In other cases, an anthropologist may be hired directly to perform a service for one group only which would mean acting in an advocacy capacity. Thus, there is a range of roles that an anthropologist could possibly adopt under various circumstances (see Hedican 1986c, 2008a: 97-107).

[24] It probably is not worthwhile dwelling on the 'what ifs' of life for very long, yet one has to wonder at time how one's life could have turned out under other unforeseen circumstances. In what one might call an 'ironic twist of fate' I had previously applied for an anthropology position at Brock University. Soon after, the chair of the department wrote a letter to me indicting that unfortunately the position had been withdrawn because of budgetary constraints. Then, when I showed up at the University of Guelph for my first day of work, another new recruit introduced himself. He said, "Your name is familiar," and as it turned out he was the former department chair at Brock who had written the letter to me about the withdrawn position. Wayne Thompson was now our new department chair, a position he filled for the next twenty years until he retired.

3. Fieldwork as a Rite de Passage

[25] Fieldwork as a Rite de Passage

[26] It is important to indicate that fieldwork in anthropology has changed considerably over the last generation or so. In my own department are several anthropologists who conducted their PhD fieldwork as part of a research team. In another case, a faculty member from Japan returned to this country to pursue further research. Another professor conducted research only several miles from their home. Obviously in each of these cases the so-called 'liminal' transitions would be different.

[27] I had originally written to the Wisconsin Historical Society requesting any information that might be available on my great-great grandfather, Edward Hedican, who had come over from Ireland about 1850. Imagine my shock when a package arrived containing a copy of a newspaper with the headline "Ed Hedican shot." As it turned out the Ed Hedican who was shot was the son of the Ed Hedican with the same name as both of us.

[28] An aspect of most ethnographies that is hardly ever mentioned, if at all, is the extent to which an anthropologist's role is explained to community members. For my part, in the Anishinaabe community of Collins, I was clearly

interested in the development of local leadership and economic change, so in this context my focus was, in my mind at least, a clearly defined one. Nonetheless, other community members might have been confused as to my role in the village. As an example, a young man brought me the bands from the legs of geese, probably thinking that I had a wildlife role because of all my questions about hunting and fishing. In another case a man appeared seeking medical attention for a wounded hand, possibly overhearing some people calling me 'doctor'.

There could be other possible misconceptions involved as well.

[29] Following Turner's concept of 'liminal transitions' a useful exercise would be to engage in some creative thinking about the stages involved in one's own fieldwork. Having a somewhat shy tendency, I was hesitant initially to participate in community affairs. Donald Patience probably noticed this and as a result pushed me to become more involved. Instead my tendency was to withdraw into the isolation of my cabin and read ethnographies and thereby convince myself that I was still doing something constructive.

[30] In another one of those interesting 'twists of fate', I have recently been contacted on Facebook and Messenger by Annie and Samson's grandchildren who I have never met yet wonder if I could tell them what their grandparents were like. I never expected that living in Collins during the 1970s would have historical value to the descendants of the community members among who I lived many decades into the future.

[31] Sidky provides a succinct account of Turner's weaknesses:

"The weaknesses of Turner's approach are the same as those perpetually besetting all other perspectives that offer interpretive accounts of cultures in terms of 'beliefs and meanings', to the exclusion of material causation and evolutionary holism. There is also the problem of validation. Interpretive accounts are immune to any systematic mode of validation or replication" (2004: 319).

It is probable here that Sidky is referring to Marvin Harris's concept of 'cultural materialism' when he uses the term 'material causation'. Of course, there are a variety of theoretical interpretations both for and against Turner's conceptual orientation.

[32] Another factor contributing to the problem of essentialism, although many anthropologists would be reluctant to admit it, is the long-standing tradition of the 'ethnographic present'. The ethnographic present can be defined as "the

use of the present tense to describe a culture, although the description may refer to situations that existed in the past" (Robbins et al. 2017: 282). As such, the use of the ethnographic present to describe cultural practices that may have existed long ago in the past but are no longer part of that culture may lead to the false impression that such a culture is somehow 'backward'. For this reason, the convention of using the ethnographic present may contribute to the view that the 'essential' aspects of a culture are still practiced in the modern world when in fact such traits may have disappeared decades ago.

[33] What might be lost in the various discussions of Victor Turner's use of the rite de passage metaphor is that his fieldwork was restricted primarily to the African society of the Ndembu and, as such, theoretical discussion beyond this particular society could lead to erroneous interpretations in other fieldwork settings. The fact is that the Ndembu people (at the time of Turner's fieldwork in the 1960s) placed a considerable emphasis on the ritual process of life's various passages at several phases in the life cycle. While most societies that anthropologists have studied place some emphasis on life's passages, even apparently somewhat trivial school graduation ceremonies, it is important to note that most societies do not place the same emphasis on rites of passage that exist in the Ndembu culture, or single out other phases in one's life that are not prominent among the Ndembu people. As such, extrapolating the characteristics of Ndembu ritual to other societies in an uncritical manner is apt to lead to an array of misinterpretations, as various authors have noted (such as Jorgensen 1992; Sidky 2004: 303-314; and Speigel 2011). In recognition of this issue of implying wider theoretical extension of the ritual concept where these might not exist, suggests that one use the rites of passage concept as more of a heuristic device (i.e. serving as an example of), than any literal or exact interpretation on the basis of Turner's fieldwork among the Ndembu.

[34] See also Agar 1980, Hedican 1994, Nash 1963 and Rabinow 1977 for further discussions of the 'anthropologist as stranger' theme, or Barley 1986 on the 'innocent anthropologist'.

[35] A topic that deserves more attention in the anthropological literature is the reciprocal relationships upon which fieldwork is often built. If one regards information as a form of currency, then it follows that those in the community who provide it deserves some recompense. This does not necessarily involve a payment in currency but more often includes some form of service as a way

of 'evening up' the reciprocal relationships upon which successful fieldwork depends. A colleague of mine taught grade school in a Nigerian village as a way of compensating his hosts for their hospitality. I hired a young man to give me lessons in the Anishinaabe language. My log cabin was not rented but my stay was recompensed with general repairs, a new window and stove with an agreement that the owner on his visits to town could stay there anytime he wished. These are the sorts of reciprocal arrangements that anthropologists build within a fieldwork community.

4. The Tourist Lodge At Whitewater Lake

[36] Decisions made during anthropological fieldwork, as with life itself, involve possibly opening up new opportunities but can incur costs as well. It is for this reason that economists have coined the phrase 'opportunity cost', a term that is useful in anthropology as well. As Harold Schneider in Economic Man explains, "The implications for this concept for anthropological work could be illustrated…when Chagga on Mt. Kilimanjaro began to grow coffee…they were faced with the problem of shifting resources to this form of production…the income from coffee being large enough to offset the opportunity costs of shifting from banana culture and cattle raising to coffee culture" (1974: 62). However, beyond the economic realm the same principles apply, which is to say, that a decision to move in one direction consequently prevents one from simultaneously moving in another. In my own case in Collins, staying solidly in the ORG camp opened up new opportunities for my research, but at the same time it more or less curtailed seeking the favors of government officials as well. As to the question as to why there was a competitive situation involved, space precludes following the avenue of discussion at this point.

[37] The issue of 'fortuitous circumstance' in ethnographic research deserves more attention in the anthropological literature. As much as one may try to anticipate unforeseen circumstances, there are always going to be occasions when a situation presents itself that merits further investigation. In this regard we need to assess the significance for our research concerning how much 'merit' this new situation deserves. As with the concept of an opportunity cost, our time in fieldwork is limited, and so probably diverting time from another task will mean that this is time that cannot be consequently spent on a matter

that we previously had hoped to investigate. On the one hand we cannot be running all over the place investigating every new situation that grabs our attention, yet, on the other, there will doubtless emerge situations that when investigated have the potential to add significantly to our overall writing project. Experience is a factor that helps sort out these options, however as has been made clear with various ethnographies we are apt not to be able to afford the time and travel to investigate a significant situation that in retrospect could add in a significant manner to our original research objective.

[38] By the use of the term 'levels of abstraction' I mean a scale of generalizations such that as one proceeds up this scale one moves farther and farther away from concrete phenomenon. Similarly, Sears and Cairns (2010: 74) use the term 'levels of generality' in which they note that "As we move into the realm of theoretical thinking, we become more conscious of the ways that abstraction is employed to frame our view of reality…The level of generality of an abstraction can range from the most specific (emphasizing the features that set a particular phenomenon apart) to the most general (emphasizing those features shared with other entities)." The process of developing abstractions involves 'separating out the essential elements which highlights only the key elements' (2010: 183).

In addition, Salzman (2001: 8, 145, 152) distinguishes between descriptive generalizations ('Formulation stating the common features of a large class including many examples'), and theoretical generalizations ('General propositions that state the relationship between factors or "variables"').

[39] The term 'unorganized community' was one which the Ontario government applied to communities without municipal status, of which Collins was an example. There are many such communities scattered throughout northern Ontario, although it is difficult to determine their exact number. As such, their characteristics are difficult to determine. From my own familiarity with a number of such communities I would say that a high proportion are comprised primarily by Indigenous peoples, especially those who, for whatever reason, have left their original reserves and are relatively small in size. However, as the Collins case illustrates, the term 'unorganized' is probably a misnomer since there is probably some form of informal political structure. In this sense the designation 'unorganized' implies an unwarranted pejorative connotation, in my opinion.

[40] In anthropology, structure can be defined as "A basic pattern of relations…the underlying conceptual and cognitive framework" (Salzman 2001: 151). The implication, then, is that members of a society understand their cultures' 'basic patterns' in term of the underlying relationships between individuals and groups. However, it could be argued that most people in a society give little thought to the 'structure' of their society.

5. Wendell, the Hermit of Best Island

[41] It is a curious matter that hermits and anthropologists should at times share certain personal characteristics. Hortense Powdermaker, in Stranger and Friend, poses the question: "Why should a contented and satisfied person think of standing outside his or any other society and studying it?" (1966: 20) She also describes growing up 'feeling somewhat apart from life', and seeking out activities of solitary involvement. Similarly, Clyde Kluckhohn writes that "The lure of the strange and far has a peculiar appeal for those who are dissatisfied with themselves or who do not feel at home in their own society" (1957: 11).

[42] George Quimby, a recognized authority on the glacial Great Lakes, suggests that "The Nipissing stage…was created by the closing of the North Bay outlet through the postglacial upwarping of the land, presumably expanding from the release of the weight of the glacial ice that covered it at an earlier time. In the southern parts of the region the land rose more than 400 feet between the time of glacial Lake Algonquin and Lake Nipissing" (1960: 16). On the subject of whales in the Great Lakes during this time period, he notes that "Sea mammals inhabiting the glacial lakes ponded by the ice were whales of several species and walruses which…entered the Lake Huron basin from the ocean by way of the Ottawa River and the North Bay channel" (1960: 20-21).

[43] According to a history of the Parker Pen Company the Jotter was introduced to the market in 1954:

"Then in 1954, another landmark innovation, the Parker Jotter, made its way onto the scene. The first quality ball pen with an unusually large cartridge design, the Jotter wrote more than five times as long as standard ball pens. The pen also featured a unique rotating point to prevent wear. In its first year, more than 3.5 million Jotters were sold" (http://www.parkerpen.com).

[44] Edward Burger (2020), in his article 'Pi: The Most Important Number in the Universe', indicates that:

"The constant π helps us understand our universe with greater clarity. The definition of π inspired a new notion of the measurement of angles, a new unit of measurement. This important angle measure is known as 'radian measure' and gave rise to many important insights in our physical world. As for π itself, Johann Lambert showed in 1761 that π is an irrational number, and later, in 1882, Ferdinand von Lindemann proved that π is not a solution to any polynomial equation with integers. However, many questions about π remain unanswered." No doubt Wendell Beckwith working in the seclusion of northern Whitewater Lake would have been intrigued by such information.

[45] There is mention in the Thunder Bay newspapers that Wendell Beckwith's various notes, drawings and other research paraphernalia had been 'assessed', yet there does not appear to be any publication of the results of this evaluation. It would be interesting, considering all the years that Beckwith conducted his research if a proper assessment of the scientific value of his work were made available to the public. In particular, probably the most important question is this: was Beckwith a 'true' scientist, or just another quack seeking refuge in the northern bush? I would imagine that this proposed assessment would be multidisciplinary in nature considering the variety of his investigative interests.

6. Emotional Experience in Fieldwork

[46] Part of the problem is that many see anthropologists as 'social scientists', and as scientists are expected to bring a detachment to their work. This attitude discourages empathy with the participants of anthropological research and thereby is seen as a means of reducing bias in the research process which could result in distorting the final conclusions. However, there is little evidence that empathy toward research participants influences or biases the course of research in fieldwork.

[47] I found it useful to engage in a period of self-reflection, usually near the end of the day when there was a quiet time. As a general rule I would go over different events that happened during the day and ask myself questions, such as, "how did I feel about this situation or that? Should I have said something when this happened?" Then, when I went to sleep, I tried not to drag the day's events into my night-time reverie which allowed me to start each day afresh, without having to deal with a backlog of troubling situations which would distract me from the work that I needed to conduct as the day went on.

[48] There was an instance during which I had a serious confrontation with a community member. While I tried to understand this event during my evening periods of reflection, my anxiety around this conflict began to build over the evening. Finally, when I tried to go to sleep, a knot began to form in my stomach. Eventually my solar plexus started to become rigid and I had trouble breathing. Even though it was about two in the morning, I put on my clothes and proceeded to run up and down the railway track behind my cabin until I was breathing heavily and started to feel exhausted. This exercise relaxed me enough to relieve the pain, after which I returned to my cabin and was able to sleep. I then realized the importance of dealing more effectively with emotional issues rather than expecting them to disappear on their own.

[49] Culture shock, in one definition, refers to a syndrome "precipitated by the anxiety that results from losing all your familiar cues, which includes frustration, repressed or expressed aggression against the source of discomfort, an irrational fervor for the familiar and comforting, and disproportionate anger at trivial interferences" (Golde 1986: 11). It results from an inadequate set of meanings that interfere with our ability to understand others' behavior but, as she indicates, "the concept includes the notion of threat to one's own system of meanings and values, and consequently to one's own identity" (1986: 12).

[50] See Hedican (2008c) for a discussion of the role of empathy in anthropological fieldwork. An attitude of empathy toward the residents of a particular field work setting has both advantages and disadvantages. One of the main advantages is that empathy toward others serves to deepen an understanding of their life's problems, however it can be disadvantageous to become too close emotionally to the inhabitants of one's research because one can lose a sense of detachment, or objectivity, which is also an important component of professional inquiry.

[51] It would have been useful if Durkheim had explained that even in scientific inquiry there really are no 'pure facts'. However, he does indicate a distinction between social facts and those existing in the physical sciences: "in reality there is in every society a certain group of phenomenon which may be differentiated from those studies by the other natural sciences" (1938: 1). Then, at the end of his chapter on 'What is a Social Fact?' he indicates in italics that "A social fact is every way of acting, fixed or not, capable of exercising on the individual an external constraint" (1938: 13). In addition, as a way of providing further clarification on the subject of 'social facts', Lett indicates that "Facts

are explained once they have been subsumed under a set of theoretical statements, although the facts themselves are determined by the theory. In the strictest meaning of the term, there is no such things as an 'objective' fact. Perception is selection and interpretation; theory tells the scientist what to select and how to interpret it" (1987: 29). Or, in a somewhat more cryptic manner, Clifford Geertz explains in Local Knowledge that "To the ethnographer the shapes of knowledge are always ineluctably local, indivisible from their instruments and encasements" (1983: 4).

[52] Reflexivity in anthropology is a term "meaning self-criticism and self-awareness in the context of research. Critical reflection upon one's own social/intellectual activities" (Sidky 2004: 437).

[53] Laing was born into a working-class family and grew up in Glasgow. He studied medicine and psychiatry and earned a doctoral degree in medicine at the University of Glasgow in 1951. After serving as a conscript psychiatrist in the British Army (1951-52) and teaching at the University of Glasgow (1953-56), he conducted research at the Tavistock Clinic (1956-60) and at the Tavistock Institute of Human Relations (1960-89). He had a private practice in London. Throughout much of his career, Laing was interested in the underlying causes of schizophrenia. In his first book, The Divided Self (1960), he theorized that ontological insecurity (insecurity about one's existence) prompts a defensive reaction in which the self splits into separate components, thus generating the psychotic symptoms characteristic of schizophrenia. He was opposed to the standard treatments for schizophrenics, such as hospitalization and electroshock therapy (https://www.britannica.com/biography/R-D-Laing, accessed 4 April 2021).

[54] When Luke Yellowhead left the train he proceeded to walk back and forth along the railway tracks, mumbling to himself. No one, not even family members, would go near him. Perhaps against my better judgement, I decided to approach him on the tracks, but kept my distance. I asked how he was doing and if he had anything to say to the people of Collins. He then reached into a jacket pocket and produced a paper, which he handed to me. He explained that it was a drawing of a church, and that the people of Collins should 'pray to be saved'. Luke planned to build this church in Collins, he said. I wished him a good day, and left, never to see him again. Presumably he stayed in the area of the railway tracks all night and left on the morning passenger train.

55 There is an old saying that hindsight is 20-20, meaning I suppose that one gains clarity about a situation over time. As far as this incident is concerned, I could have participated in the funeral procession using the participant observer technique, which is to say "the study of another culture over an extended time period during which anthropologists attempt to immerse themselves in the day-to-day activities of the group being studied" (Sidky 2004: 435). However, when I think about this situation, I was particularly interested in Peter's observation on what was happening, in the context of his long life in the village, which would not have been available to me if I were to have participated directly in the funeral.

7. The Anthropologist as Land Claims Facilitator

56 During the course of planning for the northern areas of Ontario, a more comprehensive approach was adopted for treaty negotiations, contrary to the piecemeal negotiations that had characterized earlier efforts. The Robinson-Superior and Robinson-Huron Treaties of 1850 involved an extensive tract of land, larger than the previous treaties combined. The area over which Indigenous title was ceded by these treaties extended from the north shores of Lakes Huron and Superior up to the height of land and the territory of Rupert's Land. The Hudson's Bay Company held monopoly trading and administrative rights to that territory by virtue of a royal charter. The Robinson treaties provided for annual payments or annuities, for hunting and fishing on unoccupied Crown lands, and for the establishment of reserves for the settlement of Indigenous peoples. Thus, the Robinson Treaties established a basic formula that would later act as a guide for additional treaties farther west (see Hedican 2017a: 99-124).

57 The terms of the Robinson-Superior Treaty of 1850 are clearly set out, word for word, in Canada: Indian Treaties and Surrenders (1891 [1971]). The terms of the treaty are not very extensive, covering just a little over two pages of print. Only four 'Chiefs' are listed and five 'Principal Men' whose location is not indicated. Payment for ceding this tract of land, "the sum of two thousand pounds of good and lawful money of Upper Canada to them in hand paid; and for the further perpetual annuity of five hundred pounds." Three reserves were set aside: the first one to 'commence about two miles from Fort William', the second at Michipicoton, and the third on the Gull River, near Lake Nipigon. It

appears from the names listed as signatories to the treaty that only those chiefs and principal men from the aforementioned reserves were present. There was no explanation provided for the absence of any mention of reserves for the other Indigenous populations of the area, or for any reason why representatives of the other Indigenous communities in the area were also not similarly invited to the treaty signing. There is also the question of whether or not the Indigenous people who were not signatories to the treaty ever received the payment of annuities to which they were entitled.

[58] The Museum at Nipigon, Ontario, has posted the following comments about the flooding of Lake Nipigon in the 1940s due to a water diversion project farther north:

Ogoki Diversion and Nipigon River Dams

"Through a 1940 agreement with the United States. Approval was given to Canada to utilize immediately for the increase in power output at Niagara for war purposes, an additional flow of what equivalent to that which will be added to the Great Lakes as a result of diverting water from portions of the Albany Watershed. This led to the construction of the Ogoki River Diversion which sent water south into Lake Nipigon. In 1942, the Hydro Electric Power Commission promised the diversion would increase the power resources of Southern Ontario and Quebec and improve levels of the Great Lakes for the benefit of Canada and the United States."

(http://www.nipigonmuseumtheblog.ogoki-diversion-and-nipigon-river-dams.html accessed 19 April 2021)

There can be little doubt, then, that the Ogoki River Diversion project of 1942 was a cause of the flooding of the Whitesand Reserve at the north end of Lake Nipigon, despite Ontario Hydro's denials to the contrary.

[59] The Union of Ontario Indians (UOI), also known as the Anishinabek Nation, is a political advocacy organization representing 43 Anishinabek First Nations surrounding the northern shores of the Great Lakes. There are seven tribes that make up the Anishinabek Nation. These are the Ojibway, Chippewa, Odawa, Pottawatomi, Mississauga, Algonquins and Delawares. These nations share common languages, customs, beliefs and histories (see http://www.anishinabek.ca accessed 19 April 2021).

[60] The present area of the Whitesand Reserve comprises 249 acres with a total land base of 614 acres, according to the band webpage (see http://www.whitesandfirstnation.com, accessed 19 April 2021).

[61] I have attempted to discuss and summarize several of these different roles in the following publications:

Hedican (1986c), Anthropologists and Social Involvement: Some Issues and Problems. Canadian Review of Sociology and Anthropology 23 (4): 544-558. Hedican (2008a: 97-104), Applied Anthropology in Canada: Understanding Aboriginal Issues. Toronto: University of Toronto Press. Revised 2nd edition.

8. The Ipperwash Tragedy and Settler Colonialism

[62] The title of Barrett's book Is God a Racist? is derived from the literature of the Western Guard, a white-supremacist group in Toronto. Their slogan, "God is a Racist," was once painted on the side of a Toronto church in 1977.

[63] The Report of the Ipperwash Inquiry (Linden 2007) uses both 'Stoney Point' and 'Stony Point', often employing both of these terms on the same page. It is not known if the writer(s) of this report were aware of this inconsistency, or whether these two terms were regarded as synonymous or interchangeable with one another. The present work uses only 'Stony Point' because that is the only usage employed by the Chippewas themselves.

[64] In contrast to the previous war, by virtue of the Statute of Westminster 1931, Canada instituted its measures separately from the United Kingdom. A state of apprehended war was declared on 25 August 1939, and the Defense of Canada Regulations were implemented under the Act. A state of war was declared with Germany on 10 September 1939.The extreme security measures permitted by the Defense of Canada Regulations included the waiving of habeas corpus and the right to trial, internment, bans on political and religious groups, restrictions of free speech including the banning of certain publications, and the confiscation of property. Called in Canada's Human Rights History 'One of the most notorious examples of state excess during a period of emergency was the War Measures Act'
 (https://www.history of rights.ca/encyclopedia, accessed 23 April 2021, see Canada's Human Rights History: War Measure Act and Lindsay 2014).

[65] The promise states: "if, at the termination of the war, no further use of the area is required by the Department of National Defense negotiations will be entered into with the department of Indian Affairs to transfer the lands back to the Indians at a reasonable price determined by mutual agreement" (see Koehler 1996). No reason was given as to why the Stony Point residents were

required to buy back land that was already theirs in the first place. However, in March 1992, the Standing Committee on Aboriginal Peoples recommended in its tabled report that the appropriated land be returned to its former Aboriginal inhabitants. The report also indicated that the federal government's reasons for continuing to occupy the land were 'spurious and without substance' (see Gordon 1996, Hamilton 1998, Steckley and Cummins 2008: 205).

[66] As stated in the Report of the Ipperwash Inquiry, "a fundamental problem was that the information about guns was not authenticated or verified by OPP intelligence officers" (Linden 2007: 56). Band Councilor Gerald George, who was apparently against the Ipperwash protest, reported to Detective Constable Dew that the protesters possessed firearms, although in Dew's notebook he simply wrote that the information had come from an 'anonymous source'. In the Ipperwash Report Justice Sidney Linden indicated that he found this information false and misleading, as indicated by a transcript of his comments before the Inquiry on 19 September 2007.

[67] Although certain police officers may hold racist attitudes toward members of minority groups, a related issue concerns the number of individual members of a police force in right-wing or white supremacist organizations. There are no doubt police officers who hold very conservative ideas, but this does not necessarily mean that they will ultimately join right-wing organizations. As Barrett (1987: 322) concludes, "What has been remarkable about Canada is that so few policemen have been formal members of the right wing."

[68] There is also an undercurrent of anti-Indigenous sympathies in Canada. As an example, Mark Vandermass gave a speech at the Caledonia Lions Hall on 10 June 2007 entitled 'Canada at the Crossroads: The Ipperwash Legacy'. This sort of speech is given across Ontario whose intent is to inflame anti-Indigenous opinion. In this particular diatribe, the belief is expressed that "OPP Two Tier Justice policies are based on the false premise that native people have no self-control, that they are incapable of obeying the law, that they and their children are willing to live in a lawless world ruled by criminals who take what, when they want. For more than 15 years the OPP has been sacrificing the well-being of law-abiding people—both native and non-native—for the benefit of sociopaths and demagogues" (2007: 5).

[69] Bill C-31 was passed in 1985 in an attempt to eliminate the marriage restrictions stipulated in the Indian Act, and, supposedly also the

discrimination against Indigenous women on the basis of gender. However, prior to 1972-73, minor unmarried children were also automatically enfranchised (has their Indian status taken away) with their mothers. Since that time, minors are enfranchised only when the parents request it and the request is approved by the Department of Indian Affairs. In the period between 1968-88 more than 13,000 Indians lost their legal status under various provisions of the Indian Act.

9. Anthropology in the Courtroom

[70] As an example, he had some familiarity with the Whitesand land claim and my role as a 'facilitator' through the University of Guelph.

[71] Here is a brief summary of details pertaining to each of the First Nations involved in the Williams Treaties:

Alderville First Nation (www.aldervillfirstnation.ca) is situated on a reserve located near the south shores of Rice Lake in southern Ontario, which has been this First Nation's home since the 1830s. Prior to this, the community had lived about 90 kilometers east of this location, around the Bay of Quinte, which subsequently became home to the Mohawks of the Bay of Quinte First Nation as this land had been promised to Joseph Brant and his followers by the British after the American Revolution. Residents consider themselves a band of Mississauga, a sub-nation of the Anishinaabe. In 2014, the total registered population consisted of about 1,200 people of which about 300 live on the reserve.

Beau Soleil First Nation (www.chimnissing.ca) is located on the southern tip of Georgian Bay in Simcoe County. This First Nation consists of three reserves situated on Christian, Beckwith, and Hope Islands, which are close to the communities of Midland and Penetanguishene. Traditional Aboriginal languages spoken include Ojibwa (Anishinaabe), Odawa, and Potawatomi, which are all members of the Algonquian (Algonkian) language family. In 2014, the total registered population was 2,300, of which 647 lived on these reserves.

Chippewas of Georgina Island First Nation (www.georginaisland.com) is comprised of Anishinaabe people living on the southern shores of Lake Simcoe, situated approximately 30 kilometers south of Parry Sound. The reserve consists of three islands, namely, Georgina, Snake, and Fox Islands. In

2014, the total registered population was 863 people, of whom 199 live on-reserve. Access to the reserve consists of a ferry service in the summer months. The First Nation is a member of the Ogemahwahj Tribal Council, which represents five First Nations in the Port Perry-Mactier region.

Chippewas of Rama (Mnjikaning) First Nation (www.mnjikaning.ca) is located about five kilometers northeast of Orillia between Lake Simcoe and Lake Couchiching. Around 1830, this community was moved to the Coldwater Narrows area by the Crown, part of an 'experiment' that shaped 'Indian Reserves'. Forced to move again, by the terms of what the Rama First Nation members refer to as an "illegal surrender," the First Nation purchased land in Rama Township in 1836. The land there was difficult to farm, so the First Nation pursued other entrepreneurial opportunities in the tourist market. A community referendum has recently resumed the name of Chippewas of Rama, replacing the previous name of Mnjikaning First Nation. The community comprises 1,500 total members, with approximately 750 living on the Mnjikaning Reserve, according to the First Nation's webpage (INAC does not have a population listing). It is well known for the Casino Rama and Entertainment Complex, and is a member of the Ogemawahj Tribal Council.

Curve Lake First Nation (www.curvelakefirstnation.ca) is located in Peterborough County on the Trent waterways, consisting of Mississauga Ojibwa (Anishinaabe) people who live on three reserves about 14 kilometers north of Peterborough. One of these reserves (Trent Waters Indian Reserve 36A) is also shared with the Hiawatha and Scugog First Nations. In 2014, the total registered population living on these reserves numbered 791 people, with an additional 1,458 registered band members living off-reserve. The community traces its origins to 1829, when a small band settled around Curve and Mud Lakes, but the area did not officially become a reserve until 1837. Other reserves were added in 1964.

Hiawatha First Nation (www.hiawathafirstnation.com) is located on the north shore of Rice Lake, east of the Otonabee River, approximately 30 kilometers south of Peterborough. There are extensive archaeological remains on this First Nation reserve relating to the Point Peninsula Complex, consisting of a series of earthen mounds constructed for ceremonial, religious, and burial purposes. Serpent Mounds Park includes an effigy mound, as well as nine other burial mounds, some nearly 200 feet long. In 2014, the total registered population was 606, of which 205 persons lived on-reserve.

Mississaugas of Scugog Island (www.scugogfirstnation.com) is located at Lake Scugog in the Durham Region of south-central Ontario. This community consists of two reserves, one located 42 kilometers southwest of Peterborough, and the other on the islands in Pigeon, Buckhorn, and Stony Lakes. In 2014, the total registered population was 228, of which 178 reside off-reserve. The Mississaugas moved into southern Ontario from their former homeland north of Lake Huron around the year 1700. This move followed the dispersal of the Wendat (Huron) people around 1650. By 1830, the Mississaugas began to move away from Scugog Lake because of the rising waters caused by a dam constructed at Lindsay, which flooded their wild rice beds. In 1844, Chief Crane arranged for the purchase of an 800-acre parcel of land on Scugog Island. In 1996, the Mississauga began an economic development project called the Great Blue Heron Charity Casino, which has provided much-needed local employment. This caused the population to nearly double during the decade from 2001 to 2011, with the population increasing from 51 to 93 people. The Mississauga also holds an internationally attended PowWow, which is held each summer and grows annually. The community is a member of the Ogemawahj Tribal Council, which represents six First Nations in the Port Perry-Rama region.

[72] The term 'as might be expected' refers to the fact that von Gernet had been employed by the Crown to represent their interests in numerous cases involving Indigenous land claims. A tactic that he often employed was to suggest that the evidence presented by Indigenous peoples was not reliable because it was based on oral testimony which he claimed was less historically accurate than that presented in written documents. As such, the legal representatives of the First Nations were forced into a situation of continually demonstrating the efficacy of Indigenous recollections of people, places and events.

[73] The Supreme Court ruling of the Van der Peet case, handed down on 21 August 1996, played an important role in interpreting Aboriginal rights. In this particular case Dorothy Van der Peet, a member of the Sto:lo First Nation, was charged with selling salmon that her common-law husband lawfully caught under a Native food fish license. However, in this instance, although the salmon was caught legally under existing legislation, the sale of this fish was prohibited. Chief Justice Antonio Lamer ruled that Aboriginal rights allowed for fishing for food and ceremonial purposes, but this right did not extend to

the sale of fish for commercial purposes or for monetary gain. The legal question at hand was whether or not Dorothy Van der Peet's Aboriginal rights were infringed upon under Section 35 of the Constitution Act. In the opinion of the Court, "in order to be an aboriginal right an activity must be an element of a practice, custom or tradition integral to the distinctive culture of the aboriginal group asserting the right." Subsequently, the Van der Peet decision led to a series of other court cases which attempted to delineate the nature of Aboriginal rights in Canada. In several of these cases a controversial aspect revolved around evidence pertaining to the veracity of oral history, or from the testimony of academic researchers such as anthropologists, and whether or not such evidence should be regarded as sufficiently objective enough (see Culhane 1998; Daly 2005).

[74] Tsilhqot'in Nation v. British Columbia is a landmark decision of the Supreme Court of Canada that established Aboriginal land title for the Tsilhqo'in First Nation, with larger effects. As a result of the landmark decision, provinces cannot unilaterally claim a right to engage in clear-cut logging on lands protected by Aboriginal title; they must engage in meaningful consultation with the title holder before they proceed. Although the Aboriginal title holder does not have to consent to the activity, meaningful consultation is required before infringement of the right can take place (see MacCharles 2014).

[75] Benoit v. Canada (2003) is a decision released on 7 March 2002 by the Federal Court of Canada. The central issue was whether Treaty No. 82 affords a tax exemption for Treaty 8 'Indians.'

Justice Campbell found, at paragraph seven, that when the treaty was executed, there was a 'fundamental misunderstanding' between the Government of Canada and the Cree and Dene Peoples as to whether such an exemption was provided, but that the Aboriginal People believed a tax exemption Treaty promise was made (see Oliphant 2003).

[76] The Toronto Purchase of 1805 (also known as Treaty 13) was negotiated in an attempt to clarify and confirm the terms of the Johnson-Butler Purchase of 1787-88. Ultimately, it failed to do this and additional negotiations were required. These later discussions resulted in the Williams Treaties of 1923 and a compensatory settlement between the Government of Canada and the Mississaugas of the New Credit First Nation in 2010 (see

http://www.torontopurchase-treaty13-canadianencyclopedia.com, accessed 28 April 2021).

[77] The Royal Proclamation of 1763 was issued by King George III on 7 October 1763. It established the basis for governing the North American territories surrendered by France to Britain in the Treaty of Paris, 1763, following the Seven Years' War. It introduced policies meant to assimilate the French population to British rule. These policies ultimately failed and were replaced by the Quebec Act of 1774. The Royal Proclamation also set the constitutional structure for the negotiation of treaties with the Indigenous inhabitants of large sections of Canada. It is referenced in section 25 of the Constitution Act, 1982. As such, it has been labelled an 'Indian Magna Carta' or an 'Indian Bill of Rights' (see
http://www.royalproclammation-1763-canadianencyclopedia.com, accessed 28 April 2021).

[78] The Federal Court ~ Aboriginal Law Bar Liaison Committee brings together representatives of the Federal Court, the Indigenous Bar Association, the Department of Justice (Canada), and the Canadian Bar Association to provide a forum for dialogue, review litigation practice and rules, and make recommendations for improvement. Other organizations have also participated from time to time, including members of various Canadian Courts, academics, and the National Judicial Institute. In addition, the Committee regularly consults with First Nation Community Elders from across the country. Their input and advice with respect to the Guidelines on Elder Testimony and Oral History evidence found at Part D of the Guidelines was particularly important. Committee minutes may be found on the Federal Court web site at: (http://cas-ncr-nter03.cas-satj.gc.ca/portal/page/portal/fc_cf_en/Liaison_Committees, accessed 28 April 2021).

10. Back to the Future

[79] This is the very last line of Sally Weaver's influential book. In the previous sentence she indicates that "The decade of the 1970's has proven that an experiment like the White Paper is a costly and unwise strategy, particularly for minority groups which are economically and politically marginal in society" (1981: 204). However, the White Paper nonetheless served to forge Indigenous organizations in Canada into a defensive stance out of fear of losing

Indigenous people's special rights. Further, as Weaver indicates, even though the government made an attempt to open the door to future consultations, the legacy of distrust hampered negotiations for many years after. There was a continual suspicion that the White Paper proposals were still being (secretly) implemented. Weaver then concluded that "the White Paper has become a symbol of any unpopular and unapproved government initiative" (ibid: 204), and is still remembered as such fifty years later.

[80] Canada bears some similarities to, and yet in many respects is distinctively different from the United States of America. Composed of two linguistic communities, French and English, and demographically lop-sided, with the majority of its inhabitants living within 200 miles of the U. S. border, the nation presents questions for the social scientist with applied interests which while not unique, are not easily resolved by recourse to American models. Until fairly recently, the social sciences in Canada, and anthropology in particular, were only sparsely represented within and without academia (see Practicing Anthropology 1982: 19).

[81] Fagan explains the population structure of Tenochtitlan: "the pre-Conquest population comprised about 1,00,000 people. At least half of these lived in urban centers, up to 20 percent of them based in the greater Tenochtitlan area. At least 400,00 people lived in a 231 square-mile (370 sq. km.) zone of foothills, alluvial plains, and lake bed between the Sierra de Guadalupe southward to the foothills of the Ajusco foothills...the city was the best provisioned in the world" (1984: 82).

[82] John Corbiere was a status Indian belonging to the Batchewana First Nation, an Ojibway band near Sault Ste. Marie, Ontario. He was among the two thirds of Batchewana Band members who did not live on the band's reserve land and were not permitted to vote in band elections. This restriction was imposed by section 77(1) of the Indian Act which limited the right to vote to band members who are 'ordinarily resident on the reserve'. As of 1999, almost half Canada's Indian bands elected their chiefs and councils according to the Indian Act's section 77(1) scheme that excluded non-resident members from the list of electors. The other bands held elections according to 'customary' processes, as the Indian Act provides. Corbiere claimed that section 77(1) denied him equality as guaranteed by section 15(1) of the Canadian Charter of Rights and Freedoms, which reads: Every individual is equal before and under the law and has the right to the equal protection and equal benefit of the law without

discrimination and, in particular, without discrimination based on race, national or ethnic origin, color, religion, sex, age or mental or physical disability (see http://www.constitutionalstudies.ca/2009/07/corbiere-v-canada-1999, accessed 29 April 2021).

[83] This statement is based mostly on my own personal observations concerning the Indigenous communities that I am familiar with. The main problem is that there have been so little ethnographic studies of country food production in northern areas that conclusions are therefore tentative at best.

Printed in the USA
CPSIA information can be obtained
at www.ICGtesting.com
LVHW021236240923
759052LV00008B/146